Pricing in Road Transport

Pricing in Road Transport

A Multi-Disciplinary Perspective

Edited by

Erik Verhoef

VU University Amsterdam, The Netherlands

Michiel Bliemer

Delft University of Technology, The Netherlands

Linda Steg

University of Groningen, The Netherlands

and

Bert van Wee

Delft University of Technology, The Netherlands

Edward Elgar

Cheltenham, UK • Northampton, MA, USA

Published by
Edward Elgar Publishing Limited
Glensanda House
Montpellier Parade
Cheltenham
Glos GL50 1UA
UK

Edward Elgar Publishing, Inc.
William Pratt House
9 Dewey Court
Northampton
Massachusetts 01060
USA

A catalogue record for this book
is available from the British Library

Library of Congress Cataloguing in Publication Data
Pricing in road transport : a multi-disciplinary perspective / edited by Erik Verhoef . . . [et al.].
    p. cm.
Includes bibliographical references and index.
1. Toll roads. 2. Congestion pricing. 3. User charges. I. Verhoef, E. T.
HE336.T64P75 2008
388.1'14—dc22

                                                2007038497

ISBN 978 1 84542 860 0

Printed and bound in Great Britain by MPG Books Ltd, Bodmin, Cornwall

Contents

v

Contributors

Michael Bell is Professor in Transport Operations at Imperial College London, UK.

Michiel Bliemer is Associate Professor in Transport Modelling at Delft University of Technology, The Netherlands.

Piet Bovy is Professor in Transportation Planning at Delft University of Technology, The Netherlands.

Tom de Jong is Assistant Professor in Geographic Information Science at Utrecht University, The Netherlands.

Satoshi Fujii is Professor of Civil Engineering at Tokyo Institute of Technology, Japan.

Tommy Gärling is Professor of Psychology at Göteborg University, Sweden.

David Hensher is Chaired Professor of Management and Director, Institute of Transport and Logistics Studies at the University of Sydney, Australia.

Cecilia Jakobsson is Assistant Professor of Psychology at Göteborg University, Sweden.

Dusica Joksimovic is Project Coordinator for Training and Education at the Research School for Transport, Infrastructure and Logistics (TRAIL), The Netherlands.

Peter Loukopoulos is a researcher at the Swedish National Road and Transportation Research Institute, Linköping, Sweden.

Chris Nash is Professor of Transport Economics, Institute for Transport Studies, University of Leeds, UK.

Sean Puckett is an economist at the US Bureau of Economic Analysis in Washington, DC, USA and Adjunct Researcher at the Institute of Transport and Logistics Studies at the University of Sydney, Australia.

Jan Rouwendal is Associate Professor in Spatial Economics at VU University Amsterdam, The Netherlands.

Georgina Santos is Rees Jeffreys Road Fund Lecturer in Transport and the Environment at the Transport Studies Unit, University of Oxford, UK.

Geertje Schuitema is a PhD student in Environmental Psychology at the University of Groningen, The Netherlands.

Linda Steg is Associate Professor in Environmental Psychology at the University of Groningen, The Netherlands.

Taede Tillema is a postdoctoral researcher in Transport Geography at Utrecht University, The Netherlands.

Barry Ubbels is Consultant at NEA Transport Research and Training in Rijswijk, The Netherlands.

Dirk van Amelsfort is a PhD student/researcher in Transport Planning at Delft University of Technology, The Netherlands.

Jos van Ommeren is Associate Professor in Economics at VU University Amsterdam, The Netherlands.

Bert van Wee is Professor in Transport Policy and Logistics at Delft University of Technology, The Netherlands.

Erik Verhoef is Professor in Spatial Economics at VU University Amsterdam, The Netherlands.

Muanmas Wichiensin is a doctoral research student at Imperial College London, UK.

1. Introduction

Linda Steg, Erik Verhoef, Michiel Bliemer and Bert van Wee

1.1 BACKGROUND

Various developments have put (or kept) road pricing high on the political agenda in most societies. One is the seemingly relentless growth in road transport volumes, causing side-effects such as congestion and pollution, which are among the greatest inconveniences of contemporary urban life. Another is the ongoing improvement in technologies for automated vehicle identification and charging, making sophisticated transport pricing an increasingly attractive option to deal with these side-effects. But also increasing demands on public budgets motivate the search for alternative funding of road infrastructure construction and maintenance.

Most transport analysts would agree that road pricing is a potentially effective instrument for curbing transport and transport-related problems. Likewise, many policy documents, from local authorities, as well as national and international governments, identify road pricing as one of the key cornerstones of contemporary transport policies, and support this by a variety of arguments, ranging from effectiveness and economic efficiency to considerations of fairness and transparency in the financing of infrastructure (the 'user-pays principle'). But public acceptability often seems to be lagging behind, so that actual implementations, although growing in number, remain scarce. Nevertheless, with the introduction of the London congestion charge in 2003 (see also Chapter 14), and the implementation of charging in Stockholm in the Summer of 2007 (see also Chapter 10), one might hypothesize that urban road pricing is entering a new phase in its history, and will soon spread over Europe and other parts of the world.

Although past research has produced many valuable insights into the workings and possible effects of road-pricing measures, there are still many unanswered questions, involving, *inter alia*, the optimal design of such measures, the (behavioural) effects they may induce among individuals and firms, and questions surrounding the acceptability of road pricing. These and related questions stimulated us to write this book.

1.2   AIM OF THE BOOK

This book aims to provide a multidisciplinary view on the effectiveness and acceptability of pricing in road transport.[1] After a general introduction to road pricing, four topics will be addressed. First, we elaborate on the possible behavioural responses to road pricing. Second, we illustrate how model studies may assist in designing optimal road-pricing policies, given different policy objectives. Third, we describe the acceptability of different types of road-pricing policies by the general public and firms, and indicate how such policies may affect geographical accessibility. Finally, we discuss to what extent road pricing has actually proved to be effective, and indicate the prospects for implementing transport infrastructure pricing in Europe.

1.3   OVERVIEW OF THE CHAPTERS

In Chapter 2, Erik Verhoef provides a basic introduction to the economic theory of road pricing. Introducing concepts and terminology, this chapter serves as a lead-in to the further chapters in this book. Moreover, Verhoef reviews the possible objectives of road pricing, and indicates that the optimal design of road-pricing schemes depends on the objectives set by the relevant authorities. The remainder of the book comprises four parts.

Part I elaborates on the behavioural responses to road pricing. In Chapter 3, David Hensher and Sean Puckett discuss the effects of road pricing on freight transporters and shippers. More specifically, they compare the potential effects of increases in fuel prices (the current main source of charging) and distance-based charges in freight transport. In addition, they examine which of these pricing policies is preferred most by transporters, and why this is so.

As pointed out by Hensher and Puckett, road pricing may especially result in travel-time reliability gains, which in turn have an impact on agents' decision making. Taking this subject further, in Chapter 4, Dirk van Amelsfort, Piet Bovy, Michiel Bliemer and Barry Ubbels indicate how travel-time unreliability may be taken into account in modelling travellers' choice decisions. They discuss different approaches to modelling travel-time unreliability in a discrete choice setting, which may give rise to different values of travel-time reliability, and they argue which value of travel-time unreliability is in their view most plausible. Furthermore, they examine whether it is possible and worthwhile to separate the effects of travel-time reliability on travel-choice behaviour.

Barry Ubbels, Taede Tillema, Erik Verhoef and Bert van Wee analyse the effects of kilometre charging on changes in car use, car ownership and relocation choices of households in Chapter 5. Some of these changes are more likely to occur in the short term (for example, driving at other times), while others concern long-term changes (for example, changes in car ownership or relocation decisions). The authors elaborate on which types of car trips are most likely to be affected by road pricing, and which types of charges would be most successful in bringing about changes in car use.

Chapter 6 focuses on effects of road pricing on firms. Taede Tillema, Bert van Wee, Jan Rouwendal and Jos van Ommeren argue that road pricing may affect firms' decisions in various ways: road pricing may affect not only firms' travel behaviour, but also their business and human resource policies. The authors consider the effects of kilometre charging on trip frequency, time of travel and types of trips (for example, business or transport of goods). Moreover, they examine to what extent firms intend to reimburse their employees, which may seriously affect the effectiveness of kilometre charging on commuter trips. Also, they describe to what degree firms consider mitigating (extra) costs due to a kilometre charge by increasing the price of their goods and services, and whether firms plan to relocate if a kilometre charge is implemented.

Part II focuses on the modelling effects of transport pricing. Three chapters discuss ways to design optimal road-pricing policies, given different policy objectives. Chapter 7, by Michael Bell and Muanmas Wichiensin, considers the setting of an optimal congestion charge consistent with the commercial decisions to transit operators. The authors argue that the reactions of transit operators on congestion charging should be considered, as these will influence traveller costs, which will in turn affect the optimal congestion charge. They analyse the impact of profit-maximizing transit fare setting on the social surplus under a range of congestion charges, and examine the competitive advantages of tolling for transit operators.

In Chapter 8, Dusica Joksimovic, Michiel Bliemer and Piet Bovy argue that the macroscopic results of road pricing should be understood from their micro foundations, that is, the behaviour of the individual actors. The authors introduce game theory as an appropriate way to do this, and present the results from a series of game-theoretic studies to illustrate their proposition. They show that, in this setting as well, the optimal design of a road-pricing policy (for example, toll level) depends greatly on the main policy objective set.

Chapter 9 focuses on time-varying optimal toll designs. Michiel Bliemer, Dusica Joksimovic and Piet Bovy consider uniform and time-variable tolls during the peak, taking route choice and departure time choice responses of travellers into account. They demonstrate that policy objectives can be optimized by imposing tolls, and that different policy objectives lead to different optimal tolling schemes and toll levels. Thus, this chapter once more illustrates that the optimal design of road pricing depends on the policy objectives.

Part III focuses on the acceptability of different types of road-pricing policies. The first two chapters discuss the acceptability of road pricing among the general public. In Chapter 10, Tommy Gärling, Cecilia Jakobsson, Peter Loukopoulos and Satoshi Fujii discuss how acceptability judgements may best be derived. Next, they present a theoretical framework to account for determinants of acceptability, and examine to what extent these determinants actually explain public acceptability of the Stockholm congestion charge scheme. They hypothesize that road pricing is more acceptable if individual car users are aware of the problems caused by car use, whether they expect the road-pricing scheme to be effective in reducing these problems, and whether the road-pricing scheme will affect their own car use.

Geertje Schuitema, Barry Ubbels, Linda Steg and Erik Verhoef further investigate the relationship between effectiveness and acceptability of road pricing in Chapter 11. Like Gärling et al., they argue that individual car users will consider two types of effects when evaluating the acceptability of road pricing: effects on the problems resulting from car use (for example, congestion) and effects on their own car use. They contend that the latter will depend on the degree to which a car user can cope with expected cost increases, which will be related to factors like annual kilometrage, income and price level. Next, they examine how acceptability judgements are related to possibilities of evading transport-pricing policies, and the extent to which car users are compensated for negative consequences via revenue allocations.

One way in which car users may benefit from road pricing is increased accessibility. Taede Tillema, Tom de Jong, Bert van Wee and Dirk van Amelsfort determine, in Chapter 12, to what extent various factors may affect changes in accessibility due to road pricing. Among these factors are the value of time, and characteristics of the road-pricing measure (for example, price level). They first assess the effects of a time-differentiated kilometre charge on accessibility in general, and next examine whether accessibility is sensitive to variations in value of time, characteristics of the road-pricing measure, and types of costs and benefits considered by those involved. They argue that various types of costs and benefits should be taken into account when assessing the effects of road pricing on accessibility, and that approaches focusing only on travel-time gains may not provide an accurate picture in this respect.

In Chapter 13, Linda Steg, Taede Tillema, Bert van Wee and Geertje Schuitema discuss the acceptability of road pricing by firms. As in Chapters 10 and 11, they focus on the relationships between the effectiveness and acceptability of road pricing. They start from the reasonable assumption that, if firms are more likely to suffer from road pricing, kilometre charging will be less acceptable to them, while it will be more acceptable if firms benefit from it. Firms may consider various costs and benefits, such as the expected changes in travel costs and accessibility of firms. The last two effects in particular are considered in this chapter.

Finally, Part IV discusses both the past and the future of road pricing. In Chapter 14, Georgina Santos discusses the London Congestion Charging Scheme. She provides a thorough and critical discussion of the background, design, effects, and costs and benefits of the scheme, and indicates its 'winners' and 'losers'. Furthermore, she elaborates on the possible effects of extending the scheme.

Chapter 15 identifies some prospects for transport infrastructure pricing in Europe. In this chapter, Chris Nash provides an overview of progress on the EU transport-pricing policy. He concludes that actual progress towards more efficiency in transport-pricing has been slow. He provides various reasons for this lack of progress, and indicates how some of these barriers may be overcome.

The final chapter summarizes the main conclusions of the book. On the basis of these, various suggestions for future research are indicated. Furthermore, the main implications for transport policy are described. Overall, the chapters in this book indicate that it should be feasible to implement road-pricing policies that are both effective in reducing transport and traffic problems and acceptable to the public and to firms.

NOTE

1. Many chapters report on research that was carried out in the context of the Dutch NWO/Connekt VEV project on 'A Multidisciplinary Study of Pricing Policies in Transport'; the financial support of NWO is gratefully acknowledged. This applies to all chapters, except Chapters 2, 3, 7, 10, 14 and 15.

2. Road transport pricing: motivation, objectives and design from an economic perspective[1]

Erik Verhoef

2.1 INTRODUCTION

Road pricing is gaining increasing attention in transport policy circles. After the first contemporary area-wide applications in, for example, Singapore and Scandinavia, which demonstrate the technical viability and potential effectiveness of pricing measures, more places have been following suit, either by implementing schemes or at least by considering them. The pricing schemes concerned vary from classic toll roads to express lanes, toll cordons, area charging and kilometre charges. Also charge levels, and degrees of toll differentiation, may differ quite significantly between applications. This may reflect differences both in local conditions and in the schemes' objectives, and indicate that (local or national) governments have a wide variety of road-pricing options to choose from, after deciding to implement road pricing in the first place.

This contribution reviews the various possible objectives that may motivate the practical implementation of road-pricing schemes (in Section 2.2), and to discuss (in Section 2.3) how such objectives may affect the design of schemes. These questions are, in the first place, of intrinsic interest, because any government considering the implementation of road pricing will benefit from a careful *ex ante* identification and specification of the scheme's objectives, and an assessment of how to best achieve these through optimizing the design of the measure. But, second, these same questions also allow us to provide an introduction to the remainder of the book, by presenting some of the basic (economic) theory of road pricing and linking this to the practical design of road-pricing schemes. Section 2.4 concludes.

2.2 VARIOUS OBJECTIVES OF ROAD PRICING

The implementation of road pricing in itself does not seem to be a very meaningful final objective to pursue. But it can be an effective and efficient means of pursuing other objectives. A meaningful assessment of various types of road pricing, and a motivated choice between them, can be made only in the light of the (policy) objective(s) to be pursued. It is not true that there could be only one possible objective justifying and motivating the implementation of road pricing. On the contrary, operational road-pricing schemes have varying objectives, and hence sometimes strongly differing designs and, consequently, different effects. This section therefore discusses the possible objectives of road pricing, and the possible tension and inconsistencies between these, in more detail.

It is important to emphasize from the outset that economic science cannot objectively answer the question of what the 'appropriate' objectives of (transport) policy, including transport pricing, should be. But economists *can* help to identify how to achieve a given objective in the most efficient way, that is, employing the lowest possible amount of scarce resources.

It is also important to realize that objectives can be defined at various levels of abstraction. For example, the possible objectives of economic policies in general – including policies such as road pricing – could be defined in general as (i) achieving an efficient allocation; (ii) achieving an acceptable income distribution; and (iii) stabilizing unemployment and inflation. In what follows, we shall consider often-mentioned objectives of road pricing defined at a somewhat lower level of abstraction. For example, the first possible objective to be considered – internalizing external costs – in itself could be motivated by a desire to achieve an efficient allocation. And the fifth objective – fairness – is closely related to distributional concerns. We use the lower level of abstraction mainly because it ties in more closely with how road pricing is discussed in policy circles in practice.

2.2.1 Efficiency within Road Transport Markets: Internalizing External Costs

A first important possible objective of road pricing, and the one that probably receives most attention in transport economic texts, is the internalization of external costs. This means charging for unpriced costs that a road user imposes on other individuals, who might include not only fellow road users, but also broader groups such as local residents, the whole world population and even future generations. Doing so would prevent socially excessive consumption of road trips (see below). The four most important external cost categories associated with the use of automobiles are: (i) travel-time losses through congestion; (ii) accident risks; (iii) noise annoyance; and (iv) emissions. Apart from these, there are kilometrage-independent external costs, which may, for example, result from the ownership of vehicles (externalities such as parking congestion, environmental effects from the production or scrapping of vehicles) or from the existence of infrastructure (externalities such as severance of communities or ecosystems) (see also Verhoef, 1996). These last externalities would, strictly speaking, not provide a strong motivation for road pricing when the objective is internalization of external costs, simply because the relation with the *use* of the road is only indirect or even non-existent.

When internalization is the objective, what are called the 'marginal external costs' are the relevant external cost measure: the reduction in external costs that would be achieved when removing one 'unit' of traffic (for example, a vehicle, or a vehicle-kilometre). Such marginal external costs may differ strongly by market segment, for example, over time, place, vehicle type and so on. Conventional economic theory dictates that optimal road prices should be equal to these marginal external costs for all users, at all times and at all places; see, however, Section 2.2.2 for some qualifications. This equality is typically not realized, even when, on average, it does appear to apply, as CE (2004) finds for gasoline vehicles in the Netherlands. Differences between charges and marginal external costs for specific segments can then still be significant, as shown in Figure 2.1 which is taken from the same study.

The marginal external costs of road transport thus encompass various cost categories, which in turn correspond with various other possible objectives of road pricing. For example, the internalization of external congestion costs is a specific, economically efficient implementation of the possible objective of 'curbing traffic congestion', just as the internalization of environmental externalities is an implementation of the objective of 'reducing emissions'. The consideration of all four external cost categories in setting road prices may then be taken to imply the simultaneous consideration of four objectives (that is, curbing congestion, accidents, noise and emissions), where the implied 'target' for each objective is made dependent on the levels of all marginal external cost components.

The objective of external cost internalization is consistent with the maximization of the 'social surplus' on the market under consideration. This social surplus is the most current measure for social welfare in applied economic research. It is defined as the difference between social benefits and social costs.

Why do road prices equal to marginal external costs maximize social surplus? A graphical illustration is given in Figure 2.2 for the case of congestion only (that is, ignoring other externalities), and for the short run (that

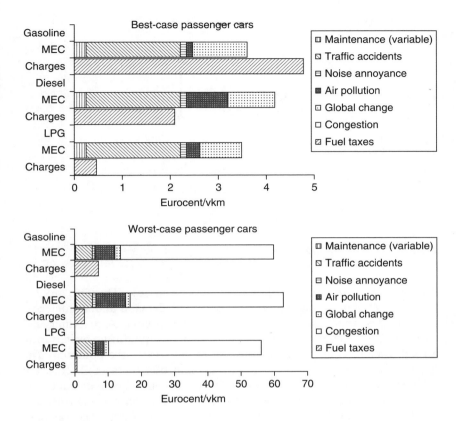

Note: 'Best case' concerns a new vehicle (2002) outside the peak period and outside built-up areas. 'Worst case' concerns an older vehicle (1993) in the peak period and inside built-up areas.

Source: CE (2004).

Figure 2.1 Marginal external costs versus variable (fuel) taxes for two representative vehicle-kilometres in the Netherlands (2004)

is, treating road capacity as fixed). It repeats textbook expositions, as can be found in, among others, Button (1993) and Small and Verhoef (2007).

When the number of road users N increases in Figure 2.2, speed will fall and average user cost c will rise because travel times rise. The marginal cost mc exceeds the average cost c because every additional user, besides incurring the average cost c, causes time losses and hence extra costs for all other users. These give the marginal external cost, *mec*. The inverse demand

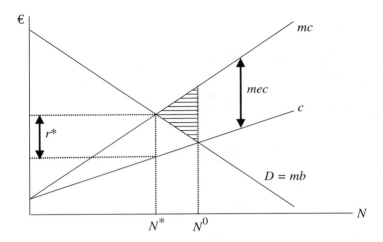

Figure 2.2   The optimal congestion charge

function *D* corresponds with marginal benefits *mb*. The free market outcome N^0 is at the intersection of the inverse demand and average cost function. The optimum is at N^*, where marginal benefit *mb* equals marginal cost *mc*. This optimum can be realized as a market equilibrium by imposing a road price r^* equal to the marginal external cost in the optimum. The hatched triangle gives the social surplus gain due to the toll. It is the difference between social cost savings due to the reduction in demand (the area below *mc* between N^* and N^0) and forgone social benefits (the area below *mb* between N^* and N^0). The inclusion of other external costs would not change the essence of this exposition. The relevant social marginal cost *smc* would be above *mc*; the optimum would therefore be to the left of the current N^*; and the social welfare gain would increase.

The example shows that the road price maximizes social surplus because it confronts every individual user with the full social cost of each kilometre travelled by car. This cost encompasses both the *internal* cost incurred by the driver (*c* in the figure) and, through the road price, the *external* costs imposed on others. A driver will then make a trip only when its associated benefits are at least equal to its social costs. And this maximizes social surplus. That is, preventing a trip that would be made under optimal road pricing would save a smaller social cost than the trip's benefit, and would thus reduce social surplus. Likewise, including a trip that is discouraged through optimal road pricing would produce a smaller benefit than the social cost it causes, and would therefore also reduce social surplus.[2] These two facts together explain the social surplus maximization.

Probably the greatest advantage of price policies, above other policies to reduce external cost, derives from the fact that road users will differ in their most preferred (or least disliked) way of reducing external cost. Some will prefer to make fewer trips, some would rather adjust the route or time of driving, some would opt for a cleaner car leaving their mobility patterns unaltered, some might go carpooling or use public transport more often, some would rather adjust their work location or residential location and so on. Yet another group might prefer not to reduce the external cost they cause, but rather pay the road price. Only (optimally differentiated) road pricing allows the road user to choose the least among these 'bads' (from the private perspective). Other policies, like direct regulation, typically leave less freedom of choice to the road user, and are therefore likely to discourage some trips (or other decisions, such as technology choice) which in fact have a social benefit exceeding the social cost; or, conversely, allow some decisions that in fact produce a social benefit that falls short of the implied social cost. Social surplus is therefore not maximized. For example, a measure like car-free Sundays will leave all week-day commutes unaffected, while also preventing the most valuable of trips made on Sundays. And it may not be worthwhile to install a mandatory cleaner technology in a car that will hardly be used.

Pricing thus offers a potentially efficient way of dealing with road transport externalities. Evidently, one also has to consider the implementation cost when the objective is to assess the overall social desirability of road pricing. The study by Prud'homme and Bocarejo (2005), who argue that the social cost of the London congestion charging mechanism may well outweigh its social benefit, is an important reminder that considering the cost of road-pricing implementation should be more than an afterthought. Recent estimates for the Randstad (CPB, 2005) and Stockholm (Stockholmsförsöket, 2006) suggest that the social benefit–cost ratio may often be more favourable than those found for London by Prud'homme and Bocarejo (and criticized by Mackie, 2005): an estimated net annual welfare gain of €1.5 billion per year was reported for the Netherlands for well-designed kilometre charges, and a projected annual benefit–cost surplus of about SEK 760 million (around €84 million) in Stockholm.

Probably the greatest disadvantage of price policies is their limited acceptability (see also Chapters 10 and 11 in this volume). An important reason for this is that road-pricing revenues are received by the government. While road users may benefit from time gains resulting from road pricing, they will suffer from this financial transfer unless the revenues are used in their own interest. Many analysts therefore believe that one of the most straightforward and effective ways of raising acceptability is to take the road users' preferences on revenue use into account when deciding on the

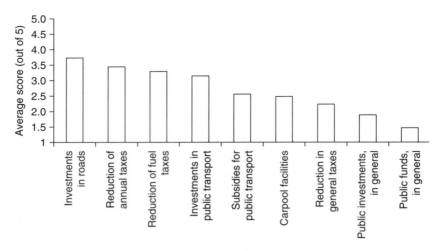

Source: Adapted from Verhoef (1996).

*Figure 2.3   Road users' preferences for the use of road-pricing revenues
            (morning peak travellers in the Randstad, 1996; N = 1327)*

use of revenues (but see also Section 2.3.4 below). Figure 2.3 illustrates
these preferences (see also Chapter 11 for more recent empirical evidence).

Besides this 'acceptability barrier', other barriers for the implementation
of road pricing have also been studied recently: for example, technical,
political, institutional and legal barriers. A recent European study (MC-
ICAM, 2004) suggests that acceptability is currently probably the greatest
of these barriers.

2.2.2   Broad Efficiency: Including Welfare Effects Elsewhere in the Economy

Road prices as described above in principle maximize social surplus in the
market in which they are implemented. However, when price distortions
occur on markets narrowly related to the transport market, for example
because of external effects or distortionary taxation, road pricing can
induce indirect welfare effects in these other markets. When such indirect
welfare effects are taken into account in the design of road pricing, along
with the effects in the market itself, as described in the previous section, the
objective can be characterized as 'broad economic efficiency', or economy-
wide welfare.

Such indirect effects from transport pricing could, in principle, arise on
nearly any market, for the simple reason that nearly all economic activities

directly or indirectly induce transport movements. Research in this field has considered various such markets, notably: labour markets with distortionary income taxation, in relation to congestion pricing (Mayeres and Proost, 2001; Parry and Bento, 2001); distorted public transport markets (Arnott and Yan, 2000; Mayeres and Proost, 2001); and environmental externalities in production in relation to freight transport charging (for example, Verhoef et al., 1997a).

Including such indirect effects can lead to upward or downward corrections on the optimal tax level, compared with charges based on marginal external cost. Furthermore, the consideration of welfare effects on other markets also implies that the allocation of revenues will have an impact on the overall efficiency of the policy (see also Section 2.3.4).

The determination of optimal charges, based on broad efficiency, may be a rather difficult task that would often require the employment of applied spatial equilibrium models with a level of accuracy that is currently not yet available. But this does not, of course, reduce the importance of considering indirect effects on distorted markets as accurately as possible when designing road-pricing and revenue-allocation schemes. Doing so would not only provide better insight into the overall desirability of the scheme, but would also increase the aggregate welfare gain it may achieve.

2.2.3 Effective Curbing of Transport-related Problems

Efficiency, whether or not defined to include welfare in related markets, is related to effectiveness – defined here as the degree to which the instrument reduces a certain undesirable side-effect of transport – but it is certainly not the same. For example, to eliminate congestion completely in Figure 2.2, a toll is required that discourages all traffic. This is the most effective way of reducing congestion but, because social surplus is even below the no-toll surplus, a very inefficient measure. The example is illustrative of the difficulties arising when effectiveness *per se* is used as an objective for road-pricing policies (or any other policy): it is sometimes but certainly not always true that a more effective policy is also more socially desirable. A secondary objective is then needed to decide on the policy's most desirable level of effectiveness, that is, to decide on the preferred target. The effectiveness of a measure can then be interpreted as the extent to which it is capable of achieving this target.

One pitfall is that the optimal target may in fact depend on the instrument chosen. This is evident when efficiency is the main objective; many studies have demonstrated how, for example, the optimal toll level and implied reduction in external effects like congestion depend on whether the toll is first- or second best (for an example, see, among many others, Verhoef and Small, 2004). The same sort of consideration is likely to be relevant in the phase of target setting when effectiveness is the primary objective, but it is not straightforward to take into account without again introducing a secondary objective.

Another complication is that, depending on the formulation of targets, it may be possible to achieve them in different ways that are indistinguishable in terms of the level of effectiveness but that differ in terms of, for example, efficiency or perceived fairness. The objective is then incapable of discriminating between these alternatives. To give an example, a certain target reduction of yearly aggregate kilometrage could be achievable by having efficient road pricing on all days, or by having zero tolls on most days and prohibitive tolls on other days. Probably not many would dispute that the former option is more desirable, but the sole objective of effectiveness cannot indicate this, and this shortcoming carries over to less obvious examples than the one just described.

All in all, although effectiveness may seem an attractive pragmatic type of objective on first sight, it easily gives rise to ambiguities that make it less attractive in practice. That is, it is certainly useful to distinguish ineffective policies from effective ones, but a more sophisticated objective is often needed in order to choose between different effective policies.

2.2.4   The Generation of Revenues and Financing of Infrastructure

Road pricing by definition implies the transfer of money. As indicated, in the first instance this will typically involve a net transfer from road users to the road operator (often the government)[3] – which, as stated, helps to explain the limited acceptability of such policies.

The generation of revenues, especially for the purpose of financing infrastructure, can be an important (fourth possible) objective for the implementation of road pricing. In fact, for a public road operator it appears more appropriate to consider the financing of infrastructure as an intermediate objective, because the supply of infrastructure itself will again be motivated by higher-order objectives such as economic efficiency. The conventional evaluation method for infrastructure investments, cost–benefit analysis (CBA), for example, has the central principle that an investment is socially desirable when the social benefits exceed the social costs. This is entirely consistent with the principle of maximizing social surplus as discussed in Section 2.2.2 above.

Nevertheless, for various political, management and social (acceptability) reasons, the financing of infrastructure appears a logical objective for imposing tolls. At first glance, there may appear to be less reason to make decisions on pricing and on investments mutually dependent through a budget constraint: both types of measure can be evaluated independently of the other measure. On second thoughts, however, there are important mutual dependencies. First, the optimal capacity will depend on whether a toll is imposed. Second, there is an important theoretical correspondence between the revenues of congestion pricing and the costs of infrastructure supply. Under certain conditions, the revenues from optimal congestion pricing will be just sufficient to cover the costs of supplying an optimal capacity (Mohring and Harwitz, 1962). In other words, an optimally designed and managed road (in terms of capacity and toll) is then exactly self-financing. In such cases, the use of road-pricing revenues for another purpose than the financing of infrastructure, and the simultaneous use of other sources for financing road investments, could be considered as unnecessarily complex and opaque. Section 2.3.5 will discuss the economic background of the Mohring–Harwitz result in greater detail.

Of course, for a private road operator, the generation of revenues can (and will) be the primary objective of road pricing. The tolls and capacities that maximize profits will typically deviate significantly from the efficient levels. Because the profit-maximizing toll internalizes the congestion externality and adds to this a demand-related mark-up that increases when demand becomes less elastic, the two outcomes are identical only when demand is perfectly elastic (for details, see Small and Verhoef, 2007). It is not inconceivable that the profit-maximizing toll reduces social welfare, compared with the absence of tolling (for example, Verhoef and Small, 2004). This means that, if the implementation of road pricing is connected to privatization of road infrastructure supply, there is good reason to develop smart concession mechanisms that aim to bring private capacity and toll choices closer to socially optimal levels.

2.2.5   Fairness: A Subjective Matter

A fifth possible objective for the implementation of road pricing could be the pursuit of some form of 'fairness' or 'justice'. Such concepts are hard to define objectively, and it is not the purpose of this chapter to go into the details of such discussions, but in broad terms the internalization of external costs through road pricing is frequently justified by the idea that it is 'fair' to have the user and/or polluter pay for the full (marginal) costs of his/her behaviour.

Because fairness cannot be defined or measured objectively and unambiguously, it would be a tricky objective for policy making. And because fairness is also a relative measure, it may often fail to provide a ranking between more and less efficient types of policies if these have comparable relative welfare effects. For such reasons, fairness is often treated as a constraint in the design of policies, rather than as a primary objective.

2.2.6 Compatibility of Possible Objectives

The five possible objectives of road pricing described above are certainly not always necessarily compatible, and may each call – certainly in the short run – for a different scheme design, different charge levels and so on (see also Chapter 9 of this book). For example, marginal external cost charges satisfy the polluter-pays principle in a marginal sense, but total charge revenues will generally be different from total external cost (unless the average external cost happens to be constant). A classic tension between efficiency and fairness will then arise. Likewise, charges that maximize revenues generally do not maximize welfare, and charges that exactly internalize marginal external costs typically do not maximize welfare when market failures occur elsewhere in the economy. The selection of one primary objective is therefore important for a consistent design of a road-pricing (and revenue-allocation) scheme. Other objectives can then still be accounted for by translating these into appropriate constraints.

In the longer run, inconsistencies between various possible objectives may diminish or even disappear altogether. An important example involves the interaction between optimal road pricing and the financing of road infrastructure. Provided that the technical conditions for self-financing are fulfilled (see Section 2.3.5), self-financing roads would in the first place help in achieving an efficient road system, in terms of optimal capacities and optimal pricing. Furthermore, it strongly reduces the need to use tax revenues from other sources for the financing of roads. This may improve economy-wide efficiency further, because these other taxes are often distortionary, and it may in addition raise public acceptability of road pricing. The resulting scheme may be perceived as 'fair' (only the users of a road pay for its capacity) and 'transparent' (there are no 'hidden' transfers surrounding the financing of roads). Although it is unlikely that self-financing will apply exactly for every road at every point in time, the fact that it may apply approximately already makes it a promising concept for reconciling potentially conflicting objectives such as efficiency, economy-wide welfare, and fairness.

2.3   DESIGNING ROAD-PRICING SCHEMES: THE DEVIL IS IN THE DETAIL

This section will address some important aspects of the design for road pricing. Section 2.3.1 will identify the choices to be made, while the following subsections present a number of considerations to be kept in mind when deciding about these choices.

2.3.1 The Major Characteristics to Consider in Designing Road-pricing Schemes

Road pricing can take on different forms. Important 'families' of road pricing include parking charging (as occurs in many cities throughout the world), toll roads (France), express lanes (US), cordon charges (Singapore, Norway), area charges (London), kilometre charges (the German MAUT), and point charges (at bridges or tunnels). Within each of these families, charges can be differentiated in various ways, revenues can be used in different ways and so on. Without any attempt to be exhaustive, Table 2.1 presents the major choices to be made in designing a road-pricing scheme, and shows a number of popular options for each of these.

Some choices implied by Table 2.1 cannot be made independently of each other, for example, a fuel tax cannot be differentiated by time of day. Nevertheless, there is still much to choose. It will be clear that the objective of road pricing will often be a decisive factor in making such choices. With efficiency as the primary objective, the differentiation of charges will be important (compare Figure 2.1), as is the careful determination of charge levels. This in turn will have implications for the tax base and the charging

Table 2.1   The major choices to be made when designing road-pricing schemes

Charging technology	Tax base	Charge level	Differentiation	Revenue use
Complements Fuel	Fuel use End point of trip (parking charge)	Marginal external cost Broad	None ('flat') Time of day Distance	Road construction and maintenance Public transport
Manual Toll plazas Parking meters	Passages (cordon, point charges) Use of roads (toll roads) or lanes (express lanes)	efficiency Cost of road construction and maintenance	Area Route Vehicle State of vehicle	Reduction or abandonment of vehicle excise duties
Electronic Cameras: number plates Microwave Tachograph Satellite	Area Kilometrage (km charge)	Current vehicle excise duties to be variable Profit (private road operator)	Driving style	Reducing fuel tax Reducing income tax Public budget

technology. Furthermore, the use of revenues will affect not only the acceptability of the scheme, but also the broader efficiency.

2.3.2 Behavioural Effects and Differentiation

As Section 2.2.1 explains, probably the biggest potential advantage of pricing over other policies to reduce external effects is that it allows different responses from individuals who will have different most-preferred ways to reduce the external effects they cause. This advantage can be exploited only when the pricing scheme is designed in such a way that does indeed provide the correct incentives to consider all the possible ways to reduce externalities. And this, in turn, will depend on the extent to which charges are differentiated by the relevant 'behavioural dimensions'. For example, a charge that is not differentiated by time of day will give little incentive to consider rescheduling of trips.

These relevant behavioural dimensions, and so the dimensions determining the levels of marginal external costs, will in turn vary by external cost category. Table 2.2 provides an indication of the major determinants by external cost category. Of course, other determinants may matter as well, but the purpose here is to identify the major determinants when an efficient reduction of external costs is the objective of the policy.

It is clear that, if road pricing is to address each of these external cost categories, there will be high demands for the differentiation of road prices, especially because different types of externalities require different types of differentiation. For the reduction of traffic jams, a refined differentiation of charges over time and place is important and the relevant basis for tolling appears to be the passage of bottlenecks. The management of flow congestion, in contrast, would require differentiation by roads used and total kilometrage. For safety, dimensions such as driving style and alcohol use ought to be considered (which is currently still hard to imagine, although fines may provide an adequate substitute for such toll differentiation). Noise and local environmental effects require differentiation by vehicle type and over space, and total kilometrage. Note that the reduction of congestion may also indirectly benefit emission reduction, by improving driving conditions and hence fuel efficiency.

Although a sophisticated differentiation of charges may create complications in terms of technology, organization and communication, one might expect important advantages in terms of:

- *efficiency*: the charge gives optimal incentives to reduce external costs at the lowest possible social cost, because individual road users can decide themselves how to achieve this reduction;

Table 2.2   The major determinants for various external cost categories

Congestion (jams)	Congestion ('flow')	Safety (external risk)	Noise	Emissions (local)	Climate
Time of day Passage-specific bottlenecks	Time of day				
	Use of certain roads		Use of certain roads	Use of certain roads	
		Driving style Tiredness and/or alcohol	Driving style	Driving style	Driving style
			Vehicle	Vehicle	Vehicle
	Kilometrage	Kilometrage		Kilometrage External determinant: congestion ('stop-and-go' traffic)	Kilometrage External determinant: congestion ('stop-and-go' traffic)

- *effectiveness*: optimal differentiation enables the optimal employment of all possible behavioural dimensions that can contribute to the reduction of external costs; and
- *acceptability*: the acceptability is likely to be higher because a stronger differentiation gives road users more possibilities to avoid paying the highest charges, and because charges more closely reflect 'polluter-pays' and 'user-pays' principles.

Next, we shall discuss these hypotheses for the example of dynamic congestion pricing.

2.3.3   Illustrating the Advantages of Charge Differentiation: Dynamic Congestion Pricing

A rather extreme illustration of the advantages of charge differentiation anticipated above is given by Vickrey's (1969) bottleneck model of traffic congestion. The main innovation from this model is that it takes a dynamic

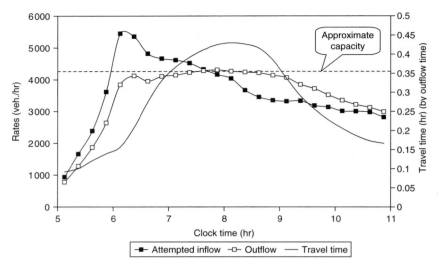

Source: Verhoef (2005).

Figure 2.4 *The average morning peak at the Coenplein in 2002: attempted inflow, outflow and travel time*

perspective and endogenizes departure time decisions. As the name of the model indicates, it is particularly targeted at describing congestion at bottlenecks – commonly known as 'queues' or 'jams' – which is arguably the most visible and pressing type of congestion. Figure 2.4 illustrates the basic mechanics of bottleneck congestion using data on traffic flows through the Coenplein, a serious bottleneck in the Netherlands (for details, see Verhoef, 2005).

Throughout the peak period, the outflow of the bottleneck is more or less constant and indicative of its capacity (around 4200 veh/hr; on a two-lane highway with a speed limit of 120 km/hr). In the first part of the peak, the attempted inflow of the bottleneck exceeds the capacity so that a queue grows and the travel time rises, while the opposite occurs in the second part. Vickrey (1969) recognized that this pattern constitutes a dynamic equilibrium when travellers have a most-desired arrival time (at work). For identical travellers, the equilibrium pattern secures that the sum of travel delay costs (the value of time lost queuing) and schedule delay costs (the value of arriving at work earlier or later than preferred) is the same at any arrival time. The queue can be eliminated by imposing a toll that has a time-varying pattern that replicates the time-varying pattern of the value of travel delays. The resulting equilibrium will have the same outflow pattern, with outflow equalling capacity over a peak period that lasts as long as the no-toll peak. The (attempted) inflow will have become equal to capacity throughout the peak, instead of a wasteful pattern of too many attempted entries in the first part, and too few in the second. This occurs because, given the toll schedule, only an inflow pattern not exceeding the capacity will satisfy the equilibrium condition that trip price (toll plus schedule delay costs plus travel delay costs) remains constant over time (for further details, see Arnott et al., 1998).

The optimal time-varying toll for a bottleneck allows the same number of vehicles to pass it over the same period of time, without queuing. Optimal time variation therefore has a great positive impact on effectiveness: in principle, the queue can be eliminated completely. It also enhances efficiency: without time variation of the toll within the peak period, queuing will continue to exist as a dynamic equilibrium phenomenon. But it is also likely to positively affect acceptability: because the toll replaces the value of travel delays of the no-toll equilibrium, the trip price does not increase, so that a worsening of welfare before revenue redistribution, as in Figure 2.2, does not occur. This case of dynamic pricing of bottleneck congestion does therefore indeed illustrate the earlier claim that differentiation may have substantial positive impacts on the efficiency, effectiveness and acceptability of pricing.

2.3.4 The Use of Revenues and Efficiency

Different options will vary in terms of efficiency, not only in the design of pricing policies but also in the choice of revenue allocation. Revenues can, for example, be used to reduce distortionary taxes on other markets, and hence the resulting welfare losses. But the use of revenues can also worsen pre-existing distortions.

Mayeres and Proost (2001), for example, present results where social welfare rises when road pricing is implemented and the revenues are used for the lowering of labour taxes or the financing of road infrastructure. However, social welfare falls when the revenues are used for subsidizing public transport, because doing this aggravates the distortions from pre-existing subsidies. Parry and Bento (2001) show that a 'lump-sum' redistribution of road-pricing revenues, which reduces labour supply in their model, can create a welfare loss in the labour market that exceeds the welfare gain in the road transport markets. But the use of revenues for reducing labour taxes, in contrast, stimulates labour supply, doubling the initial welfare gain as attained in the transport market. Clearly, therefore, the use of revenues can have decisive impacts on the eventual welfare effects of the policy, and is thus much more than just a means of 'buying' social acceptability.

2.3.5 Using Road-pricing Revenues for Financing Road Infrastructure: Self-financing?

An often-mentioned possible use of revenues, and sometimes even the primary motivation for road pricing, concerns the financing of road infrastructure. As indicated, Mohring and Harwitz's theorem states that the revenues from optimal congestion pricing are just sufficient to cover the cost of optimal capacity supply, provided that a number of technical conditions are fulfilled, involving constant economies of scale and the possibility of increasing road capacity in continuous increments (Mohring and Harwitz, 1962). The empirical evidence, in so far as it is available, suggests that the extent to which the constant-economies-of-scale condition is fulfilled, necessary for exact self-financing, may vary over applications, but on the whole it appears to be a reasonable approximation (Small and Verhoef, 2007). Capacity in practice will not be a continuous variable (for example, the number of lanes cannot be 2.3), but even with lumpy capacity, pooling of surpluses and deficits across roads or over time would make aggregate self-financing less unlikely than for every individual road segment at every instant. The self-financing result has been shown to carry over to rather general settings, including time-of-day dynamics, full networks, user heterogeneity, maintenance, external effects other than congestion, and in present-value terms when considering longer-run dynamics (for more details, see ibid.).

This suggests that two different possible objectives of road pricing – namely, efficient demand management and financing of infrastructure – may in fact be mutually consistent in the long run. Moreover, the use of revenues for the financing of infrastructure appears to improve the acceptability of road pricing (see also Chapters 10 and 11 of this volume). This particular way of using revenues may therefore be an important option for practical road-pricing applications.

Nevertheless, some issues remain. One is that the degree of economies of scale is still an issue that is under debate, partly because it may vary between cases. Another is that the theorem is frequently misinterpreted to imply that it is optimal to reinvest all toll revenues in extra road capacity. This is not true: the theorem relates toll revenues to capacity costs (for example, yearly interest and depreciation), not to investment costs. Indeed, in a steady state, the yearly toll revenues on an optimal road would cover the yearly costs of interest and depreciation, but no expansion of capacity is warranted (since we start with an optimal road by assumption).

2.3.6 Second-best Road Pricing: Express Lanes as an Example

In various places, we have already emphasized that the simple Pigouvian rule to equate charges to marginal external costs maximizes efficiency only under some conditions. In particular: the externality addressed by the charge should in fact be the final remaining distortion in the entire economy. This condition will, of course, not be satisfied in reality. This does not mean that the advantages of pricing policies would evaporate. But it does mean that, in order to reap the greatest social benefit from pricing, charges should be adjusted to optimally account for indirect effects in other (distorted) markets. Charges that are designed to do so are called 'second best' in the economics literature. Charges that ignore such indirect effects, and that are set equal to marginal external costs even though it is no longer optimal to do so, are called 'quasi first-best' charges, and are usually less efficient than second-best charges.

A simple example concerns road pricing on an express lane, with parallel untolled highway lanes available. A positive effect from tolling is then that it reduces congestion on the express lane. But the negative effect is that it increases congestion on the untolled lanes. Because of this negative side-effect, the second-best optimal level of the toll is below the marginal external cost on the express lane. Because congestion on the express lane is therefore underpriced, while that on the other lanes is not priced at all and even aggravated, the welfare gains may be substantially smaller than for first-best pricing of all lanes. Liu and McDonald (1998), for example, found welfare gains from second-best pricing of around 10 per cent from first-best gains for the Californian SR91. It is therefore not surprising that economists are often not enthusiastic about such partial schemes, unless they form some intermediate (demonstration) phase in a process that should eventually lead to more complete schemes.

The example of express lanes is illustrative of a number of more general lessons that can be drawn from the literature on second-best pricing. First, second-best charges are typically not equal to marginal external costs, but can be (sometimes much) lower or higher. Second, to set second-best charges optimally, one needs more information than just marginal external costs and use this in more complex pricing rules, so that the probability of government failures increases. Third, the social welfare gains from second-best pricing are typically below, and sometimes far below, those from first-best pricing. And fourth, the aforementioned 'quasi first-best tolls', which ignore second-best distortions and are simply equated to marginal external costs, produce welfare gains that are again smaller than those from second-best pricing, and possibly negative (that is, welfare losses).

2.4   CONCLUSION

Road-pricing schemes can be designed in many ways. Decisions have to be made on charging technology, tax base, charge levels, degree of differentiation and the use of revenues. The eventual choices on these matters may strongly depend on the objectives pursued by the policy, although we saw that sometimes different objectives may lead to the same recommendations: efficiency, effectiveness and acceptability may be served by sophisticated differentiation of charges; and acceptability may be enhanced by the use of congestion-pricing revenues for financing road capacity, which is also consistent with long-run efficiency. At the same time, second-best pricing rules may deviate from the appealing user-pays or polluter-pays principles, so that efficiency and fairness may deviate; and the often acceptable use of revenues for public transport may reduce efficiency if initial subsidies already distort the market for public transport.

Transport researchers cannot determine what should be the objective of pricing, and, as a consequence, also cannot specify the ideal design of a road-pricing scheme. They can, however, help in determining the consequences of different types of pricing in terms of, for example, efficiency, effectiveness and social acceptability. And this should help policy makers who have formulated a clear objective to design or select the most appropriate scheme. The following chapters aim to provide such information.

NOTES

1.   This chapter draws heavily from an earlier publication in Dutch entitled 'Beleidsdoelen en ontwerp prijsinstrumenten: de economische principes', which appeared as Chapter 3 of the unpublished report Verhoef et al. (2004).
2.   Note that this reasoning assumes that there are no external benefits from trips. Most benefits are normally either internal or at least pecuniary in nature, and therefore not external in a sense that would imply a deviation between marginal private benefit and marginal social benefit.
3.   This is not by definition the case. A road-pricing scheme of tradable permits, as discussed by Verhoef et al. (1997b) could be designed to be budget neutral for the government.

REFERENCES

Arnott, R., A. de Palma and R. Lindsey (1998), 'Recent developments in the bottleneck model', in Button and Verhoef (eds) (1998), pp. 79–110.
Arnott, R. and A. Yan (2000), 'The two-mode problem; second-best pricing and capacity', *Review of Urban and Regional Development Studies*, **12**, 170–99.

Button, K.J. (1993), *Transport Economics*, Aldershot, UK and Brookfield, US: Edward Elgar.

Button, K.J. and E.T. Verhoef (eds) (1998), *Road Pricing, Traffic Congestion and the Environment: Issues of Efficiency and Social Feasibility*, Cheltenham, UK and Lyme, USA: Edward Elgar.

CE (2004), *De Prijs van een Reis: De Maatschappelijke Kosten van het Verkeer* (The price of a trip: the social cost of traffic), Delft: CE.

CPB (2005), *Economische Analyse van Verschillende Vormen van Prijsbeleid voor het Wegverkeer* (Economic analysis of different types of pricing policies in road traffic), CPB Document 87, Den Haag: CPB.

Liu, L.N. and J.F. McDonald (1998), 'Efficient congestion tolls in the presence of unpriced congestion: a peak and off-peak simulation model', *Journal of Urban Economics*, **44**, 352–66.

Mackie, Peter (2005), 'The London congestion charge: a tentative economic appraisal. A comment on the paper by Prud'homme and Bocajero', *Transport Policy*, **12** (3), 288–90.

Mayeres, I. and S. Proost (2001), 'Marginal tax reform, externalities and income distribution', *Journal of Public Economics*, **79**, 343–63.

MC-ICAM (Authors: Esko Niskanen, Nicole Adler, Yossi Berechman, André de Palma, Robin Lindsey, Chris Nash, Stef Proost, Jan Rouwendal, Jens Schade, Bernhard Schlag and Erik Verhoef) (2004), *Implementation of Marginal Cost Pricing in Transport – Integrated Conceptual and Applied Model Analysis: Policy Conclusions*, Leeds: ITS.

Mohring, H. and M. Harwitz (1962), *Highway Benefits: An Analytical Framework*, Evanston, IL: Northwestern University Press.

Parry, I.W.H. and A.M. Bento (2001), 'Revenue recycling and the welfare effects of congestion pricing', *Scandinavian Journal of Economics*, **103**, 645–71.

Prud'homme, R. and J.P. Bocarejo (2005), 'The London congestion charge: a tentative economic appraisal', *Transport Policy*, **12** (3), 279–87.

Small, K.A. and E.T. Verhoef (2007), *The Economics of Urban Transportation*, New York: Routledge.

Stockholmsförsöket (2006), *Facts and Results from the Stockholm Trial – Final version – December 2006*, www.stockholmsforsoket.se/upload/ Sammanfattningar/English/Final%20Report_The%20Stockholm%20Trial.pdf. Accessed 20 February 2007.

Verhoef, E.T. (1996), *The Economics of Regulating Road Transport*, Cheltenham, UK and Brookfield, US: Edward Elgar.

Verhoef, E.T. (2005), 'Speed–flow relations and cost functions for congested traffic: theory and empirical analysis', *Transportation Research A*, **39** (7–9), 792–812.

Verhoef, E., C. Koopmans, M. Bliemer, P. Bovy, L. Steg and B. van Wee (2004), *Vormgeving en effecten van prijsbeleid op de weg. Effectiviteit, efficiency en acceptatie vanuit een multidisciplinair perspectief* (Design and effects of price policies in road transport. Efficiency, effectiveness and acceptability from a multidisciplinary perspective). Report for the Dutch Ministry of Transport and Waterworks, Directorate-General Passenger Traffic, Vrije Universiteit Amsterdam / Stichting voor Economisch Onderzoek Amsterdam / Rijksuniversiteit Groningen / Technische Universiteit Delft.

Verhoef, E.T., P. Nijkamp and P. Rietveld (1997b), 'Tradeable permits: their potential in the regulation of road transport externalities', *Environment and Planning B: Planning and Design B*, **24**, 527–48.

Verhoef, E.T. and K.A. Small (2004), 'Product differentiation on roads: constrained congestion pricing with heterogeneous users', *Journal of Transport Economics and Policy*, **38** (1), 127–56.

Verhoef, E.T., J.C.J.M. van den Bergh and K.J. Button (1997a), 'Transport, spatial economy and the global environment', *Environment and Planning A*, **29**, 1195–213.

Vickrey, W.S. (1969), 'Congestion theory and transport investment', *American Economic Review, Papers and Proceedings*, **59**, 251–60.

PART I

Behavioural responses to road pricing

3. Behavioural responses of freight transporters and shippers to road-user charging schemes: an empirical assessment[1]

David Hensher and Sean Puckett

3.1 INTRODUCTION

Congestion charging is recognised as an effective instrument in responding to the concerns about high levels of traffic congestion. Although the economic arguments have been known for decades and the technological capability is now widely available, the last bastion of constraint: namely, political will, is starting to move in support of implementation. The London experience (Transport for London, 2003; Evans, 2005) is being used as a catalyst for a broader recognition of what can be done without a political backlash in a Western democratic society. The adage 'it is not a matter of *if* but of *when*' seems to be the prevailing view in a growing number of jurisdictions, Stockholm[2] being the most recent (for a review, see Hensher and Puckett, 2005b, 2007a).

The problem of congested roads is expected to get considerably worse over the coming years. While this places traffic congestion high on government agendas, it does not mean that pricing will also be high on the agenda as a way to reduce traffic levels. Yet freight companies have much to gain from less congested roads in terms of opportunity costs, including the number of vehicles required to achieve a specific task set. Less congested roads would also have an indirect benefit for the recruitment of drivers. Indirect road-use charges via fuel taxes are remotely linked to use of congested roads, and other vehicle taxes are independent of time and location of vehicle use.

In late 2005 the European Parliament introduced a bill focused on the harmonisation of truck tolls levied on its roads. The bill, first tabled in 2003, is based on the 'user-pays principle' and aims to take account of the environmental and social impacts of heavy road freight, shifting some freight from roads onto rail or waterways. Although the proposal has given rise to much debate (see Transport Intelligence, 2005; Einbock, 2006), all European countries benefit heavily from road freight but some, such as Austria, France and Germany, also suffer high congestion and pollution levels. After heated discussions, it was agreed that these 'external costs' can include congestion costs, environmental costs, noise, landscape damage, social costs such as health, and indirect accident costs which are not covered by insurance. The Commission ended a dispute between Parliament and Council on how to integrate costs in toll prices by agreeing to develop a calculation method two years after the bill comes into force. As of 2012, the Eurovignette Directive will apply to vehicles of 3.5 tonnes or more. Member states are to be given flexibility on how to levy tolls or charges, and these can be raised on the entire road network, not just motorways, when they are part of the Trans-European Network. Toll revenue should be used, through hypothecation, for the maintenance of the road infrastructure concerned or to cross-finance the transport sector as a whole.

Although the focus of the European pricing initiative is broader than an interest in congestion (see McKinnon, 2006a), given that efficient pricing includes a large array of internal and external costs, internalizing the costs of congestion is recognized as a relevant component. This emphasis also applies to the debate in the UK on a national road-pricing scheme which would replace the road tax licence and fuel taxes with a mileage charge for all journeys (McKinnon, 2006b). Although the scheme would not be introduced for at least a decade, a feasibility study carried out in 2004 suggested that charges could range from 2p a mile (US 3.6 cents) on rural roads to £1.34 (US$2.50) a mile for peak-time journeys on the country's busiest roads and motorways.

The major challenge we face in implementing a user-charging regime is behavioural – a need to understand more fully the role that specific charging regimes might play in the distribution of freight, and who in the supply chain is affected by specific charges in terms of willingness to pay for the gains in network efficiency. This chapter investigates the potential influence of distance-based user charges, relative to fuel prices (the current main source of charging), in the freight distribution chain. A choice modelling framework is presented that identifies potential responses from the freight distribution sector to distance-based user charging within the context of the wider spectrum of costs imposed on the sector, as well as the potential benefits (for example, time savings) from alternative pricing regimes. We highlight the role that agents in the distribution chain play in influencing sensitivity to distance-based user charges.

With the growing interest in distance-based user charges (see O'Mahony et al., 2000; Forkenbrock, 2004), this chapter presents some new evidence on the role that distance-based charges might play in the formation of freight transporters' preferences. Using a computer-aided personal survey interview (CAPI), and an embedded stated choice (SC) experiment, we investigated, through a mixed logit model, the trade-offs made among a range of time- and cost-related attributes, including a distance-based charge for a sample of Sydney-based road haulage businesses. In the following sections (3.2–6), we detail the empirical context, including the SC experiment, the data collection method and the model estimation. The empirical evidence adds new insights into the influence of a distance-based charge on the value of travel-time savings and on the value of trip-time reliability. Section 3.7 concludes. This study is part of a larger research activity focused on the development and application of a new approach to studying the preferences and choices of agents in group decision-making contexts (see Hensher and Puckett (2007b) and Hensher et al. (in press) for the theoretical antecedents and an extensive literature review of other studies).

3.2   CONCEPTUAL FRAMEWORK

Road freight transport commonly involves interactions between decision makers, whether within the same organisation or across organisations (for example, between a manager of a freight transport company and the manager of a company that is paying the freight transport company to move goods). This interdependent nature of freight leads to significant obstacles when attempting to undertake an empirical study of freight stakeholders. It may be both difficult to design appropriate research frameworks for quantifying behaviour and welfare effects for interdependent stakeholders and financially prohibitive to utilise extant techniques to carry out the empirical task.

An appropriate research framework for interdependent stakeholders must reflect the nature of transactions made within interactions among decision makers. This is not impossible from a conceptual standpoint, yet it necessitates the development of research frameworks that expand either on extant frameworks that are centred on independent decision makers or are unique to the state of practice. Hence, there is a degree of burden placed upon the analyst that is greater than that within an independent decision-making setting when developing the appropriate theoretical and econometric models.

To quantify the preferences of road freight stakeholders and their clients, one appealing method is interactive agency choice experiments (IACEs), developed by Hensher (see Brewer and Hensher, 2000). IACEs involve an iterative technique by which interdependent respondents have the opportunity to amend their stated preferences within choice menus based on the preferences of other members of the group. The observed process of preference revision enables the analyst to quantify the effects of interactivity while maintaining the desirable empirical properties of discrete choice data obtained through stated choice experiments. Unfortunately, it is often infeasible, especially in a freight distribution chain context, to conduct a non-case-based IACE with a meaningful sample size because of the high level of resources required, including difficulties in matching agents.

Given these constraints, we investigated ways to make behavioural inferences for interdependent decision makers within discrete choice analysis. We first developed a general model, the 'inferred influence and integrative power' (IIIP) model, to accommodate a range of feasible empirical tasks (Hensher et al., in press). Within this broad model, we selected the minimum information group inference (MIGI) method to obtain our desired behavioural estimates. MIGI enables the analyst to model the influence structures within decision-making groups, such as the freight transport buyer–seller dyads of key interest within our research application (for a detailed justification, see Hensher and Puckett, 2005a; Puckett et al., 2006b), by inferring the effects of interactivity based upon the stated willingness of respondents to concede to the preferences of the other member(s) of their respective sampled groups. While we do not contend that MIGI is preferable to the direct observation of interactions among interdependent decision makers, we suggest that it represents a means of gaining meaningful inference with respect to group decision making when other methods are infeasible.

MIGI experiments are framed in terms of an interactive setting, within which respondents are asked to indicate their preferences among the given alternatives. Specifically, MIGI experiments prompt respondents to indicate how they would rank the alternatives if they had to attempt to reach agreement with the other member(s) of the sampled group. Importantly, the ranking process includes the option of denoting an alternative as unacceptable, in order to avoid inferring cooperative outcomes that would not likely be observed under direct interaction. In other words, allowing respondents to indicate that they would not concede to other respondent(s) to a specified degree within a given choice set preserves the potential to infer non-cooperative outcomes for a sampled group.

Unlike IACEs, MIGI does not involve an iterative process in which respondents are presented with information about the preferences of the other respondent(s) in the group and given the opportunity to revise their preferences. Rather, the influence of each respondent in a sampled group is inferred through the coordination of the preference rankings given by each respondent in a particular sampled group for a particular choice set. Influence is hypothesised to be represented within the preference rankings, in that respondents who are relatively more willing to accept less favourable alternatives are modelled as though they would be willing to offer relatively more concession within a direct interaction with the other group member(s).

That is, the preference rankings themselves are indicative of the levels of concession the respondent would offer when interacting with the other member(s) of the group.

This chapter focuses on the identification of the first preferences of each agent, without consideration of what compromises might be required to establish a cooperative outcome in the distribution chain. Fuller details are in Puckett and Hensher (2006) and Hensher et al. (in press). The focus herein is on the empirical specification of the first preference models for transporters and shippers and the estimation of a mixed logit model to reveal agent preferences for specific attributes of the freight distribution activity.

3.3   MODELLING APPROACH

To establish the distribution of preferences of transporters and shippers for the range of attributes and packages in a stated choice experiment, we need to develop and estimate a series of mixed logit models in which the sampled agents choose between bundles of attributes, including alternatives that have a distance-based user charge.

We begin by assuming that sampled firms $q = 1, \ldots, Q$ face a choice among J alternatives, denoted $j = 1, \ldots, J$ in each of T choice settings, $t = 1, \ldots, T$. The random utility model associates utility for firm q with each alternative in each choice situation:

$$U_{q,j,t} = \beta' \mathbf{x}_{q,t} + \varepsilon_{qjt}. \tag{3.1}$$

Firm-specific heterogeneity is introduced into the utility function in equation (3.1) through β. We allow the 'firm-specific' parameter vector to vary across firms both randomly and systematically with observable variables $\mathbf{z}_q$. In the simplest case, the (uncorrelated) random parameters are specified (based on Greene et al., 2006) as equation (3.2):

$$\beta_q = \beta + \Delta \mathbf{z}_q + \Sigma^{1/2} \mathbf{v}_q$$
$$= \beta + \Delta \mathbf{z}_q + \eta_q; \tag{3.2}$$

or

$$\beta_{qk} = \beta_k + \delta_k' \mathbf{z}_q + \eta_{qk},$$

where β_{qk} is the random coefficient for the kth attribute faced by firm q; $\beta + \Delta \mathbf{z}_q$ accommodates heterogeneity in the mean of the distribution of the random parameters; and δ_k' is a vector of parameters indicating the conditioning influence of the observable variables $\mathbf{z}_q$. The random vector $\mathbf{v}_q$ endows the random parameter with its stochastic properties. For convenience, denote the matrix of known variances of the random draws as $\mathbf{W}$. The scale factors which provide the unknown standard deviations of the random parameters are arrayed on the diagonal of the diagonal variance matrix $\Sigma^{1/2}$.

The *mixed logit* class of models assumes a general distribution for β_{qk}, and an IID extreme value type 1 distribution for ε_{jtq}. That is, β_{qk} can take on different distributional forms.[3] For a given value of β_q, the *conditional* (on $\mathbf{z}_q$ and $\mathbf{v}_q$) probability for choice j in choice situation t is a multinomial logit, since the remaining random term ε_{tjq} is IID extreme value:

$$\mathbf{P}_{jtq}(\text{choice } j \mid \Omega, \mathbf{X}_{tq}, \mathbf{z}_q, \mathbf{v}_q) = \exp(\beta_q'\mathbf{x}_{jtq}) \, / \, \Sigma_j \exp(\beta_q'\mathbf{x}_{jtq}), \qquad (3.3)$$

where the elements of Ω are the underlying parameters of the distribution of β_q. We label as the *unconditional* choice probability, the expected value of the logit probability over all the possible values of β_q, that is, integrated over these values, weighted by the density of β_q. The latter is conditioned on the observable firm-specific information $(\mathbf{z}_q)$, but not on the unobservable $\mathbf{v}_q$. From (3.3), we see that this probability density is induced by the random component in the model for β_q: namely, $\mathbf{v}_q$. The unconditional choice probability is given as equation (3.4) (Greene et al., 2006):

$$\mathbf{P}_{jtq}(\text{choice } j \mid \Omega, \mathbf{X}_{tq}, \mathbf{z}_q) = \int_{\mathbf{v}_q} P_{jtq}(\beta_q \mid \Omega, \mathbf{X}_{tq}, \mathbf{z}_q, \mathbf{v}_q) f(\mathbf{v}_q \mid \mathbf{W}) d\mathbf{v}_q. \quad (3.4)$$

Details on the estimation of the parameters of the mixed logit model by maximum simulated likelihood may be found in Train (2003).

One can construct estimates of 'individual-specific preferences' by deriving the conditional distribution based (within-sample) on known choices (that is, prior knowledge), (see also ibid., ch. 11; Hensher et al., 2005). These conditional parameter estimates are strictly 'same-choice-specific' parameters, or the mean of the parameters of the subpopulation of individuals who, when faced with the same choice situation would have made the same choices. This is an important distinction[4] since we are not able to establish, for each individual, their unique set of estimates, but rather we are able to identify a mean (and standard deviation) estimate for the subpopulation who make the same choice. For convenience, let $\mathbf{Y}_q$ denote the observed information on choices by individual q, and let $\mathbf{X}_q$ denote all elements of $\mathbf{x}_{jtq}$ for all j and t. Using Bayes Rule, we find the conditional density for the random parameters,

$$f(\beta_q \mid \Omega, \mathbf{Y}_q, \mathbf{X}_q, \mathbf{z}_q, \mathbf{h}_q) = \frac{f(\mathbf{Y}_q \mid \beta_q, \Omega, \mathbf{X}_q, \mathbf{z}_q, \mathbf{h}_q) P(\beta_q \mid \Omega, \mathbf{z}_q, \mathbf{h}_q)}{f(\mathbf{Y}_q \mid \Omega, \mathbf{X}_q, \mathbf{z}_q, \mathbf{h}_q}. \quad (3.5)$$

The left-hand side gives the conditional density of the random parameter vector, given the underlying parameters and all of the data on individual q. In the numerator of the right-hand side, the first term gives the choice probability in the conditional likelihood – this is in (3.4). The second term gives the marginal probability density for the random β_q implied by (3.2) with the assumed distribution of $\mathbf{v}_q$. The denominator is the unconditional choice probability for the individual – this is given by (3.4). Note that the denominator in (3.6) is the integral of the numerator. This result can be used to estimate the 'common-choice-specific' parameters, utilities, and willingness-to-pay values or choice probabilities as a function of the underlying parameters of the distribution of the random parameters. Estimation of the individual specific value of β_q is done by computing an estimate of the mean of this conditional distribution. Note that this conditional mean is a direct analogue to its counterpart in the Bayesian framework, the mean of the posterior distribution, or the posterior mean. More generally, for a particular function of β_q, $g(\beta_q)$, such as β_q itself, the conditional mean function is:

$$\mathbf{E}[g(\beta_q) \mid \Omega, \mathbf{Y}_q, \mathbf{X}_q, \mathbf{z}_q, \mathbf{h}_q] =$$

$$\int_{\beta_q} \frac{g(\beta_q) f(\mathbf{Y}_q \mid \beta_q, \Omega, \mathbf{X}_q, \mathbf{z}_q, \mathbf{h}_q) P(\beta_q \mid \Omega, \mathbf{z}_q, \mathbf{h}_q)}{f(\mathbf{Y}_q \mid \Omega, \mathbf{X}_q, \mathbf{z}_q, \mathbf{h}_q)} d\beta_q. \quad (3.6)$$

To avoid confounding our results with differentially unobserved scale effects across transporters and shippers, we pooled the choices of transporters and shippers into one model, estimating separate marginal (dis)utilities for transporters and shippers for each attribute. The value of travel-time savings (VTTS) and value of reliability gains (VRG) are obtained from the conditional estimates of the relevant time and cost parameters in the models given below.

3.4 AN EMPIRICAL FRAMEWORK FOR MODELLING THE INFLUENCE OF DISTANCE-BASED ROAD USER CHARGES

Preliminary in-depth interviews with a number of stakeholders in freight distribution chains; namely, the shipper of goods, the transporter and the receiver of goods, suggested that the majority of decisions on distribution are made by, at most, two agents (Puckett et al., 2006b). The agency set was defined as the freight transport provider carrying the goods, and the organisation paying the freight transport provider for those services. Any additional party (for example, a recipient of the goods who does not interact with the freight transport provider) was treated as an exogenous force, setting some constraints on the interaction within the two-member group.

Given the interest in evaluating a range of distance-based user charges that do not currently exist in real markets, we selected a stated choice framework (Louviere et al., 2000) within which the transporter defined a recent reference trip in terms of its time and cost attributes (detailed below), treating fuel as a separate cost item to the distance-based vehicle user charge (VUC), with the latter being zero at present. A pivot design using principles of D-optimality in experimental design (Sandor and Wedel, 2001; Rose et al., 2005) was developed to vary the levels of existing attributes around the reference levels plus introduce a VUC based on distance travelled but with varying rates per kilometre. With a focus on understanding sensitivity to varying charge levels, any consideration of tailoring a charge to the specific vehicle type in recognition of the costs it imposes on the road system is of secondary interest.

The stated choice alternatives were kept generic to one another in terms of the treatment of each parameter of the attributes, representing various options of re-routeing and rescheduling; however, these alternatives are inherently different from the reference alternative, which does not involve distance-based road user charges. We selected two stated choice alternatives, found to be sufficient to offer the desired variation in attribute bundles, giving a total of three alternatives from which to choose.

Selecting the set of attributes for the choice sets involved an iterative process of finding candidate attributes and determining how they could fit intuitively into the choice sets. While in-depth interviews and literature reviews revealed myriad attributes that influence freight decision making in one way or another (see Cullinane and Toy, 2000; Bolis and Maggi, 2001; Fowkes et al., 2004; Danielis et al., 2005; Hensher and Puckett, 2005a; Puckett et al., 2006a), we focused on the subset of these attributes that were most likely to be directly affected by congestion charges. Hence, the attributes that reside within the choice sets are: free-flow travel time; slowed-down travel time; time spent waiting to unload at the final destination; likelihood of on-time arrival; fuel cost; and distance-based road user charges. These attributes are either an input into a congestion-charging policy (that is, changes in fuel taxes, road user charges), or direct functions of such a policy. While other attributes could be hypothesised to be directly or indirectly affected by congestion charging, we found that our specification offered a useful mix of tractability and inferential power.

The levels and ranges of the attributes were chosen to reflect a range of coping strategies under a hypothetical congestion-centred road user charging regime. The reference alternative was utilised to offer a base, around which the stated choice design levels were pivoted. The resulting mixes represent coping strategies including: taking the same route at the same time as in the reference alternative under new traffic conditions, or costs, or both; and taking alternative, previously less-favourable routes, or departing at alternative, previously less-favourable times, or both, with corresponding levels of traffic conditions and costs.

Congestion charging does not yet exist in Sydney, the empirical setting, hence we needed to utilise available information to set realistic levels for the distance-based charges. Literature reviews revealed that fuel taxes are currently set as a second-best instrument to recover externality costs caused by heavy goods vehicle movements. Furthermore, the literature revealed that policy makers acknowledge that distance-based or mass-distance-based road user charging may be a more efficient method of internalising externality costs. Hence, we decided to specify the empirical study in terms of potential policy adjustments, in which fuel taxes may be amended, in preference to direct road user charges reflecting vehicle tonne kilometres travelled and congestion costs caused. To accomplish this, we utilised the fuel costs within the reference alternative as a base for the hypothetical road user charges. As fuel costs (and hence fuel taxes) increase with vehicle load and distance travelled, they form a useful, market-linked base for these hypothetical charges.

One potential complication that we identified is that changes in levels of service and operating costs (that is, changes in fuel costs and new road user charges) could lead to upward or downward adjustments in the freight rate charged by the transport company. While obvious, incorporating an endogenous (at least to the freight transport provider) choice that could dominate the changes in costs into the experimental design is not a simple matter. To combat this, we developed a method to internalise this endogeneity and uncertainty, making it exogenous to the final choice. For each stated choice alternative involving a net change in direct operating costs (that is, the change in fuel costs is not equal to the (negative) value of the new road user charges), respondents from freight firms were asked to indicate by how much of the net change in costs they would like to adjust their freight rate. Hence, the freight rate, which is not a design alternative, yet is clearly an important contextual effect, is allowed to vary across stated choice alternatives under changes in net operating costs.

The reference alternative within each choice set for respondents from freight firms is created using the details specified by the respondent for the recent freight trip. In all cases except for the distance-based charges, the attribute levels for each of the SC alternatives are related to the levels of the reference alternative (the pivot base), as detailed below. The levels are expressed as deviations from the reference level, which is the exact value specified in the corresponding non-SC questions, unless noted:

1. *Free-flow time*: -50%, -25%, 0, $+25\%$, $+50\%$.
2. *Congested time*: -50%, -25%, 0, $+25\%$, $+50\%$.
3. *Waiting time at destination*: -50%, -25%, 0, $+25\%$, $+50\%$.
4. *Probability of on-time arrival*: -50%, -25%, 0, $+25\%$, $+50\%$, with the resulting value rounded to the nearest 5 per cent (for example, a reference value of 75 per cent reduced by 50 per cent would yield a raw figure of 37.5 per cent, which would be rounded to 40 per cent). If the resulting value is 100 per cent, the value is expressed as 99 per cent. If the reference level is greater than 92 per cent, the pivot base is set to 92 per cent. If the pivot base is greater than 66 per cent (that is, if 1.5* the base is greater than 100 per cent), let the pivot base equal X, and let the difference between 99 per cent and X equal Y. The range of attribute levels for on-time arrival when $X > 66$ per cent are (in percentage terms): $X - Y$, $X - 0.5*Y$, X, $X + 0.5*Y$, $X + Y$. This yields five equally-spaced attribute levels between $X - Y$ and 99 per cent.
5. *Fuel cost*: -50%, -25%, 0, $+25\%$, $+50\%$ (representing changes in fuel taxes of -100%, -50%, 0, $+50\%$, $+100\%$).
6. *Distance-based charges*: Pivot base equals 0.5*(reference fuel cost), to reflect the amount of fuel taxes paid in the reference alternative. Variations around the pivot base are: -50%, -25%, 0, $+25\%$, $+50\%$.

The attribute levels include positive and negative deviations from the pivot bases both to cover a range of levels of service and costs that may exist for a given trip option in the future, and to represent alternative means of routeing and scheduling a given trip option at one point in time. This makes the choice data sufficiently rich to allow for inference under a range of scenarios. It is apparent that the probability of on-time arrival offers the greatest obstacle from a practical standpoint (see Fowkes et al., 2004). This is because the logical upper boundary is 1 for the attribute level (that is, the probability cannot exceed 1). As a result of the use of respondent-specified pivot bases, one cannot know a priori whether all values for the probability of on-time arrival in the SC alternatives would be less than 1 without specifying sufficient heuristics. Furthermore, the design requires sufficient variation around the pivot base, despite the mathematical constraint. Hence, for cases of reference levels very close to 1, a pivot base of 92 per cent was selected to allow for sufficient variation in the attribute, while limiting the scope for unfavourable values of the attribute in SC alternatives, relative to the reference level.

The choice experiment focuses on the reaction of firms to the introduction of a VUC system in the context of trip service levels, other trip costs, freight rates and time loading and unloading goods. The survey was conducted via a computer-aided personal interview (CAPI). This was essential if we were to seed each choice set faced by respondents with the revealed preference information they specify within the pre-choice-set phase of the questionnaire.

Given the focus herein on the role of distance-based user charges, see Hensher et al. (in press) for more details on the survey instrument and modelling of group decision making. Figures 3.1–3 reproduce the relevant CAPI screens related to the description of distance-based user charges and the SC experiment in which each sampled respondent has to review the attribute packages and make a choice. Our focus herein is on the first preference choice of the transporter and the shipper.

To familiarise respondents with VUCs, we provided an example trip situation of travel times and costs associated with taking a particular hypothetical trip during peak hours, contrasted with the travel times and costs of taking the same trip during the off-peak period (Figure 3.2). The same trip is then discussed under hypothetical VUCs, revealing altered travel times and costs for both the peak and off-peak options.

Respondents were faced with four choice sets if they represented a freight firm, and with eight choice sets if they represented a client of a freight firm. The difference is accounted for by the relatively larger burden placed on respondents from freight firms, in that they must supply the trip and relationship-specific details required to establish the choice setting and reference alternative. The exact four choice sets presented to a given respondent from a freight firm are given to the corresponding sampled client. The additional four choice sets faced by the sampled client use the same reference alternative as the other four choice sets.

Respondents were asked to assume that, for each of the choice sets given, the same goods need to be carried for the same client, subject to the same constraints faced when the reference trip was undertaken.[5] Respondents are then informed that the choice sets involve three alternative methods of making the trip (Figure 3.3): their stated trip[6] and two SC alternatives that involve VUCs. The choice tasks are described to respondents as two straightforward steps. The first step is to indicate which alternatives would be preferable if the two organizations had to reach agreement, while the second step is to indicate what information mattered when making each choice.[7]

Respondents have the option to click to find a definition for the two travel-time attributes, each of which includes an illustrative photograph.

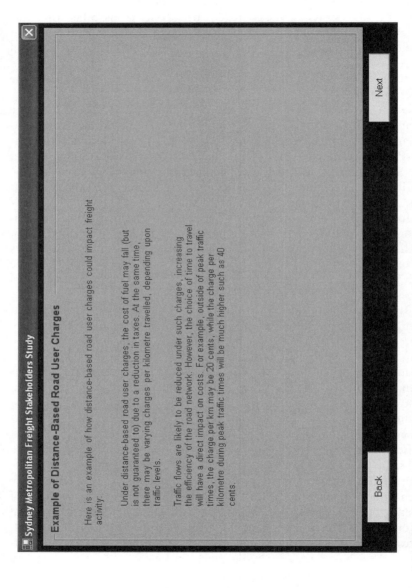

Figure 3.1   Questionnaire screen introducing distance-based user charges

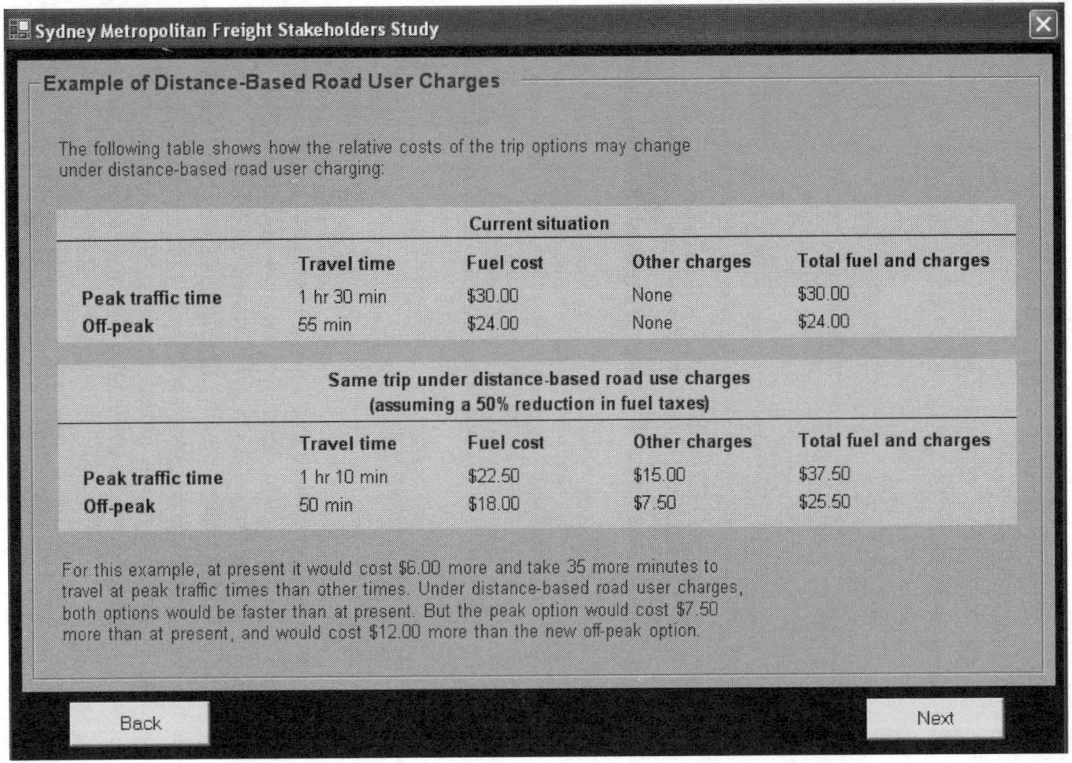

Sydney Metropolitan Freight Stakeholders Study

Example of Distance-Based Road User Charges

The following table shows how the relative costs of the trip options may change under distance-based road user charging:

		Current situation		
	Travel time	Fuel cost	Other charges	Total fuel and charges
Peak traffic time	1 hr 30 min	$30.00	None	$30.00
Off-peak	55 min	$24.00	None	$24.00

	Same trip under distance-based road use charges (assuming a 50% reduction in fuel taxes)			
	Travel time	Fuel cost	Other charges	Total fuel and charges
Peak traffic time	1 hr 10 min	$22.50	$15.00	$37.50
Off-peak	50 min	$18.00	$7.50	$25.50

For this example, at present it would cost $6.00 more and take 35 more minutes to travel at peak traffic times than other times. Under distance-based road user charges, both options would be faster than at present. But the peak option would cost $7.50 more than at present, and would cost $12.00 more than the new off-peak option.

Back   Next

Figure 3.2   *CAPI screen offering an example of the effects of VUCs*

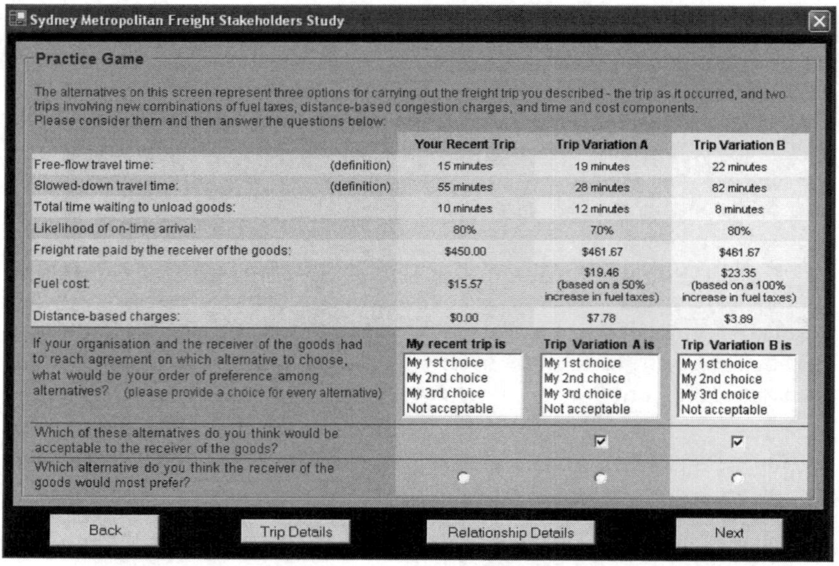

Sydney Metropolitan Freight Stakeholders Study				

Practice Game

The alternatives on this screen represent three options for carrying out the freight trip you described - the trip as it occurred, and two trips involving new combinations of fuel taxes, distance-based congestion charges, and time and cost components. Please consider them and then answer the questions below:

		Your Recent Trip	Trip Variation A	Trip Variation B
Free-flow travel time:	(definition)	15 minutes	19 minutes	22 minutes
Slowed-down travel time:	(definition)	55 minutes	28 minutes	82 minutes
Total time waiting to unload goods:		10 minutes	12 minutes	8 minutes
Likelihood of on-time arrival:		80%	70%	80%
Freight rate paid by the receiver of the goods:		$450.00	$461.67	$461.67
Fuel cost:		$15.57	$19.46 (based on a 50% increase in fuel taxes)	$23.35 (based on a 100% increase in fuel taxes)
Distance-based charges:		$0.00	$7.78	$3.89
If your organisation and the receiver of the goods had to reach agreement on which alternative to choose, what would be your order of preference among alternatives? (please provide a choice for every alternative)		**My recent trip is** My 1st choice My 2nd choice My 3rd choice Not acceptable	**Trip Variation A is** My 1st choice My 2nd choice My 3rd choice Not acceptable	**Trip Variation B is** My 1st choice My 2nd choice My 3rd choice Not acceptable
Which of these alternatives do you think would be acceptable to the receiver of the goods?			☑	☑
Which alternative do you think the receiver of the goods would most prefer?		○	○	○

Back	Trip Details	Relationship Details	Next

Note: The summary of relationship details that appears when clicking on Relationship Details includes: the length of the relationship between the two organizations; their contractual arrangement; the organizations that have input into the routeing and scheduling of the trip; and, in the case of respondents representing freight firms, the proportion of business represented by the relationship with the client. This last element is omitted from questionnaires involving sampled clients, as they may not know this information in the marketplace.

Figure 3.3   Main choice set screen

Free-flow travel time is described as: 'Can change lanes without restriction and drive freely at the speed limit', while slowed-down travel time is described as: 'Changing lanes is noticeably restricted and your freedom to drive at the speed limit is periodically inhibited. Queues will form behind any lane blockage such as a broken-down car'.

The specific choice task on the initial screen is: 'If your organisation and the client had to reach agreement on which alternative to choose, what would be your order of preference among alternatives?' Respondents are asked to provide a choice for every alternative. The available options for each alternative are: (Name of the alternative) is: {My 1st choice; My 2nd choice; My 3rd choice; Not acceptable}. At least one of the alternatives must be indicated as a first choice, which was not found to be restrictive, given that the reference alternative represents the status quo, which was clearly acceptable in the market. We focus herein on the first preference choice.[8]

The number of attributes to consider could be potentially burdensome. However, there are at least two reasons why this may not be so. First, each of the attributes is an element either of time or of cost. Therefore, although the number of attributes may be viewed as relatively high, there is an intuitive relationship between them. Second, as illustrated by Hensher (2006a, 2006b), there is not a monotonically increasing relationship between the number of attributes and the level of cognitive burden experienced by respondents. Rather, there is a local, but not global, trade-off between complexity and relevance. That is, over a finite range, decision making is relatively easier as the information presented increases. While seven attributes is a significant number, one may argue that a complex decision-making setting requires a complex, and hence relevant, array of information in order to make an informed decision. Therefore, in the case of a complex decision such as a distribution strategy, it is one thing to argue that seven is a large number, but quite another to argue that it is too large.

While the analyst must ensure that choice sets are tractable by taking care to include only those attributes that have been identified as integral to the application, there is a point at which further paring of attributes for the sake of reducing the cognitive burden becomes dangerous. Such paring may even add to the cognitive burden of respondents, as there may not be sufficient information to make an informed choice.

3.5 PROFILE OF THE DATA COLLECTION STRATEGY AND CHOICE RESPONSES

The survey was undertaken in 2005, sampling transporters who were delivering goods on behalf of a single shipper to and/or from the Sydney Metropolitan area. Initially a sample of transporters was selected and screened for participation by a telephone call. Eligibility to participate in the CAPI survey required a respondent having (i) 'input into the routeing or scheduling of freight vehicles used by your organisation' (ii) 'input into the business arrangements made with your organisation's customers', and (iii) 'your organisation carry truckloads that contain cargo either sent by, or intended for, one single company'. Each completed CAPI interview by a transporter was used to match a shipper based on a hierarchy of criteria. If the actual receiver of the goods was known, then that organisation was contacted; however, if that organisation refused to participate or was not known, a rule set was implemented that matched the transporter to the shipper. The main rules relate to the market segment of the goods (for example, perishables being delivered to a major retailer).

The resulting estimation sample, after controlling for outliers and problematic respondent data,[9] includes 108 transporters and 102 shippers, yielding 1248 observations (432 choice sets faced by transporters and 816 choice sets faced by shippers). The transporters' response rate was 45 per cent while that of the shippers is 72 per cent. The remainder of this section presents the results for models of independent preferences for transporters and shippers, based on this sample.

Tables 3.1 and 3.2 summarise the mean and standard deviation of attribute levels in the chosen alternatives, represented in terms of the specification of utility functions for transporters and shippers. The choice frequencies across alternatives are remarkably similar for both transporters and shippers, with minimal variation across the groups; alternative A (that is, the reference alternative) was chosen by 55.8 per cent of transporters and 56.3 per cent of shippers, alternative B (that is, the first stated choice alternative) was chosen by 30.6 per cent of transporters and 29.7 per cent of shippers, and alternative C (that is, the second stated choice alternative) was chosen by 13.6 per cent of transporters and 14 per cent of shippers.

While both transporters and shippers demonstrated a preference for the reference (that is, zero-distance-based-charge, zero-change-in-fuel-cost) alternative, the variation in attribute levels of chosen alternatives across the groups reveals different forces that induce transporters to choose SC alternatives relative to shippers. Transporters are willing to choose SC alternatives that offer improvements in travel quality; the mean levels of travel time and on-time reliability are more favourable in the chosen SC alternatives compared with the reference alternative. However, transporters appear willing to choose these alternatives only when the shipper covers the increase in total cost that accompanies the improved levels of service; the difference between the freight rate and the transporter's costs is larger in the SC alternatives. This is also indicative of a relatively lower disutility of the distance-based charges as the trip distance, and hence level of the charges, increases.

Shippers, on the other hand, appear willing to choose alternatives that offer improved travel times (chiefly free-flow time) and on-time reliability, as long as the proportion of charges passed on to the shipper is less than unity. That is, the mean difference between the freight rate and the transporter's costs is lower in the SC alternatives chosen by shippers than in the reference alternatives chosen by shippers. Ultimately, it appears that shippers are willing to pay some of the costs associated with the improvements offered by the SC alternatives, but are not willing to cover the costs entirely. However, as with transporters, this may also be indicative of a certain class of trips which offer relatively larger benefits of paying the distance-based charges than other trips.

Table 3.1 Descriptive statistics – transporters (chosen alternatives) (time in minutes, cost in dollars, FF*km in mins*kms/1000)

	FF/SD time	On-time reliability	FF*km	Total cost	Freight rate	Distance-based charges/km	Total cost* distance-based charges
Alternative A (55.8% choice frequency)							
Mean	250.8	85.1	75.2	193.8	753.0		
Standard dev.	102.3	14.8	68.1	179.4	382.5		
Alternative B (30.6% choice frequency)							
Mean	208.8	92.7	67.7	287.2	858.0	0.23	82.3
Standard dev.	82.8	13.0	57.0	207.5	404.7	0.14	100.3
Alternative C (13.6% choice frequency)							
Mean	240.6	88.9	70.9	361.2	1004.5	0.30	133.32
Standard dev.	127.6	17.3	68.4	237.9	523.3	0.19	136.34

45

Table 3.2   Descriptive statistics – shippers (chosen alternatives)

	Free-flow time	Slowed-down time	Waiting time	On-time reliability	Total cost	Freight rate
Alternative A (56.3% choice frequency)						
Mean	212.3	43.6	59.1	85.5	202.8	755.9
Standard dev.	100.5	33.5	70.4	13.9	146.2	405.0
Alternative B (29.7% choice frequency)						
Mean	171.5	43.0	59.3	92.5	284.6	909.2
Standard dev.	103.9	43.2	67.8	12.3	299.9	396.9
Alternative C (14.0% choice frequency)						
Mean	140.6	50.8	45.8	87.6	256.9	890.2
Standard dev.	91.6	50.4	55.6	15.8	199.1	511.2

3.6   EMPIRICAL MODEL RESULTS

Tables 3.3 and 3.4 summarize the multinomial logit (MNL) and mixed logit model results. The MNL and mixed logit models yield similar mean estimates for each measure of marginal (dis)utility; however, the mixed logit model captures elements of unobserved preference heterogeneity for the travel-time attributes. This offers an improvement over the MNL model by explaining variation around mean parameter estimates, and by relaxing the strict assumption of the independence of irrelevant alternatives. Tests for more complex models (that is, models accounting for correlations across choice sets or systematic error components) did not improve on the results of the simpler mixed logit model results, our preferred model for explaining the preferences of transporters and shippers.

The model offers rich behavioural inference. The inclusion of interaction terms with free-flow time (that is, trip distance) and distance-based charges (that is, total cost and trip distance) for transporters permits the model to account for contextual influence on preferences of transporters across types of travel time (that is, free-flow time and slowed-down time) and cost (that is, fuel cost and distance-based charges). The data are sufficiently well behaved to enable a linear representation of marginal utility for shippers that explains preferences, as well as any alternative specifications that were tested; the only restriction in the model with respect to shippers is that the model is not improved if fuel cost and distance-based charges are considered separately (that is, the model essentially assumes that shippers form an aggregate of transporters' costs).

Table 3.3 Multinomial logit model

Attribute	Parameter (*t*-statistic) Transporter	Parameter (*t*-statistic) Shipper
Marginal utility parameters		
Constant representing the reference alternative	0.6338 (2.60)	
Free-flow and slowed-down time	−0.0095 (−3.03)	
Probability of on-time arrival	0.0299 (4.25)	
Free-flow time*trip distance	0.0138 (1.95)	
Total cost	−0.0082 (−4.13)	
Freight rate	0.0045 (2.58)	
Distance-based charges per kilometre	−1.4502 (−1.87)	
Total cost*distance based-charges per kilometre	0.0028 (3.23)	
Constant representing the reference alternative		0.8229 (7.73)
Free-flow time		−0.0071 (−6.49)
Slowed-down time		−0.0173 (−5.54)
Waiting time		−0.0069 (−3.34)
Probability of on-time arrival		0.0533 (8.61)
Total cost		−0.0015 (−2.11)
Freight rate		−0.0056 (−5.80)
Model fit		
No observations	1248 (432 transporters, 816 shippers)	
LL(B)	−1039.387	

3.6.1 Marginal (Dis)utility of Travel-time Elements

For transporters, while travel time is a source of disutility, the marginal disutility of free-flow time decreases as the interaction between free-flow time and trip distance increases. This implies that transporters acknowledge an inherent value in travel quality; that is, for a given distance travelled, as the proportion of free-flow time increases, the (dis)utility decreases. The presence of this relationship has direct implications for the relative VTTS held by transporters for free-flow time and slowed-down time. These values are examined below, along with the values of reliability gains (VRG) for transporters and shippers.

The empirical marginal disutility functions for the random parameterized attributes can be written out as a set of equations, drawing on the

Table 3.4   Mixed logit model

Attribute	Parameter (*t*-statistic) Transporter	Parameter (*t*-statistic) Shipper
Mean random parameters		
Free-flow and slowed-down time (transporter)	−0.0114 (−2.90)	
Probability of on-time arrival	0.0289 (3.76)	
Free-flow time*trip distance	0.0178 (2.03)	
Free-flow time		−0.0080 (−5.95)
Slowed-down time		−0.0221 (−5.20)
Waiting time		−0.0071 (−2.79)
Probability of on-time arrival		0.0694 (7.83)
Fixed parameters		
Constant representing the reference alternative	0.6516 (2.57)	
Total cost	−0.0088 (−4.29)	
Freight rate	0.0050 (2.74)	
Distance-based charges per kilometre	−1.5119 (−1.89)	
Total cost distance-based charges per kilometre	0.0030 (3.39)	
Constant representing the reference alternative		0.9426 (8.04)
Total cost		−0.0017 (−2.05)
Freight rate		−0.0067 (−5.99)
Standard deviation of random parameters		
Free-flow and slowed-down time	0.0114 (2.90)	
Probability of on-time arrival	0.0578 (3.79)	
Free-flow time*trip distance	0.0178 (2.03)	
Free-flow time		0.0160 (5.95)
Slowed-down time		0.0441 (5.20)
Waiting time		0.0142 (2.79)
Probability of on-time arrival		0.1388 (7.83)
Model fit		
Number of observations	1248 (432 transporters, 816 shippers)	
LL(B)	−1036.369	
Adjusted pseudo R^2	0.53	

Note: 200 Halton draws used to estimate the random parameters; all random terms distributed triangular.

estimated parameters in Table 3.4. The marginal disutility is the derivative of utility with respect to the attribute. For example, the marginal disutility expressions for travel time and marginal utility of the probability of on-time arrival for transporter, based on random parameters, are:

$$Marginal\ disutility\ of\ travel\ time = -0.0114 + 0.0114*t$$

$$Marginal\ disutility\ of\ on\text{-}time\ arrival\ probability = 0.0694 + 0.0694*t,$$

where t is the triangular distribution. The marginal disutility of trip cost, based on fixed parameters, is:

$$Marginal\ disutility\ of\ trip\ cost = -0.0088 + 0.0030*dbcperkm - 1.5119,$$

where *dbcperkm* is the distance-based cost per kilometre ($/km).

The VTTS per transporter is the ratio of *Marginal disutility of travel time* to *Marginal disutility of trip cost* (in $ per trip hour), and the VRG is the ratio of *Marginal disutility of on-time arrival probability* to *Marginal disutility of trip cost* (in $ per percentage point of improvement in arrival-time probability). These estimates are obtained for each transporter, given the distribution of parameter estimates in the numerator, and these sample averages are obtained by averaging over the distributions.

Before examining the VTTS and VRG measures, it is important to contrast the marginal (dis)utility of transit time for transporters with the corresponding estimates for shippers. While free-flow, slowed-down and waiting time are technically representative of the transit time for a delivery, travel time mixes do not make a direct impact on shippers. Hence, any variation in marginal utilities across time components may serve as proxies for other factors, such as service quality. Indeed, shippers show a much stronger disutility for slowed-down time than for free-flow time or waiting time. This may be explained by a perceived relationship between slowed-down time and delay or damage risk. That is, a larger proportion of slowed-down time is indicative of travel in congested conditions, which may result in a greater probability of delay or damage relative to travel outside of congested conditions. Furthermore, strategically thinking shippers may see the benefits of reducing the transporter's costs: by reducing the amount of time the transporter spends in congested conditions, the transporter is likely to experience lower operating costs, reducing the probability that the freight rate will increase.

The presence of a significant disutility of waiting time for shippers is interesting, in that no such disutility could be identified for transporters. But the nature of the time is quite different for the two groups.

Transporters, especially owner–operators, who form the majority of the freight vehicle fleet, appear to schedule waiting time at destinations as break time. Indeed, there are limits to the amount of travel a driver may legally perform on a given shift, and hence waiting time may not lead to any wasted downtime for transporters, as long as it is within an acceptable range. However, waiting time has an impact on shippers, in that any time the transporter spends waiting to unload is time that the shipper must spend without being in possession of the goods. Nevertheless, waiting time causes less disutility than free-flow time. This is intuitive, in that arrival reliability is no longer an issue once a truck has reached its destination. Hence, time spent in a delivery queue is similar to free-flow time, in that it involves expected processes of bringing the goods into the hands of the receiver. The marked difference between slowed-down time and both free-flow and waiting times supports the notion of concerns with respect to service quality and the freight rate, and the slightly lower disutility for waiting time relative to free-flow time adds to the picture: there is a relatively higher cost to driving, even in free-flow conditions, than to waiting in a queue (that is, labour costs are involved in both cases, but asset-related operating costs are relatively low or nil when waiting). Therefore, reducing waiting time could help to decrease the transporter's costs (while also decreasing total transit time of the goods for the shipper), but not to the degree that a reduction in free-flow or slowed-down time could.

VTTS and VRG measures, given in Tables 3.5 to 3.7 and Figures 3.4 to 3.8, will be discussed as the basis of highlighting the behavioural response differences between transporters and shippers in trade-off time and cost dimensions of freight distribution.

Transporters demonstrate a clear disutility for travel in slowed-down conditions, with a mean VTTS for slowed-down time twice as high as the VTTS for free-flow time (Table 3.5, Figures 3.4–5). Furthermore, heterogeneity in preferences with respect to slowed-down time is significantly lower across transporters than heterogeneity in preferences with respect to free-flow time; the ratio of the mean VTTS for slowed-down time to its standard deviation is only approximately one-fifth of the corresponding ratio for free-flow time.

The policy implications are clear. Should the implementation of a distance-based user-charging system proceed, transporters would stand to gain from improvements in the level of service provided by the traffic infrastructure. Specifically, any reductions in travel in congested conditions would benefit most transporters at a rate that may frequently exceed the corresponding level of the charges. For example, considering a transporter at the mean of the VTTS distribution, a given trip alternative that offers a saving of 30 minutes

Table 3.5   VTTS (A$ per hour) for transporters

	Free-flow time	Slowed-down time
Mean	42.48	83.77
Standard deviation	22.95	8.88
Minimum	−22.64	55.67
Maximum	99.39	162.42
Proportion of negative values	1.9%	0%

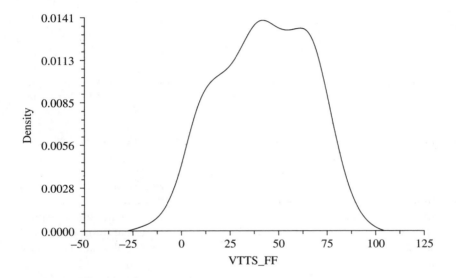

Figure 3.4   Distribution of free-flow VTTS (A$, Kernel Density Estimate)

of slowed-down time – worth A$41.89 – would benefit from the utilization of that alternative as long as the distance-based charges did not exceed A$0.41, A$0.83 or A$1.68 per kilometre for a trip of 100, 50 or 25 kilometres, respectively. Given the relatively small spread of VTTS values around the mean, the majority of transporters would experience similar opportunities.

Ultimately, the relatively large negative economic impact of traffic congestion on transporters could fuel significant changes in travel patterns under distance-based user charges. The status quo prohibits certain routeing and scheduling alternatives from being profitable, yet this may no longer be the case under distance-based charging. Not only would transporters stand to gain from an increased set of profitable routeing alternatives at a

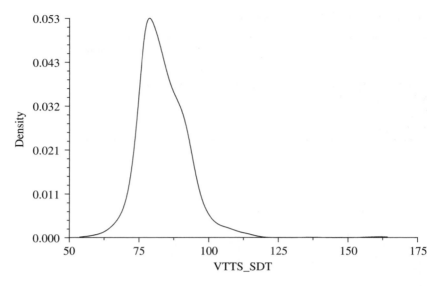

Figure 3.5   Distribution of slowed-down VTTS (A$, Kernel Density Estimate)

given time of day, but they would also stand to gain from shifting trips to times of day that are currently prohibitive for a given route. The potential for mutual gains of efficiency through tighter scheduling and more responsive, reliable travel appear significant enough to encourage transporters and shippers to work together to develop a group (that is, supply chain) response to the implementation of distance-based charging that results in a net benefit for all parties. While this has been suggested in the theoretical literature, a lack of empirical studies could not confirm this result. However, the presence of a significantly higher VTTS for slowed-down time compared with free-flow time under distance-based user charges confirms the theoretical gains to supply-chain cooperation. Furthermore, the direct gains that may be afforded to transporters go as far as to imply benefits to transporters when acting unilaterally.

Unilateral action may not be necessary, however, as Table 3.6 highlights (see also Figures 3.6–8). While transporters demonstrate a value of reliability gains of $3.54 per percentage point of improvement, shippers place an even higher value on reliability. This is intuitive, as reliability may be a larger item of concern to shippers than travel time (that is, it is more beneficial to know that shipments are likely to arrive on time than it is to know that shipments are expected to arrive within a given time frame whose reliability cannot be guaranteed). Using the shipper's only cost measure in

Table 3.6   VRG (A$ per percentage point)

	Transporters	Shippers – freight rate only	Shippers – freight rate and costs
Mean	3.54	10.32	12.67
Standard deviation	0.46	1.94	2.87
Minimum	1.62	0.61	0.72
Maximum	6.93	17.30	27.89
Proportion of negative values	0%	0%	0%

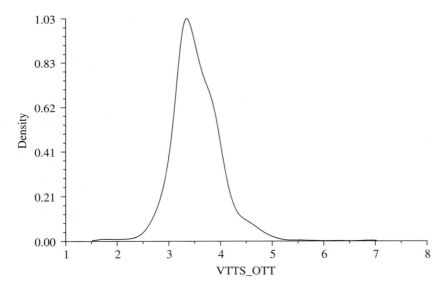

Figure 3.6   Distribution of transporters' VRG (A$, Kernel Density Estimate)

the analysis (that is, the freight rate), the mean VRG for shippers is A$10.32, or almost three times as large as the corresponding VRG for transporters. However, given the shippers' significant disutility of costs faced by the transporter, coupled with a lack of precedent for such willingness-to-pay measures, it is plausible that one must include all costs in the calculation, whether they are borne directly by the respondent or are only indirect sources of disutility (for example, through the perceived threat of an increased freight rate). Hence, we calculated a VRG for shippers based on a weighted average of the freight rate and the transporter's costs.

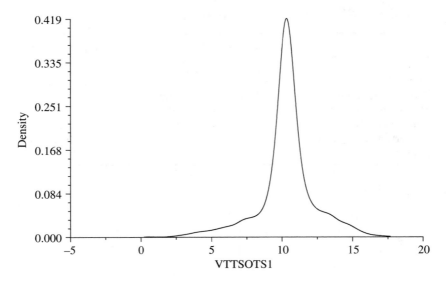

*Figure 3.7   Distribution of shippers' VRG (freight rate only in calculation –
A$, Kernel Density Estimate)*

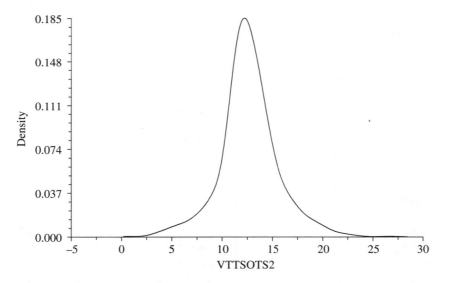

*Figure 3.8   Distribution of shippers' VRG (freight rate and transporter's
costs in calculation – A$, Kernel Density Estimate)*

This variant of VRG is somewhat higher than the VRG based solely on the freight rate; at A$12.67 per percentage point, this VRG estimate implies that shippers are approximately three-and-a-half times more sensitive to the probability of on-time arrival than transporters. Again, this is intuitive, as shippers are affected by arrival reliability both through the need to satisfy customers, and through time sensitivity in the production of items. That is, delays of incoming goods may adversely affect the production or provision of goods worth more than the incoming goods themselves. Transporters face similar concerns with respect to on-time arrival reliability; however, the scope of these concerns may be limited to customer satisfaction.

VRG measures are not inherently intuitive, to the extent that, while it is straightforward to understand the meaning of the value of an hour saved of travel time (that is, most people have been delayed for a period of time when attempting to conduct a given activity, and would be able to place a value on that lost time), it is less straightforward to understand the meaning of the value of a percentage increase in the probability of a vehicle arriving on time. However, when placed in context, VRG measures are highly insightful. Consider the mean value of on-time arrival probability in the reference alternatives recalled by transporters, which is around 85 per cent. The above estimates of VRG indicate that transporters would be willing to pay A$52.65 to eliminate all uncertainty in on-time arrival from a status quo trip at the mean, and would be willing to pay A$26.33 to eliminate one-half of the present uncertainty. When viewed in tandem with transporters' VTTS for slowed-down time, increases in travel quality offered by distance-based user charging could be of significant benefit to transporters. For example, given a trip involving the mean status quo level of slowed-down time (approximately 45 minutes) and probability of on-time arrival, and utilizing the transporters' mean VTTS and VRG measures, transporters would stand to gain benefits equivalent to A$115.48 from the elimination of both uncertainty in on-time arrival and slowed-down travel (gross of distance-based user charges), and would even stand to gain benefits equivalent to A$28.87 in the case where uncertainty and slowed-down time were pared down by only 25 per cent (gross of distance-based user charges).

The potential benefits to shippers are even stronger. Utilising the more conservative estimate of VRG for shippers, a total reduction of uncertainty in on-time arrival would be worth A$154.80, on average. More moderate reductions in uncertainty of 25 and 50 per cent would still be valued by shippers, on average, at A$38.70 and A$77.40, respectively. Hence, although transporters may stand to benefit from distance-based charging independently, the potential benefits for shippers appear sufficient for transporters and shippers to work collaboratively in their responses to a distance-based user charging system.

Table 3.7   Comparison of VTTS and VRG for transporters

	Equivalent values at the mean
One hour of free-flow time savings	12.00% increase in the probability of on-time arrival
One hour of slowed-down time savings	23.66% increase in the probability of on-time arrival
One % increase in the probability of on-time arrival	5.00 minutes of free-flow time savings
One % increase in the probability of on-time arrival	2.54 minutes of slowed-down time savings

The benefits of travel-time savings and reliability gains for transporters can be compared with one another to aid in the quantification of the value of each, as shown in Table 3.7. When considered at the mean, transporters value one hour of free-flow time savings and one hour of slowed-down time savings as equivalent to a 12 and 23.66 per cent increase in the probability of on-time arrival, respectively. The reciprocal of this relationship shows that a 1 per cent increase in the probability of on-time arrival is valued equivalently to either a savings of 5 minutes of free-flow time, or a savings of 2.54 minutes of slowed-down time. The relative values of travel-time components and on-time arrival reliability may aid in an understanding of why some trip configurations are preferred to others. That is, each routeing and scheduling alternative for a given shipment involves trade-offs not only between time and cost but also between travel time and reliability. The relative values of each influence the choice of route and time of travel; hence, any change in the levels of travel time and reliability present in each real-market alternative under distance-based charging is likely to lead to changes in travel patterns. However, this behaviour will be constrained by the costs of each alternative, which will change for alternatives, in general.

3.6.2   Marginal (Dis)utility of Monetary Measures

The preceding subsection focused on the preferences of transporters and shippers with respect to components of distribution time, utilising underlying preferences with respect to cost to establish measures of willingness to pay. However, it is important to examine preferences for the costs themselves. In a similar manner to travel-time measures for transporters, interaction terms in the model allow the transporters' disutility of distance-based user charges to be compared with their disutility of fuel cost. Specifically, the interaction between distance-based user charges and distance (that is, charges per kilometre) and the further interaction between charges per kilometre and total cost reveal distinct disutilities of distance-based user charges and fuel cost for transporters. While total cost (that is, an assumption that distance-based charges and fuel cost are valued equally) and distance-based charges per kilometre are both sources of disutility, the interaction between the two elements has a positive relationship with utility. As such, it appears that transporters are less sensitive to distance-based user charges than to fuel cost. That is, as the share of distance-based user charges in total cost increases, the disutility of paying those costs decreases. Hence, transporters demonstrate that the distance-based user charges produce a benefit (that is, improved travel quality, including time savings and reliability gains), whereas increases in fuel cost do not offer any benefit at all, or if they do, not to the same extent.

Figure 3.9 displays the relationship between the marginal utility of distance-based user charges and the charge levels for transporters. There is significant heterogeneity among those who face total user charges less than approximately A\$100, but transporters demonstrate less heterogeneity for user charges above approximately A\$100. Furthermore, it is clear that the marginal disutility of the user charge decreases as the charge increases. A simple regression of the marginal utility of the distance-based user charges reveals systematic sources of variation in marginal utility, as shown in Table 3.8.

The marginal disutility of the distance-based user charges decreases as kilometres travelled increase. Furthermore, marginal disutility decreases as years of experience in one's employment increases, and if the respondent operates a truck personally, or the sender of the goods paid for the trip, or the receiver had input into scheduling. The marginal disutility of the distance-based user charges increases if either the trip originated within a metropolitan area or the receiver of the goods had input into the scheduling of the vehicle.

These results are also intuitive. With respect to sources of relatively lower marginal disutility, the chief physical influence is trip distance. As the kilometres travelled increases, the scope of travel quality gains offered to the transporter increases. Hence, longer trips may reach a sort of critical mass, at which point the time savings or reliability gains offered through the distance-based user charges become sufficiently valuable to cover the cost of the charges. It appears that decision makers who are relatively more experienced may identify benefits of paying the charges that less-experienced decision makers may not identify. Similarly, those who operate a truck personally experience the effects of lower-quality travel on a regular

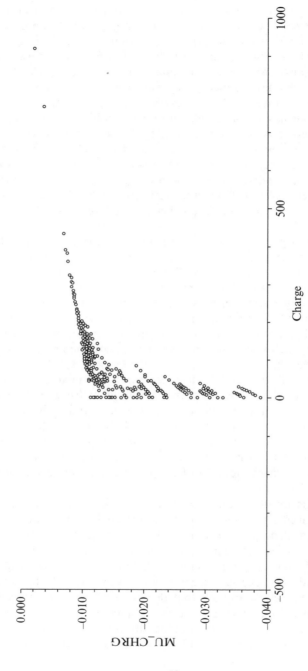

Figure 3.9 Marginal utility of distance-based charges ($) versus distance-based charges for transporters

Table 3.8   Regression of marginal utility of distance-based user charges on covariates for transporters

Attribute	Parameter (*t*-statistic)
Independent variables	
Constant	−0.0260 (−57.32)
Years working in a similar role * 10	0.0003 (2.94)
Kilometres travelled * 100	0.0028 (39.37)
Trip originated in an urban area	−0.0016 (−6.39)
Operates a truck	0.0015 (4.28)
Sender of the goods paid for the delivery	0.0015 (6.44)
Sender of the goods had input into scheduling	−0.0010 (−4.49)
Receiver of the goods had input into scheduling	0.0017 (4.83)
Model fit	
Number of observations	1296
Adjusted *R*-squared	0.68

basis, increasing their appreciation for the benefits that the distance-based user charges may offer. The results indicate that the sender of the goods may be relatively sensitive to time or reliability. That is, the sender of the goods may place a high priority on customer satisfaction, which in turn leads to a relatively higher net benefit for the transporter when paying the charges, through satisfying its customer's need to receive goods promptly, or reliably, or both. Lastly, the decrease in marginal disutility when the sender of the goods has input into the scheduling of the vehicle may be indicative of a closer relationship between the two firms, as it increases the benefits gained through paying the charges.

With respect to sources of relatively larger marginal disutility of the distance-based user charges, we could identify two systematic forces. First, trips originating within a metropolitan area lead to a higher disutility of the charges. This may be a corollary to the relationship between trip distance and marginal disutility described above; trips originating within a metropolitan area are relatively more likely to be shorter trips, and hence the distance-based user charges may not offer sufficiently large travel quality gains to justify the cost in such cases. However, as a distinct effect was identified for urban trips, there may be other physical forces apart from distance influencing marginal disutility. Second, the marginal disutility of the charges is larger if the sender of the goods has input into the scheduling of the trip. If the receiver has input into the scheduling of the trip, the relative influence that that transporter holds in scheduling the vehicle is diminished, restricting the ability of the transporter to optimise with respect to the charges, hence increasing the marginal disutility of the charges.

Shippers appear to perceive a benefit from reducing the costs of transporters. This mirrors the relationship between transit-time measures and utility for shippers, and indeed confirms what may be driving the relationship. That is, shippers may be wary of increased costs to transporters resulting in an increase in the freight rate. However, the relative sensitivity to transporters' costs is much lower for shippers than it is for transporters. This may reflect an expectation that the increases in costs can only partially be passed on to shippers.

The freight rate itself shows remarkable balance across transporters and shippers, with shippers experiencing somewhat more disutility from a given increase in the freight rate than the utility gained by transporters from the same increase, on average. That is, at the margin, there is a net loss of welfare when the freight rate increases. This may be indicative of loss-averse behaviour (that is, a dollar lost causes greater disutility than a dollar gained), or may simply be an artefact of the equilibrium forces of the market (that is, given the present levels of competition and marginal costs, the current set of freight rates results in larger price sensitivities for shippers than the corresponding sensitivity of the transporter to fluctuations in revenue).

3.7   CONCLUSION

This chapter has investigated the influence of distance-based user charges on transporters and shippers, in contrast to other sources of (dis)utility in choosing among packages of trip attributes for freight distribution. Importantly, we promote the view that an assessment of the role of distance-based user charges on behavioural response cannot be determined in isolation from the full set of attributes that drive decisions on preferred distribution strategies by transporters and shippers.

The most important policy finding is that the distinction between paying via fuel prices and via kilometre-based charges is behaviourally important. In particular, we find that transporters are much more supportive of distance-based user charges, as opposed to fuel prices, because they see a tangible benefit in terms of improved travel quality, including time savings and reliability gains. In contrast, increases in fuel prices do not offer such benefit, and if they do it is much less obvious (even if such higher prices do discourage some amount of road usage by others).

NOTES

1. Support for this research has been provided by the Australian Research Council Discovery Program under Grant DP0208269 on Freight Transport and the Environment. We also owe a great deal to Andrew Collins and John Rose for their role in the project.
2. Results from Sweden's experiment as of May 2006 show that car traffic to and from the inner city has fallen by 25 per cent since the scheme was introduced. Public transport patronage has increased by 8 per cent since last year, which translates into a daily increase of 50 000 passengers.
3. As set out in Greene et al. (2006), the random parameters' specification can accommodate correlation among the alternatives. Since β_q can contain alternative specific constants which may be correlated, this specification can induce correlation across alternatives. It follows that the model does not impose the IIA assumption. Restrictions can be imposed at numerous points in the model to produce a wide variety of specifications.
4. Discussion with Ken Train is appreciated.
5. In introducing the choice experiments, we made no explicit assumption about whether other users than freight distributors would incur the charge, although we did not say that it would apply only to freight transporters. Given that tolls are charged to all modes in Sydney, it is reasonable to assume that the sample would assume that all users would be subject to charges that currently exist on tollroads in Sydney. We also focused on a specific recent trip and did not allow for responses that might involve changing the type of vehicle or consolidating deliveries, all worthy of future investigation. It was assumed that payment would be by electronic tag and direct debit, as is the popular method in place in Sydney for all modes on tollroads.
6. The summary of trip details that appears when clicking on Trip Details includes: the name of the client or freight firm involved; the type of truck used; the primary contents of the truck; the amount paid for delivery of the goods; kilometres travelled; the last location of loading before delivery; the total number of locations at which the truck delivered goods; the allowable lead time; the time from request of delivery to departure of truck; and, in the case of questionnaires given to sampled clients, the value of the cargo. This last element is omitted from questionnaires given to representatives of freight firms, as they are not asked for this information.
7. As the tasks are likely to involve some unfamiliar terms, respondents are given definitions of the terms 'attribute' and 'alternative', and informed that a showcard is available for any unfamiliar terms in the choice sets. Respondents were also informed that any details relating either to the trip or to the relationship between the two firms that are not shown in the choice sets can be found by clicking on the buttons labelled Trip Details and Relationship Details, respectively.
8. Two further tasks are given relating to the role of the other decision maker. First, respondents are asked to indicate which of the two SC alternatives they feel would be acceptable to the other decision maker. Second, respondents are asked to indicate which of the three alternatives is likely to be most preferred by the other decision maker. These supplementary tasks serve two purposes: (i) to remind the respondent of the likely preferences of the other decision maker; and (ii) to allow the analyst to compare the perceived preferences of the other agent type with the actual preferences of that agent type. That is, the supplementary questions both reinforce the interdependent nature of the choice setting by explicitly asking respondents to consider the preferences of the other decision maker in the choice setting, and serve as a check of the degree of accuracy with which decision makers gauge the preferences of other classes of decision makers when they interact.
9. Preliminary analysis revealed that the degree of heterogeneity in reference trips was sufficiently high that some outliers obscured the inferential power of the data. After careful consideration, the following observations were removed from the final sample: (a) trips based on a fuel efficiency over 101 litres per 100 kilometres (or approximately twice the average fuel consumption for the larger trucks in the sample); (b) trips based on a probability of on-time arrival of less than 33 per cent; (c) round trips (or tours) of less

than 50 kilometres; and (d) round trips of more than 600 kilometres. The trips eliminated on the basis of low fuel efficiency may have obscured the results due to significantly prohibitive values for fuel cost and distance-based charges, reflecting reference trips that are too atypical to be pooled with other trips. An alternative source of obscuring effects via low fuel efficiency may be that the implied values of fuel efficiency were inaccurate, and hence either made the trade-offs implausible to respondents or reflect an inability of the respondent to offer meaningful information on which to base the alternatives. The trips eliminated on the basis of low probability of on-time arrival are likely to have obscured the results because the trips involved travel quality significantly worse than the remainder of the sample, making the pooling of these trips into the sample problematic. Similarly, extremely short or long trips may have involved trade-offs that are significantly different from the trade-offs made by respondents in the sample at large.

REFERENCES

Bolis, S. and R. Maggi (2001), 'Evidence on shippers' transport and logistics choice', Paper presented at the 1st Swiss Transport Research Conference, Monte Verità/Ascona, Switzerland, 1–3 March.

Brewer, A. and D.A. Hensher (2000), 'Distributed work and travel behaviour: the dynamics of interactive agency choices between employers and employees', *Transportation*, **27** (1), 117–48.

Cullinane, K.P.B. and N.R. Toy (2000), 'Identifying influential attributes in freight route/mode choice decisions: a content analysis', *Transportation Research E*, **36** (1), 41–53.

Danielis, R., E. Marucci and L. Rotaris (2005), 'Logistics managers' stated preferences for freight service attributes', *Transportation Research E*, **41**, 201–15.

Einbock, M. (2006), 'Effects of the Austrian road toll system on companies', *International Journal of Physical Distribution and Logistics Management*, **36** (2), 121–43.

Evans, J. (2005), 'London Congestion Charging Scheme and technology trials', Paper presented at the Institute of Electrical and Electronics Engineers (IEE) Road User Charging Conference, London, 6 December.

Forkenbrock, D.J. (2004), 'Mileage-based road user charge concept', *Transportation Research Record*, **1864**, 1–8.

Fowkes, A.S., P.E. Firmin, G. Tweddle and A.E. Whiteing (2004), 'How highly does the freight transport industry value journey time reliability – and for what reasons', *International Journal of Logistics: Research and Applications*, **7** (1), 33–44.

Greene, W.H., D.A. Hensher and J. Rose (2006), 'Accounting for heterogeneity in the variance of unobserved effects in mixed logit models', *Transportation Research B*, **40** (1), 75–92.

Hensher, D.A. (2006a), 'Revealing differences in behavioural response due to the dimensionality of stated choice designs: an initial assessment', *Environmental and Resource Economics*, **34** (1), May, 7–44.

Hensher, D.A. (2006b), 'How do respondents handle stated choice experiments? Attribute processing strategies under varying information load', *Journal of Applied Econometrics*, **21**, 861–78.

Hensher, D.A. and S. Puckett (2005a), 'Refocussing the modelling of freight distribution in urban areas: the role of supply chain alliances in addressing the challenge of traffic congestion for city logistics', *Transportation*, **32** (6), 573–602.

Hensher, D.A. and S. Puckett (2005b), 'Road user charging: the global relevance of recent developments in the United Kingdom', *Transport Policy*, **12**, 377–83.

Hensher, D.A. and S. Puckett (2007a), 'Congestion charging as an effective travel demand management instrument', Contribution invited for Special Issue of *Transportation Research A*.

Hensher, D.A. and S. Puckett (2007b), 'Theoretical and conceptual frameworks for studying agent interaction and choice revelation', *International Journal of Transport Economics*, XXXIV, 17–47.

Hensher, D.A., S. Puckett and J. Rose (in press), 'Agency decision making in freight distribution chains: revealing a parsimonious empirical strategy from alternative behavioural structures', *Transportation Research B*.

Hensher, D.A., J. Rose and W.H. Greene (2005), *Applied Choice Analysis: A Primer*, Cambridge: Cambridge University Press.

Louviere, J.J., D.A. Hensher and J. Swait (2000), *Stated Choice Methods*, Cambridge: Cambridge University Press.

McKinnon, A.C. (2006a), 'A review of European truck tolling schemes and assessment of their possible impact on logistics systems', *International Journal of Logistics: Research and Applications*, **9** (3), 204–16.

McKinnon, A.C. (2006b), 'Government plans for lorry road user charging in the UK: a critique and an alternative', *Transport Policy*, **13** (3), 191–205.

O'Mahony, M.D. Geraghty and I. Humphreys (2000), 'Distance and time-based road pricing trial in Dublin', *Transportation*, **27**, 269–83.

Puckett, S.M. and D.A. Hensher (2006), 'Modelling interdependent behaviour as a sequentially-administered stated choice experiment: analysis of freight distribution chains', Paper presented at the International Association for Travel Behaviour Research Conference (IATBR), Kyoto, Japan, 14–22 August.

Puckett, S.M., D.A. Hensher and H. Battellino (2006a), 'The adjustment of supply chains to new states: a qualitative assessment of decision relationships with special reference to congestion charging', *International Journal of Transport Economics*, **33** (3), October, 313–39.

Puckett, S.M., D.A. Hensher, J. Rose and A. Collins (2006b), 'Design and development of a stated choice experiment in a two-agent setting: interactions between buyers and sellers of urban freight services', UGM Paper 3, Institute of Transport and Logistics Studies, University of Sydney.

Rose, J.M., M.C.J. Bliemer, D.A. Hensher and A.T. Collins (2005), 'Designing efficient stated choice experiments involving respondent-based reference alternatives', University of Sydney, resubmitted to *Transportation Research B*.

Sandor, Z. and M. Wedel (2001), 'Designing conjoint choice experiments using managers' prior beliefs', *Journal of Marketing Research*, **38** (4), 430–44.

Train, K. (2003), *Discrete Choice Methods with Simulation*, Cambridge: Cambridge University Press.

Transport Intelligence (2005), *European Road Charging Moves Closer*, London, 6 June.

Transport for London (2003), *Congestion Charging: Six Months On*, London, October.

4. Travellers' responses to road pricing: value of time, schedule delay and unreliability[1]

Dirk van Amelsfort, Piet Bovy, Michiel Bliemer and Barry Ubbels

4.1 INTRODUCTION

In recent years considerable attention has been paid to the influence of travel-time unreliability on the choice behaviour of travellers. It is clear that the unreliability of travel time influences different choices of travellers such as mode choice, departure-time choice and route choice. These travel choices are also influenced by the introduction of road pricing, the general topic of this book. The behavioural changes as a result of road pricing are likely to cause changes in network performance, thus influencing travel-time unreliability. Our overall objective of research is to investigate and model the behavioural responses and network effects of time-varying road-pricing measures. To that end, empirical data were collected about the choice behaviour of commuters, and different choice models were estimated. This chapter focuses on how the travel-time unreliability can be taken into account in departure-time choice models and investigates how resulting values of travel time and travel-time reliability, and values of scheduling delay components compare with values found elsewhere. The aim of this chapter is to contribute to the current discussion about modelling choice behaviour, including travel-time unreliability, by presenting results from different models estimated on recently collected stated choice data from Dutch commuters. The research discussed in this chapter provides useful new insights into a relatively unknown concept (at least for the Dutch situation), and updates the value of time for an important target group (that is, commuters).

The definition of travel-time unreliability and the manner in which it affects choice behaviour is still a topic of research. Different types of travel-time unreliability can be found in the literature: for instance there is unreliability affecting traffic flow following from recurrent congestion which is to some extent predictable; and unreliability as a result of incidents or extreme weather conditions (de Jong et al., 2004; Eliasson, 2004). Apart from the question of the definition of travel-time unreliability, there is also discussion about how this factor plays a role in the choice behaviour of travellers. Noland et al. (1998) describe two sources of inconvenience of travel-time unreliability that affect choice behaviour: first, an *expected scheduling cost*, on the basis of which travellers value the likelihood of arriving on time; and second, a *planning cost*, which represents the inconvenience of the inability to precisely plan one's activities.

In this chapter we shall first discuss two approaches found in the literature to modelling travel-time unreliability (Section 4.2): namely, the direct mean-variance approach, and the indirect scheduling approach. This discussion results in our research questions (Section 4.3), leading to different possible specifications of travel-time unreliability in the utility function which may give rise to different values of unreliability. Before presenting the results of the discrete choice models estimated using these different specifications of travel-time unreliability (in Section 4.5), we first describe the most important aspects of the stated choice experiment (in Section 4.4) from which we derived the data for estimating the various utility function specifications. Finally, in Section 4.6 we compare the values of time and travel-time unreliability resulting from the models and relate these to values found in the literature.

4.2 MODELLING BEHAVIOURAL RESPONSES TO UNRELIABILITY OF TRAVEL TIME

In congested networks, the travel and departure time choices experienced by travellers are influenced by the unreliability of travel time. In their decision making on how, when and where to travel, travellers face various unreliable characteristics of the choice alternatives. Depending on the trip purpose, they will experience inconvenience if they arrive earlier or later than desired (or required). At the same time, departing earlier or later than desired also causes inconvenience to the traveller. When travel times become unreliable, the arrival times become unreliable as well, and, in order to reduce the inconvenience of especially late arrivals, travellers have to adjust their departure time. Clearly, the unreliability of travel time is an extra source of inconvenience considered in travellers' decision making. One of the questions in modelling travel unreliability is whether unreliability is an independent component in the valuation of travel-time aspects (similar to waiting time, transfer time and in-vehicle time in public transport trips), or whether, instead, the value of travel-time unreliability is completely covered by the valuation of the implied schedule delays ('early' and 'late', see Section 4.2.2) of trips. These two views on modelling travel-time unreliability and its sources of inconvenience have resulted in two modelling approaches: the mean-variance approach, and the scheduling approach. de Jong et al. (2004) and Hollander (2006) provide useful overviews of these different approaches to modelling unreliability. Below we present a short description of both methods.

4.2.1 Direct Mean-variance Approach

The mean-variance approach addresses the unreliability of travel time as a direct source of inconvenience. In the literature it is referred to as the 'mean-variance' approach because in most examples (Jackson and Jucker, 1982; Polak, 1987; Black and Towriss, 1993; Senna, 1992; Eliasson, 2004) the mean travel time and the variance of travel time are both included in the utility function. Since the mean is influenced by extreme values and out-liers, some researchers have used the median of travel time and the difference between a percentile (the 90th) and the median (Lam and Small, 2001; Brownstone et al., 2003). The mean travel time is directly influenced by the unreliability of travel time when the travel distribution is, as is typical, not symmetric but skewed to the right. A median-percentile approach avoids this dependence to some extent.

4.2.2 Indirect Scheduling Approach

In the scheduling approach, the inconvenience of unreliability in travel time reflects the inconvenience of earliness and lateness, as perceived by trav-ellers. The scheduling approach has been applied by, among others, Gaver (1968), Knight (1974), Bates et al. (1995), Noland et al. (1998) and Small et al. (1999). If the travel time is highly unreliable, as during the peak period, travellers may change their departure time (called 'rescheduling'), such that the penalties of expected early or late arrival and associated travel time are minimal. Since Small (1982) presented his framework of model-ling the scheduling of trips, this has more or less become a standard. The departure-time model he proposes includes a travel-time attribute, a travel-cost attribute and three trip-scheduling attributes. All scheduling components are based on the preferred arrival time of the trips and include a scheduling delay early (0 or number of minutes earlier than preferred), a scheduling delay late (0 or number of minutes later than preferred), and a lateness dummy (equal to 1 if late arrival).

When travel-time unreliability is introduced in this approach, the arrival time of the trip becomes uncertain and an expected arrival time is used in the model. As a result, expected scheduling delays early and late are also used in the model. Scheduling approaches mostly use a mean travel time which, depending on the definition, may correlate with unreliability in travel time. As we shall show later in this chapter, the mean travel-time variable and the schedule-delay variables may jointly cause the separate unreliability variable to be insignificant in this type of scheduling choice models, resulting in the conclusion (for example, Hollander, 2006) that unreliability is not a separate variable in the choice behaviour of travellers.

4.2.3 Values of Travel-time Unreliability for Car Trips from the Literature

Table 4.1 presents selected values of travel-time reliability for car trips found in the literature. Most results are based on the mean-variance approach since this method is more commonly applied, whereas the scheduling approach often does not contain a separate variable for travel-time unreliability. In many cases the value of reliability is presented as a ratio of the value of time (VOT). The majority of the reported travel-time reliability ratios are above 1, meaning that a unit increase in the standard deviation of travel time, reflecting unreliability, is valued more – that is, it creates more inconvenience – than a unit increase in travel time itself.

4.2.4 Discussion

Noland et al. (1998) and Small et al. (1999) conclude that including a separate variable for unreliability of travel time is often significant only when scheduling variables are not present in the utility function. Travellers seem to take unreliability into account completely by earliness and lateness variables. This finding would advocate for the scheduling approach above the mean-variance approach although the mean-variance models are more commonly applied. Hollander (2006) states that the mean-variance approach leads to the underestimation of the value of unreliability and supports the scheduling approach for modelling travel-time unreliability. Hence, in the remainder of this chapter we focus on a scheduling approach to determine the value of travel-time unreliability and other parameters, which is compatible with our overall objective to model the departure-time choice of commuters and their reactions to road pricing. This chapter therefore does not contribute to the discussion about the appropriateness of a mean-variance or a scheduling approach. The scheduling approach allows for a modelling of travel-time unreliability that takes into account both the expected scheduling cost and the planning cost.

Table 4.1   Reported values of travel-time unreliability for car trips

Study	Value of travel-time unreliability	Method
Brownstone and Small, 2002	11–14 €/h (male) 28–30 €/h (female)	RP data using percentile and median approach
Lam and Small, 2001	4.65–12.29 €/h (male)[1] 6.03–27.58 €/h (female)[1]	RP data using percentile and median approach
Copley et al., 2002	1.30 times VOT	SP data mean-variance approach
Senna, 1991	2.50 times VOT	SP data mean-variance approach
Noland et al., 1998	1.27 times VOT	SP data mean-variance approach
Black and Towriss, 1993	0.55 times VOT	SP data mean-variance approach
Transport Research Centre, 2006a	0.80 times VOT	Expert meetings
Eliasson, 2004	Travel-time variability Morning: 3.86 €/h^2 Afternoon: 1.64 €/h^2 Value of unexpected delays Morning: 42.15 €/h^2 Afternoon: 26.70 €/h^2	SP data mean-variance approach
Senna, 1991	2.5 times VOT	SP data mean-variance approach

Notes: RP = revealed preference SP = stated preference
1. February 2007 exchange rate, dollar to euro.
2. February 2007 exchange rate, Kroner to euro.

4.3   RESEARCH QUESTIONS AND METHODOLOGY

4.3.1   Research Questions

In this chapter the main focus is on the valuation of travel-time unreliability by commuters in their departure-time choice for a morning commute trip. As presented in the Introduction, a scheduling approach is used to model the departure-time choice of commuters. The starting-point is the base model given in equation (4.1) to which travel-time unreliability is added in various ways (see equations (4.2) and (4.3)). The parameter estimates resulting from the model estimations will be used to determine the value of travel-time unreliability.

$$U(k \mid p) = \beta_t T(k) + \beta_c C(k) + \beta_{asde} ASDE(k \mid p) + \beta_{asdl} ASDL(k \mid p), \quad (4.1)$$

where:

$U(k \mid p)$	=	utility of departing at time k, given preferred arrival time p;
$ASDE(k \mid p)$	=	max $\{p - [k + T(k)], 0\}$
	=	arrival-time scheduling delay early for departing at time k, given preferred arrival time p;
$ASDL(k \mid p)$	=	max $\{[k + T(k)] - p, 0\}$
	=	arrival-time scheduling delay late for departing at time k, given preferred arrival time p;
$T(k)$	=	travel time when departing at time k;
$C(k)$	=	travel cost when departing at time k.

Adding travel-time unreliability into the scheduling modelling approach raises some questions which find their origin in the fact that this unreliability affects both the travel and the arrival times of travellers while both are already variables in the utility function. The questions we shall answer in this chapter are therefore:

1. Is travel-time unreliability a separate source of inconvenience being valued independently from travel-time and scheduling delay components, and therefore needs to be included in the utility function?
2. Is it sufficient to use expected travel times and expected scheduling delays to take travel-time unreliability into account, or can the model be improved by introducing a separate variable for unreliability?
3. What values of travel-time unreliability are estimated for commuters in the Netherlands, and how do these values compare with corresponding values found elsewhere (see also Table 4.1)?

4.3.2 Methodology

In order to answer the research questions given above, discrete choice models were estimated to determine the sensitivities to different variables in the departure-time choice of commuters. A requisite for estimating discrete choice models is choice data at the individual level. Therefore dedicated data were collected using a stated choice experiment, which will be described in more detail in the next section. A first step in answering the research questions is to adapt the scheduling approach in such a way that it includes travel-time unreliability. Different approaches are examined in specifying the travel-time and scheduling variables in the utility functions. In addition, models with and without a separate variable for travel-time unreliability will be specified and tested. Based on Noland et al. (1998), a model (see equation (4.2)) with a separate variable for travel-time uncertainty is estimated. Since both the expected travel-time and expected scheduling-delay variables correlate with travel-time unreliability, some of the variables are expected to return insignificant parameter estimates. In a second and further models (see equation (4.3)) alternative specifications for travel-time and scheduling delays are used which try to eliminate the effect of unreliability from travel-time and scheduling delay variables. This may resolve the issue of insignificant travel-time unreliability parameters that some researchers have found (Ubbels, 2006).

$$U(k \mid p) = \beta_t E[T(k)] + \beta_c C(k) + \beta_{asde} E[ASDE(k \mid p)] + \\ \beta_{asdl} E[ASDL(k \mid p)] + \beta_u UNR(k) \qquad (4.2)$$

$$U(k \mid p) = \beta_t T_l(k) + \beta_c C(k) + \beta_{asde} E[ASDE(k \mid p)] + \\ \beta_{asdl} E[ASDL(k \mid p)] + \beta_u UNR(k), \qquad (4.3)$$

where:

$E[ASDE(k \mid p)]$ = expected arrival-time scheduling delay early for departing at time k, given preferred arrival time p;

$E[ASDL(k \mid p)]$ = expected arrival-time scheduling delay late for departing at time k, given preferred arrival time p;

$UNR(k)$ = travel-time unreliability for departing at time k;

$T_l(k)$ = lower-bound travel time for departing at time k;

$E[T(k)]$ = Expected travel time for departing at time k.

Before explaining the manner in which some of the variables in these utility functions are calculated, first the set-up of the stated choice experiment is explained, as the calculation of some variables is specific to the set-up of the data collection.

4.4   DATA COLLECTION

In this section we briefly present the most important aspects of the data collection including the stated choice experiment relevant for our modelling exercise. For an extensive description of the data collection, we refer to van Amelsfort and Bliemer (2006) and Tillema (2007). The data were collected in order to investigate the behavioural responses of commuters to time-varying road-pricing charges. The data collection consisted of two parts. The first part contained a questionnaire with questions about the current travel behaviour of respondents, the characteristics of their non-chosen alternatives (if available), and their socio-economic status. The second part contained a stated choice experiment, which used the answers given to the questionnaire to determine the values of attributes presented to respondents. The data were collected from 1115 commuters who travel to work by car at least twice a week, and on those journeys, face delays of at least 10 minutes. The data were collected by a market research company using an interactive Internet technique.

4.4.1 Questionnaire

The purpose of the questionnaire was twofold. First, the stated choice experiment should as much as possible evoke realistic choice behaviour from respondents. The experiment was therefore as much as possible based on the current choice situation of the respondents. The second purpose of the questionnaire was to know more about the background of the respondents in order to facilitate the explanation of differences found in the choice behaviour of respondents. The following questions were included, the answers of which were used as input in the stated choice experiment:

1. What is your free-flow travel time from home to work?
2. What is the travel distance on the route you normally choose to travel to work?
3. How long does it normally take to travel to work?
4. At what time do you normally leave home to go to work?
5. At what time would you leave if you were certain that there would never be any delays on your trip?

In addition, respondents were asked background questions, concerning income, gender, level of education, occupation, working hours, household information, availability of mode alternatives, availability of route alternatives, and availability of departure- and arrival-time alternatives.

4.4.2 Stated Choice Experiment

The main objective of the stated choice experiment is to get – as much as possible – realistic choice data from individuals about their departure-time choice when road pricing is introduced, whereas their route and mode choice behaviour were of somewhat less interest. The experiment refers to home-to-work trips of commuters who travel to work by car and face delays on a regular basis. Since the respondents frequently make home-to-work trips, our view was that it is important to take into account in the experiment the repetitive nature of this trip. Therefore, respondents were asked to distribute 10 trips among the presented alternatives, instead of choosing only one of the alternatives. In the remainder of this section the alternatives, attributes and attribute levels are presented in turn.

Choice alternatives in the experiment
The stated choice experiment contained 11 choice situations (screens), where in each screen the respondents were presented with four alternatives (A–D). Three alternatives (A–C) are car alternatives, while the fourth (D) is a public transport alternative.

A. *Paying for preferred travel conditions*   The price in this alternative is relatively high. Attribute levels are based on the preferred arrival time and free-flow travel conditions reported by the respondent. Only small deviations are made from these preferred travel conditions.
B. *Adjust departure/arrival time and pay less*   This has a lower road-pricing fee than alternative A, but in return the travel conditions are less attractive, that is, higher levels of congestion and uncertainty in travel time and arrival time. Both departing earlier and later are included.
C. *Adjust departure/arrival time and route and pay less*   Similar to alternative B, but now the respondents are provided with a detour to pay less (or avoid paying). The arrival time changes are smaller than in alternative B.
D. *Adjust mode to avoid paying charge*   There is no road-pricing fee to pay, just the fare. The public transport alternative is assumed to have a fixed travel time, hence there is no uncertainty about the arrival time.

An example of a choice screen as it was presented to respondents is given in Table 4.2.

Attributes and levels used in the experiment
Since time-varying road-pricing measures may reduce levels of congestion and consequently improve the travel time and travel-time reliability, travel-time and cost attributes are important in the experiment. The underlying experimental design is a (blocked) orthogonal design consisting of pivot levels around reported reference levels stated by each respondent.

The travel time for the car alternatives is calculated the same way for alternatives A, B and C; only the attribute levels differ among the alternatives.

Table 4.2   Example of choice screen presented to respondents (values are indicative)

Alternative A	Alternative B	Alternative C	Alternative D
Mode of transport: car	Mode of transport: car	Mode of transport: car	Mode of transport: public transport
Trip length: 35 km	Trip length: 35 km	Trip length: 49 km	Trip length: 35 km
Travel costs: €8.10 of which:	Travel costs: €4.60 of which:	Travel costs: €6.20 of which:	Price of a ticket: €3.18
fuel: €3.20	fuel: €3.20	fuel: €4.20	
charge: €4.90	charge: €1.40	charge: €2.00	
Departure time: 08.10	Departure time: 08.25	Departure time: 08.00	Departure time: 07.25
Total travel time between 40 and 50 minutes of which:	Total travel time between 50 and 60 minutes of which:	Total travel time between 55 and 65 minutes of which:	Total travel time: 72 minutes
free flow: 25 min.	free flow: 25 min.	free flow: 40 min.	
minimum time in congestion: 15 min.	minimum time in congestion: 25 min.	minimum time in congestion: 15 min.	
maximum time in congestion: 25 min.	maximum time in congestion: 35 min.	maximum time in congestion: 25 min.	
Arrival time is hence between: 8.50 and 9.00	Arrival time is hence between: 9.15 and 9.25	Arrival time is hence between: 8.55 and 9.05	Arrival time: 08.37
Assign number of trips . . .	Assign number of trips . . .	Assign number of trips . . .	Assign number of trips . . .

The total trip travel time used in the experiment is based on the reported free-flow travel time and trip length. The trip is divided into a free-flow part and a congested part. Let $\hat{\tau}_i^{ff}$ denote the free-flow travel time as reported by respondent i, and let α_{an} be the fraction of the distance in the free-flow condition used in choice situation n. Then values of travel time, τ_{ain}, shown to respondent i in choice situation n for each alternative a can be computed as:

$$\tau_{ain} = \underbrace{\alpha_{an}\hat{\tau}_i^{ff}}_{\text{uncongested}} + \underbrace{3(1-\alpha_{an})\hat{\tau}_i^{ff}}_{\text{congested}} = (3-2\alpha_{an})\hat{\tau}_i^{ff}. \tag{4.4}$$

For alternative A, the free-flow part of the trip is higher ($\alpha_{an} \in \{0.85, 0.90, 0.95, 1\}$) than for alternative B ($\alpha_{bn} \in \{0.65, 0.70, 0.75, 0.80\}$), while the free-flow part of the trip for alternative C is even lower ($\alpha_{cn} \in \{0.55, 0.60, 0.65, 0.70\}$).

The travel time of the public transport alternative is calculated in a different way. It is based on either the reported travel time using public transportation or the free-flow travel time by car (times 1.3). The levels of public transport travel time are multiplication factors (1.0, 1.2).

Arrival time

The arrival times in the experiment are based on each respondent i's preferred arrival time, p_i, which is computed by adding the reported preferred departure time and the reported free-flow travel time. The arrival time, t_{ain}^{arr}, presented to respondent i in choice situation n for alternative A is computed by making deviations δ_{an} from their preferred arrival time, as presented in equation (4.5):

$$t_{ain}^{arr} = p_i + \delta_{an}. \tag{4.5}$$

In alternative A, the arrival times have small deviations from the preferred arrival time ($\delta_{an} \in \{-10, -5, 0, 5\}$ minutes from the preferred arrival time), whereas in alternative B, these deviations are much larger ($\delta_{bn} \in \{-50, -30, -10, +10\}$ minutes from the preferred arrival time). The deviations for alternatives C and D are $\delta_{cn} \in \{-30, -20, -10, 0\}$ minutes, and $\delta_{dn} \in \{-30, -10, +10, +30\}$ minutes from their preferred arrival time, respectively.

Travel-time bandwidth

As a basis for travel-time unreliability, a travel-time bandwidth is calculated which is based on the difference between the reported congested travel time, $\hat{\tau}_i^{cong}$, and the reported free-flow travel time, $\hat{\tau}_i^{ff}$. The assumption is that this value provides a reasonable indication of the variability in travel time for that respondent. Using this value we calculate the travel-time bandwidth, ω_{ain}, as follows:

$$\omega_{ain} = \gamma_{an} (\hat{\tau}_i^{cong} - \hat{\tau}_i^{ff}). \tag{4.6}$$

Using this presentation of travel-time unreliability and its effect on arrival times, respondents are truly uncertain about the traffic conditions of a specific alternative. The lower-bound travel time is equal to τ_{ain} (see equation (4.5)), and the upper-bound travel time is equal to $\tau_{ain} + \omega_{ain}$. Furthermore, earliest and latest arrival times are presented to respondents as t_{ain}^{arr} (see equation (4.5)) and $t_{ain}^{arr} + \omega_{ain}$, respectively. Since alternative A has the preferred travel conditions, the unreliability factors are small ($\gamma_{an} \in \{0.2, 0.4, 0.6, 0.8\}$). For alternatives B and C these factors are larger: namely, $\gamma_{bn} \in \{0.8, 1.0, 1.2, 1.4\}$ and $\gamma_{cn} \in \{0.6, 0.8, 1.0, 1.2\}$, respectively.

The calculations of travel time and travel-time unreliability presented to respondents resemble a mean travel time and variance approach.

Trip length

For alternatives A, B and D a single trip-length level is presented equal to the reported actual trip length. Alternative C represents a route alternative in which respondents can avoid paying by taking a detour. This means that the distance of this trip is always longer than for the other alternatives. The trip-length attribute of alternative C has two levels, computed using a multiplication factor of 1.2 or 1.4 on the reported actual trip length.

Travel costs

The travel costs consist of fuel (car) or fare (public transport) costs and a road-pricing charge. The fuel and fare costs are calculated based on the trip length. If the travel costs of the respondent are compensated by the employer, the fuel costs are set to zero. The road-pricing charge in the experiment is assumed to be distance based, partly because of the policy relevance it has in the Netherlands. The respondents were not informed about the nature of the road-pricing charge and the manner in which it was calculated. The levels of charges are to some extent also based on prices mentioned in Dutch road-pricing proposals. Alternative A has the highest charges (8, 10, 12, 14 €ct/km) but has the best travel conditions. Alternative B has lower charges (3, 4, 5, 6 €ct/km), while alternative C has the lowest prices (levels 0, 1, 2, 3 €ct/km).

To summarize, the resulting choice experiment has some interesting features. First, the choice dimensions for route, time and mode adjustments are offered simultaneously to respondents, while for the car alternatives uncertainty in travel time is included together with a road-pricing fee. Furthermore, respondents are asked to distribute 10 trips instead of choosing one of the alternatives.

Departure time

Although presented to respondents in the screens, departure time is not an attribute that is systematically changed in the experiment. The presented departure time results from the lower-bound arrival time and the lower-bound travel time.

4.5   CHOICE MODEL ESTIMATIONS AND RESULTS

This section presents the estimation results of different choice models. In the stated choice experiment, respondents were presented with travel- and arrival-time bandwidths. The travel-time information in each choice screen consists of three elements: a free-flow part of the trip, a minimum level of congested travel time, and a maximum level of travel time. The arrival-time information includes two elements: an earliest arrival time, and a latest arrival time. The travel-time unreliability is taken into account both in the travel- and arrival-time information presented to respondents. For the travel-time and scheduling-delay variables there is a choice whether or not to take the travel-time bandwidth into account in the way the variable is calculated. For travel time there is also a distinction possible between congested and free-flow travel time.

4.5.1   Choice Model Variables: Travel Time, Travel-Time Unreliability and Scheduling Delays

Travel-time variable
In the choice models of this section, different specifications of travel time are used in the utility function. The two specifications presented below are distinguished because we as researchers are unclear about what travel time(s) respondents took into account in their decision making. Did they calculate an average travel time and, if so, in what way? Or did they use either the minimum or maximum presented travel time in their decision making? The first specification is the mean travel time assuming a uniform distribution of travel times within the presented bandwidth. The mean travel time is calculated as in equation (4.7), where ω_{ain} is the travel-time interval in what follows, and τ_{ain} the lowest possible travel time, that is, $T_l(k) = \tau_{ain}$:

$$E[T(k)] = \tau_{ain} + \tfrac{1}{2}\omega_{ain}. \tag{4.7}$$

The second specification of the travel-time variable excludes the travel-time interval unreliability and only uses τ_{ain}, the lowest possible travel time, that is, $T_l(k) = \tau_{ain}$. Because of the underlying statistical design, this specification reduces the correlation between travel time and travel-time unreliability variables in the utility function. This lower-bound travel time specification is also used because it is an actual value shown to respondents rather than an estimated mean using an assumed distribution. The lower-bound travel time is used rather than the upper-bound travel time, because the latter would lead to positive parameter estimates for the travel time bandwidth (ω) parameters in the utility function. If the travel-time bandwidth is interpreted as a measure of travel-time unreliability, a positive parameter estimate is undesirable.

Arrival-time scheduling-delay variables

The scheduling delays are calculated as differences between the actual arrival time and the preferred arrival time. Because the actual arrival time is unreliable, the scheduling delays become unreliable as well.

Three cases are distinguished. First, when the latest possible arrival time ($AATL$) is earlier than the preferred arrival time p, a schedule-delay early occurs of at least the size of ($p - AATL$). Different scheduling-delay variables to describe $E[ASDE(k \mid p)]$ in equations (4.2) and (4.3) are then calculated, as presented in (4.8). $E(SDE)$ is the expected (arrival-time) scheduling-delay early, $mSDE$ is the minimum amount of scheduling-delay early based on the latest arrival time, ωSDE is the separated unreliable scheduling-delay early effect as a result of the arrival-time bandwidth ω_{ain}.

Hence, when $AATL \leq p$, then $E[ASDE(k \mid p)]$ can be computed as:

$$E(SDE) = p - \tfrac{1}{2}(AATE + AATL) = p - AATE - \tfrac{1}{2}\omega, \quad \text{or}$$

$$mSDE = p - AATL \quad \text{and} \quad \omega SDE = \tfrac{1}{2}\omega, \tag{4.8}$$

where AATE is the earliest possible arrival time.

Second, when the earliest possible arrival time ($AATE$) is later than the preferred arrival time, a schedule-delay late occurs of at least the size of ($AATE - p$). Similarly to the scheduling-delay early variable, scheduling-delay variables to describe $E[ASDL(k \mid p)]$ in equations (4.2) and (4.3) are calculated using any of the formulae in (4.9). Hence, when $AATE \geq p$, then $E[ASDL(k \mid p)]$ can be computed as:

$$E(SDL) = \tfrac{1}{2}(AATE + AATL) - p = AATE + \tfrac{1}{2}\omega - p, \quad \text{or}$$

$$mSDL = AATE - p, \quad \text{and} \quad \omega SDL = \tfrac{1}{2}\omega. \tag{4.9}$$

Third, when p is in-between $AATE$ and $AATL$, there is uncertainty about a scheduling-delay early or late situation. Here a probability for lateness (P_l) is used to calculate the scheduling-delay variables (see equation (4.10)).

Hence, when $AATL > p$ and $AATE < p$, then $E[ASDE(k \mid p)]$ and $E[ASDL(k \mid p)]$ are computed as:

$$E(SDE) = \tfrac{1}{2}(p - AATE) \cdot (1 - P_l),$$

$$E(SDL) = \tfrac{1}{2}(AATL - p) \cdot P_l, \tag{4.10}$$

$$P_l = \frac{AATL - p}{AATL - AATE}.$$

Modelling technique
The models presented in this subsection are all multinomial logit (MNL) models. This simplifies the estimation of models, but neglects some important issues regarding the correlations between alternatives and taste-variation among respondents. Since we are using stated choice data where respondents repeatedly answered similar questions, multiple observations in the dataset are not independent. We do not explicitly model a panel structure to take into account the correlation among respondents. In addition, the models are estimated on shares or frequency data rather than on individual choice data, because we asked respondents to assign 10 trips in each choice situation. We used Nlogit for model estimations, in which discrete choice models can be estimated using share data.

4.5.2   Model Estimation Results

Using the different specifications of travel-time and scheduling-delay variables presented above, various choice models were estimated. Tables 4.3 and 4.4 present the estimation results for six different models, the utility specification of which is given in the tables. Table 4.3 contains the values of time components for car only that result from the model estimates (statistically insignificant values are in italics). Table 4.4 presents the complete estimation results.

Model 1 represents the model based on Noland et al. (1998) presented in equation (4.2) and includes a separate variable for travel-time unreliability. The parameter estimate is positive, which is not plausible, but it is also hardly significant. The values of $E(SDE)$ and $E(SDL)$ are both higher than the value of time. This is consistently found in all models, and it suggests that travellers would rather stay in their car than arrive early. This finding is unexpected and not in line with results found by others. Results from other model estimates presented by Ubbels (2006) show that the high value of $E(SDE)$ is caused by strong non-linearity in parameter sensitivity of $E(SDE)$.

In Table 4.3, Models 1 and 2, as well as Models 3 and 4, show similar results in the resulting value of time components, and are tacitly identical models. In both cases the only change is in the value of the travel-time bandwidth, which in both cases is caused by changing the travel-time variable from an expected travel time to the lower-bound travel time. The latter correlates less with the value of the travel-time bandwidth. The difference in the value of the travel-time bandwidth is equal to €5.59 per hour which is half the value of time (€11.20 per hour). This is logical because a marginal increase in travel-time bandwidth is taken into account in half of the expected travel time in Model 1 and is not taken into account in the minimum travel time in Model 2.

Table 4.3 *Values of time, travel-time unreliability and scheduling costs (euro/h), car only*

	Model 1	Model 2	Model 3	Model 4	Model 5
Exp. travel time $E[T(k)]$	11.20		11.38		
Exp. arr. sched.-delay early $E[ASDE(k\|p)] = E(SDE)$	14.29	14.29			
Exp. arr. sched.-delay late $E[ASDL(k\|p)] = E(SDL)$	13.53	13.53			
Travel-time bandwidth $UNR(k) = \omega$	*–2.17*	3.42	3.30	8.99	
Min. arr. sched.-delay early $E[ASDE(k\|p)] = mSDE$			17.13	17.13	16.16
Min arr. sched.-delay late $E[ASDL(k\|p)] = mSDL$			23.37	23.37	20.07
ω arr. sched.-delay early $E[ASDE(k\|p)] = \omega SDE$			*–2.29*	*–2.29*	17.27
ω arr. sched.-delay late $E[ASDL(k\|p)] = \omega SDL$			*–2.72*	*–2.72*	16.20
Lower-bound travel time $T_l(k) = \tau$		11.20		11.38	12.38

Note: Statistically insignificant values in italics.

Model 2, which corresponds with equation (4.3), uses the lower-bound travel time instead of the expected travel time. This results in a significant parameter for the travel-time bandwidth, as was expected because of the reduced correlation between the travel-time and the travel-time bandwidth variables, and because the unreliability variable now includes part of the expected travel time. The value of the travel-time bandwidth thus measured appears to be €3.42 per hour.

In Model 3 the expected scheduling-delay variables are replaced by the two minimum scheduling-delay variables (early and late) and two ω-scheduling-delay variables. Both coefficients for *mSDE* and *mSDL* are higher than for *E(SDE)* and *E(SDL)* in Model 1, which could be expected because the variable values are smaller. The ω-scheduling-delay variables are both insignificant. In Model 3 the expected travel time $E[T(k)]$ is used again. The ω-scheduling-delay variables, the travel-time variable, and the

Table 4.4   Estimation results for travel-time unreliability models

Variable	Model 1		Model 2		Model 3		Model 4		Model 5	
	Parameter	t-ratio	Parameter	t-ratio	Parameter	t-ratio	Parameter	t-ratio	Parameter	t-ratio
Car travel costs ($C(k)$)	−0.111	−18.5	−0.111	−18.5	−0.111	−18.43	−0.111	−18.43	−0.104	−17.46
Expected travel time ($E[T(k)]$)	−0.021	−18.5			−0.021	−18.69				
Expected arrival time scheduling-delay early ($E(SDE)$)	−0.027	−19.22	−0.027	−19.22						
Expected arrival time scheduling-delay late ($E(SDL)$)	−0.025	−12.25	−0.025	−12.25						
Travel-time bandwidth ($UNR(k)=\omega$)	0.004	2.71	−0.006	−4.81	−0.006	−2.74	−0.017	−7.81	−0.028	−15.67
Min. arrival time scheduling-delay early ($mSDE$)					−0.032	−16.95	−0.032	−16.95	−0.035	−7.53
Min. arrival time scheduling-delay late ($mSDL$)					−0.043	−9.08	−0.043	−9.08	−0.03	−8.65
ω arrival time scheduling-delay early (ωSDE)					0.004	0.76	0.004	0.76	−0.028	−9.33
ω arrival time scheduling-delay late (ωSDL)					0.005	0.97	0.005	0.97		
Lower-bound travel time ($T_l(k)=\tau$)			−0.021	−18.5			−0.021	−18.69	−0.021	−19.01
Public transport constant	−0.795	−8	−0.795	−8	−0.816	−8.2	−0.816	−8.2	−0.772	−7.77
Public transport travel costs	−0.02	−2.07	−0.02	−2.07	−0.019	−2.04	−0.019	−2.04	−0.017	−1.76
Public transport travel time	−0.024	−18.78	−0.024	−18.78	−0.024	−18.72	−0.024	−18.72	−0.024	−18.21

Public transport arrival time scheduling-delay early	−0.02	−5.51	−0.02	−5.51	−0.019	−5.37	−0.019	−5.37	−0.02	−5.58
Public transport arrival time scheduling-delay late	−0.013	−3.64	−0.013	−3.64	−0.012	−3.54	−0.012	−3.54	−0.013	−3.72
Log L	−15427.6		−15427.6		−15407.3		−15407.3		−15438.5	
N (#resp*#choices)	12,265		12,265		12,265		12,265		12,265	

travel-time unreliability variable all include the travel-time bandwidth in their calculation (see equations (4.7)–(4.10)).

In Model 4 instead of the expected travel time, the lower-bound travel time is used. Thus the travel-time variable no longer includes the interval, which changes the value of the travel-time bandwidth significantly to €8.99 per hour.

Finally, in Model 5 the travel-time bandwidth parameter is removed. Now the ω-scheduling-delay parameters become significant. The value of ωSDE is higher than the $mSDE$, while for SDL variables the opposite is the case. Interestingly, the valuation of the travel-time bandwidth is much higher when it is completely taken into account in the scheduling components (€16–€17/h) than in the case of a separate (€8.99) travel-time bandwidth variable. The value of the lower-bound travel time is also highest in Model 5, at €12.38 per hour.

Overall, the estimates show a plausible and consistent pattern of value of time components (see next section).

4.6   DISCUSSION AND COMPARISON OF ESTIMATION RESULTS

Models 1, 2 and 5 all include the travel-time bandwidth, our measure for travel-time unreliability, in the scheduling components. Noland et al. (1998), Hollander (2006) and Ubbels (2006) all show similar results where a separate variable for travel-time unreliability is insignificant and conclude that unreliability can best be taken into account by addressing it in the scheduling variables. Models 3 and 4 both contradict these results and conclusions. The parameter estimates of Models 3 and 4 show that, in a scheduling framework, it is possible to identify a separate effect of travel-time unreliability (bandwidth) in travel-choice behaviour. As a result of using a travel-time bandwidth, we can specify travel time and scheduling delays in a manner that reduces correlation with the travel-time bandwidth (unreliability). This was done in Model 4 where a lower-bound travel time and minimum scheduling delays were used. In that case, the parameter for the travel-time bandwidth is significant. Travel-time unreliability relates to both travel and arrival times, and further research is necessary to draw strong conclusions about how travellers value both aspects of unreliability, how to measure it, and how to model it.

In Model 4 both the travel-time and scheduling-delay variables are defined in such a way that they do not include the travel-time bandwidth in their calculation, while in Model 3 the travel-time variable still includes half the travel-time bandwidth. The ω-scheduling-delay parameter estimates are insignificant, which implies that besides the travel-time bandwidth as a source of inconvenience *per se*, there is no need to take other sources into account. These results answer the first two research questions (see Section 4.3.1) about how to take travel-time unreliability into account in the utility function.

The remaining third question is how the values of travel-time unreliability compare with other values found in the literature. Comparison of values is difficult because of methodological issues, differences in respondents and socio-economic variables. An added complexity here is that we use different specifications of travel time and scheduling delays than is normally done. As a result, drawing strong conclusions from direct comparison of values of time is impossible, and we therefore resort to softer plausibility checks. Our model with highest loglikelihood and with a significant travel-time bandwidth parameter (Model 4), finds a value of travel-time bandwidth of €8.99 per hour, which corresponds with a ratio of approximately 0.8 when compared with the value of lower-bound time in that model. Although comparing different methodologies for calculating the ratio, the value found is plausible when compared with values found in the literature. A ratio of 0.8 is recommended for the Netherlands by the Transport Research Centre (2006a) to be used in cost–benefit analyses. The values of travel time, mean as well as lower bound, found here are higher (€11.20–€12.38) than recommended for the Netherlands by the Transport Research Centre: €8.50 per hour (Transport Research Centre, 2006b), which can be attributed to differences in: (i) data collection (departure-time choice with road-pricing charge experiment instead of mode choice and/or time-of-day experiment); (ii) model estimation approach; and (iii) the base year of data collection.

In all the models estimated, the sensitivity of travellers to both arrival-time scheduling-delay early and scheduling-delay late appear higher (more sensitive) than to travel time. Normally, it would be expected that the sensitivity to arriving early is less high. This is caused partly by non-linear sensitivity to scheduling-delay early, which is not the topic of this chapter. In this chapter we have focused on modelling travel-time unreliability in a scheduling-choice model.

Using these data, many more relevant questions have been studied. Models have been estimated that include, for example, the heterogeneity of travellers, the departure- and arrival-time constraints (also simultaneous departure- and arrival-time scheduling delays), non-linearity in parameter sensitivity and so on. For these results we refer to van Amelsfort and Bliemer (2004, 2006) and Ubbels (2006).

NOTE

1. We are grateful for the funding this research has received from Goudappel Coffeng B.V., the NWO Multi-Disciplinary Pricing in Transport (MD-PIT) research project, and the Next Generation Infrastructures (NGI) research project in the Netherlands. We would especially like to thank Harry Timmermans (TU Eindhoven, The Netherlands) and John Rose (University of Sydney, Australia) for their help in designing the experiment.

REFERENCES

Bates, J., P. Jones and J. Polak (1995), *The Importance of Punctuality and Reliability: A Review of Evidence and Recommendations for Future Work*, Research report, Transport Studies Group, University of Westminster, London.

Black, I.G. and J.G. Towriss (1993), *Demand Effects of Travel Time Reliability*, Centre for Logistics and Transportation, Cranfield Institute of Technology, UK.

Brownstone, D., A. Ghosh, T.F. Golob, C. Kazimi and D. van Amelsfort (2003), 'Willingness-to-pay to reduce commute time and its variance: evidence from the San Diego I-15 Congestion Pricing Project', *Transportation Research A*, **37**, 373–87.

Brownstone, D. and K.A. Small (2005), 'Valuing time and reliability: assessing the evidence from road pricing demonstrations', *Transportation Research A*, **39**, 279–93.

Copley, G., P. Murphy and D. Pearce (2002), 'Understanding and valuing journey time variability', in *European Transport Conference Proceedings*, Cambridge.

de Jong, G., E. Kroes, R. Plasmeijer, P. Sanders and P. Warffemius (2004), 'The value of reliability', in *European Transport Conference Proceedings*, Strasbourg, France, 4–6 October.

Eliasson, J. (2004), 'Car drivers' valuation of travel time variability, unexpected delays and queue driving', in *European Transport Conference Proceedings*, Strasbourg, France, 4–6 October.

Gaver Jr, D.P. (1968), 'Headstart strategies for combating congestion', *Transportation Science*, **2** (2), 172–81.

Hollander, Y. (2006), 'Direct versus indirect models for the effects of unreliability', *Transportation Research A*, **40**, 699–711.

Jackson, W.B. and J.V. Jucker (1982), 'An empirical study of travel time variability and travel choice behavior', *Transportation Science*, **16** (4), 460–75.

Knight, T.E. (1974), 'An approach to the evaluation of changes in travel unreliability: a "safety margin" hypothesis', *Transportation*, **3**, 393–408.

Lam, T.C. and K.A. Small (2001), 'The value of travel time reliability: measurement from a value pricing experiment', *Transportation Research E*, **37**, 231–51.

Noland, R.B., K.A. Small, P.M. Koskenoja and X. Chu (1998), 'Simulating travel reliability', *Regional Science and Urban Economics*, **28**, 535–64.

Polak, J. (1987), 'A more general model of individual departure time choice transportation planning methods', in *Proceedings of Seminar C held at the Planning and Transport, Research and Computation (PTRC) Summer Annual Meeting*, University of Bath, P290, 247–58.

Senna, L.A.D.S. (1991), 'The influence of travel time variability on the value of time', *Transportation*, **21**, 203–28.

Small, K.A. (1982), 'The scheduling of consumer activities: work trips', *American Economic Review*, **72**, 467–79.

Small, K.A., R. Noland, X. Chu and D. Lewis (1999), *Valuation of Travel-time Savings and Predictability in Congested Conditions for Highway User-cost Estimation*, Transportation Research Board, NCHRP Report 431.

Tillema, T. (2007), 'Road pricing: a transport geographical perspective', PhD thesis, University of Utrecht, The Netherlands.

Transport Research Centre (2006a), Ministry of Transport Public Works and Water Management, The Netherlands, http://www.rws-avv.nl/pls/portal30/docs/13135.PDF, 28 February 2006.

Transport Research Centre (2006b), Ministry of Transport Public Works and Water Management, The Netherlands, http://www.rws-avv.nl/pls/portal30/docs/15837.PDF, 28 February 2006.

Ubbels, B. (2006), 'Road pricing: effectiveness, acceptance and institutional aspects', PhD thesis, Free University of Amsterdam, The Netherlands.

van Amelsfort, D.H. and M. Bliemer (2004), *Modeling Behavioral Responses to Road Pricing using Stated Choice Data, 8th TRAIL Congress 2004, A World of Transport, Infrastructure and Logistics*, Selected Papers, November 2004, TRAIL Conference Proceedings, P2004/1, Delft: Delft University Press.

van Amelsfort, D.H. and M. Bliemer (2006), 'Alternative specifications of scheduling delay components: the effect of travel time uncertainty and departure time rescheduling', in *Proceedings of the 85th TRB Annual Meeting*, Washington, DC, 22–26 January, paper number 06-2182, pp. 1–16.

5. Effects of a kilometre charge on car use, car ownership and relocation

Barry Ubbels, Taede Tillema, Erik Verhoef and Bert van Wee

5.1 INTRODUCTION

People's responses to transport pricing may be multifold. Price increases need not exclusively lead to trip suppression, they may also induce travellers to change their modal use, change their departure time, or even decide to move or change job, depending on the type of measure. Pricing may thus affect many behavioural dimensions, most of which have been studied, both theoretically and empirically. Empirical studies often focus on conventional pricing measures, such as fuel taxes and parking pricing, and the practical experiences of road tolls. This is relevant in many situations, and provides useful insights into the potential effects road pricing may have. For instance, Goodwin (1992) reports that the price elasticity of gasoline demand is −0.27 in the short run and −0.71 in the long run. The case of Singapore has shown that time-dependent charges will affect time of driving (Olszewski and Xie, 2005). In addition, relocation effects may be expected (for example, Banister, 2002; Eliasson and Mattsson, 2002; and Vickerman, 2005). However, currently in several countries the attention is shifting toward charges on a kilometre basis, the UK and the Netherlands being examples. Research into the possible short- and long-term effects of a kilometre charge in its different possible forms is rather poor. In this chapter we try to reduce this gap by presenting the results of research carried out in the Netherlands, focusing on the present debates on introducing a kilometre charge, including on the use of revenues.

The Netherlands has a long history of policy debates about the implementation of road pricing. Recently, the Dutch government has focused on the introduction of a nationwide system where by drivers have to pay according to the number of kilometres driven. At the same time, it is foreseen that drivers will be compensated and that revenues will be returned in one or another way (revenue neutrality is seriously considered). Variabilization is a specific example where a kilometre charge replaces the existing taxes on car ownership (which are independent of car use). Fairness is one of the main reasons for implementation of this measure. Moreover, proposals also indicate that the system will be used to reduce congestion levels and mitigate environmental consequences by differentiating the charge according to time and place. This survey therefore evaluates not only alternatives consisting of flat kilometre charges, but also variants that are more targeted to congestion (bottleneck and peak charges) or the environment (weight differentiated).

This chapter summarizes the most important findings from an empirical survey among car owners in the Netherlands with the aim of investigating behavioural responses to different types of kilometre charge. Three different types of responses are discussed: a number of short-term responses; car ownership responses; and spatial responses. We emphasize that the aim of this contribution is to provide a rather general overview of the behavioural responses that we found. Note that it is difficult to compare the effects found, given the difference in purposes. The reader interested in more background and details of the analysis is referred to the underlying studies in the various (sub)sections.

This chapter is organized as follows. Section 5.2 discusses the survey and presents the short-term responses to various road-pricing measures. Section 5.3 focuses on the car ownership effects. Section 5.4 continues with the relocation effects. Finally, Section 5.5 concludes.

5.2   SHORT-TERM RESPONSES

5.2.1   Data Collection

Because a kilometre charge for all cars at a network level has not been implemented anywhere yet, a stated preference approach is used to gain insights into possible responses. We presented the respondents with a number of hypothetical situations and asked how they would respond. The data have been obtained through an (interactive) Internet survey among Dutch car owners. The total sample consists of 562 respondents, of whom half are car commuters who experience congestion on a regular basis. These respondents were presented with three different road-pricing measures, and we asked them if and how they would expect to change their behaviour in response to these measures.

The aim of the survey was to analyse behavioural responses to realistic and policy-relevant road-pricing measures. Road pricing can have many different types of response, which cannot all be included here. This section focuses on the sensitivity and the type of particular short-term response to different road-pricing measures presented to the respondents for three different trip purposes (that is, commuting, social travel (visits) and other (for example, shopping)). Trips for business purposes are not included. Three different pricing measures were considered, each in multiple variants. Table 5.1 shows the various measures that have been considered: six different variants (1A–1F) for measure 1; two variants (2A and 2B) for measure 2; and again six variants (3A–3F) for measure 3. The variants were divided randomly over the respondents, and each respondent evaluated one variant of each measure (so three in total).

All descriptions of the measures, as shown to respondents, consisted of two major components: an explanation of both the structure and level of the charge, and the allocation of the revenues. Furthermore, each respondent was individually provided with an estimation of his or her potential financial consequences of the implementation of the proposed measure (on the basis of self-reported current (unchanged) travel behaviour and type of car ownership). This estimation of course depends on the charge level (costs) and on the type of revenue use (benefits). Information on the annual number of kilometres driven, and for some measures also on the type of vehicle (measure 2B) and time of driving (measures 2A and 3A–F), is the input for the cost estimation based on present behaviour. The financial benefits shown to the respondent depend on the type of revenue use. Because it was impossible to give respondents a personal estimate of the financial benefits resulting from recycling revenues via lower-income taxation, we presented only the savings for those measures where existing car taxes are abolished.[1] Some specific issues that were meant to prevent various practical considerations from affecting the response were mentioned: in the described system, the privacy of car users is guaranteed, electronic equipment registers the toll, and the driver can choose the preferred payment method (for example, credit card, bank transfer and so on).

If respondents indicated that they did expect to adjust their travel behaviour in response to the measure,[2] they were next asked to indicate the share of trips that would be changed, and also how these would be changed. Depending on the type of measure (for instance, it makes little sense to ask whether respondents will change their departure time when a flat kilometre charge is presented), various possibilities for adjusted behaviour were presented:

- public transport;
- non-motorized transport (walking, bicycle);
- motorized private transport (motorbike, motor);
- carpool (only asked for commuting trips);
- work at home (only asked for commuting trips);

Table 5.1 Description of measures

Measure	Variants
1. Flat kilometre charge, with different revenue allocations	**A**: €0.03, revenues used to abolish car ownership taxes (MRB) **B**: €0.06, revenues used to abolish existing car taxation (purchase (BPM) and ownership (MRB)) **C**: €0.12, revenues used to abolish existing car taxation and construct new roads **D**: €0.03, revenues used to lower income taxes **E**: €0.06, revenues used to lower income taxes **F**: €0.12, revenues used to lower income taxes
2. Flat kilometre charge, with additional bottleneck charge (2A) or differentiated according to weight of the car (2B)	**A**: €0.02, additional multi-step toll during peak times (morning and evening) on working days at daily bottlenecks: 6:00–7:00 €0.50; 7:00–7:30 €1.00; 7:30–8:00 €1.75; 8:00–8:30 €2.50; 8:30–9:00 €1.75; 9:00–9:30 €1.00; 9:30–10:00 €0.50. The same structure for the evening peak (16.00–20.00). Revenues used to abolish car ownership taxes (MRB) **B**: Light cars pay €0.04 per kilometre; middle weight cars pay €0.06 per kilometre; heavy cars pay €0.08 per kilometre, revenues used to abolish existing car taxation (MRB and BPM)
3. Peak and off-peak kilometre charge and different revenue allocations	**A**: €0.02 outside peak times and €0.06 in peak times on working days (7.00–9.00 and 17.00–19.00), abolition of car ownership taxes **B**: €0.04 outside peak times and €0.12 in peak times on working days (7.00–9.00 and 17.00–19.00), abolition of existing car taxation **C**: €0.08 outside peak times and €0.24 in peak times on working days (7.00–9.00 and 17.00–19.00),

Table 5.1   (continued)

Measure	Variants
	abolition of existing car taxation and new roads
	D: €0.02 outside peak times and €0.06 in peak times on working days (7.00–9.00 and 17.00–19.00), revenues used to lower income taxes
	E: €0.04 outside peak times and €0.12 in peak times on working days (7.00–9.00 and 17.00–19.00), revenues to lower income taxes
	F: €0.08 outside peak times and €0.24 in peak times on working days (7.00–9.00 and 17.00–19.00), revenues used to lower income taxes

- travel at other times (only when measure is time dependent);
- give up the trip.

In order to analyse the behavioural responses to the proposed pricing measure in a quantitative way, we asked the respondents to indicate for each purpose how many trips they made in a normal week. Because some (types of) trips are made only once a week, we asked the respondents to indicate how many trips they would change in a period of 4 weeks (by presenting their total number of trips made for each purpose (four times the number of trips in a week)). Hence, a respondent indicating that he/she makes 5 commuting trips a week can change 20 trips at most. Next, it was asked how these trips would be changed. Respondents had to make sure that the number of trips changed was equal to the number of trips allocated over the different alternatives.

The trips changed already provided an indication of the people's responses. We moved a step further, and applied a statistical analysis with the aim of explaining the level of self-reported effectiveness for the various measures. The dependent variable is the fraction of the total trips made during 4 weeks that will be adjusted as indicated by the respondents, that is, a number between 0 (no change) and 1 (all car trips will be adjusted). Hence, the effect of the measures is defined as the fraction of current trips adjusted as a result of pricing. The fraction of trips has been used, rather than vehicle-kilometres, for reasons of reliability. Since the number of kilometres driven per purpose for each respondent is known, it is also possible to calculate the effect in terms of kilometres. The information on reported behaviour is only available for a trip when the respondent indicated that they made that type of trip in the current situation.

5.2.2 Results

The first measure was a flat kilometre charge with different charge levels of 3, 6 and 12 eurocents, and different types of revenue use. The qualitative analysis suggested that trips to visit people are relatively most sensitive (about 14 per cent of this type of trips will be adjusted: see Table 5.2). Commuting trips are hardly changed at all. This may be explained by the fact that a trip suppression is not a feasible alternative for commuting trips (only 0.5 per cent of trips to be adjusted will no longer be made), whereas for other reasons people can seriously consider the alternative of not making the trip. Popular alternatives for car trips include non-motorized transport (all purposes) and public transport (commuting). Cycling and walking in particular are an alternative for visits and other trips, as apparently these trips are often of short distance. The effect in terms of adjusted number of kilometres is smaller than for number of trips; it is likely that people who drive relatively less are more likely to adjust their behaviour.

A statistical analysis[3] for this measure shows that the type of measure (split into charge level and type of revenue use) has a significant impact on the individual effectiveness scores. As expected, the measures with lower charge levels (3 eurocents and 6 eurocents compared with 12 eurocents) are in general less effective. Surprisingly, the abolition of car taxation seems to have less effect in terms of reducing trips than the reduction of income taxes. This might be explained by the fact that for income tax reductions we were unable to specify the expected benefits for the respondents, so the respondents might have overestimated the effect on their kilometrage.

Also, the purpose of the trips is relevant. The statistical analysis confirms the qualitative findings: commuting trips are significantly less sensitive to pricing than 'other' and 'visiting' trips.

Within the group of employed people driving from home to work, it makes a difference whether they have the opportunity to work at home on certain days. This group is more flexible and hence tends to change behaviour sooner than others who do not have this possibility. Respondents driving to work (at least once a week) who obtain partial compensation for their costs tend to change behaviour sooner than drivers who have no commuting costs at all (this group may work at home, for instance). Such

Table 5.2   Aggregate results for all three measures

		Measure 1: flat kilometre charge; different revenue use	Measure 2		Measure 3: peak and off-peak km charge
			2A: peak period with flat fee	2B: weight-differentiated charge	
Effectiveness (trips adjusted)	Commuting	5.9 %	11.2%	4.0%	14.8%
	Visits	14.2%	9.1%	8.4%	14.6%
	Other	10.9%	9.2%	7.9%	13.2%
Two most-preferred alternatives	Commuting	Non-motorized transport, and public transport	Travel at other times, and public transport	Non-motorized travel, and motorized transport	Travel at other times, and public transport
	Visits	Non-motorized transport, and give up trip	Travel at other times, and non-motorized transport	Non-motorized transport, and give up trip	Travel at other times, and non-motorized transport
	Other	Non-motorized transport, and give up trip	Travel at other times, and non-motorized transport	Non-motorized transport, and give up trip	Travel at other times, and non-motorized transport

a result may have been expected for the group who receive no compensation at all. One explanation might be that compensation is in many cases rather modest.

Respondents in the highest income category tend to be less price sensitive, and this is also what we found here. People without children are also less inclined to change behaviour. Other variables, such as age, car usage (yearly number of kilometres), frequency of experiencing congestion, gender (not included) or education (not included and correlated with income) do not seem to have an important impact on the level of self-reported effectiveness.

The variants of the second measure are very different (Table 5.2 therefore shows outcomes for both variants). The first variant 2A is a peak-period charge combined with a flat kilometre fee, while measure 2B is differentiated according to the weight of the vehicle. Compared with the previous measure, one type of response has been added for variant 2A: travel at other times. The qualitative part of the analysis revealed that changing departure time is very attractive for all trip purposes: people prefer car use at other times over public transport and non-motorized travel, especially for commuting trips. The respondents will try to avoid the bottlenecks at certain times, and are less inclined to give up trips for social or other purposes (relative to measure 2B). Note that this variant has a fine differentiation compared with measure 3, and only applies to certain (bottleneck) locations. The charge differentiated according to car weight (2B) seems relatively less effective for commuting trips: only 4 per cent of the total number of commuting trips will be changed. Finally, it appears that slower travel modes are an attractive alternative, especially for social purposes. These trips are likely to have nearby destinations.

The Tobit analysis confirmed that the peak-period variant has more effect than the weight-differentiated charge (especially for commuting trips). Commuters tend to be more sensitive to a bottleneck charge than to a flat kilometre charge. Measure 2A is a bottleneck charge affecting car drivers during peak hours on congested roads. It is therefore understandable that the measure tends to change the behaviour of people who regularly experience congestion more strongly than that of others. Measure 2B has relatively more impact on respondents who own a heavier car, which is rather plausible given the higher charge applying to these car types. Other explanatory variables of the effect of measure 2B include the age of the respondents (with older people being less inclined to change), employment (working people tend to change less) and the compensation of commuting costs by the employer. The measure has more effect for those who have to pay these costs themselves, which seems rather plausible.

The third measure is a kilometre charge differentiated crudely according to time (peak and off-peak only) with different revenue use allocations. Compared with the previous measures, this measure is, in terms of total number adjusted trips (for all purposes), most effective (14.1 per cent versus 9.7 per cent (first measure) and 7.6 per cent (second measure)). This measure has relatively more impact on commuting trips. The number of commuting trips changed is 1004 (about 15 per cent of the total trips made for commuting reasons), considerably more than for measure 1 (400) and for measure 2 (503). Almost half of the trips that would be adjusted would be replaced by trips made off-peak. Non-motorized travel is also an attractive alternative, but again only for the non-commuting purposes (see Table 5.2). The motor or motorbike is not a serious alternative for the respondents, and the same holds for carpooling.

The impact of the type of measure on the effect level was not entirely clear. The level of the charge is less significant, and the type of revenue use is not significant at all. The individual costs and the benefits, however, were presented differently to the respondents than for measure 1. The difference is that here the level of the charge depends on the time of driving. And, since information on the number of kilometres driven during these peak periods was not available, both extremes were presented to each respondent (that is, costs when all or no kilometres are driven during peak hours). While the off-peak charges are lower than with measure 1, the peak charges are considerably higher. The benefits from lower car taxation may be perceived by the respondents as being rather low, which may explain the stronger effect levels for measure 3 relative to measure 1 for the first three variants. This may then also be an explanation for the low level of significance of revenue use here.

In contrast with most previous measures, employment does make a difference. Employed respondents (not necessarily making a commuting trip by car) seem to be less tempted to change behaviour in general (for all types of trips). Also new is the importance of the number of times during a week that people usually experience congestion. This measure leads car drivers who drive regularly in congestion to make more trip adjustments. The structure of the measure, mainly affecting peak-hour drivers (when congestion is usually most severe), is the most likely reason for this. Similarly, we find a significant impact (with the expected sign) of the possibility of working at home. This measure, however, has no differentiated effect on trips made for a certain purpose. This finding corresponds with the general finding that effect sizes are similar for different purposes. Respondents with a higher income are also less price sensitive here, which is rather plausible.

5.2.3 Overview

In terms of trips, the effect of the measures is in the range of 6 to 15 per cent for all trip purposes. There are considerable differences between trip purposes. Measures 1 and 2B seem to have less effect on commuting trips, which is an expected result. In contrast, measures 3 and 2A seem to have a stronger effect on commuting trips. A common characteristic of both these measures is the differentiation according to time. Clearly, the effect level is related to the main purpose of these measures: congestion reduction. Measure 3 seems to adjust nearly all trips, especially commuting trips.

Non-motorized transport is a popular alternative for trips to visit people or shopping trips, especially when it concerns a flat kilometre charge. This suggests that people often take the car for short trips that could easily be replaced by walking or cycling. Giving up social trips is also an option for many respondents. Driving at different times from before is also a popular alternative, especially for (car-dependent) commuting trips. Commuting trips are hard to forgo (working at home or not making the trip are not serious options for most respondents), but there does seem to be some flexibility to allow the rescheduling of trips. This is confirmed by the empirical results from Singapore (see Olszewski and Xie, 2005). Revenue use and charge level have an impact on effect levels, but to a different extent for the discussed measures. There are, of course, two opposing effects: a price increase caused by the kilometre tax, and the indirect subsidy of revenue spending. The abolition of present taxation may be considered as an income effect that gives purchasing power to the consumer (countervailing force). Given the nature of the measures – revenue neutral to the government – the level of compensation of both types of revenue use is similar. But we do find a difference in consequences: those measures with revenues allocated to lower income taxes generally have more effect on car use. Although difficult to explain, it may be caused by the difference in perception of both types of income compensation. The financial consequences of the abolition of car taxation were estimated and presented to the individuals. This was not the case for those variants where income taxation was lowered. In addition, respondents may reserve a certain budget for travel-related expenses. It may then be justified to spend transport-related bonuses on transport matters, and keep the number of kilometres travelled constant. Compensation by means of income taxation may be used previously for purposes outside the transport area, thus reducing the travel budget relatively more.

This approach, as with most research on future, hypothetical situations, may involve some drawbacks that affect the presented response levels. Respondents may answer strategically ('I want this measure not to be implemented, so I will not change behaviour') or give socially desirable answers. It may also be the case that respondents indicated that they would not change their behaviour (respondents currently driving outside the peak hours), but in the future situation (with road pricing) would return to the peak period because of (unexpected) improved travel conditions. This would mitigate the effects of pricing on congestion. Uncertainties about the compensation of commuting costs by employers when road pricing is implemented are also relevant in this context. It is difficult to predict the impact of this issue on our findings. Respondents who receive compensation at present may have answered the questions assuming that future commuting expenses (including tolls) would also be compensated by their employers. As will be described in Chapter 6, such expectations may only partly be fulfilled. Around 70 per cent of the employers, for example, do not intend to provide any compensation for a road tax.

5.3   CAR OWNERSHIP

There are hardly any studies on the relationship between pricing and car ownership, although research has been done on the effects of fuel prices on car stock (see, for example, Goodwin, 1992). The effects are likely to be modest, with elasticities of around -0.2, and lower than fuel consumption elasticities. But the increased policy interest in variabilization in the Netherlands has also entailed increasing attention for the impact of this measure on vehicle ownership. The impact on car ownership is ambiguous, due to opposite changes in two categories: lower fixed costs and higher variable costs. People without a car may decide to purchase one after variabilization, as cars become cheaper to own. Theoretically, one might expect that this would lead to an increase in car ownership, but modelling studies have shown some mixed results on this. A stated preference survey by MuConsult in 2002 does indeed report an increase in car ownership when variabilization is implemented (by an average of 3 per cent). The effect of car owners deciding to sell their car was present (ranging from 1.3 per cent (MRB only) to 4.6 per cent (MRB and BPM)), but the effect on people buying an extra car or a first car (by respondents presently not owning a car) was higher.

This suggests that it is not completely clear what can be expected in terms of car ownership; much depends on the price structure and the type of revenue allocation. Variabilization tends to increase car ownership, while road pricing alone seems to have a (mild) limiting effect on the car stock. But, given the few studies available to date, and the uncertainties in effect sizes, there is scope for further research on this issue. Below, the most important findings on a few car ownership questions that we included in our survey are briefly presented (for a more detailed analysis, see Ubbels, 2006).

5.3.1 Survey

After questions about each measure (1–3), as presented in Section 5.2, the respondents were asked whether they would consider selling their car in response to the measure. With measure 2 (including a variant that is differentiated according to the weight of the car), we added the possibility of replacing the existing car with a heavier vehicle or with a lighter one. Buying a heavier car may seem implausible (because of the higher charge for measure 2B), but this may happen as a result of the abolition of fixed taxes on car ownership and car purchase, which currently rise with vehicle weight.

Our survey did not include respondents who at present do not own a car, but the expected impact of variabilization on car ownership levels depends a great deal on their reaction. To get an impression of the behavioural response (in terms of car ownership) to variabilization of the group that is close to indifference about owning a car (but that owns a car now and is therefore included in our sample), we considered a measure that was the opposite of variabilization. An increase in the fixed costs and a decrease in variable costs may stimulate people to sell (one of) their car(s). The measure (measure 4) was presented as an increase in car ownership taxes by €150 per year (independent of car type) and a decrease in the fuel price by 10 euro-cents per litre (as an average for all fuel types). Since the annual number of kilometres driven and the fuel type of the car for each respondent were available, it was possible to estimate the financial consequences on an annual basis. The reactions of car owners who are close to selling their car should be a good indicator for the reactions of people who currently do not have a car, but are considering buying one. But there may be asymmetries between car owners and non-car owners who are both close to indifference. This all means that we have analysed four questions in total. In addition, we asked the respondents how probable it is that they would sell one of their cars, or in the case of measure 2 also how likely it is that they would buy another type of car. People could indicate this probability on a 7-point scale, ranging from 'very unlikely' (score 1) to 'very likely' (score 7).

5.3.2 Results

The differences between the measures are rather small, with an average score on the question whether people will sell their car of about 1.6 (with score 2 being 'unlikely' and score 1 'very unlikely'). Only 2 per cent of the respondents answered that they would be 'likely' or 'very likely', to sell their car. These effects seem very marginal, but are in the range of the previous mentioned results of variabilization among car owners found by MuConsult (2002).

It may be difficult to explain the differences in probability scores by the structure of the measure because the variabilization measures (1A to 1C and 3A to 3C) contain two opposing effects, which makes it hard to predict the overall consequences for car ownership (and the decision to sell a car or not). On the one hand, the fixed tax decreases (providing an incentive to keep a car), while on the other, a price per kilometre replaces this (discouraging car use and, indirectly, ownership). The presence of opposing effects becomes clear when we look at the results. A higher charge does not lead to a higher probability of selling a car, either for measure 1 or measure 3. Revenue use does matter, but only for measure 1. For equal charge levels, we find that income tax reduction leads to a higher probability of selling the car, while measure 2 seems to generate a slightly lower probability. It is true, however, that both variants include an abolition of fixed taxation and only modest charge levels compared with the other measures. However, measure 2A may have considerable financial consequences for those driving in peak hours. But most of these drivers are commuters who are relatively more car dependent and less inclined to sell their car.

Only a few respondents (1.6 per cent) seriously consider giving up car ownership when car ownership taxes are increased and fuel taxes decreased (measure 4: the opposite of variabilization). This may suggest that the effect on non-car owners buying a car may also be limited. However, we should not forget that both groups are not necessarily equal and comparable. For instance, respondents who have recently purchased a car may be little inclined to give up their car soon afterwards.

A statistical (ordered probit approach) analysis for measure 4 showed that few variables have a significant impact on this probability of selling one of the cars available (Ubbels, 2006). The expected effect of income is present, but not as strong as anticipated. Only the lowest income group has a higher probability of selling their car (but only significant at the 10 per cent level). We have also tested the impact of education instead of income, but the results were no different. Younger people (with lower incomes) generally have a higher probability of selling their car. These may, for instance, be students who buy very cheap second-hand cars for which the fixed taxes become too high a burden. Location has been included to test for different responses by city people. Parking problems in city centres and good public transport accessibility may be an incentive for urban residents with a car to reconsider ownership sooner than people living in more rural areas. But the results do not confirm this assumption. In contrast, the number of cars available in households is important. People with (only) one car available seem to be less tempted to give up their car than households who own more cars. Apparently, the presence of at least one car is important.

These results reveal some of the characteristics of the group that reconsiders car ownership when fixed and variable costs change. Our results suggest that variabilization tends to increase car ownership, especially among younger people with lower incomes. In most cases vehicles will be purchased, with an increasing number of households having a second or third car as a consequence. However, it is still recommended that more in-depth research on car ownership behaviour among non-car owners should be conducted in order to obtain better insight into the effects of variabilization on car ownership levels.

5.4   RELOCATION EFFECTS

5.4.1 Introduction

This section focuses on the work and residential relocations of households. Relocation decisions consist of several stages. Wong (2002) formulates two major stages within the relocation process: (i) the decision to move; and (ii) the selection of a new location. These two stages of the housing decision tree are likely to be interdependent and linked. Road-pricing costs might have an impact on the (perceived) travel impedance and form a trigger for households to make a decision to relocate (that is, to decide to look for a new location). Apart from that, pricing measures might also influence the actual choice of an activity location (for example, where to settle, work and so on).

Thus, road pricing might have an impact on both phases of the relocation decision. In this section, we concentrate only on the influence of the same three kilometre charges (see Table 5.1) on the decision to change the residential and/or work location. For insight into the impact of these kilometre charges on the search process and final location decision, see Tillema et al. (2006). As a result of activity relocations, the equilibrium between demand and supply of locations and houses (in certain areas) might become distorted (on an aggregate level). These changes in demand and supply can, along with other influencing factors, lead to movements in housing and land prices. These changes in their turn influence the choices to relocate but also the final location choices. We shall not study these 'secondary effects' on the relocation choice in this section, but shall focus on the primary effect of road pricing on relocation decisions.

Only employed respondents (in total 465 of 562) were asked to indicate the probability of relocating as a result of a road-pricing measure. Respondents had to indicate the probability that they would relocate to another dwelling (closer to work) or would search for another job (closer to home) on a 7-point ordinal scale ranging from 'highly unlikely' (score 1) to 'highly likely' (score 7). Below, we present the most important findings with respect to the relocation probability as a result of a kilometre charge. For a more detailed analysis, see Tillema et al. (ibid.).

5.4.2 Results

The average percentage of respondents (taken over all three measures) who reported a 'quite high', 'high' or 'extremely high' probability of moving house if a kilometre charge were to be implemented, amounts to 4.1 per cent (see Table 5.3). Some 2.1 per cent indicated the probability of moving as 'high' or 'extremely high'. The relocation probabilities do not clearly differ for the three kilometre charges. Only a slightly lower relocation probability was observed for kilometre charge measure 2. For job relocation we find a significantly ($\alpha \leq 0.05$) higher probability if road pricing were to be implemented. Averaged over the measures, 10.8 per cent of the respondents indicated that the probability is 'quite high', 'high' or 'extremely high', and 5.3 per cent reported a 'high' to 'extremely high' probability. Again, differences between the measures are small.

These figures include responses from people who have plans to change their residence or job location (within 2 years) regardless of the introduction of road pricing. The propensity to move house or job in response to road pricing is significantly higher for those considering a move anyway.

Table 5.3   Relocation probabilities

Probability of relocating (%)	Residential relocation (%)	Work relocation (%)
1 Extremely low	69.6	58.6
2 Low	20.9	22.3
3 Quite low	2.5	2.2
4 Not low/high	3.1	5.0
5 Quite high	2.0	5.5
6 High	1.4	3.9
7 Extremely high	0.7	1.4
Sum 5 to 7: quite to extremely high	4.1	10.8
Sum 6 to 7: high to extremely high	2.1	5.3

Around 75 per cent of the previously mentioned 4.1 per cent group indicated that they had a 'quite high', 'high', or 'extremely high' probability of relocating for whatever reasons within two years. Thus, it is especially those respondents who are already intending to relocate who are expected to be influenced in their relocation decision by the introduction of a road-pricing measure. Furthermore, a significant relation between changing the residential or work location and (road) pricing has been found. However, most respondents who indicated that they would relocate as a result of pricing, chose to adjust only one location (either the job or the residential location).

As far as is known, there are only a very few studies that report on the (to be expected) relocation probabilities/chances of households in response to road pricing. One of these studies, MuConsult (2000), estimated the percentage of people who would relocate as a result of a pricing measure. The reported relocation percentages due to a kilometre charge[4] are within the range of 3 to 5 per cent. MuConsult expects a higher percentage change for job relocation compared with residential relocation. Moreover, Arentze and Timmermans (2005) studied the relocation intention of Dutch households on the basis of a stated adaptation experiment. The road-pricing scenario used consisted of a time-differentiated kilometre charge with a higher price level during the peak period. Different price levels were used. For the off peak, charge levels of 7 and 9 Dutch guilder cents per kilometre were used (that is respectively, 3.2 and 4.1 euro-cents/kilometre). For the peak charge, an extra 15 or 20 guilder cents were added to the off-peak charge (that is, an extra charge of 6.8 or 9.1 euro-cents, respectively). This makes the charge quite comparable to the average price level in measure 3 (see price measures 3B and 3E in Table 5.1). Arentze and Timmermans found that 88.2 per cent of the respondents would not consider a change; 2.0 per cent would change their work location and 11.1 per cent would change their home location. Neither study reported the intention of respondents to relocate anyway (without road pricing).

Overall, it can be concluded that the relocation intentions presented in MuConsult (2000) and Arentze and Timmermans (2005) are more or less the same as the results presented in this section. However, comparisons can only be made on a very rough basis, on account of likely sample differences but especially because the dependent variable varies. In our research we focused on the probability of changing location, whereas MuConsult used the formulation of 'residential change percentage' and Arentze and Timmermans asked respondents about their intention to relocate. Such differences in the (formulation of the) dependent variable might influence the 'relocation results' to a considerable extent. Although the process of comparing results must be undertaken with some care, at least one appealing difference is that Arentze and Timmermans find a substantially higher residential compared with job location change, whereas on the basis of household questionnaire 2 the opposite emerged: a higher job compared with a residential location change.

Several variables were found to explain the probability of changing the residential location or searching for another job specifically as a result of a road-pricing measure. Important influencing factors for relocation (based on the total sample, including those who have the intention anyway) are gross yearly household income, the yearly number of kilometres driven, the degree of travel-cost compensation from employers, the education level and the probability of relocating within 2 years for whatever reason. Households within the lowest distinguished income class (<28 500 euros/year) indicated a higher relocation probability. Households who drove more than 19 000 km/year and also those households who already had a (quite) high probability of relocating within 2 years, indicated that they had a relatively higher relocation probability specifically due to the kilometre charges. For respondents with a higher education (university) and for households who received a total travel-cost compensation, a relatively lower residential and job relocation probability was found.

The observed explanatory factors for relocating as a result of (road-) pricing measures are often comparable and of the same sign as can be found in general 'relocation' studies (van Wee, 1994; Kim et al., 2005). The most important difference is that factors such as income and travel-cost compensation seem to play a more important explanatory role in the relocation decision due to road pricing. Moreover, in contrast to 'normal' relocation studies, where respondents with a higher income often have a higher (residential) relocation intention, in our survey people with a higher income show a lower relocation intention due to road pricing.

In general, differences between influencing factors for the work or residential relocation probability due to road pricing are small. Somewhat unexpectedly, the price level of the road-pricing measure does not seem to be important. The number of kilometres driven can (especially in the case of a kilometre charge) be seen as a proxy for generalized road-pricing costs. This kilometre-variable, however, has a higher explanatory power, causing the price variable to become insignificant. Research by Arentze and Timmermans (2005) confirms this; they also find no significant influence of car commuting costs (including the congestion charge) on the relocation probability. Thus, it seems that the price level has a weaker influence on long-term (relocation) behaviour than on the short-term car trip behaviour (see Section 5.2).

5.5   CONCLUDING REMARKS

The results presented in this chapter confirm that road pricing may have a considerable effect on car use, but much depends on the design of the measure. In terms of trips adjusted, the effects of the measures are in the range of 6 to 15 per cent for all purposes. There are considerable differences between trip purposes, with commuting generally being least sensitive (as is well known from the literature) when the charge is time independent. Trips made to visit people or for shopping purposes will be modified first, with non-motorized transport (walking, cycling) being the most frequently chosen alternative for the car. This suggests that car use for short-distance trips will be reconsidered.

When policy makers want to affect peak-time (commuting) road traffic, a time-differentiated measure seems most appropriate. The kilometre charge with additional peak charge is the most effective overall, especially for commuting trips. The implementation of these (time-dependent) charges is likely to lead to driving at other times, especially for commuting trips. Commuting trips are necessary (working at home or not making the trip are not feasible options for most of the respondents), but there seems to be some level of flexibility which allows the scheduling of trips.

Road pricing can have considerable consequences for road usage, but policy makers should be aware that it may also affect car ownership (with indirect effects on road use). The effects of road pricing and revenue recycling on the car stock are an as yet unsettled issue, given the mixed results in the literature. Our own results indicate that about 2 per cent of the respondents will most probably sell their car, or one of their cars, if a variable charge is implemented. Variation between measures is low, indicating that revenue use and type of charge have a minor impact on car ownership. We have also considered the opposite of variabilization, with the aim of analysing the behaviour of (car-owning) respondents if car ownership becomes more expensive. The case where road pricing is implemented and revenues are recycled by an abolition of ownership taxes may lead to a reduction of car use, or at least a change in mobility patterns. However, policy makers should not forget that car usage may actually increase if non-car owners decide to buy a car. Our findings suggest that only a few respondents (1.6 per cent) would seriously consider giving up car ownership under reversed variabilization. This is only a proxy for behaviour of non-car owners. A statistical analysis revealed that younger people and households owning two or more cars are more likely to sell their (one of their) car(s), which suggests that the total number of kilometres driven will be reduced only slightly (or increased in the case of variabilization).

Apart from trip and car ownership changes, the residential and/or job relocation probabilities due to kilometre charges were also studied. About 4 per cent of the households indicated a 'reasonably high' probability of changing their residence location. In contrast, a substantial larger group (that is, 11 per cent) of respondents had a '(quite) high' job relocation probability. Approximately half of these respondents indicated a 'high' or 'extremely high' probability: 2.1 per cent residential change and 5.3 per cent job relocation. Note that most of the respondents who indicated that they would most probably relocate when road pricing becomes a reality, already had this intention to start with.

Although it was found that the residential and especially work relocation probabilities due to pricing are substantial, especially for people who were already intending to relocate within 2 years, the results must be handled with some care. The implicit assumption within the stated preference questionnaire was that house prices would not change with the introduction of transport pricing. In reality, a new market equilibrium in house prices might occur, because of changing demands. Some locations might become more, and others less, desirable as places to live. Furthermore, possibly increasing costs of living due to transport pricing might cause house prices to decrease in general.

Finally, it is difficult to determine whether these results can be generalized to other countries. For example, the availability (for example, of public transport) and the inherent popularity of alternatives (for example, cycling) may differ between countries; with respect to relocation, the spatial structure and/or transfer costs for relocation might be different, possibly leading to somewhat different relocation probabilities due to a road-pricing measure in other countries. Although it is tempting to present, for example, the conclusion on the importance of time-differentiation of charges for effectiveness in commuting as a more general result, we cannot draw such conclusions from our study and therefore leave it as material for further (local) study.

NOTES

1. The benefits from paying less car taxation depend on the type of car the respondents own (that is, on fuel type and weight). We have estimated average savings for nine categories (a combination of three fuel types and three weight categories), for an abolition of annual car ownership taxes (MRB) only, and an abolition of all existing car taxation: namely, MRB and the fixed purchase tax (BPM).
2. It was made possible for people to indicate that they intended to make more car trips due to the measure; in this case we only asked how many extra trips that person would make.
3. Because of the large number of zero observations, censored regression models, in which the dependent variable is observed in only some of the ranges, are more appropriate. Tobin

(1958) analysed this problem, and formulated a regression model that was later called the Tobit model. We applied this type of methodology to analyse the level of self-reported effectiveness. For more detailed information on methodology and results, see Ubbels (2006).
4. MuConsult (2000) estimates the relocation chances on the basis of, among other things, elasticities. Within their relocation chance computations they assume a 10 per cent increase in transport costs due to a kilometre charge. The charge in itself is not specifically defined/operationalized.

REFERENCES

Arentze, T. and H. Timmermans (2005), *Spatial Impact of Congestion Pricing Scenarios*, Tweede Belgischse Geografendag, Gent.

Banister, D. (2002), *The Integration of Road Pricing with Land Use Planning*, Brussels: Imprint-Europe.

Eliasson, J. and L.G. Mattsson (2002), 'Transport and location effects of road pricing: a simulation approach', *Journal of Transport Economics and Policy*, 3, 417–56.

Goodwin, P.B. (1992), 'Review of new demand elasticities with special reference to short and long run effects of price changes', *Journal of Transport Economics and Policy*, 26 (2), 155–71.

Kim, J.H., F. Pagliara and J. Preston (2005), 'The intention to move and residential location choice behaviour', *Urban Studies*, 42 (9), 1621–36.

MuConsult (2000), *Ruimtelijke Effecten Prijsbeleid (Hoofdrapport)* ('Spatial effects of pricing policy (main report)'), Amersfoort: MuConsult.

MuConsult (2002), *Onderzoek naar de Effecten van Kilometerheffing* (Study into the effects of a kilometre charge), concept Onderzoeksrapport, Amersfoort: MuConsult.

Olszewski, P. and L. Xie (2005), 'Modelling the effects of road pricing on traffic in Singapore', *Transportation Research A*, 39, 755–72.

Tillema, T., D. Ettema and G.P. van Wee (2006), 'Road pricing and (re)location decisions of households', Paper presented at the 85th Transportation Research Board (TRB) Annual Meeting, Washington, DC, 22–26 January.

Tobin, J. (1958), 'Estimation of relationships for limited dependent variables', *Econometrica*, 26, 24–36.

Ubbels, B. (2006), 'Road pricing: effectiveness, acceptance and institutional issues', PhD thesis, Vrije Universiteit, Amsterdam.

van Wee, B. (1994), *Werklocaties, woonlocaties en woon-werkverkeer*, Work locations, residential locations and commute traffic (trans.), RIVM (Rijksinstituut voor Volksgezondheid en Milieu), Bilthoven.

Vickerman, R.W. (2005), 'Evaluating the wider economic impacts of congestion charging schemes: the limitations of conventional modelling approaches', Paper presented at the 45th European Regional Science Association (ERSA) meeting, Amsterdam, 23–27 August.

Wong, G.K.M. (2002), 'A conceptual model of the household's housing decision-making process: the economic perspective', *Review of Urban and Regional Development Studies*, 14 (3), 217–34.

6. Firms: changes in trip patterns, product prices, locations and in the human resource policy due to road pricing

Taede Tillema, Bert van Wee, Jan Rouwendal and Jos van Ommeren

6.1 INTRODUCTION

Road-pricing policies are increasingly being implemented in urbanized areas around the world, with the aims of alleviating congestion,[1] maintaining the accessibility of urban regions and minimizing negative environmental effects of road traffic (van Wee, 1995; de Wit and van Gent, 1998; Verhoef, 2000). An additional motivation is the generation of revenues that can be used to build and maintain infrastructure.

The introduction of road-pricing measures might have an effect on both household and firm behaviour. Whereas Chapter 5 in this volume has already focused on the behavioural responses of households to road pricing, this chapter shifts attention to the behavioural changes of firms.

6.2 THEORY AND OUTLINE

Transport costs are generally regarded as a main determinant of the location of economic activity. This is true for both classical location theory (Max Weber) and for the new economic geography. For instance, Krugman's (1991) core–periphery model stresses the interrelationship between transport costs and the polarization of regions. The model shows that, in particular settings, the (long-run) effects of modest changes in transport costs on location patterns of industries can be large and this conclusion has been repeated in numerous later variants of the model. This suggests that measures that influence transport costs in a systematic manner, such as road pricing, may have potentially large effects on the spatial distribution of firms and employment. However, the effect of changes in transport costs on the concentration of economic activity is ambiguous. New economic geography models tend to predict increased concentration as a consequence of lower transport costs, but the literature on urban sprawl, recently surveyed in Glaeser and Kahn (2004) suggests that deconcentration should be expected. It is therefore a priori unclear what the impact of road pricing on location patterns will be.

One may even go one step further and question the presence of any effect of road pricing on generalized transport costs, at least in particular circumstances. For instance, in the well-known bottleneck model with inelastic demand (see Arnott et al., 1990), the introduction of an optimal toll leads to a change in the composition of total travel costs: the queue in front of the bottleneck disappears, and drivers no longer pay in terms of time, but in terms of money to arrive at their place of work at or close to their preferred time. The times at which workers reach their employment location will not change and the introduction of an optimal congestion toll does not seem to provide any incentive for firms to relocate. However, in most other cases one would expect that the internalization of external effects, which is the main economic motivation for road pricing, will cause transportation costs to increase. Note, however, that the decrease in congestion will usually provide partial compensation for the higher costs resulting from the toll, and that further compensating effects may be achieved when toll revenues are used to improve transport infrastructure.

Even though the effects of changes in transport costs on location patterns are ambiguous, according to economic theory, the welfare effects should be positive. To the extent that the increased transport costs serve to internalize external effects, such as pollution and congestion, welfare may increase, and the people who gain will be able to compensate the losers.[2] This conclusion is generally reached in transport economic models and does not depend on the possibility of firms or workers (or other economic actors) changing their location. Even if all these actors were unable or unwilling to change their location, road pricing may be beneficial to all. The conclusion is, therefore, that road pricing is on average not a net burden, but a benefit. Even though one should not expect actual road-pricing measures to come in such a form that the net benefit will be positive for every actor, a substantial share of the actors should experience net benefits.[3] The possibility that a firm's situation will improve as a result of the introduction of road pricing increases when the revenues are used in such a way that many 'losers' receive compensation or transport infrastructure is substantially improved.

This rather positive theoretical perspective on the effects of road pricing seems to differ markedly from the perceptions of workers and managers.

Their common sense is that road pricing is an increase in costs. This perception is perfectly understandable. After all, if road pricing is meant to internalize costs that used to be external, it implies that some of the costs that used to be paid by others now appear on the bill of those who cause them.

This change in costs may invoke a number of reactions. In the short term, firms may decide, depending on the type of pricing, to make changes in the trip pattern and in their product/service prices. Possible short-term trip changes due to road pricing are in: route choice so as to decrease the number of kilometres driven (probably at the expense of more travel time); departure time (so as to avoid the high tariff during rush hours); transport mode (from car to public transport); and the frequency of travelling (May and Milne, 2000; Verhoef et al., 2004). Such changes may occur in the transport of inputs, goods produced and business trips. If the firm does not itself transport its inputs and completed products, it may be confronted with higher transport prices, which may induce it to change the frequencies of transport and other trip characteristics in much the same way. Higher costs of transport (whether undertaken by the firm itself or by others) may induce a firm to switch to other suppliers of inputs and/or to change its output prices.

If customers visit the firm so as to make purchases, higher transport costs due to road pricing may be beneficial to easily accessible firms and detrimental to others. The firm may react to these changes in its attractiveness, by changing its prices. Depending on its degree of market power, it may also attempt to transfer its increased transport costs to consumers. Note also here that road pricing does not necessarily increase every firm's and customer's costs. The net effect depends on the change in travel time and possibly its reliability that results from road pricing. Road pricing may also affect a firm's accessibility to workers. In some cases, its relative accessibility may improve, but in others it may deteriorate. Also here, there may be reactions in terms of prices. The firm may decide to offer higher wages or increase compensation for commuting costs.

These effects illustrate the way in which road pricing can have its efficiency-improving effect on road pricing in the short run, when location is taken as given. They have been studied in theoretical models, but, given the limited experience with actual road pricing, not much is known about their actual size. Business travel accounts for a substantial part of overall travel (approximately 10–25 per cent of the person-kilometres[4]). Changes in the trip behaviour of firms might therefore have important consequences for the level of service of the infrastructure network. Apart from that, changes in employee (cost) compensation might affect the commuting travel pattern of employees.

Although it is, therefore, clearly relevant to study the behavioural changes of firms due to a pricing measure, only very few studies have made an attempt to gain insight into these effects (for example, MuConsult, 2000; Vervoort and Spit, 2005). MuConsult expects only small changes in the behaviour of firms, because transport costs form only a small proportion of their total operational costs. Moreover, firms might try to mitigate possibly higher costs due to a charge by trying to further increase the efficiency (for example, using larger vehicles for transport if possible), or by transferring costs to others such as customers (see also Vervoort and Spit, 2005). In advance of implementing a pricing measure, it is not clear whether firms would be worse off. A charge might lead to benefits in the form of travel-time and/or travel-time reliability gains, and if these benefits occur, firms might be better off. In addition, whether firms will benefit or lose because of the charge will depend not only on the type and size of the benefit but also on the (main) type of activity of the firm. Firms within the goods transport sector (that is, freight traffic) might, for example, be influenced more directly by a pricing measure than other firms. On the other hand, labour-intensive firms might more often be confronted with higher costs to compensate employees. Verhoef et al. (1998) studied (in this respect) the effects of road pricing for different types of trips in the Randstad area within the Netherlands. They report that a cordon charge leads to gains mainly for freight traffic and to a somewhat lesser extent for business traffic. These gains result from the expected travel-time improvements, in combination with a high value of time for these kinds of trips. Commuters are expected to be worse off, at least if revenue investments are not taken into account. Vervoort and Spit (2005) quantitatively assessed the influence of a motorway kilometre charge[5] for freight traffic on (short-term) travel behaviour. The study expects on average a 2.7 per cent decrease in vehicle-kilometres (that is, those made by firms) for the transport of goods. This effect might look small, but it must be emphasized that because of the type of measure, transport trips by (heavy) lorries are charged only on the motorways and not on the secondary roads.

In the urban economics literature, spatial variation in wages due to differences in commuting costs is an active field of study (see Timothy and Wheaton, 2001). In the standard monocentric model, workers have to pay all their own commuting costs. The empirical literature usually finds that house prices reflect accessibility to jobs, but not that wages reflect accessibility to residential areas, which suggests that wages will not react strongly to road pricing. Finally, to the authors' knowledge, very little literature is available on the impacts of road-pricing measures on other compensation measures such as fringe benefits offered by firms. Exceptions are van Ommeren et al. (2006) and van Ommeren and Rietveld (2007). In the former study, it is shown empirically that reimbursement of travel costs (for example, by means of a company car), is positively related to the length of the commute. A possible explanation of this finding is that employers use such reimbursements to attract workers with long commutes to their firm. If true, this suggests that the employees' costs of road pricing may be reimbursed by their employers. In the latter study, it is theoretically supported that firms are more likely to reimburse residential moving costs as road pricing is introduced. But there seem to be no studies that investigate the reaction of commuting-cost reimbursement to the introduction of road pricing. Given the scarcity of studies on the effects of road pricing on firms, it is clearly important to improve our knowledge of the size of these effects before such measures are actually introduced, as was the purpose of the questionnaire that will be discussed in the following sections.

In the longer run, road pricing can also have an influence on the location pattern of firms. Indeed, the introduction of road pricing may act as a trigger for location change (Tillema et al., 2006). Such changes in location are a derived effect of the short-run impact of road pricing discussed above. We noted at the beginning of this section that spatial economic theory (and especially the new economic geography) suggests that the long-run changes in locational patterns induced by road pricing may be large. Nevertheless, the influence of road pricing on the (re)location choices of firms has also received limited attention to date. The empirical literature that addresses the effect of travel cost (in general; not road-pricing costs) and travel time on (re)location decisions tends to downplay the importance of transport costs on relocation decisions, which, however, is emphasized in neoclassical and new economic geography location theories (see, for instance, Pellenbarg, 1999; van Dijk and Pellenbarg, 2000; Pen, 2002; McQuaid et al., 2004). Possible reasons for this relatively limited influence of transport on firm relocation decisions are that, as described above, transport costs form only a small proportion of firms' total operational costs, and that transaction costs for relocating may in general be too high to enable firms to react 'freely' to transport or accessibility changes/differences (see McQuaid et al., 2004). Apart from the empirical studies, which do not focus specifically on road-pricing issues, there is a literature that investigates the potential effect of this policy on relocation decisions with micro-simulation models (for example, Anas and Xu, 1999; Eliasson and Mattsson, 2001; Mattsson and Sjölin, 2002). The results from such studies are not further discussed here. It may, however, be concluded that better information about the effects of road pricing on location decisions is needed. The questionnaire that is the central subject of the present chapter is also intended to make a contribution in this respect.

It can be concluded that very few research studies on the behavioural changes of firms due to pricing have been undertaken,[6] and the studies that were carried out often do not give quantitative indications of changes in firm behaviour. Moreover, no empirical studies were found in which firms were asked about (intended) changes in their behaviour due to a pricing measure. This chapter attempts to fill (some of) these gaps by shedding light on the intended behavioural changes of firms due to a (road-)pricing measure. More specifically, the aim is to gain insight into the extent to which firms intend to change their trip behaviour, product prices, locations and their human resource policy as a result of a pricing measure. Section 6.3 describes the main characteristics of the data. Section 6.4 gives insight into intended trip changes and product price changes by firms. Section 6.5 analyses shifts in the human resource policy (for example, employee compensation and offers) due to pricing. The relocation probabilities of firms due to road pricing are described in Section 6.6. Finally, conclusions follow in Section 6.7.

6.3 DATA AND METHODOLOGY

To the authors' knowledge, no databases of observed firm responses to road pricing exist. Therefore, a stated preference approach was followed to investigate the impact of road pricing on the behaviour of firms. A survey was held among 485 firms that operate in the business service or in the manufacturing industrial sector.[7] These types of firm were selected, first, because firms within these categories are relatively autonomous in their behaviour and policy. Within the limits of laws and general agreements, they can decide themselves to what extent they want to compensate their employees or want to adjust their trip behaviour. Moreover these firms, and especially firms within the business service sector, are free to choose their settlement locations.[8] Therefore, such firms are able to indicate behavioural changes due to a pricing measure. For those same reasons, public organizations or firms working within the retail sector were not included (that is, they are more constrained in changing their behaviour[9]). Moreover, the decision to select firms in the business service or in the manufacturing industrial sector was also made because together these types of firm form a substantial part of firms in the Netherlands (according to the Dutch Chamber of Commerce (2006), almost 50 per cent of the establishments). This makes possible changes in their behaviour of general importance, and it also makes it easier to obtain sufficient respondents. Finally, the choice to focus on only two sectors was made to avoid running the risk of not getting enough data to assess (significant) effects for various sectors.

The questionnaire included only one pricing measure: a kilometre charge, which was described as follows:

> Imagine that the government introduces a kilometre charge. The level of the charge is dependent on the time of travel. On working days, a car/lorry driver has to pay 12 eurocents per kilometre during rush hours (between 7.00 and 9.00, and between 17.00 and 19.00), and 4 eurocents per kilometre outside rush hours. Electronic devices register travel behaviour, and compute the total costs per trip. Payments may be made via automatic debit notices, credit card, giro, smart cards, or prepaid cards. The registration and payment systems have no technical defects. The privacy of travellers will not be threatened. The government decided to use the revenues for decreasing income taxes.

Respondents were then asked to indicate the expected short-term behavioural changes of their establishment due to the charge. The short-term behavioural questions can be classified into two groups: (i) changes in the trip pattern; and (ii) changes in product prices. Questions had to be answered on a 7-point ordinal response scale. With respect to long-term behavioural changes, only one question was posed: respondents had to indicate (on a 7-point scale) the probability that their establishment would relocate within 2 years specifically as a result of the kilometre charge.

The final part of the questionnaire contained questions about the last-recruited employee. The main advantage of this procedure is that this employee can be considered as a randomly chosen employee on which the respondents are most likely to have detailed information, thus making it possible to investigate the effect of road pricing on individual workers more precisely. Firms were asked to indicate which transport-related fringe benefits (for example, company cars) they offered to the last recruited employee. Subsequently, the same kilometre charge as presented earlier in the questionnaire was displayed once more, after which firms were asked to point out (again) which of the facilities would have been offered to the last-recruited employee if the kilometre charge had already been implemented when the employee was recruited. The following benefits were included: residential relocation reimbursement, company car, and compensation for kilometre/fuel costs or public transport expenses.

6.4   SHORT-TERM REACTIONS OF FIRMS: INTENDED TRIP AND PRODUCT PRICE CHANGES

The trip consequences of the charge fall into three categories: (i) changes in the number of business trips by car in general, and in those made within and outside the peak period; (ii) changes in the number of trips for the transport

Table 6.1   Intended changes in firms' current trip pattern for business trips

Consequences of km charge compared to current situation for number of business trips . . .	By car (overall)		By car outside peak period		By car within peak period	
	%	(no.)	%	(no.)	%	(no.)
1. Far fewer	1.2	(6)	0.2	(1)	2.5	(12)
2. Fewer	3.1	(15)	0	(0)	7.7	(37)
3. Slightly fewer	14.5	(70)	3.9	(19)	27.5	(132)
4. Stays the same	77.6	(374)	56.0	(270)	57.8	(277)
5. Slightly more	1.0	(5)	22.8	(110)	2.1	(10)
6. More	1.5	(7)	13.2	(64)	1.5	(7)
7. Far more	1.0	(5)	3.7	(18)	1.0	(5)
Do not know/not relevant		3		3		5
Total fewer trips (sum categories 1, 2, 3)	18.8		4.1		37.7	
Total more trips (sum categories 5, 6, 7)	3.5		39.7		4.6	

of goods by car or lorry in general, and alterations in those made within and outside the peak period; and (iii) the effect of the kilometre charge on the extent to which firms use (or allow employees to use) information and communication technologies (ICTs) as a substitute for car trips. Table 6.1 shows the firms' intended changes to their current trip pattern for business trips. The respondents could indicate the changes on a 7-point ordinal scale ranging from 'far fewer' to 'far more' trips compared with the current situation. The table shows the results in three columns. Column 1 represents the changes in the number of car trips in general. Columns 2 and 3 describe the alterations in trips within and outside of the peak period. Apart from giving the percentages of respondents who chose each of the 7 categories, the sum of the percentages of the two groups of categories (1–3 and 5–7) are also given at the bottom of the table. The sum of the percentages of categories 1–3 represents the total percentage of respondents who expected that their establishment would make fewer trips as a result of the charge; in contrast, the combined categories 5–7 give the total percentage of firms that want to make more trips. Respondents who had no idea of the change in business trips by car due to the charge, or respondents whose firm did not undertake any business trips by car, could choose the option 'do not know/not relevant'.

In total, roughly 19 per cent of the firms responded that they expected to make fewer business trips by car relative to the current situation. Only

3.5 per cent decided to make more trips, possibly because they expected to benefit from travel-time gains. Most firms (77.6 per cent) did not intend to change anything. From the 19 per cent that intended to make fewer business trips by car, most firms (that is, 14.5 per cent) chose the class 'slightly fewer'. Changes in the travel behaviour in the period during which the trips are made appear more likely than the reduction of the total number of business trips. Around 40 per cent indicated that they would make business trips more often outside the peak period, in which the kilometre charge level is higher. Only about 4 per cent decided to make fewer trips outside the peak. As an extra check for consistency, the opposite behavioural change was also studied (see Column 3): the percentage travelling more or less within the peak period. These percentages (about 38 per cent less, 4.6 per cent more) are as expected and comparable to the results in Column 2.

Table 6.2 presents the intended changes for the car/lorry trips made for the transport of goods. The presentation of the table is comparable to Table 6.1. Column 1 shows that firms intended to make fewer changes in the number of trips for goods transport compared with changes in business trips. Approximately 6 per cent chose to make fewer trips. The percentage of firms that intended to make more trips approximates to 3.5 per cent and is in line with the percentage observed in Table 6.1. An important difference

Table 6.2   *Intended changes in firms' current trip pattern for transport of goods*

Consequences of km charge compared to current situation for transportation of goods . . .	By lorry/car (overall)		By lorry/car outside peak period		By lorry/car within peak period	
	%	(no.)	%	(no.)	%	(no.)
1. Far fewer	0.7	(3)	0.4	(2)	1.3	(6)
2. Fewer	1.1	(5)	0.7	(3)	7.0	(31)
3. Slightly fewer	4.3	(19)	1.1	(5)	18.4	(82)
4. Stays the same	90.5	(402)	70.2	(314)	69.7	(310)
5. Slightly more	1.1	(5)	14.8	(66)	2.0	(9)
6. More	1.4	(6)	10.7	(48)	0.9	(4)
7. Far more	0.9	(4)	2.0	(9)	0.7	(3)
Do not know/not relevant		41		38		40
Total fewer trips (sum categories 1, 2, 3)	6.1		1.9		26.7	
Total more trips (sum categories 5, 6 ,7)	3.4		27.5		3.6	

between the two tables is that the option 'do not know/not relevant' was chosen far more often in the case of transport of goods. This indicates that business trips are more likely to be made by each firm than trips for the transport of goods. With regard to the intention to make alterations in the period in which the firm undertakes transport trips (that is, Columns 2 and 3), Table 6.2 shows that around 27.5 per cent of the firms indicated that they would make more trips outside the peak period if the time-differentiated kilometre charge were to be implemented. This percentage is somewhat lower than in Table 6.1 where it was nearly 40 per cent. Again, the results of changes in the trips made within the peak, period (that is, to check for consistency) are in line with the results from changes in trips made outside of the peak: the results are opposite and of the same size. Finally, most firms that wanted to change trips did so only to a small extent.

Table 6.3 shows the intended changes of firms in the use of ICT. Column 1 describes to what extent firms expected to make more or less use of ICT as a means of changing the number of commuter car trips made by employees. An example of ICT use in this case is teleworking. Some 35 per cent of the firms intended to make more use of ICT if the kilometre charge were to be introduced. Of these 35 per cent, most (23.4 per cent) chose the

Table 6.3   Intended change in the use of ICT as a substitute for commute and business trips

Consequences of km charge for use of ICT as a substitute for current trips compared with use in current situation	ICT as a substitute for commuter trips (e.g., teleworking)		ICT as a substitute for business trips (e.g., email, video conferencing)	
	%	(no.)	%	(no.)
1. Far fewer	0.7	(3)	0.6	(3)
2. Fewer	–	–	–	–
3. Slightly fewer	1.5	(7)	1.5	(7)
4. Stays the same	62.9	(288)	62.8	(290)
5. Slightly more	23.4	(107)	24.5	(113)
6. More	10.3	(47)	9.1	(42)
7. Far more	1.3	(6)	1.5	(7)
Do not know/not relevant		27		23
Total fewer trips (sum categories 1, 2, 3)	2.2		2.1	
Total more trips (sum categories 5, 6, 7)	35.0		35.1	

option 'slightly more' usage of ICT. Roughly 2 per cent of the firms wanted to use ICT less often than they currently did. No clear explanation can be given for this finding. It might be the case that those firms (2 per cent) expected travel-time gains, making it more feasible to request teleworkers to come to the office more often. On the other hand, this 2 per cent might also be explained by some firms being opposed to a pricing measure, and therefore they gave strategic answers. The observed results for the use of ICT as a substitute for current business car trips (that is, Column 2) are in line with the results for commuting. Some 35 per cent of the respondents said that they would make more use of ICT as a substitute for current business trips by car. Moreover, the distribution of the answers over the seven classes in the case of business trips is also comparable to the results observed for the commuter trips by car.

Apart from alterations in the current trip pattern of firms due to pricing, another 'short-term' behavioural reaction was measured: increases in product/service prices. Some 41.4 per cent of the firms regarded it as 'quite likely' or 'likely' that product prices would be raised due to the kilometre charge. As many as 9.3 per cent selected the category 'extremely likely'. The remaining 49.3 per cent did not really expect any price changes. Thus, the results show that increases in product/service prices are quite likely to occur if the kilometre charge is implemented.

Overall, it can be concluded that a substantial number of firms would consider making changes in their current trip pattern by car (or lorry) as a result of the presented kilometre charge. Changes in the period of driving (that is, avoiding the high-charge peak period) seem more likely to be made than reductions in the overall frequency of travelling by car/lorry. Furthermore, trip alterations occur more often for current business trips compared with trips made for the transport of goods. It is likely that the transport of goods is of more important for the existence of firms that undertake such trips, which makes trip changes less attractive. However, fewer changes in transport trips might also be a consequence of not many alternatives (for example, other transport modes) that can be chosen for goods transport compared with those available for business trips. Whereas the intended changes in the trip pattern are substantial, most firms who chose to adapt current trips wanted to do so only to a limited extent. Apart from more 'regular' changes in the trip pattern, such as time changes, the use of ICT also seems to be a promising alternative to save extra costs for business or commuting traffic due to pricing. Finally, the expected increases in the product/service prices of firms due to the kilometre charge were measured. Around 50 per cent of the firms expected their prices to increase, which might imply that a large share of firms intend to transfer part of the possibly higher costs to, for example, customers.

6.5 CHANGES IN HUMAN RESOURCE POLICY OF FIRMS

The introduction of road pricing will probably change employers' human resource policy. To get some idea of the effects to be expected, we concentrated on a number of transport-related fringe benefits: residential relocation reimbursement; company car; and compensation for kilometre/fuel costs or public transport expenses. It has been shown in the literature that employers are more likely to offer these benefits to workers with a long commute. The common perception of road pricing as an increase in travel costs suggests that its introduction will encourage employers to offer more of these benefits to compensate workers. It also suggests that employers will reimburse (part) of the road tax. Further, it has been suggested in the literature that employers may change their policy regarding teleworking, flexible working hours and so on, as a reaction to road pricing.

Our analysis focused on responses to a range of questions, related to the latest staff appointment the respondent was personally involved with. The respondent had to answer questions on a number of fringe benefits offered to the applicant, including a company car, compensation for kilometre/fuel costs, flexible working hours or a residential relocation reimbursement. The respondent had to exclude internal and part-time appointments. Furthermore, we investigate whether the employer would reimburse (part of) the (hypothetical) road tax, free of income tax. The specific charge is identical to the one described in the previous section. Table 6.4 gives the relevant information on transport-related fringe benefits offered to the

Table 6.4   Share of employees (%) who are offered fringe benefits in the situation without and with a charge

Offered fringe benefits (% of employees)	No charge	With charge	Difference
Residential relocation reimbursement	3.5	15.3	11.8
Company car	20.4	20.6	0.2
Compensation for kilometre/fuel costs	49.7	50.1	0.4
Compensation for cost of public transport	21.9	39.8	17.9
Flexible working hours	18.6	21.9	3.3
Compensation for tax per driven kilómetre	0.0	30.5	30.5

applicant in the current situation (with no charge) and the benefits that would be offered with a road tax present (with a charge).

Table 6.4 suggests that, generally speaking, compensation for commuting expenses is an important phenomenon in the Netherlands. About 50 per cent of the applicants receive an offer for kilometre/fuel compensation, whereas nearly 22 per cent receive a similar offer for public transport. It also appears that about 20 per cent of the employees receive a company car offer, and almost 20 per cent are given the opportunity to benefit from flexible working hours.

In interpreting the figures in the table, it must be noted that employers may offer more than one type of compensation. The average number of compensation types offered to an employee is 1.1 in the situation without charge,[10] but 37 per cent of newly appointed employees are not offered any compensation at all for their commuting expenses. Hence, instead many employers offer their new employees two or even more transport-related fringe benefits. The table shows that, at most, 22 per cent of the newly appointed employees are offered compensation for kilometre/fuel cost *and* compensation for cost of public transport. In fact only 9 per cent of these employees are offered both types of compensation. The probable reason is that compensation is only offered for the relevant transport mode.

The effect of the kilometre charge on the probability that employers offer the fringe benefits described above is given in the last column of Table 6.4. It appears that, as a consequence of the introduction of the charge, employers would be more responsive regarding the offer of residential relocation reimbursements (about 12 per cent), the compensation for the cost of public transport (about 18 per cent) and the reimbursement of the road tax (about 31 per cent). The charge appears not to have any substantial effect on the probability of being offered a company car (0.2 per cent), or on compensation for kilometre/fuel costs (0.4 per cent). These results are in line with the study by van Ommeren et al. (2006). In conclusion, we have established that reimbursement of the charge and an increase in fringe benefits may be important reactions to a kilometre charge.

The reaction of employers regarding the choice of these fringe benefits will be relevant for the effect of road tax on the behaviour of workers. If employers are more inclined to reimburse residential relocation costs, or put more emphasis on the possible reimbursement of the costs of public transport, then it is plausible that the negative effect of the tax on the length of the commute is reinforced. In contrast, if employers reimburse the road tax, then this effect will be (strongly) mitigated. However, it is noteworthy that 70 per cent of the employers did *not* intend to provide any compensation for the road tax. It seems therefore unlikely that the effectiveness of road pricing will be undermined by a widespread practice among employers to reimburse these costs.

An interesting aspect of Table 6.4 is that it suggests that the average number of transport-related benefits offered to newly appointed employees would increase from 1.1 to almost 1.8. Even if we correct for the part of the increase that is caused by employers offering compensation of the road tax, an increase from 1.1 to 1.5 still remains. The reason for this increase is that employers expect to put more emphasis on residential relocation reimbursement and compensation of the cost of public transport. Such a shift in the fringe benefits menu offered to newly appointed employees will stimulate substitution from the car to public transport and the realization of shorter commutes through relocation. This contributes to the effectiveness of road pricing in decreasing congestion.

6.6   LONG-TERM REACTIONS OF FIRMS: RELOCATION PROBABILITY DUE TO PRICING

Besides the discussed short-term trip reactions of firms and their intended changes in their human resource policy, in addition relocation probabilities were studied. Table 6.5 shows the distribution across probability categories of changing the firm's location due to the kilometre charge. Again seven categories are distinguished, ranging from 'extremely unlikely' to relocate specifically as a result of the pricing measure to 'extremely likely'. As well as this, the sums of the categories (5–7 and 6–7) representing the highest probabilities are shown.

In total, 7.8 per cent of the respondents indicated that it was 'quite likely', 'likely' or 'extremely likely' that the firm would relocate as a consequence of

Table 6.5   Probability (%) of relocating to another settlement due to the km charge

Probability of relocation	Probability	
	%	(no.)
1. Extremely unlikely	41.0	(199)
2. Unlikely	26.6	(129)
3. Quite unlikely	4.5	(22)
4. Not unlikely/likely	20.0	(97)
5. Quite likely	4.3	(21)
6. Likely	2.5	(12)
7. Extremely likely	1.0	(5)
Sum 5 to 7: quite to extremely likely	7.8	(38)
Sum 6 to 7: (extremely) likely	3.5	(17)

the charge. Somewhat less than half of these respondents (that is, 3.5 per cent) regard it as 'likely' or 'extremely likely'. In a separate place in the questionnaire, before the kilometre charge was introduced, firms were also asked about the probability of relocating within the coming 2 years (thus without them realizing at that point that a charge was being implemented). It was found that roughly half of the firms that indicated they had a high probability of relocating specifically due to the charge also indicated earlier in the questionnaire that they had a '(quite) high' probability of relocating within 2 years anyway.

This 'relation' between relocating due to the kilometre charge and the probability of relocating anyway (within 2 years) is statistically significant with a reliability of 95 per cent. Thus it seems likely that especially those firms that already have a high probability of relocating within 2 years, might see the charge as the (final) push to relocate. As described in Section 6.2, (mainly) two groups of firms were selected: namely, firms working in the business service sector or those in the industrial sector. However, no significant difference in relocation probability between these types of firms was found.

It would be interesting to compare the firm relocation probability results with the expectations from the literature, and to examine differences with the relocation probabilities for households that were described in Chapter 5, Section 5.4 of this volume. As mentioned in Section 6.2, there are only a limited number of studies that have examined the influence of transport-pricing policies on firms' relocation probabilities. Moreover, most of these studies are based on modelling approaches. No empirically based research into the relocation intention of firms due to pricing is known to exist. The only study that was found to report specifically on the relocation chances of firms is MuConsult (2000), which anticipates that the relocation probability of firms due to a kilometre charge would be negligible, because transport costs form only a small part of the operational costs of firms. No quantitative indication is given of the share of firms that are expected to relocate. If, however, a relocation decision has already been taken (for another reason), MuConsult reckons that firms will take pricing costs into account in selecting their new location. When the firm relocation probabilities presented above are compared with the expectations of MuConsult, the results in this chapter seem to point to a stronger influence of the charge on relocation. But comparisons are difficult to make, as MuConsult does not give a quantitative insight into the relocation likelihood of firms.

We can also compare the probability of firms relocating as a result of a pricing measure with the residential and job relocation probabilities for households, which were described in Section 5.4 of the previous chapter. The kilometre charge that was presented within the firm questionnaire is the same as kilometre charge variant 3E for households (see Table 5.1). Kilometre charge 3, which was presented to the households, consisted of six alternatives: three pricing levels and two different types of revenue use. Because a medium price level was selected for the firm questionnaire and no clear price level or revenue-use effects on the relocation probability of households were found in Chapter 5, it seems to be legitimate to compare the firm relocation probability described above with the household relocation probabilities of measure 3. A comparison shows that the observed probabilities for firms are higher than the residential relocation probabilities found for households. Some 7.8 per cent of the firms indicated a 'quite high', 'high', or 'extremely high' probability of relocating compared with 3.8 per cent of the households. This higher relocation probability for firms does not directly correspond with some expectations in the literature (for example, MuConsult, 2000; McQuaid et al., 2004) that firms are rather insensitive to changes in transport costs as these costs form only a small part of their total operational costs. However, if only the response categories 'likely' and 'very likely' are selected, the difference is slightly smaller: 3.5 per cent for firms against 2.3 per cent for households. On the other hand, the observed percentages for the firm relocation probabilities are lower than the job relocation probabilities of households: 11.6 per cent of the households indicated a 'quite high', 'high', or 'extremely high' probability; 64 per cent a 'high' or 'extremely high' job relocation probability.

A striking difference between the firm and household relocation probabilities due to pricing is related to the probability of changing location anyway within 2 years. In the case of the firm relocation decision due to pricing, 47 per cent of the firms that indicated they were likely to relocate as a result of the kilometre charge also have a '(quite) high' probability of relocating for whatever reason. In contrast, for households the majority of the respondents who indicated they were likely to relocate as a result of pricing already had a '(quite) high' intention to relocate within 2 years. Some 80 per cent of the respondents who indicated that they would change their residential location due to a pricing measure also meant to change residence within 2 years for whatever reason. For job relocation this is 72 per cent. This means, that with respect to firms, the relocation due to pricing is less related to already-existing plans to relocate.

To gain insight into the actual influence of the kilometre charge on relocation, relocation probabilities due to the charge must consider the probability that firms and households are planning to relocate anyway. For example, a small change due to pricing might in fact be important if in a 'normal' situation very few firms or households relocate. On the other hand, if the pricing measure leads to a 'quite high' percentage of actors who will relocate, whereas every year all actors relocate anyway, the (relative) influence of the pricing measure on relocation frequencies is limited. Within the sample, 13.8 per cent of the firms have a 'quite high', 'high', or 'extremely high' probability of relocating within 2 years for whatever reason. For households' residential and job relocation, these percentages amount to, respectively, 23.5 and 30.3 per cent. Thus, the relocation probability for households is higher than for firms. Given the relocation probability percentage of firms due to the charge (7.8 per cent), which is in-between those observed for households' residential and job relocation (respectively, 3.8 and 11.6 per cent), the influence of the kilometre charge on the relocation probability of firms seems to be relatively higher compared with the influence on household relocations.

In the discussion above, we saw that a substantial share (that is, 47 per cent) of firms that intended to relocate due to the kilometre charge were also planning to relocate for whatever reason (within 2 years). Therefore, a comparison of the relocation intentions (for whatever reason) of firms within the sample with the average percentage of Dutch firms that relocate within a year might give a first indication of the relocation probability of all (types of) firms within the Netherlands due to a kilometre charge. Pellenbarg (2005) reports that per year, on average, around 7.5–8 per cent of Dutch firms relocate. This seems to correspond with (that is, is marginally higher than) the 13.8 per cent of firms within the sample that are likely to relocate within 2 years: 13.8 per cent in 2 years would quite likely lead to a maximum percentage change of around 7 per cent per year. The percentage reported by Pellenbarg is based on an average over all firm sectors. Pellenbarg (2005) also shows the number of firms per sector which relocated, on average, over 2001 and 2002. If we relate these numbers to the total number of firms per sector in 2005 (see Dutch Chamber of Commerce, 2006) we can (roughly) estimate the relocation percentage per sector. By doing this, we find that, on average, 7.8 per cent of the firms in the advice/business service sector relocate per year. For the manufacturing industrial sector this amounts to 6.1 per cent. These sector-specific numbers are (overall) also quite in line with the findings in the dataset used here. Given that, on average, firms that are intending to relocate anyway more often also mean to relocate specifically as a result of the kilometre charge, the observed relocation probability percentage in the sample (that is, 7.8 per cent) might also be quite comparable to the possible relocation probability in reality (taking all types of firms into account).

Finally, whereas this study focused on only studying the probability of relocation, it is at least as interesting and important to know where exactly (individual) firms are going to settle. Are they going to locate nearer to specific other firms (that is, forming clusters)? Or, are they changing regions (for example, going back to the western part of Holland because traffic congestion decreases due to pricing), and so on? It would be interesting to focus on these actual spatial consequences in further research.

6.7 CONCLUSIONS

On the basis of a questionnaire held among 485 firms operating in the manufacturing industrial or business service sector, this chapter has analysed changes in the behaviour of firms due to a kilometre charge. More specifically intended changes in the trip pattern and expected alterations in product prices were studied, as well as changes in firms' human resource policy (for example, travel-cost compensations, possibility of working at home and/or flexibility in choosing working hours). Finally, relocation probabilities were examined.

Around 30 to 40 per cent of the firms considered making changes in their current trip pattern by car (or lorry) due to the presented kilometre charge. Changes in the period of driving (that is, avoiding the high-charge peak period) seem more likely to be made than reductions in the overall frequency of travelling by car/lorry. Furthermore, trip alterations occur more often for current business trips compared with trips made for transport of goods. This lower likelihood of trip change probably occurs because the transport of goods is more important for the existence of firms that undertake such trips or because trips for the transport of goods are less easily adjustable. Whereas the intended changes in the trip pattern were substantial, most firms that chose to adapt current trips wanted to do so only to a limited extent. Apart from more 'regular' changes in the trip pattern, such as time changes, the use of ICT also seemed to be a promising alternative to save extra costs for business or commuter traffic due to pricing. Changes in product prices were also examined briefly. It seems that a large number (that is, approximately 50 per cent) of firms would try to mitigate (extra) costs due to pricing by increasing prices.

Moreover, it appears that the introduction of a kilometre charge could have an important effect on the way that employees are compensated by employers. The results indicate that about 30 per cent of the employees would be fully reimbursed by their employer. Hence, the direct effect of road pricing on employees may be (much) less than if this effect of full compensation is ignored. Furthermore, employers are likely to change the fringe benefits package offered to employees. It appears that employers would be more likely to offer a residential relocation reimbursement, and reimburse the costs of *public* transport. This may have the effect that employees would be more likely to switch to public transport or reduce their commuting distance.

A final topic of research was the relocation probability due to the kilometre charge. Some 7.8 per cent of the firms indicated that it is likely that their firm would relocate as a result of the kilometre price measure. However, roughly half of these firms indicated that they already had a '(quite) high' probability of relocating within 2 years (for another reason). Thus, firms that were already planning to relocate, on average, also indicated that they had a significantly higher probability of changing specifically as a result of the charge. In addition, we can compare the likelihood of firms relocating as a result of a pricing measure with the average (that is, over different kilometre charges) residential and job relocation probabilities for households, which were described in Chapter 5, Section 5.4. A comparison shows that the observed probabilities for firms were higher than the residential relocation probabilities found for households. Some 7.8 per cent of the firms indicated a 'quite high', 'high' or 'extremely high' probability of relocating compared with 4.0 per cent of the households. The observed percentages for the firm relocation probabilities are lower than the job relocation probabilities of households: 10.7 per cent of the households indicated a 'quite high', 'high' or 'extremely high' probability. To gain insight into the actual influence of the kilometre charge on relocation, relocation probabilities due to the charge must take into account the (revealed preference-based) likelihood that firms and households in reality are planning to relocate anyway. As reported above, 13.8 per cent of the firms within the sample have a '(quite) high' probability of relocating within 2 years for whatever reason. For households' residential and job relocation, these percentages amount to, respectively, 23.5 and 30.3 per cent. Thus, the relocation probability for households is higher than for firms. Given the relocation probability percentage of firms due to the charge (7.8 per cent) which is in-between the percentages observed for households' residential and job relocation, the influence of the kilometre charge on the relocation probability of firms seems to be relatively higher compared with its influence on household relocations.

Although the results of the questionnaire described within this section give a first insight into the probability of firms relocating as a result of the charge, at least one important aspect was left unanswered: the influence on behavioural changes of travel time or reliability gains that might occur as a result of a (road-)pricing measure. If respondents are explicitly confronted with possible travel-time (or travel-time reliability) benefits that may occur due to a toll, their perceived accessibility is substantially higher than if benefits are not clearly presented (see Chapter 13, Section 13.3.3). If quantitatively expressed benefits had been shown to respondents, perhaps short-term changes and relocation probability alterations might have been different. Therefore, in a more ideal situation, the influence of travel-time (and reliability of time) benefits must be systematically included when studying the relocation probability of firms.

NOTES

1. For an extensive overview of congestion (data, factors influencing congestion and so on), see Bovy and Salomon (1999) and Bovy (2001).
2. Note, however, that, even in this respect, there are exceptions. Under specific circumstances, road pricing may be welfare decreasing.
3. Much depends on the details. For a discussion, see, for instance, Small (1992).
4. In the Netherlands in 2003, 14.5 per cent of the total car-kilometres (as a car driver) are made with the purpose of 'work-related business visits' (Ministerie van Verkeer en Waterstaat, 2004). Besseling et al. (2005) have predicted that, in 2020, 25 per cent of the person-kilometres are likely to be generated by business and transport of goods trips of firms.
5. The price level is 9 eurocents/km for 3-axle lorries above 12 tonnes and 10 eurocents/km for 4-axle lorries above 12 tonnes.
6. There is, however, some empirical evidence from the evaluation of the London Congestion Charging Scheme that the charge does not have medium- and long-term negative impacts (for example, with respect to business performance, retail sales) on businesses in the charging zone (TfL, 2006).
7. Approximately 22 per cent of the Dutch employees worked in the manufacturing industrial sector in 2003, and around 14 per cent worked in the business service sector. If the mineral extraction sector, the energy and water supply sector and the building sector are also regarded as being in the industrial sector, then approximately 36 per cent of Dutch employees worked in the industrial sector in 2003 (CBS, 2006).
8. Of course, the freedom of choice is to a large extent defined by employee locations (for example, employee pools) and links with, and locations of, other firms or organizations.
9. For example, public organizations (and also firms within the retail sector) are often embedded in their current locations (cities, regions). A town hall, for example, cannot be moved to an entirely different city just because of a pricing measure.
10. Adding up the figures in the column 'no charge' gives a total of 114.1 per cent.

REFERENCES

Anas, A. and R. Xu (1999), 'Congestion, land use, and job dispersion: a general equilibrium model', *Journal of Urban Economics*, **45**, 451–73.

Arnott, R., A. de Palma and R. Lindsey (1990), 'Economics of a bottleneck', *Journal of Urban Economics*, **27**, 111–30.

Besseling, B., W. Groot and R. Lebouille (2005), 'Economische analyse van verschillende vormen van prijsbeleid voor het wegverkeer' ('An economic assessment of various methods of road pricing'), Den Haag: CPB.

Bovy, P.H.L. (2001), 'Traffic flooding the low countries: how the Dutch cope with motorway congestion', *Transport Reviews*, **21**, 89–116.

Bovy, P.H.L. and I. Salomon (1999), 'The spread of congestion in Europe: A prospective assessment of the problem', in *European Council of Transport Ministers* (ECMT), Roundtable 110, European Conference of Ministers of Transport, Paris, 85–154.

CBS (2006), 'CBS Statline' ('Statistics Netherlands Statline'), http://statline.cbs.nl.
de Wit, J. and G. van Gent (1998), *Economie en transport* ('Economics of Transport'), Utrecht: Lemma B.V.
Dutch Chamber of Commerce (2006), 'Starters en bestaande bedrijven: Kerncijfers bedrijven' ('Starting and existing firms: core figures firms'), www.kvk.nl/artikel/artikel.asp?artikelID=46702, 28 March.
Eliasson, J. and L.G. Mattsson (2001), 'Transport and location effects of road pricing: a simulation approach', *Journal of Transport Economics and Policy*, **35** (3), 417–56.
Glaeser, E.L. and M.E. Kahn (2004), 'Sprawl and growth', in J.V. Henderson and J.F. Thisse (eds), *Handbook of Regional and Urban Economics*, vol 4, Amsterdam: Elsevier, pp. 2481–527.
Krugman, P. (1991), 'Increasing returns and economic geography', *Journal of Political Economy*, **99**, 483–99.
Mattsson, L.G. and L. Sjölin (2002), 'Transport and location effects of a ring road in a city with or without road pricing', 6th Workshop of the Nordic Research Network on Modelling Transport, Land-Use and the Environment, Haugesund, 27–9 September.
May, A.D. and D.S. Milne (2000), 'Effects of alternative road pricing systems on network performance', *Transport Research Part A*, **34**, 407–36.
McQuaid, R.W., M. Greig, A. Smith and J. Cooper (2004), *The Importance of Transport in Business' Location Decisions*, Edinburgh: Napier University Press.
Ministerie van Verkeer en Waterstaat (2004), 'Kerncijfers personenvervoer' (Basic data passenger traffic), Ministerie van Verkeer en Waterstaat, Rijkswaterstaat, Adviesdienst Verkeer en Vervoer, Den Haag.
MuConsult (2000), *Ruimtelijke Effecten Prijsbeleid (Hoofdrapport)* ('Spatial effects of pricing policy (main report)'), Amersfoort: MuConsult.
Pellenbarg, P.H. (1999), 'Het huidig belang van infrastructuur en vervoer voor regionale en nationale vestigingsbeslissingen' ('The current importance of infrastructure and transport for regional and national settlement decisions'), in J.P. Elhorst and D. Strijker (eds), *Het belang van het vervoer: verleden, heden en toekomst*, (*The Importance of Transport: Past, Present and Future*), Groningen: Universiteitsdrukkerij RUG.
Pellenbarg, P.H. (2005), 'Firm migration in the Netherlands', Paper presented at the 45th European Regional Science Association (ERSA) congress, Amsterdam, 23–27 August.
Pen, J.C. (2002), 'Wat beweegt bedrijven (Besluitvormingsprocessen bij verplaatste bedrijven)' ('*What moves firms (decision-making processes of relocated firms)*'), Faculteit der Ruimtelijke Wetenschappen, Rijksuniversiteit Groningen.
Small, K. (1992), 'Using the revenues from congestion pricing', *Transportation*, **19**, 359–81.
Tillema, T., D. Ettema and G.P. van Wee (2006), 'Road pricing and (re)location decisions of households', Paper presented at the 85th Transportation Research Board (TRB) Annual Meeting, Washington, DC, 22–26 January.
Timothy, D. and W. Wheaton (2001), 'Intra-urban wage variation, employment location and commuting times', *Journal of Urban Economics*, **50**, 338–66.
Transport for London (TfL) (2006), 'Central London congestion charging, impacts monitoring', fourth annual report (overview), London: Transport for London.
van Dijk, J. and P.H. Pellenbarg (2000), 'Firm relocation decisions in the Netherlands: an ordered logit approach', *Papers in Regional Science*, **79**, 191–219.

van Ommeren, J.N. and P. Rietveld (2007), 'Commuting and reimbursement of residential relocation costs', *Journal of Transport Economics and Policy*, forthcoming.
van Ommeren, J.N., A. van der Vlist and P. Nijkamp (2006), 'Transport-related fringe benefits: implications for moving and the journey to work', *Journal of Regional Science*, **46** (3), 493–506.
van Wee, B. (1995), 'Pricing instruments for transport policy, environment, incentives and the Common Market', in F.J. Dietz, H.R.J. Vollebergh and J.L. de Vries (eds), *Environment, Incentives and the Common Market*, Dordrecht/Boston/London: Kluwer Academic Publishers, pp. 97–124.
Verhoef, E.T. (2000), 'Second-best congestion pricing in general static transportation networks with elastic demands', Tinbergen Institute Discussion Paper, 078/3, 1–24.
Verhoef, E.T., C. Koopmans, M. Bliemer, P. Bovy, L. Steg and B. van Wee (2004), 'Vormgeving en effecten van prijsbeleid op de weg. Effectiviteit, efficiëntie en acceptatie vanuit een multidisciplinair perspectief' ('Design and effects of road pricing. Effectiveness, efficiency and acceptability from a multidisciplinary perspective'), Amsterdam: Vrije Universiteit/SEO, Delft: Technische Universiteit Delft, Groningen: Rijksuniversiteit Groningen.
Verhoef, E., M. Lijesen and A. Hoen (1998), 'The economic effects of road pricing in the Randstad area', Tinbergen Institute Discussion Paper, 98-078/3.
Vervoort, K. and W. Spit (2005), 'Economische toets variant 3: Betalen per kilometer vracht' (*'Economic Test Alternative 3: Pay Per Freight Kilometre'*), Rotterdam: ECORYS.

PART II

Modelling effects of transport pricing

7. Transit market effects on socially optimal congestion charging

Michael Bell and Muanmas Wichiensin

7.1 INTRODUCTION

Traffic congestion in urban areas is one of the most serious problems for the government and transport planners. Since a congestion charging scheme was first introduced in Singapore more than 30 years ago, big cities like Seoul and Tokyo have considered such schemes, with London implementing congestion charging in 2003 (see reviews in Gomez-Ibañez and Small, 1994; May and Milne, 2000). From this evidence, many studies have been made for the auto mode network in order to determine the optimal congestion charge (see, for example, Arnott and Small, 1994; Liu and McDonald, 1999).

However, congestion charging affects not only car drivers who must pay the charge but also the users of alternative modes, as well as decisions about whether to travel in the first place. Hence, a model which allows for variable demand, as well as mode choice, is required for a comprehensive assessment of the impact. In particular, cities considering congestion charging will normally have two transit modes (bus and train). These services are often provided by the private sector in some regulated way.

In the UK, following bus privatization in 1980, several studies have focused on the characteristics of the transit market. Some say that the market is contested (Beesley and Glaister, 1985), while others that the evidence is inconclusive or disputable (Gwilliam et al., 1985; Evans, 1991). Some say that the tendency for an operator seeking to enter a market is to merge with an operator already present in this market (Mackie et al., 1995). The merging of operators has also been studied (Salant et al., 1983; Perry and Porter, 1985; Beesley, 1990; McAfee et al., 1992).

In this chapter we focus on the level of competition in the transit market, assuming that the market is in fact not contested, by considering two situations: the first is where one agency/company runs both transit modes (the 'monopoly' case) and the second is where each mode is run by an individual company (the 'duopoly' case). We assume that competition between duopolists is *strict*, that is, there is no price communication, no merging and no collusion. In both the monopoly and the duopoly markets, operators pursue the same objective, namely, profit maximization.

Conventionally, research has focused on supply-side competition, where the operator varies the capacity (seats or standing room offered per unit of time) and accepts whatever fares travellers are willing to pay. In this chapter we consider instead fare competition. We assume that there is sufficient capacity to carry any demand that may arise, so vehicle occupancy adjusts to the demand rather than constrains it. One may argue that in many urban transit networks it is difficult in any case to increase or decrease transit capacity dramatically.

In the duopoly case, we adopt the Bertrand (simultaneous) game (Bertrand, 1883; Maskin, 1986) to set bus and train fares. We assume that transit operators accept the equilibrium price (they do not collude, compensate each other, or maximize their joint profits).

We seek the congestion charge which maximizes social surplus, using a bi-level problem formulation which maximizes social surplus at the upper level and maximizes operator profits subject to an inter-modal network equilibrium at the lower level. Transit operators set profit-maximizing fares at the lower level. Network equilibrium takes account of congestion created in the road network by car and bus flows.

In determining network equilibrium, we adopt a frequency-based user equilibrium transit assignment, whereby transit users are assumed to know transit attributes, including fares, precisely. Le Clerq (1972) pointed out that the difference between transit and auto assignment is that the former also includes waiting time and transfer time, leading to the common line problem. The effect of common lines (shared stops) is allowed for in this chapter by adopting the strategy proposed by Spiess and Florian (1989). This involves defining a set of attractive elemental routes (referred to collectively as a 'hyperpath') and a route choice rule (take whichever attractive line arrives first). A route is attractive if it is optimal for certain departure times.

Regarding network equilibrium for multi-modal transport, most research has focused on the impact of private and transit (bus) vehicles sharing the same road links (Florian, 1977; Dafermos, 1982; Hamdouch et al., 2007). Florian incorporated the interaction between modes in the network formulation. Dafermos presented a general multi-modal network equilibrium model with elastic demand. Hamdouch et al. fixes the demand for car and metro modes to address the problem of an inter-modal network equilibrium with a congestion charge. This chapter extends this work to demonstrate the impact of profit-maximizing transit and socially optimal congestion charging on the car, bus and train sub-networks.

This chapter stems from Wichiensin et al. (2007) which considered the case of a deregulated transit market with a limited number of operators making commercial decisions regarding fares and services. Here we extend the model to include both a distance-based transit fare and the common line problem, so choice of line is affected by its frequency. This necessitates the adoption of a somewhat more complex network.

The model formulation is presented in Section 7.2. Section 7.3 presents the example network. Section 7.4 demonstrates the impact of profit-maximizing fare setting by the transit operator(s) on the optimal congestion charge. We also analyse the effect of social welfare maximization on consumer surplus and government revenues. Furthermore, the effect of the common line problem is shown. Finally, conclusions and policy implications are summarized in Section 7.5.

7.2   THE MODEL

The model framework is formulated as a bi-level programme illustrated in Figure 7.1. At the upper level, the government determines the congestion charge based on social welfare maximization. At the lower level, there is a process of fare setting by profit-maximizing monopoly or duopoly transit operator(s) who take into account traveller mode choices. The travellers choose whether to travel and, if so, by which mode according to the perceived costs of each mode. The network flows then feed back to the upper level.

The notation used in this chapter is defined as follows:

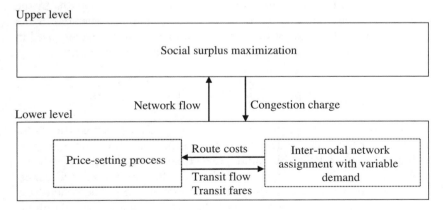

Figure 7.1   Model framework

a	:	link;
i	:	origin zone;
j	:	destination zone;
m	:	mode index (1 = auto, 2 = bus, 3 = train);
r	:	route;
h_r	:	total vehicle flow on route r per hour;
v_{am}	:	flow by mode m on link a;
$c_{am}(v_{a1}, v_{a2})$	:	cost of travel by mode m (for $m = 1$, 2) on link a;
t^0_{am}	:	free-flow travel time by mode m on link a (minutes);
p_m	:	congestion charge p_1 or distance based fare p_2, p_3;
ω	:	value of time;
f_a	:	line frequency of link a;
C_{ij}	:	generalized travel cost for origin i and destination j;
C^0_{ij}	:	observed minimum generalized travel cost for origin i and destination j (per trip);
q_{ij}	:	person trips between origin i and destination j (per hour);
q^0_{ij}	:	observed demand between origin i and destination j corresponding to the observed minimum generalized travel cost C^0_{ij};
θ	:	positive dispersion parameter related to auto and transit mode choice, that is, the parameter for the log sum function (estimated from data);
γ	:	sensitivity parameter for the travel demand function (also estimated from data); and
D	:	product of passengers and average kilometre per trip.

As is made clear later, there are a number of links and paths in the network but only one origin and destination. Demand is elastic. For the demand function, we adopt the exponential form, which is widely used in urban transport models. We represent the demand function q_{ij} as:

$$q_{ij} = q^0_{ij} \exp\left(-\frac{C_{ij} - C^0_{ij}}{\gamma} \right) (q^0_{ij} > 0,\ C^0_{ij} > 0,\ \gamma > 0), \qquad (7.1)$$

where q^0_{ij} is an observed demand corresponding to an observed travel cost C^0_{ij}, together locating the demand curve. In the context of the numerical example presented later, this could be set equal to the average travel cost.

As for mode choice, it is assumed that travellers minimize their generalized cost of travel with imperfect travel information. The generalized cost for the car mode is composed of the cost of the least-cost path plus the congestion charge. For the road links, travel cost is flow dependent.

Buses running on shared links are assumed to share the same congestion as the cars and therefore benefit from the decongestion effect of the congestion charge. In-vehicle travel time on the road link is a non-negative, increasing function of link flow. The relationship between link flow and link travel time is represented by the Bureau of Public Roads (BPR) functional form (see equation (7.2)). Travel time is converted into generalized cost to which is added the direct cost of travel (the congestion charge in the case of the car and the fare for the bus). The congestion charge is levied on an area, while bus fares are a function of distance. Buses do not pay the congestion charge, but bus riders must pay the fare for each link (see equation (7.3)).

$$c_{a1}(v_{a1}, v_{a2}) = \omega t_{a1}^{(0)} \left[1 + 0.15 \left(\frac{v_{a1} + bv_{a2}}{k_a} \right)^4 \right] \tag{7.2}$$

$$c_{a2}(v_{a1}, v_{a2}) = p_2 d_a + \omega t_{a2}^{(0)} \left[1 + 0.15 \left(\frac{v_{a1} + bv_{a2}}{k_a} \right)^4 \right]. \tag{7.3}$$

Note that, in general (as opposed to the example presented later), the congestion charge cannot be included in the link cost function as it is area rather than link related. In equations (7.2) and (7.3), k_a represents the capacity of link a measured in equivalent car trips. We assume that a transit vehicle is equivalent to a multiple b of private cars on account of its higher occupancy, where b converts trips by bus into equivalent trips by car. Note that $0 < b < 1$, to reflect that, *ceteris paribus*, transfer of trips from car to bus would reduce congestion and therefore in-vehicle travel time.

Out-of-vehicle travel time consists of waiting time at the stop and time for walking to and from the stop. The frequencies are assumed to be constant, which means that public transport has enough capacity to absorb any increase in patronage. Trains are assumed to run to a fixed schedule, so the generalized in-vehicle cost of travel by train is:

$$c_{a3} = p_3 d_a + \omega t_{a3}^{(0)}. \tag{7.4}$$

It is assumed in the numerical example that walking time to and from bus stops is less than for train stations in the base case. The route cost for car and bus mode is:

$$c_r = \sum_{a \in A} \delta_{ar} c_{am}, \quad m \in 1, 2. \tag{7.5}$$

The expected perceived cost of travel, assuming that the least-cost mode is chosen, is:

$$C_{ij} = -\frac{1}{\theta}\ln\left[\sum_{m \in (\text{car, transit})}\exp\left(-\theta g_{ijm}\right)\right], \forall i \in I, \forall j \in J, \qquad (7.6)$$

where g_{ijcar} is the cost of travel by car by the least-cost route (which includes p_1 if the least-cost path passes through the congestion charging zone), and $g_{ijtransit}$ is the least cost of travel by transit. Flow conservation is assumed, hence:

$$h_{ijcar} + h_{ijtransit} = q_{ij}, \quad \forall i \in I, \forall i \in J, \qquad (7.7)$$

where h_{ijcar} is the number of car trips and $h_{ijtransit}$ is the number of transit trips. Mode choice is calculated by assuming that travellers minimize their travel costs subject to imperfect information. The number of car trips from the origin to the destination is given by:

$$h_{ijcar} = q_{ij}\frac{1}{1 + e^{\theta(g_{ijcar} - g_{ijtransit})}}, \quad \forall i \in I, \forall j \in J. \qquad (7.8)$$

We solve the transit assignment problem by calculating the least-cost path to the destination according to link travel times and expected waiting times. If there are several attractive paths (paths that may be optimal depending on the precise arrival time of the service), we consider the common lines, which has the effect of reducing the waiting time as passengers will choose the common line that arrives first (Le Clerq, 1972; Spiess and Florian, 1989). The method used to solve transit assignment follows Spiess and Florian (1989). This method seeks an optimal strategy $\overline{A}$, that is, $\overline{A}$ is the set of used (attractive) links. Links not included in strategy are never used. Denote $\overline{A}^+$ the set of outgoing attractive links at any stop. The expected combined waiting time $W(\overline{A}^+)$ at a particular stop can be derived from the frequencies in equation (7.9):

$$W(\overline{A}^+) = \frac{\alpha}{\sum_{a \in A}f_a}, \alpha > 0, \qquad (7.9)$$

where α depends on the punctuality of service. A uniform passenger arrival rate is assumed. The case where α equals 1 is when the services have an exponential distribution of inter-arrival times with mean $1/f$; α equals $\frac{1}{2}$ when the services have constant arrival time. In this chapter we assume that there is a distribution of arrival time, that is, $\alpha = 1$.

Since different objectives will result in different networks, the choice for a specific objective is important. Yang and Bell (1997) stated that social welfare, that is, the sum of consumer surplus and operator surplus or profit, is a good objective to be considered in this context as it is a measure that can be used to evaluate the efficiency of a proposed policy (in this case congestion charging) and the consequences associated with it. Consumer surplus, equal to γq, expresses the perceived benefits experienced by potential travellers (see equation (7.10)). This simple expression for consumer surplus comes from the integration of the exponential demand function (Evans, 1992). The second term is government surplus or the revenue which is received from collecting the congestion charge. The producer surplus is the third term and represents operator profits. The objective is therefore:

$$\max_{p_1} \sum_i \sum_j \left[\gamma q_{ij} + p_1 q_{ij1} + \sum_{m=2,\,3} (p_m - ac_m)D_{ijm} \right], \qquad (7.10)$$

where ac_m is the average cost to operator $m = 2,\ 3$ of supplying a unit of service. We assume that the average cost is constant, although in practice this will not be true. D_{ijm} is the passenger-kilometres transported by each transit mode, which can be calculated by equations (7.11) and (7.12):

$$D_{ijm} = \sum_a v_{ijam} d_a, \quad \forall\ i, j, m, \qquad (7.11)$$

where d_a is the length of link a (kilometres) and

$$v_{ijam} = \sum_r h_{ijmr} \delta_{ijmar}, \quad \forall\ i, j, m, a, \qquad (7.12)$$

where $\delta_{ijmar} = 1$ if link a belongs to route r connecting i to j by mode m, and 0 otherwise. In the subsequent numerical example, there is only one origin and destination.

In optimal fare setting for the duopoly, we suppose that U_2, U_3 are the profits of the two operators, and that R_2, R_3 are their best response fare functions according to the Bertrand equilibrium. The best response fare function of an operator is defined in a way that gives this operator the best profit for any choice of fare by its competitor. According to Bertrand's concept of equilibrium, we obtain equations (7.13) and (7.14):

$$U_2\,[R_2(p_3), p_3] \geq U_2(p_2, p_3); \qquad (7.13)$$

$$U_3\,[p_2, R_3(p_2)] \geq U_3(p_2, p_3). \qquad (7.14)$$

By the definition of the Bertrand equilibrium solution, the optimal fares p_2^* and p_3^* satisfy equations (7.15) and (7.16):

$$p_2^* = R_2(p_3^*); \tag{7.15}$$

$$p_3^* = R_3(p_2^*). \tag{7.16}$$

7.3 THE EXAMPLE NETWORK

Our hypothesis is that when stops are shared, people get more benefits, that is, consumer surplus and social surplus should increase and the fares should go down, provided that more than one line using the stop is attractive. We use the network represented in Figures 7.2 and 7.3 to show the impact of privatized transit in two situations. There are two layers which represent the car network and the transit sub-network connecting an origin to a destination. Figure 7.2 shows the base case where the lines do not share stops, so choice of transit line does not take into account which line arrives first. The auto sub-network has road links 3–4. In the transit layer, there is a one bus line, one train line and four stops; two bus stops (stops 1 and 2) and two train stops (stops 5 and 6). In the transit sub-network, each stop is represented by line-specific nodes. Each link belongs to a specific transit line and connects to boarding links and alighting links as in Fearnside and Draper (1971). Trains run through nodes 7–8. Buses run through nodes 3–4 which correspond to the road nodes 3–4 in the car sub-network. The walking times to bus stop (node 1) and to train stop (node 5) are equal at 9 minutes.

Since there is one line serving nodes 1 and 5, the waiting time at these nodes equals the inverse service frequency at these stops. Note that the frequency matters at the stop where travellers wait for the service.

Figure 7.3 shows the network where the transit lines share the same stop. Passengers walk to a stop and choose from the possible lines using the stop, provided that more than one line is attractive. When a passenger arrives at stop 1, the links 1–3 and 1–5 represent the boarding/waiting links for getting on the chosen vehicle. At node 1, people choose a line. The walking time to the first stop (node 1) is 9 minutes, which is equal for both bus and train as they share the stop. The waiting time in this case is less than or equal to the former case, being equal to the inverse of combined frequencies of the attractive lines at that stop. As in the common line problem, people take the first line in an attractive set to arrive. Users also consider the distance-based fare and the waiting time at the station when deciding whether a line is attractive.

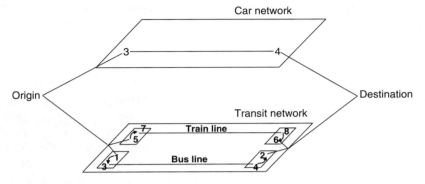

Figure 7.2   The base case where the stops are mode specific

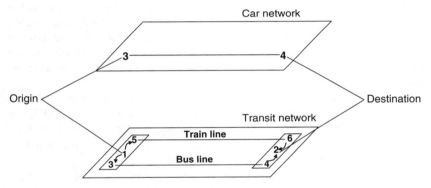

Figure 7.3   The common line case where modes share stops

The model is fitted to 2002 Edinburgh data taken from the Statistical Bulletin Transport Series Trn/2004/4 (Scottish Executive, 2004). The number of trips q^0 is assumed to be 78 000. In the absence of a congestion charge, the data shows the mode share for car, bus and train is 78, 16 and 6 per cent, respectively. Travel time is available in the form of duration ranges. The average travel time for car, bus and train fell most frequently in the range of 11–20 minutes for car journeys, 21–30 minutes for bus journeys and 30–40 minutes for train journeys. The average trip length corresponds to the average trip length in Edinburgh of 5 km. The length of links in Figures 7.2 and 7.3 are 5 km. Taking as the value of time that quoted in Transport Economic Notes (DfT, 2001), namely £9.23/hour, and converting this to correspond to Scotland by the conversion in Graham and Glaister (2002), we estimated a value for Edinburgh of £6.47. Regarding the parameters, values of γ and θ are calibrated so that the above statistics were more-or-less reproduced. This led to γ and θ equal to 8 and 0.35, respectively.

7.4　RESULTS

The toll is varied in steps of £0.5. Figures 7.4 to 7.10 show the comparison between the base (non-common line) case and the common line case. Note that there is a discontinuity in the graphs presented. This is as a consequence of grid search combined with abrupt changes in mode choice. The base case is on the left and the common line case is on the right. The social surplus as a function of the toll is shown in Figure 7.4. In general, the difference between the two cases is marginal. However shared stops can improve social surplus. There is an optimal toll under both forms of transit market. The tolls at the optimum are about the same in both cases. We cannot see the optimal toll clearly from the figure. However the calculation shows that shared stops have optimal tolls lower than the base case. For the base case, the optimal tolls are closer £3.5 and £2 for the monopoly and the duopoly market, respectively. For the common line case, the optimal tolls are closer to £3 and £1.5.

A duopoly market produces a higher social surplus than the monopoly market. In both cases where the toll is high, there is a possibility that the monopoly market is better overall. Monopoly might be preferable at high road taxes because it matches overpriced road transport with overpriced public transport, reducing inefficient consumer substitution.

Figure 7.5 shows the results of fare determination. It compares how the profit-maximizing bus and train fares change with the toll in the two cases. In general, the profit-maximizing fares in the monopoly market are greater than those in the duopoly market. The profit-maximizing train fare is greater than the profit-maximizing bus fare in the monopoly market. The fares generally move together. However, in both monopoly and duopoly markets, increasing the toll can decrease congestion, leading to benefits for the bus from congestion charging because it can speed up. This gives a competitive advantage to the bus mode, which is reflected in an increase in its fares relative to rail fares, which show only a slight increase. When a small toll is charged, the market with no competition acts differently in the two transit line configuration cases. In the separate stops case, the train fare decreases. In the shared stop case, the train fare increases.

Figure 7.6 shows that consumer surplus falls with increasing tolls in both cases. The effect on consumer surplus is directly due to the implied market equilibrium prices. Consumer surplus is lower for all tolls in a monopoly market when compared with a duopoly market. The sharing of stops

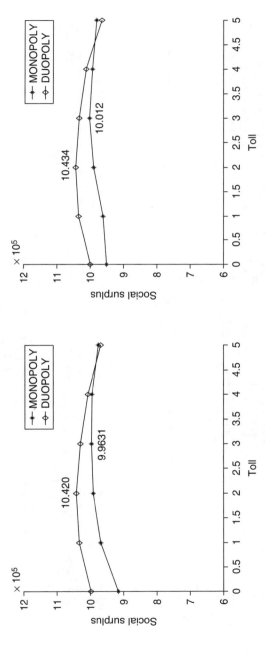

Figure 7.4 Social surplus with increasing toll (base case on left, common line case on right)

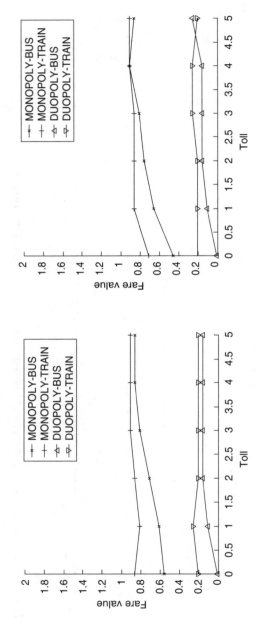

Figure 7.5   Optimal fare with increasing toll (base case on left, common line case on right)

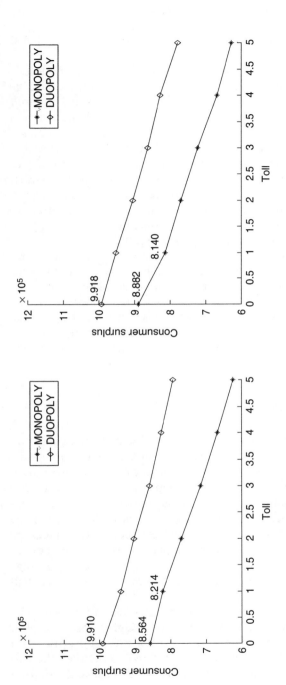

Figure 7.6 Consumer surplus with increasing toll (base case on left, common line case on right)

appears to create slightly more consumer surplus, which suggests that it would be preferable for users.

Figure 7.7 shows that, in general, the operator profits in the monopoly market mostly increase with tolls in both cases. In the duopoly market, the train company gains at lower tolls, while the bus company starts to profit at a higher toll in the base case because of congestion relief. In the common line case, there is fluctuation in profit as the set of attractive lines changes. No trend can be observed because the mode can be switched more easily.

Figure 7.8 shows how government revenue increases with the toll, up to a limit. This limit is lower and reached more rapidly in a duopoly market. The maximum revenue occurs at a lower toll level in a duopoly market because its lower price implies that public transport is a more attractive substitute, limiting market power for the road operator. From the figure, sharing stops can increase government revenue slightly.

Figures 7.9 and 7.10 show the changes in car and transit mode shares with respect to the toll. Car use falls with increasing tolls in both markets, and is lower in the duopoly than in the monopoly market. The lower transit prices in a duopoly market makes car users less willing to drive in a high toll situation. When the stops are separate, there is a switch to bus at some point. Where stops are integrated, mode switch is easier. In the duopoly market, however, the bus appears to become unattractive again for very high tolls, suggesting that the train can compete more effectively.

7.5   CONCLUSIONS

This chapter has investigated the impact of profit-maximizing transit on optimal congestion charging. We used an inter-modal equilibrium model which has auto, bus and train modes, and showed the impact of two market types, monopoly and duopoly, for two cases, separate stops (the base case) and shared stops (the common line case). In the base case, travellers choose the path with the least expected cost at the outset, while in the common line case travellers choose a transit mode based on frequency if both modes are attractive. This allows us to investigate the impact of competition, both at the corporate and the street levels. Our analysis assumes that the average operating cost is constant, though this is not the case in reality. We shall seek to relax this assumption in future work.

We found that, in general, the duopoly transit market is more beneficial than a monopoly transit market as it leads to a higher social surplus, driven by a higher consumer surplus because public transport prices are closer to marginal cost. We found that the differences between the two cases (with or without stop sharing) are minor. None the less, the sharing

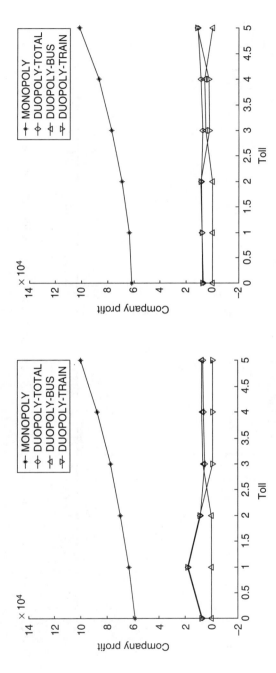

Figure 7.7   Company profits with increasing toll (base case on left, common line case on right)

145

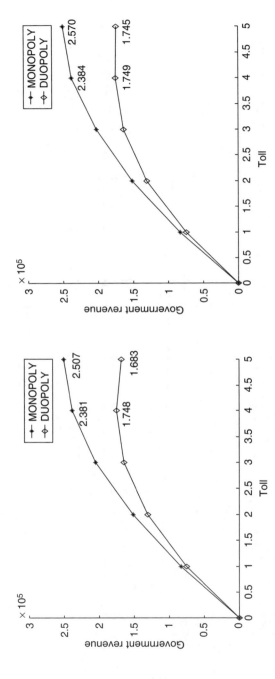

Figure 7.8   Government revenue with increasing toll (base case on left, common line case on right)

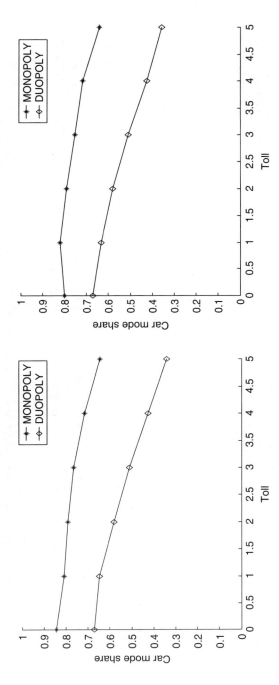

Figure 7.9   Car mode share with increasing toll (base case on left, common line case on right)

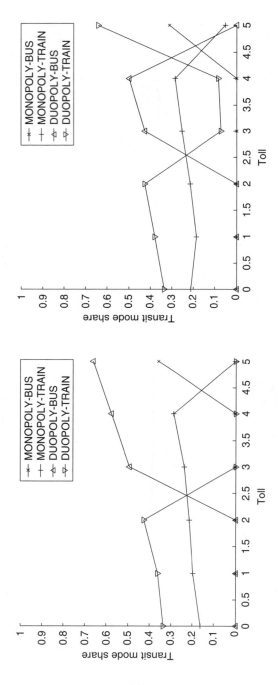

Figure 7.10 Transit mode share with increasing toll (base case on left, common line case on right)

of stops is preferable to separating them as it produces more social surplus, induced mainly by more consumer surplus and more government revenue.

In general, the optimal fares for bus and train tend to move together with an increasing toll, but bus fares tend to increase while train fares remain stable or increase only slightly. The toll gives a competitive advantage to the bus mode in terms of increased speed, which enables the operator(s) to increase fares. Fares are lower in a duopoly market as compared with a monopoly market.

REFERENCES

Arnott, R. and K.A. Small (1994), 'The economics of traffic congestion', *American Scientist*, **82**, 446–55.

Beesley, M.E. (1990), 'Collusion, predation and merger in the UK bus industry', *Journal of Transport Economics and Policy*, **24**, 295–310.

Beesley, M.E. and S. Glaister (1985), 'Deregulating the bus industry in Britain: (C) a response', *Transport Reviews*, **5**, 133–42.

Bertrand, J. (1883), 'Review of Cournot's "Rechercher sur la théorie mathématique de la richesse"', *Journal des Savants*, 499–508.

Dafermos, S.C. (1982), 'The general multimodal network equilibrium problem with elastic demand', *Networks*, **12**, 57–72.

Department for Transport (DfT) (2001), 'Transport economic note: values of time and operating costs', www.webtag.org.uk/webdocuments/3_Expert/5_Economy_Objective/3.5.6.htm, October 2006.

Evans, A. (1991), 'Bus competition: economic theories and empirical evidence', *Transportation Planning and Technology*, **15**, 295–313.

Evans, A. (1992), 'Road congestion pricing: when is it a good policy?', *Journal of Transport Economics and Policy*, **26** (3), 213–42.

Fearnside, K. and D.P. Draper (1971), 'Public transport assignment: a new approach', *Traffic Engineering and Control*, **12**, 298–99.

Florian, M. (1977), 'A traffic equilibrium model of travel by car and public transit modes', *Transportation Science*, **11** (2), 166–79.

Gomez-Ibañez, J.A. and K.A. Small (1994), *National Cooperative Highway Research Program Synthesis 210: Road Pricing Congestion Management: A Survey of International Practices*, Transportation Research Board, National Research Council, Washington, DC.

Graham, D.J. and S. Glaister (2002), *Review of Income and Price Elasticities of Demand for Road Traffic*, Imperial College London, Final Report.

Gwilliam, K.M., C.A. Nash and P. Mackie (1985), 'Deregulation of the British bus industry', *Transport Review*, **5**, 105–32.

Hamdouch, Y., M. Florian, D.W. Hearn and S. Lawphongpanich (2007), 'Congestion pricing for multi-modal transportation systems', *Transportation Research B*, **41**, 275–91.

Le Clerq, F. (1972), 'A public transport assignment method', *Traffic Engineering and Control*, **14**, 91–6.

Liu, L.N. and J.F. McDonald (1999), 'Economic efficiency of second-best congestion pricing schemes in urban highway systems', *Transportation Research B*, **33**, 157–88.

Mackie, P., R. Preston and C.A. Nash (1995), 'Bus deregulation: ten years on', *Transport Review*, **15** (3), 229–51.

Maskin, E. (1986), 'The existence of equilibrium with price-setting firms: some observations on duopoly theory: firm decision-making processes and oligopoly theory', *American Economic Review, Papers and Proceedings*, **76** (2), 382–6.

May, A.D. and D.S. Milne (2000), 'Effects of alternative road pricing systems on network performance', *Transportation Research A*, **34** (6), 407–36.

McAfee, R.P., J.J. Simons and M.A. Williams (1992), 'Horizontal mergers in spatially differentiated noncooperative markets', *Journal of Industrial Economics*, **40** (4), 349–58.

Perry, M.K. and R.H. Porter (1985), 'Oligopoly and the incentive for horizontal merger', *American Economic Review*, **75** (1), 219–27.

Salant, S.W., S. Switzer and R.J. Reynolds (1983), 'Losses from horizontal merger: the effects of an exogenous change in industry structure on Cournot–Nash equilibrium', *Quarterly Journal of Economics*, **98** (2), 185–99.

Scottish Executive (2004), 'Scottish Household Survey Travel Diary results for 2002', Statistical Bulletin Series Trn/2004/4, Edinburgh, Scotland.

Spiess, H. and M. Florian (1989), 'Optimal strategies: a new assignment model for transit networks', *Transportation Research B*, **23** (2), 83–102.

Wichiensin, M., M.G.H. Bell and H. Yang (2007), 'Impact of congestion charging on the transit market: an inter-modal equilibrium model', *Transportation Research A: Special Issue* (accepted for publication).

Yang, H. and M.G.H. Bell (1997), 'Traffic restraint, road pricing and network equilibrium', *Transportation Research B: Methodological*, **31** (4), 303–14.

8. Different policy objectives of the road-pricing problem: a game-theoretic approach

Dusica Joksimovic, Michiel Bliemer, Piet Bovy

8.1 INTRODUCTION AND BACKGROUND

This chapter considers road pricing from its microscopic foundations, meaning that interactions among individual actors are taken into account and analysed. The motivation for using such a concept was to obtain a better understanding of the pricing phenomenon among policy makers by explaining that the macroscopic results of pricing should be understood from their micro foundations (that is, the behaviour of the individual actors), in line with the more general arguments of Schelling (1978). Ideas from microeconomic theory have been applied to congestion problems in the work of Walters (1961) and Mohring (1970). More recently, Arnott et al. (2005) basically argue in favour of a microscopic approach in many different respects, including modelling road pricing and traffic congestion. This part of our research adopts this approach, which aims to build the simplest possible road-pricing model that reflects individual behaviour of the actors in road pricing (the road authority, on the one side, and travellers, on the other).

The road-pricing problem is a complex and controversial issue (Verhoef et al. 1999) including different actors who influence one another in different ways. In order to gain more insight into the nature of the optimal toll design problem, we shall approach the road-pricing problem by considering the simplest case of pricing and network description. On the one hand, the road authority, as one of the actors in the road-pricing problem, influences other actors (travellers) in their travel decision making. On the other, travellers react to the influence of the road authority by changing their travel choices. From the behavioural point of view, we are dealing with the route and trip choice of travellers (the travellers have the opportunity to decide which route to take or to decide to stay at home and not take a trip) on a small hypothetical network.

In this chapter we analyse in a game-theoretic framework a simple route choice problem with elastic demand, where road pricing and different policy objectives are introduced. First, the road-pricing problem is formulated using game theory notions whereby different games are described. After that, a game-theoretic approach is applied to formulate the road-pricing game as, in turn, the social planner (monopoly), the Stackelberg and the Cournot games. The main purpose of the experiment reported here is to show the outcomes of different games and different policy objectives established for the optimal toll design problem.

8.2   LITERATURE REVIEW

8.2.1   Transportation Problems and Game Theory

Game theory first appeared in solving transportation problems in the form of what was called the 'Wardropian equilibrium' of route choice (see Wardrop, 1952), which is similar to the Nash equilibrium of an N-player game (see Nash, 1950). For the definition of a Nash equilibrium, see Section 8.5.

8.2.2   Optimal Traffic Control Problems and Game Theory

Fisk (1984) was the first to propose the game theory approach for solution algorithms to solve different problems in transport systems modelling. In that paper, relationships are drawn between two game theory models based on the Nash non-cooperative and Stackelberg games.

In Wie (1995), the dynamic mixed behaviour traffic network equilibrium problem is formulated as a non-cooperative N-person, non-zero sum differential game. A simple network is considered where two types of players (called user-equilibrium (UE) players and Cournot–Nash (CN) players, respectively) interact through the congestion phenomenon. A procedure to compute system-optimal routings in a dynamic traffic network is introduced by Garcia et al. (2000). Fictitious play is utilized within a game of identical interests wherein vehicles are treated as players. In the work of Bell (2000), a two-player, non-cooperative game is established between the network user seeking a path to minimize its expected trip cost, on the one hand, and an 'evil entity' choosing link performance scenarios to maximize the expected trip cost, on the other. An application of game theory to solve risk-averse UE traffic assignment can be found in Bell and Cassir (2002). Network users have to make their route choice decisions in the presence of uncertainty about route costs, a reason why they need to have a strategy towards risk. In Zhang et al. (2005), a preliminary model of dynamic multilayer infrastructure networks is presented in the form of a differential game. In particular, three network layers (car, urban freight and data) are modelled as CN dynamic agents. In Chen et al. (1998), the integrated traffic control and dynamic traffic assignment problem is presented as a non-cooperative game between the traffic authority and highway users. The objective of the combined control-assignment problem is to find dynamic system-optimal signal settings and dynamic user-optimal traffic flows. The combined control-assignment problem is first formulated as a single-level Cournot game: the traffic authority and the users choose their strategies simultaneously. Then, the combined problem is formulated as a bi-level Stackelberg game in which the traffic authority is the leader who determines the signal settings in anticipation of the user's responses.

8.2.3   Road-pricing Problems and Game Theory

The problem of determining optimal tolls in transport networks is a complex issue. Levinson (1988) examines the question of what happens when jurisdictions have the opportunity to establish tollbooths at the frontier separating them. If one jurisdiction is able to set its policy in a vacuum, it is clearly advantageous to impose as high a toll on non-residents as can be supported. However, the neighbouring jurisdiction can set a policy in response. This establishes the potential for a classical prisoner's dilemma consideration: in this case to tax or to toll. In Levinson (2003), there is an application of game theory and queuing analysis to develop micro formulations of congestion. Only departure time is analysed in the context of a two- and three-player game, respectively, where interactions among players affect the pay-offs for other players in a systematic way. In Joksimovic et al. (2004), route choice and the elastic demand problem are considered with a focus on different game concepts of the optimal toll problem. Their experiments show that the Stackelberg game is the most promising game between the road authority and the travellers if only one road authority's objective is considered.

There is a gap in the literature concerning the importance of the different policies that the road authority may adopt, and the outcomes that can be the result of the different objectives and games played with the travellers. Therefore, different policy objectives of the road authority in the optimal toll design problem, as well as the consequences of different game concepts consequences, will be the focus of this chapter.

8.3 PROBLEM STATEMENT (NON-COOPERATIVE GAME THEORY)

The interactions between travellers and the road authority can be seen as a non-cooperative, non-zero sum, $(N + 1)$ players game between a single traffic authority, on the one hand, and N network users (travellers), on the other. The objective of the road-pricing problem, which is the combined optimal toll design and traffic assignment problem, is to determine system-optimal tolls and user-optimal traffic flows simultaneously. However, this road-pricing problem is an example of a bi-level optimization problem. The UE traffic-assignment problem (lower-level problem) can be formulated as a non-cooperative, N-person, non-zero sum game solved as a Nash game. The upper-level problem may have different objectives depending on what the road authority would like to achieve. This question as well as the outcomes of different game theory concepts will be the focus of this chapter.

A conceptual framework for the optimal toll design problem in the case of elastic demand addressed from different objectives of the road authority is given in Figure 8.1. The road authority sets tolls on the network while travellers respond to tolls by changing their travel decisions. Depending on travel costs, they can decide to travel along a certain route or decide not to travel at all in the tolled network.

In the road-pricing problem, we are dealing with an $(N + 1)$ player game, where there are N players (travellers) making a travel choice decision, and one player (the road manager) making a control or design decision (in this case, setting road tolls). However, adding the traffic authority to the game is not as simple as extending an N-player game to an $(N + 1)$ player game, because the strategy space and the pay-off function for this additional player

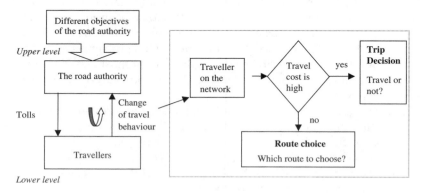

Figure 8.1   Conceptual framework for optimal toll design with route and trip choice

differ from those of the rest of the N players. In fact, there are two games played in conjunction with each other. The first game is a non-cooperative game where all N travellers aim to maximize their individual utility by choosing the best travel strategy (that is, trip choice and route choice), taking into account all other travellers' strategies. The second game is a game between the travellers and the road manager, where the road manager aims to maximize some network performance by choosing a control strategy, taking into account that travellers respond to the control strategy by adapting their travel strategies. The two games can be described as follows.

The outer-level game, being the toll design problem, consists of the following elements:

1. players: the authority, on the one side, and N potential travellers, on the other;
2. strategies of players: (a) toll levels (for the authority), and (b) travel choices such as route and trip choice (for travellers);
3. pay-off function of players: (a) pay-off for the authority (for example, social welfare, revenues), and (b) pay-off for the travellers (travel utilities);
4. rule of the game: the authority sets the tolls taking the travellers' behaviour and responses into account in order to optimize a certain objective.

The inner-level game, being the network equilibrium problem, consists of the following elements:

1. players: N travellers;
2. strategies of the players: travel choices such as route and trip choice;
3. pay-off functions of players: travel utilities;
4. rule of the game: travellers make their optimal trip and route choices; decisions to maximize their individual subjective utilities given a specific toll pattern over space.

Our main focus in this chapter is to investigate the outer-level game between the road authority and the users, although the inner-level game between travellers is part of it.

8.4   MODEL STRUCTURE

The objectives of the road authority and the travellers are different and sometimes even opposite. The upper-level objective may be to minimize total travel time, relieve congestion, improve safety, raise revenue, improve total system utility and so on. The lower-level objective may be the individual travel time, travel cost, or the individual travel utility. In this chapter, we use the individual travel utility as the objective to maximize for travellers.

Since the purpose of this chapter is to gain more insight into the structure of the optimal toll design problem under different policy objectives by using game theory, we restrict ourselves to the case of a simple network in which only one origin–destination (OD) pair is considered. Between this OD pair, different non-overlapping route alternatives are available. The generalized route travel cost function c_{pi} of traveller i for path p includes the travel-time costs and the toll costs,

$$c_{pi} = \alpha \tau_p + \theta_p, \tag{8.1}$$

where τ_p is the travel time of path p; θ_p is the toll costs of path p; and α denotes the value of time (VOT) which converts the travel time into monetary costs. Let U_{pi} denote the trip utility for making a trip along path p of traveller i. This trip utility consists of a fixed net utility $\overline{U}$ for making the trip (or arriving at the destination), and a disutility consisting of the generalized path travel costs c_{pi}:

$$U_{pi} = \overline{U} - c_{pi}. \tag{8.2}$$

According to utility maximization theory, a trip will be made only if the utility of doing an activity at a destination minus the utility of staying at home and the disutility of travelling is positive. In other words, if $U_p \leq 0$, then no trip will be made. By including a *fictitious* path in the path choice set representing the travellers' choice not to travel, and attaching a disutility of zero to this 'path' alternative, we combine path choice and trip choice in the model. Travellers are assumed to respond according to Wardrop's equilibrium law extended with elastic demand: at equilibrium, no user can improve its trip utility by unilaterally making another path choice or trip choice decision.

8.5   GAME THEORY APPLIED TO ROAD PRICING

Let us first consider the N-player game of the travellers, where S_i is the set of available alternatives for traveller i, $i \in \{1, \ldots, N\}$. The strategy $s_i \in S_i$ that traveller i will play depends on the control strategy set by the road manager, denoted by vector θ, and on the strategies of all other players, denoted by $s_{-i} \equiv (s_1, \ldots, s_{i-1}, s_{i+1}, \ldots, s_N)$. We assume that each traveller decides independently to seek unilaterally the maximum utility pay-off, taking into account the possible rational choices of the other travellers. Let $Ji\,[s_i(\theta), s_{-i}(\theta), \theta]$ denote the utility pay-off for traveller i for a given control strategy θ. This utility pay-off can include all kinds of travel utilities and travel cost. Utility pay-off for traveller i can be expressed as follows:

$$J_i[s_i(\theta), s_{-i}(\theta), \theta] = U_{i_{s_i}}, \qquad (8.3)$$

where C_{pi} is defined in expression (8.1), and $U_{i_{s_i}}$ denotes a specific path p (including the fictitious path) in equation (8.2).

If all other travellers play strategies s_{-i}^*, then traveller i will play the strategy that maximizes his/her pay-off utility, that is,

$$s_i^*(\theta) = \arg \max_{s_i \in S_i} J_i[s_i(\theta), s_{-i}^*(\theta), \theta]. \qquad (8.4)$$

If equation (8.4) holds for all travellers $i \in \{1, \ldots, N\}$, then $s_i^*(\theta) \equiv [s_i^*(\theta), s_{-i}^*(\theta)]$ is called a 'Nash equilibrium' for the control strategy θ. In this equilibrium, no traveller can improve his/her utility pay-off by unilateral change of behaviour. Note that this coincides with the concept of Wardrop's user equilibrium.

Now consider the complete $N + 1$-player game where the road manager faces the N travellers. The set Θ describes the alternative strategies that are available to the road manager. Suppose he/she chooses strategy $\theta \in \Theta$. However, depending on this strategy and on the strategies $s^*(\theta)$, chosen by the travellers, the manager's utility pay-off is $R[s^*(\theta), (\theta]$ (which may represent, for example, the total system utility or the total profits made). The road manager chooses the strategy θ^* by which he/she aims to maximize his/her utility pay-off, depending on the responses of the travellers:

$$\theta^* = \arg \max_{\theta \in \Theta} R[s_i^*(\theta), \theta]. \qquad (8.5)$$

If equations (8.4) and (8.5) are satisfied for all $(N + 1)$ players, where $\theta = \theta^*$ in equation (8.4), then this represents a Nash equilibrium in which no player can be better off by unilaterally following another strategy. Although all equilibria use the Nash concept, a different equilibrium or game type can be defined in the $N + 1$-player game depending on the influence that each of the players has in the game. Game theory notions used in this chapter are adopted from the work of Altman et al. (2003).

8.6 DIFFERENT OBJECTIVES OF THE ROAD AUTHORITY

Which objective the road authority will apply will have an influence on the optimal toll levels. Depending on the authority's objective, different utility pay-off functions can be formulated. We can also say that the objective of the road authority is a system-optimal solution, while the objective of the travellers is to reach a user-optimal solution.

First, assuming that the road authority's objective is to *maximize total travel utility* (the utility of all network users together), the objective is defined as the sum of the pay-off values of all travellers:

$$\max R[s^*(\theta), \theta] = \sum_{i=1}^{N} J_i[s^*(\theta)]. \tag{8.6}$$

Second, if the road authority aims at *maximizing total toll revenues*, they may have the following objective:

$$\max R[s^*(\theta), \theta] = \sum_p q_p[s^*(\theta)] \theta_p, \tag{8.7}$$

where $q_p(s^*)$ denotes the number of travellers using path p, which can be derived from the optimal strategies s^*. Clearly, setting tolls equal to zero does not provide any revenues, while setting very high tolls will make all travellers decide not to travel at all.

Third, combining these two objectives leads to the notion of *social surplus maximization*. The social surplus can be computed by adding the toll revenues to the total trip utilities, such that the following problem will maximize social surplus as an objective:

$$\max R[s^*(\theta), \theta] = \sum_{i=1}^{N} J_i[s^*(\theta)] + \sum_p q_p[s^*(\theta)] \theta_p. \tag{8.8}$$

The formulated policy objectives will be used in the experimental part of this chapter.

8.7 DIFFERENT GAME CONCEPTS

In the following we shall discuss in turn three different types of games between the road authority and the travellers: namely, the social planner (monopoly), the Stackelberg and the Cournot games.

8.7.1 The Social Planner (Monopoly) Game

In this case, the road manager not only sets his/her own control, but is also assumed able to control the strategies that the travellers will play. In other words, the road manager sets θ^* as well as s^*. This case will lead to what is called a 'system-optimal solution' of the game. A social planner (monopoly or solo player) game represents the best system performance and thus may serve as a 'benchmark' for other solutions. This game solution shows what is best for one player (the road manager), regardless of the other players. From an economic point of view, in this case the road authority has complete (or full) market power. Mathematically, the problem can be formulated as follows:

$$(s^*, \theta^*) = \arg \max_{\theta \in \Theta, s \in S} R(s, \theta). \tag{8.9}$$

8.7.2 Stackelberg Game

In this case, the road manager is the 'leader' by setting the control, thereby directly influencing the travellers who are considered to be 'followers'. The travellers may only influence the road manager indirectly by making travel decisions based on the control. It is assumed that the road manager has complete knowledge of how travellers respond to control measures. The road manager sets θ^* and the travellers follow by playing $s^*(\theta^*)$. From an economic point of view, in a Stackelberg game one player has more market power than the other players in the game (in this case the road authority has more market power than the travellers).

The problem can be mathematically formulated so as to find (s^*, θ^*), such that:

$$\theta^* = \arg \max_{\theta \in \Theta} R[s^*(\theta), \theta],$$

$$\text{where } s_i^*(\theta) = \arg \max_{s_i \in S_i} J_i(s_i, s_{-i}^*, \theta), \forall i = 1, \ldots, N. \tag{8.10}$$

8.7.3 Cournot Game

In contrast to the Stackelberg game, in this case the travellers are now assumed to have a direct influence on the road manager, having complete knowledge of the manager's responses to their travel decisions. The road manager sets $\theta^*(s^*)$, depending on the travellers' strategies s^* (θ^*). This type of 'duopoly game', in which two players choose their strategies simultaneously, and therefore one player's response is unknown in advance to the other, is known as a Cournot game. Mathematically, the problem can be formulated as follows. Find (s^*, θ^*), such that:

$$\theta^* = \arg \max_{\theta \in \Theta} \; R(s_i^*, s_{-i}^*, \theta), \text{ and } s_i^* = \arg \max_{s_i \in S_i} J_i(s_i, s_{-i}^*, \theta^*), \; \forall i = 1, \ldots, N.$$

$$(8.11)$$

The proposed different game concepts will be illustrated in the next section. Note that the Stackelberg game is the most realistic game approach in our pricing context because of the nature of pricing. More about game theory concepts can be found in Basar and Olsder (1995) and Ritzberger (2002). Moreover, mathematical bi-level problem formulations can be used to solve more complex games (see, for example, Joksimovic et al., 2005).

Some of the games presented may be less relevant in practice. For example, a game where road authority and road users are engaged in a pure Nash game seems rather odd, compared with the more realistic case where the road authority has Stackelberg leadership. Similarly, some objective functions may not be realistic.

8.8 SOME EXPERIMENTS

Let us now look at the following simple problem to illustrate how the road-pricing problem can be analysed using game theory. Suppose there are two individuals wanting to travel from A to B. There are two alternative paths available to go to B. The first path is tolled (toll is equal to θ), the second path is untolled. Depending on the toll level, the travellers decide to take either Path 1 or Path 2, or not to travel at all. The latter choice is represented by a third virtual path, such that we can consider three path alternatives as available strategies to each traveller, that is, $S_I = \{1, 2, 3\}$ for traveller $i =$

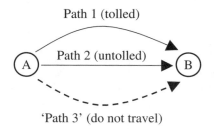

Figure 8.2   Network description for the road-pricing problem

1, 2. Figure 8.2 illustrates the problem.

In equation (8.2), $\overline{U}$ represents the trip utility when making the trip to destination B (in the calculations we assume $\overline{U}=210$); $\tau_p^{rs}(\cdot)$ denotes the path travel time for path p depending on the chosen strategies; and α represents the VOT (we assume $\alpha = 6$ for all travellers). Note that negative net utilities on Paths 1 and 2 imply that one will not travel, that is, if the cost (disutility) of making the trip is greater than the utility of the trip itself. The path travel times are given as a function of the chosen strategies, in that the more travellers use a certain path, the longer the travel time:

$$\tau_1[s_1(\theta), s_2(\theta)] = \begin{cases} 10, \text{ if } s_1(\theta) = 1 \text{ or } s_2(\theta) = 1 \text{ (e.g., flow on Path 1 is 1)}, \\ 18, \text{ if } s_1(\theta) = 1 \text{ and } s_2(\theta) = 1 \text{ (e.g., flow on Path 1 is 2)}, \end{cases}$$

$$(8.12)$$

and

$$\tau_2[s_1(\theta), s_2(\theta)] = \begin{cases} 20, \text{ if } s_1(\theta) = 2 \text{ or } s_2(\theta) = 2 \text{ (e.g., flow on Path 2 is 1)}, \\ 40, \text{ if } s_1(\theta) = 2 \text{ and } s_2(\theta) = 2 \text{ (e.g., flow on Path 2 is 2)}, \end{cases}$$

$$(8.13)$$

Each strategy yields a different pay-off, depending on the utility of making the trip, the travel time on the path (which increases whenever more travellers use it), and a possible path toll. We assume that traveller i aims to maximize his/her individual travel utility (pay-off) given by:

$$J_i[s_1(\theta), s_2(\theta)] = \begin{cases} \overline{U} - \alpha\tau_1[s_1(\theta), s_2(\theta)] - \theta & \text{if } s_i(\theta) = 1, \text{ Path 1 (tolled)} \quad (8.14) \\ \overline{U} - \alpha\tau_2[s_1(\theta), s_2(\theta)], & \text{if } s_i(\theta) = 2, \text{ Path 2 (untolled)} \\ 0, & \text{if } s_i(\theta) = 3, \text{ Path 3 (do not travel)}. \end{cases}$$

Solving the game between the two travellers for a Nash equilibrium corresponds to a Wardrop equilibrium with elastic demand, in which no traveller can improve his/her utility by unilaterally changing path or deciding not to travel. For the sake of clarity, we shall look only at pure strategies in this example, but the case may be extended to mixed strategies as well. In pure strategies, each player is assumed to adopt only one strategy, whereas in mixed strategies, the players are assumed to adopt probabilities for choosing each of the available strategies. In our example, we are thus looking at discrete flows instead of continuous flows, so Wardrop's first principle according to which all travel utilities are equal for all used alternatives may no longer hold in this case. In fact, the more general equilibrium rule applies in which each traveller aims to maximize his/her personal

Table 8.1   Utility pay-off table for travellers

		Traveller 2		
		Path 1	Path 2	Path 3
Traveller 1	Path 1	$(102-\theta, 102-\theta)$	$(150-\theta, 90)$	$(150-\theta, 0)$
	Path 2	$(90, 150-\theta)$	$(-30, -30)$	$(90, 0)$
	Path 3	$(0, 150-\theta)$	$(0, 90)$	$(0, 0)$

trip utility. The utility pay-off table, depending on the toll θ, is given in Table 8.1 for the two travellers, where the values between brackets are the pay-offs for Travellers 1 and 2, respectively. For example, if Traveller 1 chooses Path 1 and Traveller 2 chooses Path 2, then the travel utility for Traveller 1 is $J_1(1, 2) = 210-6\cdot10-\theta = 150-\theta$.

In the experiments we shall consider three different objectives of the road authority: total travel utility, 'social surplus' and generating revenues. For the first objective, three different game concepts are applied in turn: the social planner, the Stackelberg and the Cournot games. Because the Stackelberg game is the most realistic, we present it as the only game for the other two objective functions.

8.8.1   Case Study 1: Maximize Total Travel Utility

Now, let us add the road manager as a player, assuming that he/she tries to maximize total travel utility, that is,

$$\text{Max } R[s^*(\theta), \theta] = J_1[s^*(\theta)] + J_2[s^*(\theta)]. \tag{8.15}$$

The strategy set of the road manager is assumed to be $\Theta = \{\theta | \theta \geq 0\}$. The pay-offs for the road manager are presented in Table 8.2 depending on the strategy $\theta \in \Theta$ that the road manager plays and depending on the strategies that the travellers play.

Let us solve the previously defined pay-off tables for different game concepts and different values of tolls. First, we discuss the social planner game, then the Stackelberg game and finally the Cournot game.

The social planner game
In the social planner game, the road manager sets the toll as well as the travel decisions of the travellers such that his/her pay-off is maximized. Note that the travel utility always decreases as θ increases, hence $\theta^* = 0$. In this case, the maximum utility can be obtained if the travellers take both

Table 8.2   Utility pay-off table for the road manager if his/her objective is to maximize the total travel utility

		Traveller 2		
		Path 1	Path 2	Path 3
Traveller 1	Path 1	$204-2\theta$	$240-\theta$	$150-\theta$
	Path 2	$240-\theta$	-60	90
	Path 3	$150-\theta$	90	0

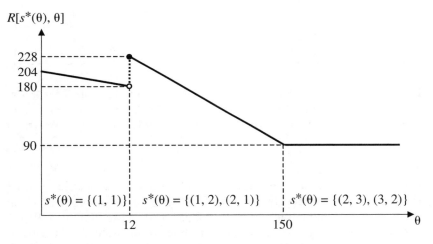

Figure 8.3   Total travel utilities depending on toll value for the objective of maximizing total travel utility

Paths 1 and 2, that is, $s^* = \{(1, 2), (2, 1)\}$. Hence, in this system optimum, the total travel utility in the system is 240. Note that this optimum would not occur if travellers have free choice, since $\theta = 0$ yields a Nash–Wardrop equilibrium for both travellers to choose Path 1.

The Stackelberg game
After the toll is set by the road authority, the travellers react to this toll by reconsidering their travel choices, perhaps choosing different paths. Now the travellers will individually maximize their own travel utility, depending on the toll set by the road manager. Figure 8.3 illustrates the total travel utility for different values of θ, with the corresponding optimal strategies played by the travellers. When $0 \leq \theta < 12$, travellers will both choose Path 1.

Table 8.3   *Cournot game solutions for the objective of maximizing total travel utility*

		Strategy of the road authority		
		$\theta=0$	$\theta=15$	$\theta=170$
Combined	$s=(1, 1)$	$(102, 204)^*$	$(87, 174)$	$(-68, -136)$
strategies	$s=(1, 2)$	$(90, 240)$	$(90, 225)$	$(-20, 70)$
for both	$s=(1, 3)$	$(0, 150)$	$(0, 135)$	$(-20, -20)$
travellers	$s=(2, 1)$	$(90, 240)$	$(90, 225)$	$(-20, 70)$
	$s=(2, 2)$	$(-30, -60)$	$(-30, -60)$	$(-30, -60)$
	$s=(2, 3)$	$(0, 90)$	$(0, 90)$	$(0, 90)^*$
	$s=(3, 1)$	$(0, 150)$	$(0, 135)$	$(-20, -20)$
	$s=(3, 2)$	$(0, 90)$	$(0, 90)$	$(0, 90)^*$
	$s=(3, 3)$	$(0, 0)$	$(0, 0)$	$(0, 0)$

If $12 \le \theta < 150$, travellers will take both Paths 1 and 2, while for $\theta \ge 150$ one traveller will take Path 2 and the other traveller will not travel at all. Clearly, the optimum for the road manager is $\theta^* = 12$, yielding a total travel utility of 228.

The Cournot game
It can be shown that if the travellers and the road manager have equal influence on each other's strategies, multiple Cournot solutions exist. There is, however, one dominating strategy, that is, the travellers both take Path 1 and the road manager sets zero tolls, yielding a total system utility of 204 (indicated with an asterisk in Table 8.3). According to Table 8.3, multiple Nash equilibria exist.

Comparison of games for the policy objective of maximizing the total time utility
Table 8.4 summarizes the outcomes for the three different games presented in the previous section. According to Table 8.4, the Stackelberg game yields a pay-off for the road authority of 228, setting its strategy to the optimal toll equal to 12. Taking into account the nature of road pricing and the results of the experiments, we conclude that the Stackelberg game is the most realistic game concept for the optimal toll design problem.

8.8.2   Case Study 2: Maximize Revenues

Now, let us add the road manager as a player, assuming that he/she tries to maximize revenues (see equation (8.7)). The strategy set of the road

Table 8.4   Comparison of outcomes of different games for the objective of maximizing total travel utility

Game	θ^*	$s_i^*(\theta)$	R	J_i
Social planner	0	{(1, 2), (2, 1)}	240	{(90, 150), (150, 90)}
Stackelberg	12	{(1, 2), (2, 1)}	228	{(90, 138), (138, 90)}
Cournot	0	{(1, 1)}	204	{(102, 102}

Table 8.5   Utility pay-off table for the road manager if his/her objective is to maximize revenues

		Traveller 2		
		Path 1	Path 2	Path 3
Traveller 1	Path 1	2θ	θ	θ
	Path 2	θ	-60	90
	Path 3	θ	90	0

manager is assumed to be $\Theta = \{\theta | \theta \geq 0\}$. Depending on the strategy $\theta \in \Theta$ that the road manager plays, and depending on the strategies the travellers play, the pay-offs for the road manager are presented in Table 8.5.

The Stackelberg game
Figure 8.4 illustrates the revenues for different values of θ, with the corresponding optimal strategies played by the travellers. When $0 \leq \theta < 12$, travellers will both choose Path 1. If $12 \leq \theta < 150$, travellers will take both Paths 1 and 2, while for $\theta \geq 150$ one traveller will take Path 2 and the other traveller will not travel at all. Clearly, the optimum for the road manager is $\theta^* = 150$, yielding a total system utility of 240.

8.8.3   Case Study 3: Maximize Social Surplus

Now, the road manager is assumed to maximize social surplus (see equation (8.8)). The strategy set of the road manager is assumed to be $\Theta = \{\theta | \theta \geq 0\}$. The pay-offs for the road manager are presented in Table 8.6 depending on the strategy $\theta \in \Theta$ that the road manager plays and depending on the strategies that the travellers play.

The Stackelberg game
Figure 8.5 illustrates the social surplus for different values of θ with the corresponding optimal strategies played by the travellers. When $0 \leq \theta < 12$,

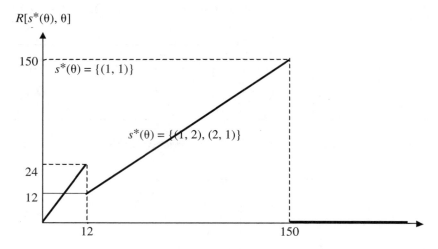

Figure 8.4   Total travel utilities depending on toll value for the objective of maximizing revenues

Table 8.6   Utility pay-off table for the road manager if his/her objective is to maximize social surplus

		Traveller 2		
		Path 1	Path 2	Path 3
Traveller 1	Path 1	204	240	150
	Path 2	240	−60	90
	Path 3	150	90	0

the travellers will both choose Path 1. If $12 \leq \theta < 150$, the travellers will take both Paths 1 and 2, while, for $\theta \geq 150$, one traveller will take Path 2 and the other traveller will not travel at all. Clearly, the optimum for the road manager is $12 \leq \theta^* \leq 150$, yielding a total system utility of 240.

8.8.4   Comparison among Different Policy Objectives with Regard to the Stackelberg Game

Considering all three case studies (Table 8.7) some conclusions can be drawn:

● different objectives can all be applied, depending on what the road

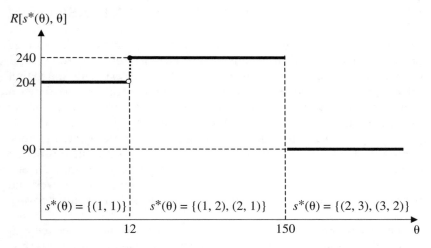

Figure 8.5 Total travel utilities depending on the toll value, given the objective of maximizing social surplus

Table 8.7 Comparison of different policy objectives

Policy objectives	Optimal strategy		Maximum pay-offs	
	Road authority	Travellers	Road authority	Travellers
	(θ^*)	$s^* = (s_1^*, s_2^*)$	(R)	(J_1, J_2)
Total travel utilities	12	(1, 2) (2, 1)	228	(90, 138) (138, 90)
Total toll revenues	150	(2, 3) (3, 2)	150	(90, 0) (0, 90)
Social surplus	{12, 150}	(1, 2) (2, 1)	240	({138, 0}, 90) (90, {138, 0})

    authority would like to achieve;
- different objectives lead to different outcomes, both in terms of the optimal toll system, as well as in pay-offs for players;
- looking at different game types shows the span of outcomes of an optimal design and their relative worth;
- there are multiple optimal solutions (multiple Nash equilibria); and
- the objective function may have a non-continuous shape (jumps).

8.9   CONCLUSIONS AND FURTHER EXTENSIONS

The purpose of this chapter was to gain more insight into the road-pricing problem using concepts from game theory, as well as different toll designs depending on different policy objectives. It should be explicitly stated that the aim of this chapter is simply to provide an introduction to a microscopic approach to road pricing based on game theory. To that end we presented the notions of game theory and presented three different game types in order to elucidate the essentials of the game-theoretic approach. These game types were applied to three different toll design objectives exemplified on a simplistic demand–supply network system. This clearly revealed differences in design results in terms of toll levels and pay-offs for the actors involved, that is, the road authority and network users.

The theory presented here can be extended to include other relevant travel choices, such as departure time choice, as well as heterogeneous travellers and imperfect information on the part of the road users. An important extension is to apply the proposed game-theory framework to large cases (for example, for a large number of players or on a bigger network). For practical use, the presented game-theoretic analysis should be translated into a modelling system for which tolling designs for more realistic road networks become feasible. For that purpose, the bi-level optimization framework will be used (see Joksimovic et al., 2005).

REFERENCES

Altman, E., T. Boulogne, R. El-Azouzi, T. Jiménez and L. Wynter (2003), 'A survey on networking games in telecommunications', Working Paper, INRIA (Institut National de Recherche en Informatique), France.

Arnott, R., T. Rave and R. Schob (2005), *Alleviating Urban Traffic Congestion*, CESifo book series, Cambridge, MA: MIT Press.

Basar, T. and G.J. Olsder (1995), *Dynamic Non-Cooperative Game Theory*, New York: Academic Press.

Bell, M. (2000), 'A game theory approach to measuring the performance reliability of transport networks', *Transportation Research B*, **34**, 533–45.

Bell, M. and C. Cassir (2002), 'Risk-averse user equilibrium traffic assignment: an application of game theory', *Transportation Research B*, **36**, 671–81.

Chen, O.J. and M.E. Ben-Akiva (1998), 'Game-theoretic formulations of the interaction between dynamic traffic control and dynamic traffic assignment', *Transportation Research Record: Journal of the Transportation Research Board*, No. 1617, TRB, National Research Council, Washington, DC, 178–88.

Fisk, C.S. (1984), 'Game theory and transportation systems modelling', *Transportation Research B*, **4**, 301–13.

Garcia, A., D. Reume and R.L. Smith (2000), 'Fictitious play for finding system optimal routings in dynamic traffic networks', *Transportation Research B*, **34**, 147–56.

Joksimovic, D., M.C.J. Bliemer and P.H.L. Bovy (2004), 'Road pricing problem with route choice and elastic demand – a game theory approach', *Triennial Symposium on Transportation Analysis (TRISTAN)*, CD-ROM, Le Gosier, Guadeloupe.

Joksimovic, D., M. Bliemer and P.H.L. Bovy (2005), 'Optimal toll design problem in dynamic traffic networks – with joint route and departure time choice', *Transportation Research Record: Transportation Modelling*, no. 1923, 61–72.

Levinson, D. (1988), 'Tolling at a frontier: a game theoretic approach', *Proceedings of the 14th International Symposium on Transportation and Traffic Theory*, Jerusalem: Pergamon, pp. 665–83.

Levinson, D. (2003), 'Micro-foundations of congestion and pricing', paper presented at International Symposium: The Theory and Practice of Congestion Charging, London, 23–25 August.

Mohring, H. (1970), 'The peak load problem with increasing returns and pricing constraints', *American Economic Review*, **60**, 693–705.

Nash, J.F. (1950), 'Equilibrium points in *n*-person games', *National Academy of Sciences*, **36**, 48–9.

Ritzberger, K. (2002), *Foundations of Non-Cooperative Game Theory*, Oxford: Oxford University Press.

Schelling, T.C. (1978), *Micromotives and Microbehaviour*, New York: W.W. Norton.

Verhoef, E.T., J. Boot and P. Boot (1999), 'The long road towards the implementation of road pricing: the Dutch experience', in ECMT/OECD (eds), *Managing Car Use for Sustainable Urban Travel*, Dublin.

Walters, A.A. (1961), 'The theory and measurement of private and social cost of highway congestion', *Econometrica*, **29**, 676–99.

Wardrop, J.G. (1952), 'Some theoretical aspects of road traffic research', in *Proceedings of the Institute of Civil Engineers II*, **1**, 278–325.

Wie, B.W. (1995), 'A differential game approach to the dynamic mixed behavior traffic network equilibrium problem', *European Journal of Operational Research*, **83**, 117–36.

Zhang, P., S. Peeta and T. Friesz (2005), 'Dynamic game theoretic model of multi-layer infrastructure networks', *Networks and Spacial Economics*, **5** (2), 147–78.

9. Optimal toll design problem: a dynamic network modelling approach

Michiel Bliemer, Dusica Joksimovic and Piet Bovy

9.1 INTRODUCTION

9.1.1 Background

Road pricing is one of the market-based policy instruments that influences the travel behaviour of users of a transportation network. Road pricing is a type of responsive pricing that can change travel patterns by influencing users' travel choices at various levels (for example, departure time choice, route choice). Many researchers have been working on road-pricing problems (see, for example, May and Milne, 2000; Verhoef, 2002), but almost all of these modelling studies consider only static traffic models. Dynamic models, however, describe the problem more accurately and are required for studies that look at time-varying road pricing. However, formulating and solving dynamic models with time-varying pricing is much more complex than with static models.

In this chapter we are dealing with the time-varying optimal toll design problem for planning purposes. Uniform and variable (time-varying) tolls during the peak are considered, and travellers' responses (route choice and departure-time choice) to these tolls are taken into account. Charging will, in general, also lead to a lower travel demand. However, for simplicity, the total number of travellers is assumed constant in this chapter. We shall consider tolling schemes in which the road authority has already decided on which links to toll and which period to toll. Then, for different tolling patterns (for example, uniform or time varying), the aim is to determine optimal toll levels given a certain policy objective, such as minimizing total travel time or maximizing total revenues. The problem of finding the optimal toll levels can be formulated as a network design problem.

The focus of this chapter is to describe the framework of the optimal toll network design problem and to formulate the problem mathematically. Furthermore, it will be illustrated that different objectives of the road authority and different tolling schemes can lead to different optimal toll levels. The main contributions of this chapter are the following. First, we propose a dynamic, instead of static, traffic model with road pricing. This includes not only route choice but also departure-time choice. Second, heterogeneous travellers with high and low value of time are considered. Third, different objectives of the road authority are explored: namely, maximizing revenues and minimizing total network travel time. Finally, different tolling schemes and their impact on the objective of the road authority are analysed.

9.1.2 The State of the Art

The problem of road pricing has been studied in the literature from different modelling perspectives and under various assumptions. The (economic) theory of road pricing dates back to Pigou (1920), and first-best congestion tolls are derived in static deterministic models (Beckmann et al., 1956; Dafermos, 1973; Yang and Huang, 1998) and static stochastic models (Yang, 1999).

Dynamic pricing models in which network conditions and link tolls are time varying, have been addressed in Wie and Tobin (1998), who compare the effectiveness of various pricing policies (time varying, uniform and step tolls). A limitation of these models is that they are restricted to a bottleneck or a single destination network. Mahmassani and Herman (1984) and Ben-Akiva et al. (1986) developed dynamic marginal (first-best) cost-pricing models for general transportation networks. As indicated by these authors, the application of their model is limited to destination-specific (rather than route or link-based) tolling strategies, which might not be easy to implement in practice. Moreover, since tolls are based on marginal cost pricing, it is implicitly assumed that all links can be priced dynamically, which is not feasible in practice.

Second-best pricing models, in which typically only a subset of links, time periods and/or travellers are tolled, put practical restrictions on the marginal cost-pricing models. In Viti et al. (2003) a dynamic congestion-pricing model is formulated as a bi-level programming problem, in which the prices are allowed to affect the (sequentially) modelled route and departure-time choice of travellers. Abou-Zeid (2003) developed some models for pricing in dynamic traffic networks. In Joksimovic et al. (2005), the time-varying pricing problem including route and departure choice is solved using a simple algorithm for the road authority's objective of minimizing total travel time on the network. In this chapter these models are extended to include heterogeneous travellers, different and more general tolling schemes, and different objectives of the road authority.

9.1.3 Chapter Outline

In Section 9.2 the optimal toll design problem is described, while in Section 9.3 the framework and all components are discussed and mathematically formulated. Then, in Section 9.4 a simple solution algorithm is proposed for finding the optimal toll levels. Section 9.5 illustrates and discusses, with reference to a small hypothesized network, how the model works under different tolling schemes and different objectives of the road authority. Finally, conclusions are drawn in Section 9.6.

9.2 OPTIMAL TOLL DESIGN PROBLEM

In the optimal toll design problem described in this chapter, the links and time periods to toll are given. The aim is to determine optimal toll levels for different tolling patterns, given a specific objective of the road authority (such as minimizing congestion, maximizing total toll revenues, maximizing accessibility, maximizing social welfare and so on). The resulting road-pricing scheme describes for each link and each time period how much a traveller has to pay for entering the link at that particular time.

When the road authority has determined the toll levels, the travellers are faced with these tolls while traversing the network and may change their travel behaviour in order to optimize their own objective, following random utility theory. It is assumed that each traveller individually chooses his or her subjective most preferable route. We assume that each traveller can choose the route and departure time for his or her trip. It has been argued in the literature that these two choices are the most important behavioural responses to road pricing. No other choices, such as trip choice, mode choice and destination choice, are considered in this chapter.

When travellers make route and departure-time changes for their trips after the road authority has introduced tolls on the network, the network conditions (traffic flows and travel times) may change. This may be a reason for the road authority to reconsider their tolling scheme in order to optimize its objective. Hence, there is an interaction between the road authority and the travellers, as depicted in Figure 9.1. On the left-hand side in the road-pricing model, the road authority sets levels for the link tolls based on a given tolling pattern (spatial and temporal pattern of tolls, stating when and where to toll) and the objective considered. On the right-hand side in

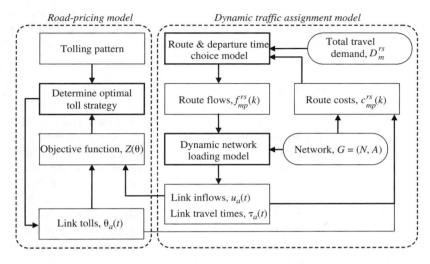

Figure 9.1   Optimal toll design model framework

the dynamic traffic assignment model, the travellers are simulated on a transportation network which aims for a (stochastic) dynamic D_m^{rs} equilibrium state taking the link tolls into account. In the next section the framework will be formulated and described in more detail.

9.3   MODEL FORMULATION

Let $G = (N, A)$ denote a given transport network G with nodes N and directed links A. Furthermore, let D_m^{rs} describe the given travel demand (total number of travellers) for each origin–destination (OD) pair (r, s) and for each user class $m \in M$. Between each OD pair there exist routes $p \in P^{rs}$, where P^{rs} denotes the set of all feasible routes.

All user classes are assumed to use the same infrastructure. In this chapter the problem is considered in discrete time, and is hence defined in terms of time intervals instead of time instants. The total time horizon considered is denoted by set T, and each time interval is denoted by $t \in T$. The travel demand period is defined by subset $K \subset T$, where each $k \in K$ is a feasible departure-time interval. Not all links and all time intervals need to be tolled. The set of tolled links is denoted by $\overline{A} \subseteq A$, while the tolled time intervals (in terms of link entrance) for each link $a \in \overline{A}$ are defined by $\overline{T}_a \subseteq T$.

As depicted in Figure 9.1, the model framework consists of two main parts: namely, a road-pricing part, and a dynamic traffic assignment part.

This framework essentially describes a bi-level problem. The upper level is the road-pricing part, while the lower level is the dynamic traffic assignment for given toll levels. Both parts will be explained in more detail in the following subsections.

9.3.1 Road-pricing Model

In the road-pricing model, the road authority aims to introduce the best tolling scheme depending on its goals. A tolling scheme is defined as a package in which a set of links and time intervals is chosen to be tolled, together with the toll levels corresponding to certain time-varying tolling patterns. The road authority may have different goals, leading to different objective functions in the model. Depending on its goal, the road authority has to select the best tolling scheme. We assume that the tolled links, $\overline{A}$, are given, as well as the tolled time period, $\overline{T}_a$, for each tolled link a. First, some possible link tolling patterns will be described. Second, potential objective functions are mathematically formulated.

Link tolling patterns
Different link tolling patterns over time can be considered by the road authority. As illustrated in Figure 9.2, we distinguish (i) a uniform tolling scheme (toll levels are constant over the entire study time period); (ii) a quasi-uniform tolling scheme (tolls levels are constant over a specified time period and zero otherwise); and (iii) a variable tolling scheme (tolls levels are time varying).

The three different tolling patterns in time can be formulated as follows:

$$\text{Variable: } \theta_a(t) = \begin{cases} \phi_a(t)\overline{\theta}_a, & \text{if } a \in \overline{A}, t \in \overline{T}_a; \\ 0, & \text{otherwise,} \end{cases} \text{ where } 0 \le \phi_a(t) \le 1. \quad (9.1)$$

$$\text{Quasi-uniform: } \theta_a(t) = \begin{cases} \overline{\theta}_a, & \text{if } a \in \overline{A}, t \in \overline{T}_a; \\ 0, & \text{otherwise.} \end{cases} \quad (9.2)$$

$$\text{Uniform: } \theta_a(t) = \begin{cases} \overline{\theta}_a, & \text{if } a \in \overline{A}, t \in T; \\ 0, & \text{otherwise.} \end{cases} \quad (9.3)$$

| Uniform | Quasi-uniform | Variable |

Figure 9.2 Different tolling patterns

In all cases, there is only a single toll level $\bar{\theta}_a$ to be determined for each tolled link $a \in \bar{A}$, which indicates the maximum toll to be paid for that link. Clearly, the quasi-uniform tolling pattern is a special case of the variable tolling pattern (assuming that $\phi_a(t) = 1, \forall t \in \bar{T}_a$), while the uniform pattern is a special case of the quasi-uniform pattern (by furthermore assuming that $\bar{T}_a = T$). In the case of uniform tolls, the toll levels for all time intervals are set to toll level $\bar{\theta}_a$ for tolled link a. In the case of quasi-uniform tolls, only the tolls in the time intervals $t \in \bar{T}_a$ will be set to the toll level $\bar{\theta}_a$, and will be zero outside that time period. For variable tolls we assume that there is a given predefined function $\phi_a(t)$ over time for each tolled link. In other words, the proportions of the time-varying tolls are fixed (hence, the shape of the toll levels over time is given). All three toll patterns will be used in the case study in this chapter.

A tolling scheme indicates a combination of a tolling pattern and corresponding maximum toll levels, hence describing the following variables:

1. set of tolled links $\bar{A}$ (assumed given);
2. set of tolled time intervals $\bar{T}_a, \forall a \in \bar{A}$ (assumed given);
3. link tolling pattern $\phi_a(t), \forall a \in \bar{A}, \forall t \in \bar{T}_a$ (assumed given);
4. maximum toll levels $\bar{\theta}_a, \forall a \in \bar{A}, \forall t \in \bar{T}_a$ (to be optimized).

This means that, for each tolling scheme, toll levels $\theta_a(t)$ are known for each link a and each time interval t. In this chapter the tolled links, the tolled time intervals, and the link tolling patterns are assumed to be input. The road authority aims to find optimal maximum toll levels $\bar{\theta}_a^*$ that optimize some given objective. The next subsection will discuss these objectives further.

Road authority objectives
In Chapter 2 of this book a detailed discussion on different objectives for road pricing can be found. For illustration purposes, in our experiments two different objectives are chosen: namely (i) maximization of total toll revenues; and (ii) minimization of the total travel time.

The road authority seeks to optimize its objective by selecting the optimal maximum toll levels $\bar{\theta}^*$, that is,

$$\bar{\theta}^*, = \arg \min_{\bar{\theta} \in \Theta} Z(\bar{\theta}). \tag{9.4}$$

The set Θ denotes the set of feasible maximum toll levels, which typically includes upper and lower bounds $\bar{\theta}_a^{\min}$ and $\bar{\theta}_a^{\max}$ for each tolled link:

$$\Theta = \{\bar{\theta} : \bar{\theta}_a^{\min} \leq \bar{\theta}_a \leq \bar{\theta}_a^{\max}, \forall a \in \bar{A}\}. \tag{9.5}$$

For each evaluation of the objective function $Z(\bar{\theta})$, a dynamic traffic assignment problem has to be solved (see Figure 9.1).

The total revenues on the network are a product of the inflows into tolled links and the corresponding toll levels at the link entrance times. Given some maximum toll levels $\bar{\theta}$, $Z_{\text{revenue}}(\bar{\theta})$ describes the total toll revenues (to be maximized, hence the negative sign):

$$Z_{\text{revenue}}(\bar{\theta}) = -\sum_a \sum_t u_a(t)\theta_a(t), \qquad (9.6)$$

where $\theta_a(t)$ is the toll level on link a at time interval t (according to the different tolling patterns described in equations (9.1–3), and $u_a(t)$ is the number of vehicles flowing into link a at time interval t.

Instead of maximizing total toll revenues, the road authority may be more interested in minimizing total travel time (for example, as a proxy for minimizing congestion or pollution). Objective function $Z_{\text{time}}(\bar{\theta})$ describes the total travel time on the network,

$$Z_{\text{time}}(\bar{\theta}) = \sum_a \sum_t u_a(t)\tau_a(t), \qquad (9.7)$$

where $\tau_a(t)$ is the link travel time when entering link a at time interval t.

9.3.2 Dynamic Traffic Assignment Model

The dynamic traffic assignment (DTA) model consists of two components: (i) a simultaneous route choice and departure-time choice component; and (ii) a dynamic network loading component. In the route and departure-time choice component, travellers are modelled as utility maximizers, who choose the route and departure time that minimizes certain generalized costs, thus yielding dynamic route flows. Heterogeneous travellers are considered in which travellers may differ only in their values of time (VOTs). The dynamic loading component then dynamically propagates these route flows over the network, yielding (new) experienced travel times and toll costs. The interaction between the two components is depicted in Figure 9.1. Both components will be explained in more detail below.

Simultaneous route choice and departure-time choice component
Let the class m experienced generalized travel costs for each route p from origin r to destination s and departure-time interval k (denoted by $c^{rs}_{mp}(k)$) be given by a linear combination consisting of the route travel time $\tau^{rs}_p(k)$, penalties for scheduling delays, and route toll costs $\theta^{rs}_p(k)$:

$$c^{rs}_{mp}(k) = \alpha_m \tau^{rs}_p(k) + \beta|k - s^{rs}| + \gamma|k + \tau^{rs}_p(k) - \xi^{rs}| + \theta^{rs}_p(k), \qquad (9.8)$$

where $k - \varsigma^{rs}$ denotes the deviation of the actual departure time k from the preferred departure time ς^{rs}, and where $k + \tau_p^{rs}(k) - \xi^{rs}$ denotes the deviation of the actual arrival time $k + \tau_p^{rs}(k)$ from the preferred arrival time ξ^{rs}. The parameters α_m, β, and γ convert time to a monetary value. Parameter α_m denotes the VOT of class m travellers. Note that the VOT is the only class-specific parameter. The travel times (speeds) and tolls are assumed to be the same for all types of traveller. Hence, we are not assuming different vehicle types, but focus on travellers with, for example, different purposes such as business trips (high VOT) versus leisure trips (low VOT).

The route travel times and the route toll costs are determined from the corresponding link travel times and toll costs along the route. Let $\delta_{ap}^{rs}(k, t)$ be a dynamic route-link incidence indicator, which is 1 if link a is reached on route p from r to s at time t when departing at time k, and 0 otherwise. This indicator can be computed when the link travel times $\tau_a(t)$ are known. Then the route travel time can be computed from consecutive link travel times,

$$\tau_p^{rs}(k) = \sum_{a \in p} \tau_a(t) \delta_{ap}^{rs}(k, t). \tag{9.9}$$

Similarly, the route toll costs can be computed from consecutive link toll costs $\theta_a(t)$,

$$\theta_p^{rs}(k) = \sum_{a \in p} \theta_a(t) \delta_{ap}^{rs}(k, t). \tag{9.10}$$

Given the experienced generalized travel costs $c_{mp}^{rs}(k)$, each traveller is assumed to simultaneously choose the route and departure time that he or she perceives to have the least travel costs, yielding a stochastic user-equilibrium assignment. Assuming that the random components of the generalized travel costs are independently (which may not hold if routes overlap) and identically extreme value type I distributed, then, according to McFadden (1974), the joint probability of choosing route p and departure time k is given by the following multinomial logit (MNL) model:

$$\psi_{mp}^{rs}(k) = \frac{\exp[-\mu c_{mp}^{rs}(k)]}{\sum_{p' \in P^{rs}} \sum_{k'} \exp[-\mu c_{mp'}^{rs}(k')]}, \forall (r, s), p \in P^{rs}, m. \tag{9.11}$$

Given the class-specific travel demand D_m^{rs}, the dynamic class-specific route flows can be determined by:

$$f_{mp}^{rs}(k) = \psi_{mp}^{rs}(k) D_m^{rs}, \forall (r, s), p \in P^{rs}, m. \tag{9.12}$$

Solving the DTA model is basically a fixed-point problem since generalized route-travel costs yield route flows, while route flows affect the travel times and therefore the generalized route-travel costs. The relationship between the route flows and the travel times is given by the dynamic network loading component.

Dynamic network loading component
The dynamic network loading (DNL) component 'simulates' the route flows on the network, yielding link flows, link volumes and link travel times. The DNL model used in this chapter is a simple system of equations adapted from Chabini (2000) and Bliemer and Bovy (2003), in which the flow propagation equation is simplified by assuming that there are no subintervals within one time interval, and that the link travel time is stationary. In this case, the equations are similar to those proposed by Ran and Boyce (1996).

The following set of equations describe the dynamic network loading model:

$$v_{ap}^{rs}[t + \tilde{\tau}_a(t)] = u_{a\pi}^{rs}(t), \qquad (9.13)$$

$$u_{ap}^{rs}(t) = \begin{cases} \sum_m f_{mp}^{rs}(t) & \text{if } a \text{ is the first link on route } p, \\ v_{a'p}^{rs}(t), & \text{if } a' \text{ is the previous link on route } p. \end{cases} \qquad (9.14)$$

$$u_a(t) = \sum_{(r,s)} \sum_{p \in P^{rs}} u_{ap}^{rs}(t). \qquad (9.15)$$

$$v_a(t) = \sum_{(r,s)} \sum_{p \in P^{rs}} v_{ap}^{rs}(t). \qquad (9.16)$$

$$x_a(t) = \sum_{w \le t} u_a(w) - v_a(w). \qquad (9.17)$$

$$\tau_a(t) = \tau_a^0 + b_a x_a(t). \qquad (9.18)$$

The flow propagation equations in equation (9.13), which describe the propagation of the inflows through the link and therefore determine the outflows, relate the inflows $u_{ap}^{rs}(t)$ and outflows $v_{ap}^{rs}(t)$ of link a at time interval t of vehicles travelling on route p from r to s. This equation simply states that traffic that enters link a at time t will exit the link when the link travel time $\tau_a(t)$ elapses. Note that since we are dealing with a discrete-time problem, the link exit time $t + \tau_a(t)$ needs to be an integer value. Therefore,

$\tilde{\tau}_a(t)$ is used, which simply rounds off the travel time (expressed in time intervals) to the nearest integer.

Equation (9.14) describes the flow conservation equations. If link a is the first link on a route, the inflow rate is equal to the corresponding route flows determined by the simultaneous route and departure-time choice model. Since we have assumed that all vehicles travel at the same speed, all travellers can be combined in the DNL model by summing them up. If link a is not the first link on a route, then the link inflow rate is equal to the link outflow rate of the previous link.

Equations (9.15–17) are definitions. The first two simply state that the total link inflows $u_a(t)$ (or outflows $v_a(t)$) are determined by adding all link inflows (or outflows) for all routes that flow into (out of) link a at that time interval. Equation (9.17) defines the number of vehicles on link a at the beginning of time interval t, $x_a(t)$, which is by definition equal to the total number of vehicles that have entered the link until time interval t, $\sum_{w \leq t} u_a(w)$, minus the total number of vehicles that have exited the link, $\sum_{w \leq t} v_a(w)$.

Finally, equation (9.18) relates, for each link a, the number of vehicles to the travel time on that link as an increasing function, where each link has a free-flow travel time τ_a^0, and a delay component $b_a x_a(t)$ (with b_a a non-negative parameter).

9.4 SOLUTION ALGORITHM

Each component of the optimal toll design problem can be solved using various types of algorithms. The outline of the complete algorithm for the case of variable tolls is as follows. The algorithm starts with specifying the grid of considered toll levels for all links to be tolled, satisfying the constraints (lower and upper bounds). In each iteration, the algorithm solves a DTA problem (that is, finds a dynamic stochastic multiclass user equilibrium solution) based on the current toll levels and sets new tolls that can potentially optimize the objective functions described in equations (9.6) or (9.7). Because the algorithm is a grid-search method it stops after all feasible toll levels in the grid have been considered. At this stage of the research, the focus is mainly on investigating the framework of the model and the properties of the (upper-level) solutions for different objectives and tolling schemes, and not on the development of algorithms. More efficient algorithms will be developed in future research. Moreover, although interesting, properties of the lower level (DTA problem), such as existence, uniqueness and convergence of the algorithm, will not be discussed here, as this is beyond the scope of the chapter. The interested reader is referred to, for example, Bliemer (2001). The two-stage iterative grid-search procedure for the optimal time-varying toll problem with DTA (including joint route and departure-time choice) can be outlined as follows:

Input: Network $G = (N, A)$, set of tolled links $\overline{A}$, set of tolled time intervals $\overline{T}_a$, link tolling patterns $\phi_a(t)$, travel demand D_m^{rs}, logit scale parameter μ, free-flow link travel times τ_a^0, link delay parameters b_a, number of DTA iterations J, grid dimensions I_a, road authority objective.

Output: Optimal maximum toll levels $\overline{\theta}^*$, optimal value of objective function Z_{rev}^* or Z_{time}^*.

1. *Outer loop: PRICING*
    Step 1:   [Initialization] The maximum toll-level grid for each link a is given by:

$$\overline{\theta}_a^{(i)} = \overline{\theta}_a^{min} + \frac{i}{I_a}(\overline{\theta}_a^{max} - \overline{\theta}_a^{min}), \ i = 0, \ ..., \ I_a.$$

All combinations of all maximum toll levels for all links determine the set of grid vectors $\overline{\theta}^{(i)} \equiv [\overline{\theta}_a^{(i)}]$, which contains $I \equiv \Pi_a(I_a + 1)$ elements. Set $i := 1$ and set $Z^* = +\infty$.

    Step 2:   [Set toll values] Select grid point i for the toll levels, yielding tolls $\theta_a^{(i)}(t)$ from equations (9.3–5).

2. *Inner loop: DTA*
    Step 3a: [Initialization] Set $j := +1$. Assume an empty network and free-flow network conditions, that is $\tau_a^{(j)}(t) = \tau_a^0$.

    Step 3b: [Compute dynamic route costs] Compute travel costs $c_{mp}^{rs,(j)}(k)$ using equations (9.8–10).

    Step 3c: [Compute new intermediate route flows] Determine the new intermediate dynamic route flow pattern $\tilde{f}_{mp}^{rs,(j)}(k)$ using equations (9.11–12).

    Step 3d: [Flow averaging] Use the method of successive averages (MSA) to update the route flows, that is,

$$f_{mp}^{rs,(j)}(k) = f_{mp}^{rs,(j)}(k) + \frac{1}{j}[\tilde{f}_{mp}^{rs,(j)}(k) - f_{mp}^{rs,(j)}(k)].$$

    Step 3e: [Perform dynamic network loading] Dynamically load $f_{mp}^{rs,(j)}(k)$ onto the network using equations (9.13–18), yielding new link travel times $\tau_a^{(j+1)}(t)$.

    Step 3f: [Convergence of DTA level] If convergence has been reached (for example, if the dynamic duality gap is sufficiently small), go to Step 4; otherwise set $j: = j + 1$ and return to Step 3b.

Step 4: [Compute objective function] Compute the objective function $Z(\theta^{(i)})$ using equations (9.6) or (9.7). If $Z(\theta^{(i)}) < Z^*$, then set $Z^* = Z(\theta^{(i)})$ and set $\overline{\theta}^* = \overline{\theta}^{(i)}$.

Step 5: [Convergence of road-pricing level] While $i < N$, set $i := i + 1$ and return to Step 2. Otherwise, the algorithm is terminated and $\overline{\theta}^*$ is the set of optimal toll levels.

Performing this simple iterative procedure, we explore all possibilities for all toll-level combinations and find the optimal value of the objective function. Regarding the convergence of this algorithm, the inner DTA loop using the widely used heuristic MSA procedure typically converges to an equilibrium solution, although convergence cannot be proven. In the outer road-pricing loop the whole solution space is investigated with a certain grid accuracy (yielding a finite number of solutions that are evaluated).

9.5   CASE STUDIES

9.5.1   Network Description, Travel Demand and Input Parameters

The solution procedure proposed in the previous section has been applied to a small network (see Figure 9.3). The network consists of just a single OD pair connected by two non-overlapping paths where only link 2 is tolled. Since there is only one OD pair, we shall ignore the OD subindices (r, s), in the variables.

Two user classes with a different VOT are distinguished. The total travel demand for departure period $K = \{1, \ldots, 20\}$ from node 1 to node 3 is $D = 86$, 50 per cent of which are high VOT travellers and 50 per cent low VOT travellers. The following parameter values are used on the route level: preferred departure time $\varsigma = 10$; preferred arrival time $\xi = 15$; VOT for class

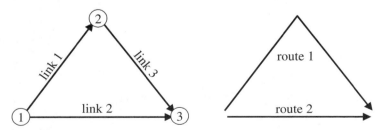

Figure 9.3   Network for case studies

1 $\alpha_1 = 0.25$; VOT for class 2 $\alpha_2 = 0.75$; penalty for deviating from preferred departure time $\beta = 0.25$; penalty for deviating from preferred arrival time $\gamma = 1$; and the scale parameter in the MNL model is $\mu = 0.8$. On the link level, we assume that route 1 with a free-flow travel time of 7.0 time intervals is longer than route 2 (3.0 time intervals) by setting the free-flow link travel times in equation (9.18) to $\tau_1^0 = \tau_3^0 = 3.5$ and $\tau_2^0 = 3.0$. Furthermore, it is assumed that the first route never has congestion, hence $b_1 = b_3 = 0$, while congestion is possible on link 2 for which we set $b_2 = 0.005$ in equation (9.18).

9.5.2   Zero Toll Case

For the case in which the tolls are zero on link 2, the route flows and costs are depicted in Figure 9.4. The flows are almost evenly spread between the two routes. The departure-time profiles indicate that travellers who use the longer route 1 will depart earlier in order to arrive as close as possible to their preferred arrival time. Since high VOT users attach a higher weight to the travel time in their costs, more high VOT users will be using route 2 as this route will typically have a lower travel time (even with some congestion), whereas route 1 is primarily used by low VOT users who mainly take the penalty for arriving late or early at the destination into account.

In Section 9.3.1 three different tolling schemes were mentioned: namely, uniform, quasi-uniform and variable (see equations (9.1–3)). All three tolling regimes will be considered in the case studies below. Note that, in this case study, with only a single link (link 2) tolled, determining the optimal toll for each tolling regime (even for the variable tolling scheme) requires that only a single optimum toll level, $\bar{\theta}_2^*$, be found. The uniform tolling scheme does not have any parameters. For the quasi-uniform tolling scheme, we assume that a toll will be levied in the peak period, that is, the tolling period is $\bar{T} = \{8, 9, 10, 11, 12,\}$ in equation (9.1). In the variable tolling scheme only periods 9, 10 and 11 will be tolled, with fixed proportions 0.6, 1.0, and 0.6, that is:

$$\phi_2(t) = \begin{cases} 1.0, & \text{if } t = 10; \\ 0.6, & \text{if } t = 9, 11; \\ 0, & \text{otherwise.} \end{cases} \qquad (9.19)$$

9.5.3   Optimal Tolls for Maximizing Total Revenues

Assume that the road authority aims to maximize total revenues, as formulated in equation (9.6), by selecting the best tolling scheme and the best

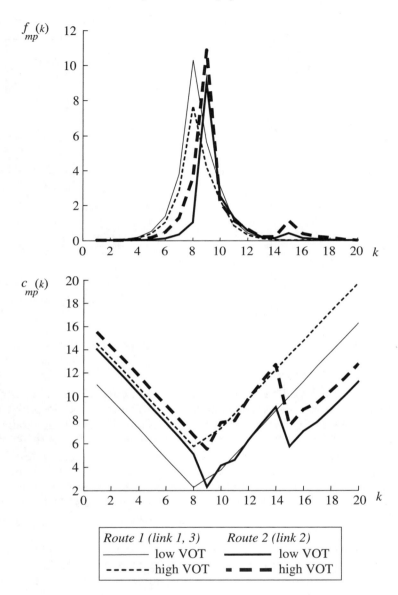

Figure 9.4   Route flows and costs in the case of zero tolls

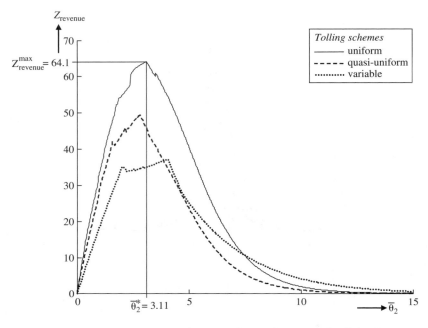

Figure 9.5   Total revenue for different tolling schemes and toll levels

toll level. The three different tolling regimes mentioned above will be considered. For each tolling scheme and for each toll level, the DTA problem can be solved. In Figure 9.5, the total revenues are plotted for each tolling scheme for all $0 \le \bar{\theta}_2 \le 15$ (although not shown here, in all cases the DTA model converged). If the toll level is zero, there are clearly no revenues. For very high toll levels, all travellers will choose to travel on the untolled route, which also results in zero revenues. As can be observed from Figure 9.5, uniform tolling with $\bar{\theta}_2 = 3.11$ yields the highest revenues. The variable tolling scheme is not able to provide high revenues because of the small number of tolled time periods.

The route flows and costs are also depicted in Figure 9.6, together with the optimal toll levels for the objective of maximizing revenues. Compared with the case of zero tolls in Figure 9.4, it can be seen that travellers shift towards (non-congested and untolled) route 1 and also shift their departure time (mostly later). Furthermore, it can be observed that there are many more travellers with a high VOT on tolled route 2 than travellers with a low VOT. This is to be expected, as travellers with a high VOT care less about toll costs and more about a short trip time.

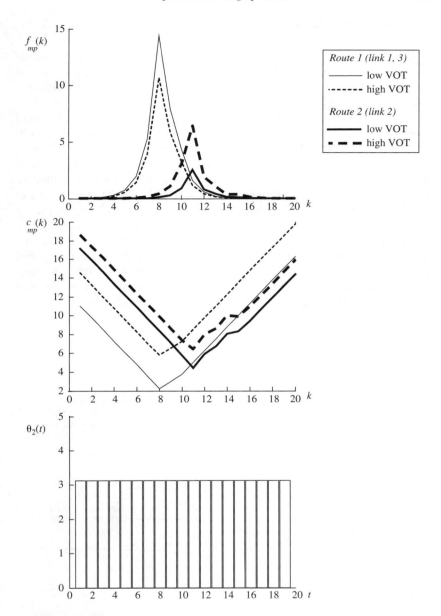

Figure 9.6   Route flows, costs and toll levels when maximizing revenues

9.5.4 Optimal Tolls for Minimizing Total Travel Time

In this case study, the road authority aims at minimizing total travel time on the network (see equation (9.2)) by selecting the best tolling scheme and the best toll level. Figure 9.7 depicts the total travel times for different tolling schemes and toll levels.

As can be observed from Figure 9.7, it seems possible to decrease the total travel time on the network by imposing a toll on congested route 2. High toll levels will push all travellers during the tolled period away from route 2 to the longer route 1, again yielding higher total travel times. Variable tolling with $\bar{\theta}_2^* = 3.24$ (yielding $\theta_2^*(10) = 3.24$ and $\theta_2^*(9) = \theta_2^*(11) = 1.99$, according to equations (9.1) and (9.17)) results in the lowest total travel time. The objective function looks somewhat irregular. However, this can be explained by the rounding off of the link travel times in flow propagation equation (9.13).

The route costs and flows are depicted in Figure 9.8, together with the optimal toll levels for the objective of minimizing total travel time. Compared with Figure 9.6, it can be clearly seen that there are more departure-time changes because only the peak period is tolled, leading to a better spread of traffic over space and time, and therefore lower total travel time.

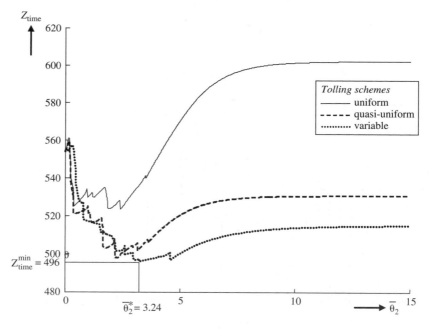

Figure 9.7   Total travel time for different tolling schemes and toll levels

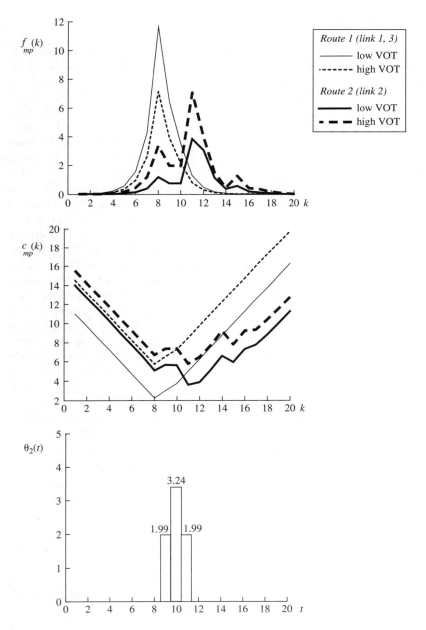

Figure 9.8   Route flows, costs and toll levels when minimizing total travel time

9.5.5   Discussion

The results of both objectives (maximizing total toll revenues and minimizing total travel time) where different tolling schemes (uniform, quasi-
uniform and variable) are applied are given in Table 9.1.

These results show that, in the case of maximizing total toll revenues, the
best tolling scheme is uniform with toll level $\bar{\theta}_2 = 3.11$. However, this toll
will yield a high total travel time (534.48). On the other hand, in the case of
minimizing total travel time, the variable tolling scheme with $\bar{\theta}_2 = 3.24$ per-
forms best. However, this toll will yield a low total toll revenue (35.25). In
other words, maximizing total toll revenues and minimizing total travel
time are opposite objectives. This can be explained as follows. In maximizing toll revenues, the road authority would like to have as many travellers
as possible on the tolled route, and hence try to push as few of them as possible away from the tolled alternative by imposing the toll. In contrast,
when minimizing total travel time, the road authority would like to spread
the traffic as much as possible in time and space, and hence try to influence
as many travellers as possible to choose other departure times and routes.
Using a uniform tolling scheme, travellers do not change their departure
times, making it suitable for maximizing revenues. In the variable tolling
scheme, on the other hand, other departure times are good alternatives,
making it suitable for minimizing travel time. In any case, depending on the
objectives of the road authority, there are different optimal tolling schemes
with different toll levels.

*Table 9.1   Comparison of toll revenues and total travel time for different
objectives*

Objective: maximize total toll revenue

Tolling scheme	Optimal toll	Total revenue	Total travel time
Uniform	3.11	*64.15*	534.48
Quasi-uniform	2.82	49.50	503.42
Variable	4.04	37.13	498.26

Objective: minimize total travel time

Tolling scheme	Optimal toll	Total revenue	Total travel time
Uniform	2.41	60.81	523.56
Quasi-uniform	2.27	45.56	497.91
Variable	3.24	35.25	*496.02*

9.6 CONCLUSIONS

A mathematical bi-level optimization problem has been formulated for the optimal toll network design problem. The road authority has some policy objectives, which they may optimize by imposing tolls. Second-best scenarios are considered in this chapter, assuming that only a subset of links can be tolled. Different tolling schemes can be selected by the road authority, such as (quasi-)uniform and variable tolling schemes, each having a different impact on the policy objective. As a result of tolls, travellers may change their route and departure times. Heterogeneous travellers with high and low VOTs are considered.

The aim of the research was to investigate the feasibility of the dynamic model framework proposed in this chapter and to investigate properties of the objective function for different objectives and tolling schemes. The complex optimization problem has been solved using a simple grid search method, but for more practical case studies more sophisticated algorithms will be developed in the future.

In the case studies it is shown that policy objectives can indeed be optimized by imposing tolls, and that different policy objectives lead to different optimal tolling schemes and toll levels. Keeping the total travel demand fixed, and introducing a uniform (fixed) toll, travellers can avoid the toll only by route changes, not by changing departure time, a scheme which leads to higher toll revenues. On the other hand, having a variable toll enables travellers to avoid tolls by changing their departure time, a scheme which yields lower total travel times.

REFERENCES

Abou-Zeid, M. (2003), 'Models and algorithms for the optimization of traffic flows and emissions using dynamic routing and pricing', MSc thesis, Massachusetts Institute of Technology, Cambridge, MA.

Beckmann, M.J., C.B. McGuire and C.B. Winsten (1956), *Studies in the Economics of Transportation*, New Haven, CT: Yale University Press.

Ben-Akiva, M., A. De Palma and P. Kanaroglou (1986), 'Dynamic model of peak period traffic congestion with elastic arrival rates', *Transportation Science*, **20** (2), 164–81.

Bliemer, M.C.J. (2001), 'Analytical dynamic traffic assignment with interacting user classes: theoretical advances and applications using a variational inequality approach', PhD Thesis, Delft University of Technology, The Netherlands.

Bliemer, M.C.J. and P.H.L. Bovy (2003), 'Quasi-variational inequality formulation of the multiclass dynamic traffic assignment problem', *Transportation Research B*, **37**, 501–19.

Chabini, I. (2000), 'The analytical network loading problem: formulation, solution algorithms and computer implementations', *Transportation Research Record*, no. 1771, 191–200.

Dafermos, S. (1973), 'Toll patterns for multiclass-user transportation networks', *Transportation Science*, 7, 211–23.

Joksimovic, D., M.C.J. Bliemer and P.H.L. Bovy (2005), 'Optimal toll design problem in dynamic traffic networks – with joint route and departure time choice', *Transportation Research Record*, no. 1923, 61–72.

Mahmassani, H.S. and R. Herman (1984), 'Dynamic user equilibrium departure time and route choice in idealized traffic arterials', *Transportation Science*, 18 (4), 362–84.

May, A.D. and D.S. Milne (2000), 'Effects of alternative road pricing systems on network performance', *Transportation Research A*, 34 (6), 407–36.

McFadden, D. (1974), 'Conditional logit analysis of qualitative choice behaviour', in P. Zarembka (ed.), *Frontiers of Econometrics*, New York: Academic Press, pp. 105–42.

Pigou, A.C. (1920), *Wealth and Welfare*, London: Macmillan.

Ran, B. and D.E. Boyce (1996), *Modeling Dynamic Transportation Networks: An Intelligent Transportation System Oriented Approach*, 2nd edn, Berlin: Springer-Verlag.

Verhoef, E.T. (2002), 'Second-best congestion pricing in general static transportation networks with elastic demand', *Regional Science and Urban Economics*, 32, 281–310.

Viti, F., S.F. Catalano, M. Li, C.D.R. Lindveld and H.J. van Zuylen (2003), 'An optimization problem with dynamic route-departure time choice and pricing', in *Proceedings of the 82nd Annual Meeting of the Transportation Research Board*, Washington, DC.

Wie, B. and R.L. Tobin (1998), 'Dynamic congestion pricing models for general traffic networks', *Transportation Record B*, 32 (5), 313–27.

Yang, H. (1999), 'System optimum, stochastic user equilibrium and optimal link tolls', *Transportation Science*, 33, 354–60.

Yang, H. and H.-J. Huang (1998), 'Principle of marginal-cost pricing: how does it work in a general road network?', *Transportation Research A*, 32 (1), 45–54.

PART III

Acceptability of different road-pricing policies

10. Acceptability of road pricing[1]

Tommy Gärling, Cecilia Jakobsson, Peter Loukopoulos and Satoshi Fujii

10.1 INTRODUCTION

The urgent economic, social and environmental problems now being experienced worldwide as a result of increasing trends in car ownership and use have been amply documented (for example, Goodwin, 1996; Crawford, 2000; Black, 2001; Hine and Grieco, 2003; Whitelegg, 2003). Various policy measures that aim to reduce the levels of car-use-related congestion, noise and air pollution have been proposed and implemented. Since the proposed policy measures focus on changing or reducing demand for private car use, they are generally referred to as either 'mobility management' or 'travel demand management' (TDM) (Pas, 1995; Kitamura et al., 1997).

Road pricing (RP) has, in its various forms, been on the political agenda for a long time. One of the first mentions of charging motorists for using urban road space in order to moderate traffic levels can be found in the Smeed Report (Ministry of Transport, 1964). Yet, since the report was issued, very few successful implementations have been made, notable exceptions being those in Singapore and a host of Norwegian cities. On the other hand, reports of failures abound, as in Hong Kong (for example, Hau, 1990), Stockholm (for example, Ahlstrand, 1998), and the Netherlands (for example, Hårsman, 2003). A critical turning-point appears to have been reached, however, following the successful implementation of the London Congestion Charging Scheme on 17 February 2003 – a response to that city's severe congestion and environmental problems (Richards, 2006; Santos, Chapter 14 of this volume). This success, coupled with the re-election of London's Mayor Ken Livingstone, whose election platform included enlarging the scheme, has given a new lease of life to many schemes that have been contemplated but never implemented. Even cities which had previously failed, notably Stockholm, have taken steps towards the implementation of such schemes.

While RP has been endorsed by transport economists (for example, Ubbels and Verhoef, 2007), the public's response has almost always been negative at the outset and pre-implementation stage (Jones, 1995, 2003). Yet, in fact, after experiencing such schemes in practice, public acceptance tends to increase (Tretvik, 2003), in fact, even to the point where, as in London, a majority may support further extensions of a current scheme. It is such documented differences across time that has prompted Stockholm to take up the RP issue again, several years after failing in its attempts to implement such a scheme. This time, however, the authorities have planned a full-size, fully operational field trial so that the public has a chance to experience the scheme in practice and before a referendum[2] is held at a later point (17 September 2006) concerning whether the scheme is to be made a permanent fixture.

In this chapter, Section 10.2 discusses some issues related to the measurement of the acceptability of RP. Section 10.3 presents a theoretical framework to account for determinants of acceptability. In Section 10.4 we test a model derived from this theoretical framework using data from a survey made in conjunction with the Stockholm RP field trial. Section 10.5 presents the conclusions, including some implications for future research.

10.2   MEASUREMENT OF ACCEPTABILITY AND ACCEPTANCE OF RP

In research on how car users and the general public at large respond to proposed or implemented RP schemes, their responses are frequently referred to as 'acceptability' or 'acceptance'. 'Acceptance' denotes a positive evaluation of an implemented RP scheme, implying perhaps that there are no or only a few protests to be expected. In contrast, acceptability is used to refer to 'prospective acceptance', that is, a statement to the effect that, if the RP scheme is implemented, it will be accepted. A related issue is whether acceptability, acceptance or both refer to a dichotomous or continuous response scale, and if the latter is the case, what scale properties (ordinal, interval or ratio) the resulting measures have. For instance, if dichotomous responses are analysed, does this mean that researchers assume that there is a *true* dichotomy? Or is their aim only to present a simplified picture of the public response (for example, the percentage of people who believe that it is acceptable or who accept)? Is it theoretically sound to assume one or the other? Schade (2003) highlights additional conceptual fuzziness by noting that it is frequently unclear what one wants to know. Questions that need to be carefully addressed include: what should be accepted? By whom (the general public, car users, and so on) should it be accepted? Under which conditions will it be accepted (for example, for what purposes the fees will be used, how charging is made)?

Measurement issues like those discussed here have been dealt with in social psychological research on attitudes (Gärling et al., 1998, 2003). Drawing on this research may therefore help to clarify the issues. 'Attitude' refers to a relatively stable evaluative response to some attitude object (Eagly and Chaiken, 1993, 1998; Gärling et al., 2003). An attitude is less influenced by situational factors than preferences are but is less stable than personality traits (Ajzen, 1987). An 'attitude object' can be anything that is discriminated or held in mind. It may be abstract such as a value (freedom, equality or health) or concrete, such as an activity (driving), a person (a politician or a political ideology), or a transport policy such as road pricing.

Over the years a number of methods for measuring attitudes have been developed (for an overview, see Dawes and Smith, 1985) including self-report, physiological and behavioural. For instance, a commonly used self-report method is to ask participants in a survey to check numerical scales anchored by adjective pairs such as positive–negative, attractive–unattractive and good–bad. Including several such scales makes it possible to use multivariate statistical methods for determining the reliability and construct validity (dimensionality) of the composite measure (averaged across the scales) of a positive–negative attitude. A more tedious method is to ask participants to agree or disagree with factual statements. Such a method assesses *opinions* but may be turned into an attitude measure if the statements are independently scaled on a positive–negative attitude dimension. However, without such scaling, the degree of positive or negative attitude from expressions of opinions remains speculative.

In some previous research (as reviewed by, for example, Steg and Schuitema, 2007), an analysis of the acceptability and acceptance of road pricing has drawn on the theory of reasoned action (TRA) (Fishbein and Ajzen, 1975), or its predecessor the theory of planned behaviour (TPB) (Ajzen, 1991). In both these theories, attitude (A) is defined as the aggregated positive or negative evaluations (e) of salient beliefs about the properties of the attitude object (or outcomes of a choice), multiplied by the probability (b) that the attitude object has these properties (or that the outcomes are materialized):

$$A = \Sigma be.$$

Acceptability may be interpreted as an attitude towards RP in general, a particular RP scheme, or, possibly, the implementation of a particular RP scheme (say, in three months). As an example, if reduced congestion is a *desired* outcome of a particular RP scheme, the attitude would be positive if one believes that this is a *likely* outcome. The positive attitude would, however, be reduced if diminished air pollution is considered to be a desirable but unlikely outcome.

Another relevant concept in TRA and TPB is 'behavioural intention' (I), defined as either the perceived likelihood that an individual will perform a particular kind of behaviour (also referred to as an 'expectation' that the kind of behaviour will be performed) or the degree of commitment to a plan to perform the kind of behaviour (Ajzen and Fishbein, 1980). In TRA, intention is related to attitude and 'subjective norm' (SN) as follows:[3]

$$I = w_A A + w_{SN} SN,$$

where SN is a measure of perceived social pressure. It is defined in an analogous way to attitude as $SN = \Sigma bm$ expressing the aggregated belief (b) of approval from salient referents (society, influential family members, or friends) multiplied by the motivation (m) to comply. The ws are weights that are allowed to vary with the particular kind of behaviour and context.

Acceptance may alternatively be interpreted as an attitude towards the RP scheme after its implementation, or an *intention* of behaving in a certain way, for instance, not to protest. Acceptance may thus be related to different kinds of overt behaviours such as voting in a referendum. However, this is only a possibility – the correspondence between attitudes, intentions and behaviour is less than perfect (for a review, see Eagly and Chaiken, 1993). We may also mention the construct of consumer satisfaction, as defined in, for instance, the 'expectancy–disconfirmation' model proposed by Oliver (1997). A third interpretation of acceptance is thus that it reflects that people (after some time) are *satisfied* with the outcome of the implementation of an RP scheme.

In discrete choice theory (McFadden, 2001), a binary choice is mapped on a continuous preference (or utility). In revealed preferences, the binary choice is 'forced' on the person: for instance, a choice between voting for or against an alternative (or possibly to abstain). Note that the behaviour is dichotomous whereas the latent preference is continuous. Given this latter theoretical assumption, no objection would be raised to measuring acceptability and acceptance as continuous variables if this is feasible. Methods developed for measuring attitudes may be used. In fact, when more information is thus collected, the better the possibility to model the determinants of acceptance.

10.3   THEORETICAL FRAMEWORK

In this section we introduce a theoretical framework (Gärling et al., 2002) that has been used to understand behavioural responses to TDM measures.

We shall propose how the theoretical framework can be extended to account for the acceptability of RP.

Starting with the observation that car users make choices among various travel options, we can ask under what circumstances such choices are changed. It appears to be believed that this depends exclusively on whether the travel options are changed: for instance, if car use becomes more expensive than the alternatives. However, this belief is based on the false view that car users are completely stimulus bound. A more valid conceptualization is that the changes in travel options (and other factors such as information campaigns and word of mouth) trigger *deliberation*. Such deliberation may not otherwise take place since car-use choices are frequently automatized (Verplanken et al., 1997; Fujii and Gärling, 2005, 2007), implying among other things that information about alternatives are frequently not sought and processed. A field experiment by Garvill et al. (2003) obtained support that deliberation is a necessary step for change in car use. Likewise, in another field experiment, Jakobsson et al. (2002) showed that increased monetary costs of car use had little effect unless participants were forced to make plans for how to change their car use. The additional charges probably motivated them to do this more meticulously than they would have done otherwise.

The outcome of deliberation is not easily predicted. It can at least be assumed that it takes some time. In addition, changes in car use extend in time and need to be described as a process of change and non-change. Thus, any instant effect is unlikely. Furthermore, car-use change is not always unidimensional. An RP scheme may in fact lead to different patterns of *adaptations* among different car users (Arentze et al., 2004; Loukopolous et al., 2005).

Gärling et al. (2002; and see also Loukopoulos et al., 2007a) drew on one social–psychological theory (Carver and Scheier, 1998) in their theoretical analysis of car users' adaptations to TDM measures such as RP. In this analysis the setting of goals[4] (Locke and Latham, 1990) is posited to be the outcome of the deliberation process. In the case of the implementation of RP, such goals may be a certain degree of car-use change or reduction, but it may also be some other change in spending (or no change in a high-income household). A high degree of commitment and a large specific goal are known to increase the likelihood that the goal is attained. Whether the goal is forced on the car user or self-imposed does not seem to be important, however (Locke et al., 1988).

Impediments to the attainment of car-use change goals were analysed by Fujii and Gärling (2003). They noted that such impediments include both habits and impulses (no, or less deliberation). As demonstrated by Loukopoulos et al. (2005), attainment of car-use change goals is a process entailing choices of adaptation alternatives, such as car pooling, trip chaining, trip suppressing and mode switching contingent on subjective assessments of cost and effectiveness (degree of goal attainment). Of importance here is that car users (like people in general) are unwilling to change activities they like and have become used to. A number of well-known phenomena such as status quo or inaction bias (Samuelson and Zeckhausen, 1988), as well as habit formation (Ouellette and Wood, 1998), bear witness to this. Car users are, according to a 'minimal cost of change' principle, likely to start by making the less costly changes. If these changes are insufficient, as determined by negative feedback, other more costly changes are chosen. However, in this process several things may go wrong. First, the more costly changes may be too costly, in which case the change goal is abandoned or reduced. Second, information about effectiveness is generally delayed and likely to be imprecise. This is known to have detrimental effects on goal attainment (Brehmer, 1995). Cost is also directly felt and may therefore override effectiveness, leading to short-sightedness.

Why should road pricing ever be acceptable to car users? Our hypothesis is that acceptability (and acceptance) increases with benefits and decreases with costs. Thus, if a car-use change goal has been set, acceptability is inversely related to the perceived cost of its implementation: for instance, depending on whether or not viable alternatives exist. In addition, if no car-use change goal has been set, the anticipated benefits obtained from observing others doing this would increase acceptability.

However, car users (like people in general) are not only self-interested (Stern and Dietz, 1994; Garvill, 1999). They are also concerned about their fellow citizens. Being aware of the problems for others (unfairness, health hazards) has been shown to be a motivating factor that increases acceptability (Jakobsson et al., 2000).

In summary, both factors related to self-interest (set car-use change goal) and a concern for others (fairness, health hazards) are conjectured to be determinants of the acceptability of RP schemes. Previous research has demonstrated a strong and direct relationship between perceptions of fairness of an RP scheme, anticipated infringement of freedom (Jakobsson et al., 2000; Bamberg and Rölle, 2003), and acceptability of the scheme, which together account for nearly 70 per cent of the variance. When also including perceived effectiveness as a direct determinant, and problem awareness (of health hazards and environmental effects) as an indirect determinant of acceptability, Bamberg and Rölle (2003) found that both were important, with the proportion of variance accounted for increasing to approximately 80 per cent. The intention to change car use was also found to have an influence on acceptability.

10.4   AN EMPIRICAL STUDY OF PUBLIC ACCEPTABILITY

10.4.1   Hypotheses

In connection with the planned field trial in Stockholm, an opportunity arose to use collected evaluation data (Trivector, 2004) to examine the determinants of acceptability and car-change goals prior to the beginning of the field trial. The following hypotheses were derived and tested.

An awareness of the extent and seriousness of the problems associated with car traffic should be associated with greater acceptability, as should greater perceived effectiveness. Furthermore, the more a person expects to have to change his/her car use (that is, size of car-use change goals), the lower the acceptability. Car users are assumed to reduce or change their car use by first choosing less costly (and less effective) change alternatives; costlier and more effective alternatives are only chosen after negative feedback indicating that the desired level of change has not been achieved. Loukopoulos et al. (2005) noted that the costliness of a given alternative varies as a function of socio-demographic characteristics (for example, cycling is costlier for the elderly), trip purpose (for example, cycling for grocery shopping) and characteristics of the local area or transport system (for example, walking is costlier in suburban neighbourhoods built around cul-de-sac systems). It may then be hypothesized that individuals residing in areas where it is easier to use public transport set higher car-use change goals. Thus, when greater ease of using public transport is the determinant of higher car-use change, the less freedom is limited (in so far as a person is able to conduct activities without the car) and the less costly is the adaptation. Thus, perceived ease of public transport use would counteract the negative effect of car-use change goal on acceptability.

To test these hypotheses, two models were estimated from survey data collected in November and December 2004, more than a year before the commencement of the field trial on 3 January 2006 (for further details, see Loukopoulos et al., 2007b). Although the questions in the survey were framed as attitudes to the RP *trial*, it may be assumed that the public's reactions would not differ much if the implementation were permanent.

10.4.2   The Stockholm RP Field Trial

The main purpose of the Stockholm RP field trial was to assess whether the efficiency of the traffic system can be enhanced by congestion charges. The objective is to test the effects of a charge (varying from SEK 10 to 20 (SEK $1.00 \approx €0.09$) from 06.30 to 18.30 hours on weekdays) on congestion, accessibility, and the environment. The aim is to obtain a 10–15 per cent reduction in traffic, higher average speeds, less air pollution, more resources for public transport, and a general improvement in the city environment.

The system is an electronically managed charging system. Given that the appropriate equipment is installed in a vehicle, drivers are charged automatically when passing into or out of the charging zone. The maximum charge per day is SEK 60.

The first stage of the trial began on 22 August 2005 by improving the public transport system. To further assist travel by alternative modes, a large number of new park-and-ride facilities are currently being built in the region and already existing park-and-ride facilities are being made more attractive.

10.4.3 Survey

The total sample recruited to the survey included 1600 respondents (200 respondents drawn from each of the eight following regions: southern and northern inner-city areas, southern and northern outer-city areas, inner and outer northern regional areas, and inner and outer southern regional areas). The response rate was 59 per cent.

Only automobile drivers *not* residing in the southern and northern inner-city areas, and who also had answered the questionnaire fully with no missing answers, were included in the present analyses. This resulted in a sample of 265 persons (176 or 66 per cent male and 89 or 34 per cent female) divided into six age classes: 18–24 years (10.9 per cent), 25–34 years (17.7 per cent), 35–44 years (27.5 per cent), 45–54 years (18.9 per cent), 55–64 years (20 per cent) and over 65 years (4.9 per cent). No questions concerning income were asked in order to minimize non-response.

The survey obtained the following information: (i) problem awareness; (ii) perceived effectiveness; (iii) acceptability; (iv) car-use change goal; and (v) perceived ease of public transport (PT) use.

Problem awareness was measured with five questions regarding environmental problems (congestion on arterial roads leading into the city; congestion in the inner city; noise; air pollution; and traffic safety for pedestrians and/or cyclists) in Stockholm inner city during the hours 6.30–18.30 on weekdays. Responses were coded from 1–3 (no problem; minor problem; and serious problem). Averaging across questions yielded a composite measure with a Cronbach's alpha of 0.72. The mean problem awareness in the sample was 1.9 (SD = 0.5).

Perceived effectiveness was measured with six questions assessing beliefs concerning the extent to which the trial will affect and reduce environmental problems (less congestion on the arterial roads leading into the city; less congestion in the city; less air pollution; less noise from traffic; improved safety for pedestrians and cyclists; and improved public transport services). Responses were coded from 1–3 ('not at all' to 'a great extent') with a composite measure formed by averaging across questions (Cronbach's alpha = 0.86) and with the mean perceived effectiveness being 1.8 (SD = 0.5).

Acceptability was measured with a single question asking respondents to evaluate from 1–4 (very bad to very good) the decision to go ahead with a full-scale trial. The mean level of acceptability was 2.5 (SD = 0.5).

Car-use change goal was measured by asking respondents how their car use (that is, driving to, through, and within the inner city area of Stockholm) would be affected during the charging period. Their car use was assessed on a 5-point scale ('substantially more use of the car' to 'substantially less use of the car'), with a mean change goal of 3.2 (SD = 0.6).

Finally, *perceived ease of PT use* was measured by asking respondents if it would be easy or difficult for them to use PT instead of the car for trips to/from or within Stockholm city during the charging period. Responses were dummy-coded (1 = easy, 0 = difficult) with 90 (34 per cent) respondents finding it easy to use public transport and 175 (66 per cent) finding it difficult.

10.4.4   Results

A regression analysis was conducted with *acceptability* as the dependent variable. The independent variables were *problem awareness, perceived effectiveness, car-use change goal* and *perceived ease of PT use*. The interactions between each of the first three variables and the fourth variable were also included, because their effect on acceptability may depend on the service level of PT offered by the municipality. The adjusted R^2 of the model was 0.34 ($F(7, 257) = 19.98, p < 0.001$); the interactions between perceived ease of PT use and both perceived effectiveness and problem awareness were not significant. These were, therefore, excluded and a reduced model was estimated. As seen in Table 10.1, the reduced model accounts for as much variance as the full model. Acceptability increases with problem awareness and perceived effectiveness, while acceptability decreases with the size of the car-use change goals. However, the main effect of the car-use change goal is modified by the interaction with perceived ease of PT use. This interaction suggests that the sign of the coefficient of goal varies as a function of perceived ease of PT use: when PT use is perceived to be difficult, the standardized regression coefficient for the car-use change goal is −0.34, while the corresponding figure is 0.23 when PT use is perceived to be easy. That is, high car-use change goals as a result of the RP trial are associated with higher acceptability when PT use is perceived to be easy than when it is perceived to be difficult.

Table 10.1   Results of regression analysis with acceptability as the dependent variable

Independent variable	r	p	b	β	t	p
Constant			0.636	–	1.33	0.184
Problem awareness	0.265	<0.001	0.276	0.13	2.47	0.014
Perceived effectiveness	0.545	<0.001	1.040	0.47	8.62	<0.001
Car-use change goal	0.128	0.038	−0.341	−0.19	−2.55	0.012
Perceived ease of PT use	0.218	<0.001	−1.523	−0.67	−2.45	0.015
Goal × Perceived ease of PT use	0.261	<0.001	0.569	0.90	3.04	0.003
Adj. $R^2 = 0.339$, $F(5, 259) = 28.12$, $p < 0.001$						

Note: PT = public transport.

Table 10.2   Results of regression analysis with car-use change goal as the dependent variable

Independent variable	r	p	b	β	t	p
Constant			2.610	–	15.68	<0.001
Problem awareness	0.125	0.042	0.110	0.09	1.50	0.135
Perceived effectiveness	0.199	0.001	0.161	0.13	2.06	0.040
Perceived ease of PT use	0.293	<0.001	0.350	0.27	4.62	<0.001
Adj. $R^2 = 0.107$, $F(3, 261) = 11.51$, $p < 0.001$						

Note: PT = public transport.

Another regression analysis was conducted with the *change goal* as the dependent variable. The independent variables were *problem awareness*, *perceived effectiveness*, and *ease of public transport use*; interaction effects were excluded from this model, which is presented in Table 10.2. The adjusted R^2 is significant but not larger than 0.107 (10.7 per cent of the variance accounted for). As can be seen, a higher goal to reduce car use is not affected by increases in problem awareness but by perceived effectiveness and ease of PT use.

10.4.5   Discussion

It may first be noted that, as compared with previous research (Jakobsson et al., 2000; Bamberg and Rölle, 2003), the percentages of variance accounted for in the regression analyses were substantially less. The likely

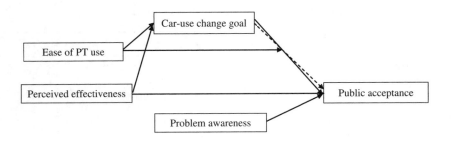

Note: The broken line denotes a negative effect; PT = public transport.

*Figure 10.1   Merged models of determinants of acceptability of road
pricing and car-use change goal*

reason is that *perceived fairness* was not included in the estimated models.
This factor has previously been found to have strong effects. Nevertheless,
putting the results together in Figure 10.1, additional insights are still provided into the other factors that influence car users' acceptability of road
pricing, as well as their stated car-use changes in response to any such
scheme. For example, while greater problem awareness is associated with
higher acceptability, it is not associated with a greater tendency to change
one's car use, presumably because the relevant factor here is perceived ease
of public transport use: when using public transport is less costly, then
greater car-use change goals are possible in response to an RP scheme. It
was also demonstrated that the perceived ease of public transport use (that
is, costliness of adaptation) is a particularly important factor as it interacts
with the car-use change goal, implying that an RP scheme that is implemented without considering the availability of public transport in an area
and that forces people to have high car-use change goals is likely to be unacceptable. The analyses also revealed that for an RP scheme to be acceptable,
it needs to be designed and planned in such a way that it is perceived to be
effective.

10.5   CONCLUSIONS

A main conclusion of this chapter is that acceptability of road pricing
reflects a conflict between self-interest (car-use change goal) and concern
for others (fairness, health hazards). In a series of experiments, Baron and
Jurney (1993) showed that participants were strongly opposed to the
implementation of a policy measure (increased gasoline taxes) that

Table 10.3   Proposed classification of TDM measures

Attribute	Definition
Market-based (vs. regulatory) mechanism	Increasing voluntary control at a cost
Targeting latent (vs. manifest) demand	Changing unobserved (vs. observed) car use
(Restriction of) Time scale	Hours of operation
(Restriction of) Spatial scale	Area of operation
Degree of coerciveness	Reducing car users' voluntary control
Bottom-up (vs. top-down) process	Empowering car users and increasing voluntary control

Source: Loukopoulos et al. (2007a).

required personal sacrifices, even though it was considered highly valuable for society to implement it. This is one of many demonstrated examples of collective irrationality (Dawes, 1980). On the other hand, the public may be rational in being opposed to RP because it is an ineffective measure to solve what are the worst threats to urban quality of life (most likely health hazards due to air pollution and traffic accidents). Needless to say, political decision making must counteract collective irrationality. Thus, politicians need to have the courage to implement unpopular policy measures if this is what it takes. However, goal conflicts and conflicts between political ideologies appear to be severe obstacles (Johansson et al., 2003).

RP takes various forms. Other chapters in this volume are devoted to discussing and evaluating these different forms. As noted by Loukopoulos et al. (2007a), such discussions tend to overlook that RP is only one of several TDM measures that may be more or less effective. The classification of such measures proposed by Loukopoulos (2007) thus identifies market-based (versus regulatory) mechanisms as only one of several dimensions that distinguish the different measures. Other dimensions include targeting latent (versus manifest) demand, (restriction of) time scale, (restriction of) spatial scale, degree of coerciveness, and bottom-up (versus top-down) process (for definitions, see Table 10.3). A recent broader analysis of the relative benefits of other measures in modifying travel behaviour appears in Gärling and Fujii (2007).

Microeconomic theory (for example, Quinet and Vickerman, 2004) is not the only relevant theory of behavioural change. In fact, this theory is silent on the question of whether RP is more effective than other measures such as legislation, physical changes, individualized marketing or education.

This chapter has proposed an alternative (Gärling et al., 2002) that does not suffer from such a limitation.

Any policy measure needs to be evaluated with respect to its effectiveness before being implemented. Such evaluations require a satisfactory evaluation design, which includes adequate control groups (Gärling and Fujii, 2007). If it could be shown in flawless evaluation studies that RP (alone or in conjunction with other TDM measures, such as individualized marketing, prohibition and improvements of alternatives) is effective, then communicating such positive outcomes should have a positive effect on acceptability. Unfortunately, in some discussions of the issue (for example, Emmerink et al., 1995), acceptability of RP seems to be considered in isolation from effectiveness. As this chapter has shown, this would not be a productive way to achieve a solution of the urgent problems caused by the excessive use of private cars.

NOTES

1. This research was financially supported by grant #2002-00434 from the Swedish Agency for Innovation Systems and grant #25.9/2001-1763 from the Swedish Research Council for Environment, Agricultural Sciences, and Spatial Planning.
2. It is now known that a majority of residents of the city of Stockholm voted for a continuation of the RP scheme. However, because the referendum is non-binding and advisory in nature, the ultimate decision lies with elected officials and politicians. In this context, it is relevant that residents in municipalities surrounding the city of Stockholm have expressed strong opposition.
3. In the theory of planned behaviour (TPB) (Ajzen, 1991), the equation is $I = w_A A + w_{SN} SN + w_{PBC} PBC$. PBC or perceived behavioural control is relevant when the intention is to reach a goal that is only partly under volitional control, for instance, a student who intends to reach the goal of passing an exam. This does not seem to apply to a decision to accept or not accept road pricing.
4. The setting of goals is closely related, if not identical, to forming intentions.

REFERENCES

Ahlstrand, I. (1998), 'The rise and fall of the heroic transport plan for Stockholm', *Transport Policy*, **5**, 205–11.

Ajzen, I. (1987), 'Attitudes, traits, and actions: dispositional prediction of behavior in personality and social psychology', in L. Berkowitz (ed.), *Advances in Experimental Social Psychology*, Vol. 20, San Diego, CA: Academic Press, pp. 1–63.

Ajzen, I. (1991), 'The theory of planned behavior', *Organizational Behavior and Human Decision Processes*, **50**, 179–211.

Ajzen, I. and M. Fishbein (1980), *Understanding Attitudes and Predicting Social Behavior*, Englewood Cliffs, NJ, Prentice-Hall.

Arentze, T., F. Hofman and H.P.J. Timmermans (2004), 'Predicting multi-faceted activity-travel adjustment strategies in response to possible pricing scenarios using an Internet-based stated adaptation experiment', *Transport Policy*, **11**, 31–41.

Bamberg, S. and D. Rölle (2003), 'Determinants of people's acceptability of pricing measures: replication and extension of a causal model', in J. Schade and B. Schlag (eds), *Acceptability of Transport Pricing Strategies*, Oxford: Elsevier, pp. 235–48.

Baron, J. and J. Jurney (1993), 'Norms against voting for coerced reform', *Journal of Personality and Social Psychology*, **64**, 347–55.

Black, W.R. (2001), 'An unpopular essay on transportation', *Journal of Transport Geography*, **9**, 1–11.

Brehmer, B. (1995), 'Feedback delays in complex dynamic decision making', in P.A. Frensch and J. Funke (eds), *Complex Decision Making: The European Perspective*, Hillsdale, NJ: Erlbaum, pp. 103–30.

Carver, C.S. and M.F. Scheier (1998), *On the Self-Regulation of Behavior*, Cambridge: Cambridge University Press.

Crawford, J.H. (2000), *Carfree Cities*, Utrecht: International Books.

Dawes, R.M. (1980), 'Social dilemmas', *Annual Review of Psychology*, **31**, 169–93.

Dawes, R.M. and T.L. Smith (1985), 'Attitude and opinion measurement', in G. Lindzey and E. Aronson (eds), *Handbook of Social Psychology*, Vol. 1, 3rd edn, New York: Random House, pp. 509–66.

Eagly, A.H. and S. Chaiken (1993), *The Psychology of Attitudes*, Fort Worth, FL: Harcourt Brace Jovanovich.

Eagly, A.H. and S. Chaiken (1998), 'Attitude structure and function', in D.T. Gilbert, S.T. Fiske and G. Lindzey (eds), *Handbook of Social Psychology*, Vol. 1, 4th edn, Englewood Cliffs, NJ: McGraw-Hill, pp. 269–322.

Emmerink, R.H.M., P. Nijkamp and P. Rietveld (1995), 'Is congestion pricing a first-best strategy in transport policy? A critical review of arguments', *Environment and Planning B*, **22**, 581–602.

Fishbein, M. and I. Ajzen (1975), *Belief, Attitude, Intention, and Behavior: An Introduction to Theory and Research*, Reading, MA: Addison-Wesley.

Fujii, S. and T. Gärling (2003), 'Application of attitude theory for improved predictive accuracy of stated preference methods in travel demand analysis', *Transportation Research A*, **37**, 389–402.

Fujii, S. and T. Gärling (2005), 'Temporary structural change: a strategy to break car-use habit and promote public transport', in G. Underwood (ed.), *Traffic and Transport Psychology*, Amsterdam: Elsevier, pp. 585–92.

Fujii, S. and T. Gärling (2007), 'The development and impact of car-use habit', in T. Gärling and L. Steg (eds), *Threats from Car Traffic to the Quality of Urban Life: Problems, Causes, and Solutions*, Amsterdam: Elsevier, pp. 235–50.

Gärling, T., D. Eek, P. Loukopoulos, S. Fujii, O. Johansson-Stenman, R. Kitamura, R. Pendyala and B. Vilhelmson (2002), 'A conceptual analysis of the impact of travel demand management on private car use', *Transport Policy*, **9**, 59–70.

Gärling, T. and S. Fujii (2007), 'Travel behaviour modification programs: theory, method, and empirical evaluations', manuscript, Department of Psychology, Göteborg University, Sweden.

Gärling, T., R. Gillholm and A. Gärling (1998), 'Reintroducing attitude theory in travel behavior research: the validity of an interactive interview procedure to predict car use', *Transportation*, **25**, 129–46.

Gärling, T., P. Loukopoulos and M. Lee-Goselin (2003), 'Public attitudes', in K. Button and D. Hensher (eds), *Handbooks in Transport, Vol. 4: Transport and the Environment*, Oxford and Amsterdam: Pergamon/Elsevier, pp. 725–37.

Garvill, J. (1999), 'Choice of transportation mode: factors influencing drivers' willingness to reduce personal car use and support car regulations', in M. Foddy, M. Smithson, S. Schneider and M. Hogg (eds), *Resolving Social Dilemmas*, Philadelphia, PA: Psychology Press, pp. 263–79.

Garvill, J., A. Marell and A. Nordlund (2003), 'Effects of awareness on choice of travel mode', *Transportation*, **30**, 63–79.

Goodwin, P.B. (1996), 'Simple arithmetic', *Transport Policy*, **3**, 79–80.

Hårsman, B. (2003), 'Success and failure: experiences from cities', in J. Schade and B. Schlag (eds), *Acceptability of Transport Pricing Strategies*, Oxford: Elsevier, pp. 137–51.

Hau, T.D. (1990), 'Electronic road pricing: developments in Hong Kong 1983–1989', *Journal of Transport Economics and Policy*, **24**, 203–14.

Hine, J. and M. Grieco (2003), 'Scatters and clusters in time and space: implications for delivering integrated and inclusive transport', *Transport Policy*, **10**, 299–306.

Jakobsson, C., S. Fujii and T. Gärling (2000), 'Determinants of private car users' acceptance of road pricing', *Transport Policy*, **7**, 153–58.

Jakobsson, C., S. Fujii and T. Gärling (2002), 'Effects of economic disincentives on private car use', *Transportation*, **29**, 349–70.

Johansson, L.-O., M. Gustafsson, G. Falkemark, T. Gärling and O. Johansson-Stenman (2003), 'Goal conflicts in political decision making: a survey of municipality politicians' views of road pricing', *Environment and Planning C*, **21**, 615–24.

Jones, P.M. (1995), 'Road pricing: the public viewpoint', in B. Johansson and L.-G. Mattsson (eds), *Road Pricing: Theory, Empirical Assessment and Policy*, Dordrecht: Kluwer Academic Publishers, pp. 159–79.

Jones, P.M. (2003), 'Acceptability of road user charging: meeting the challenge', in J. Schade and B. Schlag (eds), *Acceptability of Transport Pricing Strategies*, Oxford: Elsevier, pp. 27–62.

Kitamura, R., S. Fujii and E.I. Pas (1997), 'Time-use data, analysis and modeling: toward the next generation of transportation planning methodologies', *Transport Policy*, **4**, 225–35.

Locke, E.A. and G.P. Latham (1990), *A Theory of Goal-Setting and Task Performance*, Englewood Cliffs, NJ: Prentice-Hall.

Locke, E.A., G.P. Latham and M. Erez (1988), 'The determinants of goal commitment', *Academy of Management Review*, **13**, 23–39.

Loukopoulos, P. (2007), 'A classification of travel demand management measures', in T. Gärling and L. Steg (eds), *Threats from Car Traffic to the Quality of Urban Life: Problems, Causes, and Solutions*, Amsterdam: Elsevier, pp. 275–92.

Loukopoulos, P., T. Gärling, C. Jakobsson and S. Fujii (2007a), 'A cost-minimization principle of adaptation of private car use in response to road pricing', in C. Jensen-Butler, B. Madsen, O. Anker Nielsen and B. Sloth (eds), *Road Pricing, the Economy, and the Environment*, Amsterdam: Elsevier, in press.

Loukopoulos, P., T. Gärling, C. Jakobsson, S. Meland and S. Fujii (2005), 'Choices of activity- and travel-change options for reduced car use', in H.P.J. Timmermans (ed.), *Progress in Activity-Based Analysis*, Amsterdam: Elsevier, pp. 489–501.

Loukopoulos, P., C. Jakobsson, T. Gärling and S. Fujii (2007b), 'Determinants of public acceptability and car-use change goal: the Stockholm road pricing field trial', manuscript, Swedish National Road and Transport Research Institute, Linköping, Sweden.

McFadden, D. (2001), 'Disaggregate behavioral travel demand's RUM side – a 30 years retrospective', in D.A. Hensher (ed.), *Travel Behavior Research*, Amsterdam: Elsevier, pp. 17–63.

Ministry of Transport (1964), *Road Pricing: Economic and Technical Possibilities*, London: HMSO.

Oliver, R.L. (1997), *Satisfaction: A Behavioral Perspective on the Consumer*, New York: McGraw-Hill.

Ouellette, J.A. and W. Wood (1998), 'Habit and intention in everyday life: the multiple processes by which past behavior predicts future behavior', *Psychological Bulletin*, **124**, 54–74.

Pas, E.I. (1995), 'The urban transportation planning process', in S. Hanson (ed.), *The Geography of Urban Transportation*, Amsterdam: Elsevier, pp. 53–77.

Quinet, E. and R. Vickerman (2004), *Principles of Transport Economics*, Cheltenham, UK and Northampton, MA, USA: Edward Elgar.

Richards, M.G. (2006), *Congesting Charging in London: The Policy and Politics*, Basingstoke, UK and New York: Palgrave Macmillan.

Samuelson, W. and R. Zeckhausen (1988), 'Status quo bias in decision making', *Journal of Risk and Uncertainty*, **1**, 7–59.

Schade, J. (2003), 'European research results on transport pricing acceptability', in J. Schade and B. Schlag (eds), *Acceptability of Transport Pricing Strategies*, Amsterdam: Elsevier, pp. 109–23.

Steg, L. and G. Schuitema (2007), 'Behavioural responses to transport pricing: a theoretical analysis', in T. Gärling and L. Steg (eds), *Threats to the Quality of Urban Life from Car Traffic: Problems, Causes, and Solutions*, Amsterdam: Elsevier, pp. 347–66.

Stern, P.C. and T. Dietz (1994), 'The value basis of environmental concern', *Journal of Social Issues*, **50**, 55–84.

Tretvik, T. (2003), 'Urban road pricing in Norway: public acceptability and travel behaviour', in J. Schade and B. Schlag (eds), *Acceptability of Transport Pricing Strategies*, Oxford: Elsevier, pp. 77–92.

Trivector (2004), *Plan för utvärdering av försök med miljöavgifter i Stockholmstrafiken* (Plan for evaluation of road pricing field trial in Stockholm), Lund, Trivector Inc. (www.Trivector.se), accessed 12 August 2007.

Ubbels, B. and E. Verhoef (2007), 'The economic theory of transport pricing', in T. Gärling and L. Steg (eds), *Threats from Car Traffic to the Quality of Urban Life: Problems, Causes, and Solutions*, Amsterdam: Elsevier, pp. 325–45.

Verplanken, B., H. Aarts and A. van Knippenberg (1997), 'Habit, information acquisition, and the process of making travel mode choices', *European Journal of Social Psychology*, **27**, 539–60.

Whitelegg, J. (2003), 'Transport in the European Union: time to decide', in N. Low and B. Gleeson (eds), *Making Urban Transport Sustainable*, Basingstoke, UK: Palgrave Macmillan, pp. 115–31.

11. Car users' acceptability of a kilometre charge

Geertje Schuitema, Barry Ubbels, Linda Steg and Erik Verhoef

11.1 INTRODUCTION

Worldwide, car traffic has increased by almost 70 per cent between 1980 and 1998 (OECD, 2001). This increase in road transport causes various problems, such as congestion, accidents and noise. Various policies may be implemented to reduce these problems, transport pricing being one of them. In this chapter, transport pricing refers to cost increases for car use or car ownership. In general, transport-pricing policies are considered to be fairly effective in reducing problems resulting from increased car use. In particular, economists plead for the implementation of transport-pricing policies, because of the welfare gains of these pricing tools (for an overview of the theory and effectiveness of transport pricing, see Ubbels, 2006; see also Ubbels et al., Chapter 5 of this volume). The London congestion charge and the Singapore area licence scheme are examples of effective transport-pricing schemes (see Small and Gomez-Ibañez, 1998; Santos, 2004; Santos et al., 2004). Six months after the introduction of the congestion charge in London, the total number of vehicles entering the charged zone reduced by 14 per cent compared with the pre-charge period (Transport for London, 2006; Santos, Chapter 14 of this volume). Since 1998, vehicles entering the city centre of Singapore have been charged between 7.30 p.m. and 19.00 a.m. As a result, traffic volumes have decreased by 15 per cent all through the day, and during rush hours by 16 per cent (Menon, 2000). Outside the evening peak, increases in car use were hardly registered.

Technically, transport-pricing measures can easily be implemented. However, such policies often meet public resistance. Therefore, acceptability is one of the major barriers to successfully implementing transport-pricing schemes (Jones, 1995; Niskanen et al., 2003; Schade and Schlag, 2003). Acceptability of policies is related to various features of the policies (see, for example, Schuitema, 2003) as well as to individual factors, such as environmental concern (Loukopoulos et al., 2005) and problem awareness (Steg and Vlek, 1997; Jones, 2003). Furthermore, transport-pricing policies appear to be more acceptable if people consider the policy as fair (Jakobsson et al., 2000; Bamberg and Rölle, 2003; Jones, 2003). In addition, acceptability judgements are related to the perceived effects of the policy. Individual car users may consider two types of effects. First, they may consider the effects of transport-pricing policies on their own car use. Such policies may elicit changes in, for example, transportation mode, route, departure time or destination. If costs increase, car users may feel forced to either change their car use or pay higher prices, for example, when they have little opportunity to evade the measure. As a result, car users may feel restricted in their freedom to move. In such cases, transport-pricing policies are probably not acceptable (Jakobsson et al., 2000; Schuitema and Steg, 2005). Second, car users may consider the effects of transport-pricing policies on problems resulting from car use, such as congestion. Individual car users may benefit from these positive effects, which may increase the acceptability of transport-pricing policies (for example, Bartley, 1995; Schlag and Teubel, 1997; Rienstra et al., 1999; Gärling et al., Chapter 10 of this volume). If individual car users profit from reduced societal problems, it does not necessarily mean that their own car use is affected.

Thus, on the one hand, individual car users may be negatively affected by transport pricing (namely, their costs increase), while, on the other, they may also benefit from transport pricing (namely, collective problems reduce). The aim of the present study is to examine how perceived effectiveness relates to the acceptability of transport-pricing policies. Both types of effects will be considered. In addition, it is examined how acceptability judgements relate to possibilities of evading transport-pricing policies, and the extent to which car users are compensated for negative consequences. These issues are elaborated on in the next section.

This chapter describes an empirical study focusing on the acceptability of a specific type of transport pricing, that is, kilometre charging among Dutch car owners.[1] Kilometre charging implies that car users have to pay for each kilometre driven. This charge may be differentiated, for example on time, place or type of car. The Netherlands has long experience in developing new transport-pricing measures to reduce congestion levels. However, none of these policy proposals has ever been implemented, mainly because of low levels of public acceptability. Car owners were selected for this study because this is a large and influential group with regard to the implementation of kilometre charges in the Netherlands. This chapter is organized as follows. Section 11.2 discusses important factors that may be related to acceptability levels of kilometre charging. On the basis of this, several hypotheses are formulated, which will be tested in a field study. The design and results of this study are presented in Sections 11.3 and 11.4. Section 11.5 discusses the main findings.

11.2   ACCEPTABILITY OF KILOMETRE CHARGING

The acceptability of kilometre charging depends on the perceived effectiveness of the measure. As was explained in the previous section, both the effects on individual car users and on the expected outcomes in terms of reduced congestion are relevant in this respect. On the one hand, it may be expected that acceptability increases for people who expect to benefit from kilometre charging, for example, if congestion decreases (Hypothesis 1).

On the other hand, acceptability is likely to decrease if people expect to be negatively affected by the measure, for example, if travel costs increase, or if they have to reduce their number of kilometres driven (Hypothesis 2). The extent to which people expect to be negatively affected by kilometre charging may depend on their current travel behaviour, household characteristics and the design of the particular policy.

First, current travel behaviour may influence the extent to which car users are negatively affected by kilometre charging. In this respect, the annual kilometrage may be especially relevant. After all, the more kilometres people drive, the more strongly they are negatively affected by a kilometre charge, that is, they have to pay higher costs or have to reduce the number of kilometres they drive to avoid cost increases (Hypothesis 2a). Commuters usually have a high annual kilometrage, and consequently, may be more strongly affected if kilometre charging is implemented. On the other hand, commuters are more likely to be involved in traffic jams, and, consequently, kilometre charging may also have positive consequences for them (provided that congestion levels do indeed reduce). Thus, kilometre charging may have significant positive as well as negative effects on commuters. We shall examine how both mechanisms affect acceptability levels of commuters (research question).

Second, the extent to which car users are negatively affected by kilometre charging is probably dependent on their income. Lower-income groups intend to reduce their car use relatively more strongly when kilometre charging is implemented (Jakobsson et al., 2000). This suggests that people with a lower income perceive more infringement on their freedom to drive than those with a higher income, that is, lower-income groups may feel forced to change their car use because they cannot afford to pay the kilometre charge. This is in line with economic research about the valuation of travel time. Car drivers with a higher income generally tend to have a higher value of time (willingness to pay to save one hour of travel time) than those with a lower income (see, for example, Gunn, 2001). Therefore, it is expected that kilometre charging has more negative effects for lower-income groups than for higher-income groups (Hypothesis 2b).

Third, the extent to which car users are affected by kilometre charging may depend on the price level. It is likely that car users change their car use more strongly when price levels are high than if price levels are low. Thus, we expect that kilometre charging is less acceptable when price levels are high rather than low (Hypothesis 2c).

Kilometre charging is expected to be less acceptable when people have few or no opportunities to evade the measure. Opportunities to work at home may give commuters the possibility of evading kilometre charging. In addition, commuting distance may be relevant, because long commuting distances may result in fewer opportunities to use non-motorized travel modes, such as walking or cycling. Thus, it may be expected that commuters who are able to work at home and have short commuting distances evaluate pricing policies as more acceptable than commuters who are not able to work at home and have long commuting distances (Hypothesis 3).

Pricing policies are likely to be more acceptable if people are compensated for possible negative consequences. The way in which revenues of kilometre charging are allocated may therefore be important. In general, revenues may be used in three different ways. First, they can be allocated to the sector 'car transport' (for example, for reducing road taxes, fuel taxes or improving road infrastructure), and therefore benefit those who pay them directly. Second, revenues can be used to finance the general transport sector, including public transport. Third, they can be used to fund general public expenses, in which case there is no hypothecation to the transport sector. In each case, car users may potentially profit from the allocation of revenues, although this may not always be clear to those involved. Research has shown that the use of revenues from transport-pricing policies affects acceptability judgements. Verhoef (1996), for instance, asked morning-peak road users their opinion on transport-pricing policies. An overwhelming majority (83 per cent) stated that their opinion depends on the allocation of revenues. Schade and Schlag (2000) found that the vast majority of respondents favoured using revenues for transport purposes such as traffic flow and public transport improvements. Vehicle tax reductions were also supported, whereas income tax reductions were not. From the perspective of policy makers, car users may always benefit from the revenues of kilometre charging, irrespective of how they are invested. However, from the perspective of individual car users, they may feel compensated more if revenues are invested in the car transport sector instead of in general public funds, because the former is directly linked to the payments they made. Linking behaviour (paying) directly to rewards (compensating for possible negative consequences) is an important psychological mechanism (see also Geller, 1989). Car users may not perceive they are being compensated if they do not benefit directly from the allocation of the revenues. Moreover, since only car users are paying for kilometre charging, investing revenues in the road system may be perceived as more fair than investing in general public funds (see also Steg and Schuitema, in press). Therefore, it may be expected that kilometre charging is more acceptable if revenues are allocated to investments in the 'car transport' sector instead of to general public funds (Hypothesis 4).

11.3 FIELD STUDY ON ACCEPTABILITY AND PERCEIVED EFFECTIVENESS OF A KILOMETRE CHARGE

11.3.1 Sample

Because a kilometre charge for all cars on a network level has not yet been implemented anywhere in the Netherlands, we used a questionnaire to examine the acceptability of charging per kilometre. Data were collected through an (interactive) Internet survey conducted with a panel of the Dutch Institute for Public Opinion and Market Research. Only regular car users were invited to participate. The total sample consisted of 562 respondents, of whom 257 commuted by car and experienced congestion on a regular basis (at least twice a week for 10 minutes or more); this group was labelled 'commuters'. The remaining 305 car users were randomly selected from regular car users from the total panel; this was a representative sample of Dutch car users (labelled 'general car users'). Since we aimed to select a representative sample, this group also included commuters (63 per cent), of which 14 per cent experienced congestion on a regular basis. These respondents were included in the group 'general car users' in order to be able to compare commuters with a representative sample of the Dutch population of car users.

The mean age was 42 years (SD = 13.2), and 61 per cent of the respondents were male. About 46 per cent of the respondents had completed lower education, 29 per cent middle education, and 8 per cent higher education. For 17 per cent, the educational level was unknown. The average gross household income per year was classified into 4 classes: less than €28 500 a year (21 per cent of the respondents); between €28 500 and €45 000 (32 per cent), between €45 000 and €68 000 (29 per cent), and more than €68 000 (16 per cent). For 3 per cent of the respondents, data on income levels are missing. Almost 22 per cent of the respondents were single; 2 per cent were single with children; 32 per cent had a partner but no children; and 44 per cent had a partner and children. Almost one-third of the respondents lived in the western part of the Netherlands (the area with the highest congestion levels).

The sample of car users was representative for the Dutch population (CBS, 2005), although the average age was a bit higher: in this sample, the average age was 42 years whereas the average age of the Dutch population is 39 years. This is because the sample consisted only of car users, with a minimum age of 18. The sample of commuters had more male respondents (70 per cent), with a higher income (20 per cent had an income of more than €68 000) and educational level (12 per cent had a higher education level). This is comparable with other samples of Dutch car users who often experience traffic jams (Bureau Goudappel Coffeng, 1997; Steg, 2005).

11.3.2   Data Collection

The data presented in this chapter were part of a larger questionnaire study, and only those parts of the questionnaire that are relevant for the present study are described here. Respondents evaluated a kilometre charge. In the description of the kilometre charge, every car user had to pay for each kilometre driven by car (see Table 11.1). Six versions of the kilometre charge were distinguished, by systematically varying price level and allocation of the revenues.

Price level was systematically varied: per kilometre, 3, 6 and 12 eurocents had to be paid. Revenues were either used to decrease income taxes or returned to the car user by abolishing road taxes (if the price level was 3 eurocents), by abolishing road taxes and taxes on the purchase of cars (if the price level was 6 eurocents), or by abolishing both these taxes and improving existing and building new infrastructure (if the price level was 12

Table 11.1   Description of kilometre charge

Measure	Variants
Flat kilometre charge, systematically varying price level and allocation of revenues	A: 3 €cents, revenues used to abolish car ownership taxes (MRB)
	B: 6 €cents, revenues used to abolish existing car taxation (purchase (BPM) and ownership (MRB))
	C: 12 €cents, revenues used to abolish existing car taxation and construct new roads
	D: 3 €cents, revenues used to decrease income taxes
	E: 6 €cents, revenues used to decrease income taxes
	F: 12 €cents, revenues used to decrease income taxes

eurocents). All variants were budget neutral for an average Dutch house-hold (Table 11.1). Each respondent evaluated one version only (that is, a between-subjects design was followed).

For each respondent, an estimation of potential financial consequences of the kilometre charge was shown on the basis of self-reported current travel behaviour and type of car they owned. This estimation depended on the charge level (costs) and on the type of revenue use (benefits). Because it was impossible to give respondents a personal estimate of the financial benefits resulting from the allocation of revenues via lower-income taxa-tion, we presented the savings only for those measures where current car taxes are abolished.[2] We also explained some practical issues to prevent such considerations from affecting responses. More specifically, we indi-cated that the privacy of car users is guaranteed, electronic equipment reg-isters the charge, and drivers can choose their preferred payment method (for example, credit card, bank transfer and so on).

After reading one version of the kilometre charge, respondents indicated how acceptable the kilometre charge was to them (on a 7-point answering scale ranging from 1 – very unacceptable – to 7 – very acceptable). For the univariate analyses (described in subsection 11.4.1) that did not aim to examine the relationship between price level and revenue use, average acceptability judgements were calculated. Respondents also indicated to what extent they expected congestion to reduce after implementation of the kilometre charge (on a 7-point answering scale ranging from 1 – very unlikely – to 7 – very likely).

The questionnaire included general questions about socio-demographics (for example, income), annual kilometrage, car weight and fuel type (in order to estimate the potential financial consequences, see above) and employment status. Commuters were asked to answer additional questions about the possibility of working at home (answering categories were: yes, most days (1), yes, every now and then a full day (2), yes, every now and then a part of the day (3), no (4)), and commuting distance (single journey).

Two types of analyses were conducted. First, we examined to what extent the single factors, described in 11.4.1, are related to car users' evaluation of the acceptability of kilometre charging (univariate analyses). Second, we examined to what extent each of these factors contributed to the explan-ation of acceptability judgements by means of a regression analysis (multi-variate analyses). Some extra factors were included in the regression analyses: vehicle weight (which partly determined the financial benefits of the kilometre charge due to the revenue allocation), age, residential location, being employed, weekly number of times they experienced congestion and self-reported effects on changes in car use. The last factor was measured in terms of the proportion of the trips that car users intended to change if the kilometre charge were to be implemented (for more details, see Ubbels, 2006). The added factors were included to examine whether they contribute to the explanation of the acceptability of kilometre charging. The aim of this regression analysis was to examine the impacts of the various determinants upon acceptability simultaneously, hence correcting for possible correlations between determinants, and thus isolating the pure marginal effect of each determinant upon acceptability ('keeping everything else constant').

11.4 RESULTS

11.4.1 Factors Related to Acceptability Judgements

Generally, the kilometre charge was fairly unacceptable ($M = 3.0$; SD = 1.78). Figure 11.1 shows the average acceptability judgements on the six versions of the kilometre charge. Most variants are close to a score of 3: this is 'somewhat unacceptable'. The kilometre charge is less unacceptable if price levels are 3 or 6 eurocents, and if revenues are used to reduce car-related taxes (versions A and B).

About 86 per cent of the respondents do not expect congestion levels to reduce ($M = 2.2$, SD = 1.12) if the kilometre charge were to be

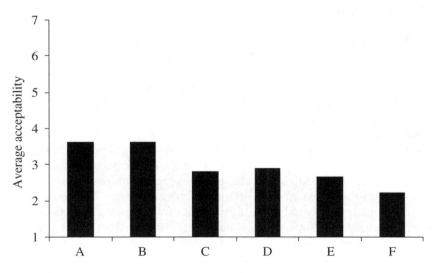

Note: For the meaning of the letters A–F, see Table 11.1.

Figure 11.1   Average acceptability of 6 versions of the kilometre charge

implemented. In line with our expectations, the expected effects on congestion were related to the acceptability judgements of the kilometre charge (Hypothesis 1). It appeared that the less people expected congestion levels to reduce, the less acceptable the kilometre charge was to them (Pearson's $r = 0.30, p < 0.001$).

In line with our Hypothesis (2a), it appeared that the more kilometres people drive a year, the less acceptable the kilometre charge was to them (Pearson's $r = -0.18, p < 0.001$). Contrary to our expectations, income appeared not to be related to acceptability of the kilometre charge (Pearson's $r = 0.06, p = 0.174$) (Hypothesis 2b). Furthermore, as expected, (Hypothesis 2c) a kilometre charge of 12 eurocents per kilometre was less acceptable than a charge of 3 or 6 eurocents per kilometre ($F (2, 559) = 9.70, p < 0.001$; see Figure 11.2). No differences in acceptability judgements were found for a charge of 3 eurocents per kilometre compared with 6 eurocents per kilometre.

Car users in general find the kilometre charge more acceptable ($M = 3.3$, SD = 1.84) than commuters ($M = 2.6$, SD = 1.62; $F (1, 560) = 23.4, p < 0.001$; see Figure 11.3). Commuters have a higher annual kilometrage ($M = 25.848$ km/year) than car users in general ($M = 13.356$; $F (1, 560) = 63.9, p < 0.001$), which may explain why commuters find the kilometre charge less acceptable than general car users. Of all commuters, 93 per cent did not expect congestion to reduce if the kilometre charge were to be implemented. The less

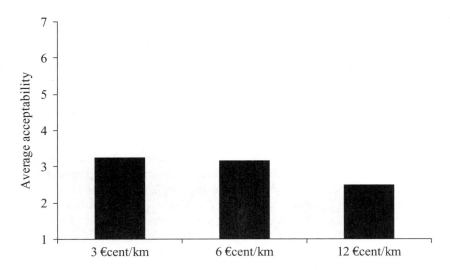

Figure 11.2   Average acceptability judgements of kilometre charge with three different price levels

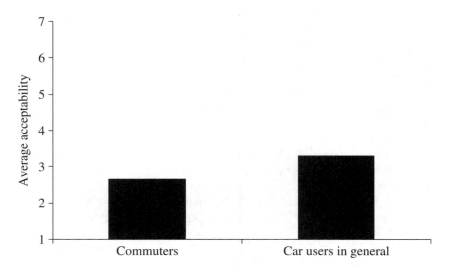

Figure 11.3   Average acceptability judgements of kilometre charge for commuters and car users in general

Table 11.2   Correlations between acceptability judgement, ability to work at home, and commuting distance

	Acceptability of kilometre charge	
	Pearson's *r*	*p*
Ability to work at home	−0.04	0.521
Trip distance (single journey)	−0.08	0.184

commuters expected congestion to reduce, the less acceptable kilometre charging was for them (Pearson's $r = 0.30$, $p < 0.001$).

Next, we examined to what extent acceptability depended on the extent to which commuters are able to evade kilometre charging. On average, commuters travelled 40 kilometres (single journey) to their work. For a minority of the commuters (5 per cent) it was always possible to work at home, while for 47 per cent of the commuters working at home was not possible at all. Contrary to our expectations, acceptability judgements of the kilometre charge did not appear to be related to the possibility of working at home and commuting distance (see Table 11.2) (Hypothesis 3).

Finally, the relationship between acceptability and the extent to which car users are compensated for possible cost increases was examined. In line

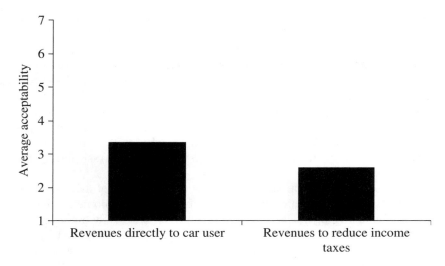

Figure 11.4   Average acceptability of kilometre charge when revenues returned to car user or used to reduce income taxes

with our expectations, the kilometre charge was more acceptable if revenues were returned to the car user instead of being allocated to reducing income taxes (Hypothesis 4). If revenues were used to decrease taxes on driving and the possession of a car, and to improve road infrastructure, the kilometre charge was far more acceptable ($M = 3.4$, SD $= 1.94$) than if revenues were used to decrease income taxes ($M = 2.6$, SD $= 1.53$; $t\,(560) = 5.1$, $p < 0.001$; see also Figures 11.1 and 11.4).

11.4.2   Predicting Acceptability Judgements

The previous section considered the relationship between each of the various factors and the acceptability of a flat kilometre charge. Here, we examine to what extent acceptability may be explained by these variables, together with age, vehicle weight, residential location, being employed, weekly number of times they experienced congestion, and self-reported effects on changes in car use. Various econometric techniques are available to investigate the relationship between the different variables. The methodology to be applied depends to a large extent on the structure of the data. Here, an ordered probit (OP) technique was used. For more information about the applied method, see Ubbels (2006).

It appears that the type of measure (in terms of charge level and revenue use) is very important for the level of acceptability of the kilometre charge.

The signs of the coefficients are as expected: the kilometre charge of 3 and 6 eurocents per kilometre is more acceptable than the 12 eurocents charge. Allocating revenues to reduce income taxes is less popular than a decrease of current car taxation. This result may be explained by the lower perceived costs for the individual. This effect may have been overestimated to some extent, because we have indicated the financial benefits only from an abolition of car-related taxes, and presented this to the respondents together with the estimated costs due to the charge. Unfortunately, it was not possible to also estimate the actual financial benefits of the other type of revenue use (lower income taxes and improving road infrastructure) for each individual.

The weight of the car and the number of kilometres driven yearly are also significant predictors of acceptability of the kilometre charge. Respondents owning a heavy car find this measure relatively more acceptable than people with smaller cars. This may partly be explained by the impact of the type of revenue use, since current Dutch car taxation is differentiated according to the weight of the car. Owners of heavier cars pay relatively more taxes and would benefit more from a kilometre charge than owners of light cars. But this only holds for three of the six variants where fixed car taxes are abolished. We assume that heavier (and more expensive) cars are owned by those on a higher income, and this is the same group that benefits relatively more from an income tax reduction. This may also explain the importance of weight for the acceptability of the other three variants (D, E and F, see Table 11.1). As expected, people who drive many kilometres are relatively more opposed to a kilometre charge than others. It is this group who will pay most.

The expected effects of the charge on the reduction of congestion have a significant relationship with acceptability as well. Respondents who think that the measure will be effective in reducing congestion, also tend to find it more acceptable. Since we have information on the self-reported behavioural changes of the respondents (in terms of the proportion of trips that will be changed), it is also possible to include 'personal effectiveness' in the analysis. The 'self-reported behavioural change' dummy is not significant, suggesting no difference in acceptability between respondents who do, and those who do not, expect to change their behaviour.

The previous section indicated that income is not related to acceptability of the kilometre charge. This analysis generally confirms this: only the highest income group (inc4) is slightly more positive about the kilometre charge than the other income groups (as may be expected). Commuting has not been included as a separate variable in this analysis. Instead, we have included employment and number of kilometres driven yearly as explanatory variables as it is a good proxy. People who have a job are more

Table 11.3   *Results of OP analysis with acceptability of kilometre charge as the dependent variable*

Variable	Probit ACC measure 1	Sign.
Threshold (μ's)		
μ_1	−3.451 (0.739)	***
μ_2	−2.617 (0.737)	***
μ_3	−2.214 (0.736)	***
μ_4	−1.827 (0.735)	**
μ_5	−1.360 (0.733)	*
μ_6	−0.285 (0.732)	
Age	−0.003 (0.004)	
Income (inc5 (do not know/won't say) = base)		
Inc1 (< €28 500)	0.226 (0.280)	
Inc2 (€28 500–45 000)	0.314 (0.276)	
Inc3 (€45 000–68 000)	0.299 (0.280)	
Inc4 (>€68 000)	0.523 (0.291)	*
Type of measure (charge, dummy 12 €cents = base)		
Charge 3 €cents	0.606 (0.114)	***
Charge 6 €cents	0.486 (0.114)	***
Type of measure (revenue use)		
Dummy income taxes	−0.457 (0.093)	***
Number of kilometres driven yearly	−7.27E–06 (0.000)	**
Vehicle weight (dummy weight3 = base)		
Weight1 (low weight)	−0.408 (0.134)	***
Weight2 (middle weight)	−0.306 (0.116)	***
General effectiveness (less congestion) (Geff7 = base)		
Geff1	−2.341 (0.642)	***
Geff2	−1.917 (0.639)	***
Geff3	−1.763 (0.649)	***
Geff4	−1.462 (0.668)	**
Geff5	−1.321 (0.653)	**
Geff6	−0.948 (0.734)	
Self-reported behavioural change (dummy = yes)	0.057 (0.099)	
Employed (dummy = yes)	−0.494 (0.148)	***
Residential location (south = base)		
Loc1 (3 large cities)	−0.238 (0.150)	
Loc2 (rest west)	−0.166 (0.124)	
Loc3 (north)	−0.126 (0.201)	
Loc4 (east)	−0.231 (0.134)	*
Weekly number of times in congestion	−0.030 (0.017)	*
N	562	
Log-likelihood	−917.490	***

Table 11.3 (continued)

Variable	Probit ACC measure 1		Sign.
Pseudo *R*-square	Cox and Snell		0.250
	Nagelkerke		0.258
	McFadden		0.081

Notes: Standard errors are shown in brackets. *, ** and *** denote significance at the 10%, 5% and 1% level, respectively (two-sided *t*-test).

opposed to the measure than others. This group may also use the car for commuting reasons (though not every employed person makes commuting trips by car; about 9.5 per cent of this group uses another mode), and our data confirm that commuters in most cases drive more kilometres. It is also this group who tend to experience congestion relatively more often, so the employment dummy may include this effect. However, we included a separate variable accounting for the number of times in congestion. The effect is modest (with the expected sign), but becomes stronger when the employment dummy is left out of the analysis, thus confirming our previous suspicion. This confirms the previous finding that commuters are less positive about this kilometre charge. This indicates that this group does not expect the measure to be effective, even though they may benefit relatively most from reduced levels of congestion.

11.5   SUMMARY AND DISCUSSION

Public acceptability is a major barrier for implementing transport-pricing policies. The literature suggests that there is some degree of variation in the level of acceptability: for instance, depending on the type of the measure proposed and the way in which revenues are used. In addition, individual characteristics play a role, such as expected increases in travel costs. In order to implement transport-pricing policies successfully, the policy should be effective in reducing problems resulting from car use, as well as being acceptable to the public. Therefore, the relationship between acceptability and perceived effectiveness of transport-pricing policies is particularly important. Such policies may have positive effects for car users when collective problems, such as congestion are reduced. On the other hand, transport pricing may have negative effects, for example, as a result of higher travel costs. The acceptability of transport-pricing policies probably increases if people expect to benefit from the positive effects, whereas acceptability is likely to decrease if they expect to be negatively affected. Thus, if transport-pricing policies maximize the positive effects and mini-mize the negative effects for individual car users, such policies may be effective as well as acceptable. The study presented focused on the relation-ship between perceived effectiveness (both positive and negative) and the acceptability of one specific transport-pricing policy: kilometre charging.

We have examined the acceptability levels of a kilometre charge, which is being seriously considered by Dutch policy makers. Different versions of a flat kilometre charge were investigated, by systematically varying the price level and revenue use. We questioned two different groups of respondents: commuters who regularly experienced congestion, and car users in general. The importance of individual characteristics and the type of kilometre charge for explaining acceptability levels were tested in two different ways. First, univariate analyses were conducted. We examined relationships between acceptability and the expected positive effects (due to decreased congestion) and negative effects (for example, due to cost increases) of kilo-metre charging, the possibility of evading kilometre charging (in particular by commuters), and compensation for car users. Second, we conducted a multivariate analysis, in order to examine how various factors contributed to the explanation of acceptability judgements, taking the relationships among determinants into account. The results of the univariate analyses are consistent with the results of the multivariate analysis.

In line with our expectations, it appeared that the perceived effects of the kilometre charge on congestion are related to the acceptability levels of the kilometre charge (Hypothesis 1): kilometre charging is more acceptable when respondents expect congestion to reduce. This conclusion also holds for commuters who experience congestion on a regular basis. Despite the fact that most people did not expect congestion to reduce if kilometre charging is implemented, the results suggest that acceptability increases for those who do expect reduced congestion levels. This is in line with previous studies, which have shown that acceptability judgements of transport pricing are more related to its perceived effects on collective problems than to the financial and behavioural effects on individual car users (Schlag and Teubel, 1997; Rienstra et al., 1999; Gärling et al., Chapter 10 of this volume). This is a promising result, since it implies that acceptability levels may increase if people are aware of the positive consequences that kilome-tre charging may have on congestion. Communication strategies which explain the aims and intended effects of kilometre charging on congestion are therefore highly recommended.

Our hypotheses about the relationship between acceptability and the extent to which car users are negatively affected were partly confirmed. As expected, kilometre charging is less acceptable for car users with a high annual kilometrage compared with those who have a low annual kilometrage (Hypothesis 2a). Contrary to our expectations, income was unrelated to the acceptability of kilometre charging (Hypothesis 2b). This result is in line with previous studies (for example, Odeck and Bråthen, 1997; Jaensirisak et al., 2005). As expected, price level is related to the acceptability of kilometre charging: the higher the price level, the less acceptable the kilometre charge was (Hypothesis 2c). In sum, acceptability of kilometre charging decreases if car users are more strongly financially affected, as a result of a higher annual kilometrage and higher price levels. However, this relationship is less strong than might have been expected: annual kilometrage did not correlate very strongly with acceptability levels ($r = -0.18$), and only in the case of a fairly high price level (12 eurocents) did acceptability decrease.

Contrary to our expectations, for commuters, the acceptability of kilometre charging is not related to possibilities of evading the measure (Hypothesis 3). The opportunity to work at home and commuting distance are not related to the acceptability of kilometre charging. It is possible that changing starting hours or working at home may not be perceived as a feasible way to avoid the kilometre charge.

As expected, kilometre charging is more acceptable when revenues are used to decrease car taxes instead of decreasing income taxes (Hypothesis 4). From the perspective of policy makers, car users should benefit equally from allocating revenues to decrease road taxes as they do from allocating revenues to reduce income taxes. However, the results suggest that individual car users do not perceive that they are equally compensated if revenues are returned to the car user via reducing income taxes. These results should be interpreted with care: we were able to estimate and provide feedback only about the financial benefits of the kilometre charge in the case where revenues were allocated to decreasing car-related taxes and not if revenues were allocated to road infrastructure or to decreasing income taxes. This may have affected acceptability judgements.

It is clear that policy makers will face some level of opposition when considering the implementation of kilometre charging, which makes the job rather difficult. The empirical work reported in this chapter suggests that it may be possible to implement policies that are effective in reducing problems related to car use and at the same time are acceptable. To increase acceptability, the negative effects for individual car users should be minimized, whereas positive effects should be maximized. Despite negative consequences (increased costs), acceptability may increase if respondents expect congestion to reduce. Thus, a broad range of costs and benefits should be considered, and not just the financial consequences.

NOTES

1. Parts of this study have been presented at the European Regional Science Association, Amsterdam, 2005.
2. The benefits from paying less car taxation depended on the type of car the respondents owned (that is, on fuel type and weight). We estimated average savings for nine categories (a combination of three fuel types and three weight categories), for an abolition of only annual car ownership taxes (MRB), and an abolition of all existing car taxation: namely, MRB and the fixed purchase tax (BPM).

REFERENCES

Bamberg, S. and D. Rölle (2003), 'Determinants of people's acceptability of pricing measures – replication and extension of a causal model', in J. Schade and B. Schlag (eds), *Acceptability of Transport Pricing Strategies*, Oxford: Elsevier Science, pp. 235–48.

Bartley, B. (1995), 'Mobility impacts, reactions and opinions', *Traffic Engineering and Control*, **36** (11), 596–603.

Bureau Goudappel Coffeng (1997), *Marktprofiel van een Filerijder, Eindrapport* (Profile of a Car Driver in a Traffic Jam, Final Report), Deventer: Bureau Goudappel Coffeng.

CBS (Statistics Netherlands) (2005), *Bevolking: Kerncijfers* (Population: Key Figures), www.statline.nl, accessed February 2006.

Geller, E.S. (1989), 'Applied behavior analysis and social marketing: an integration for environmental preservation', *Journal of Social Issues*, **45** (1), 17–36.

Gunn, H. (2001), 'Spatial and temporal transferability of relationships between travel demand, trip cost and travel time', *Transportation Research E*, **37** (18), 163–98.

Jaensirisak, S., M. Wardman and A.D. May (2005), 'Explaining variations in public acceptability of road pricing schemes', *Journal of Transport Economics and Policy*, **39** (2), 127–54.

Jakobsson, C., S. Fujii and T. Gärling (2000), 'Determinants of private car users' acceptance of road pricing', *Transport Policy*, **7** (2), 153–8.

Jones, P.M. (1995), 'Road pricing: the public viewpoint', in B. Johansson and L.G. Mattsson (eds), *Road Pricing: Theory, Empirical Assessment and Policy*, Boston, MA: Kluwer Academic Publishers, pp. 159–80.

Jones, P. (2003), 'Acceptability of transport pricing strategies: meeting the challenge', in J. Schade and B. Schlag (eds), *Acceptability of Transport Pricing Strategies*, Oxford: Elsevier Science, pp. 27–62.

Loukopoulos, P., C. Jakobsson, T. Gärling, S. Schneider and S. Fujii (2005), 'Public attitudes towards policy measures for reducing private car use', *Environmental Science and Policy*, **8** (1), 57–66.

Menon, A. (2000), 'ERP in Singapore: a perspective one year on', *Traffic Engineering and Control*, **41** (2), 40–45.

Niskanen, E., A. De Palma, R. Lindsey, N. Marler, T. May, C. Nash, J. Schade, B. Schlag and E. Verhoef (2003), *Pricing of Urban and Interurban Road Transport: Barriers, Constraints and Implementation Paths*, Deliverable 4, EU-project MC-ICAM, funded by the European Commission, 5th Framework Transport RTD, Leeds.

Odeck, J. and S. Bråthen (1997), 'Public attitudes towards toll roads', *Transport Policy*, **4** (2), 73–83.

Organization for Economic Cooperation and Development (OECD) (2001), *Environmental Outlook*, http://213.253.134.29/oecd/pdfs/browseit/9701011E. PDF, accessed February 2006.

Rienstra, S.A., P. Rietveld and E.T. Verhoef (1999), 'The social support for policy measures in passenger transport. A statistical analysis for the Netherlands', *Transportation Research D*, **4** (3), 181–200.

Santos, G. (2004), 'Urban road pricing in the UK', in G. Santos (ed.), *Road Pricing: Theory and Evidence*, Amsterdam: Elsevier, pp. 251–82.

Santos, G., W.W. Li and T.H. Koh (2004), 'Transport policies in Singapore', in G. Santos (ed.), *Road Pricing: Theory and Evidence*, Amsterdam: Elsevier, pp. 251–82.

Schade, J. and B. Schlag (2000), *Acceptability of Urban Transport Pricing* (AFFORD publication), VATT research report 72, Helsinki.

Schade, J. and B. Schlag (2003), 'Acceptability of urban transport pricing strategies', *Transportation Research Part F: Traffic Psychology and Behaviour*, **6** (1), 45–61.

Schlag, B. and U. Teubel (1997), 'Public acceptability of transport pricing', *IATSS Research*, **21** (1), 134–42.

Schuitema, G. (2003), 'Pricing policies in transport', in L. Hendrickx, W. Jager and L. Steg (eds), *Human Decision Making and Environmental Perceptions: Understanding and Assisting Human Decision Making in Real-life Settings*, Groningen: University of Groningen Press, pp. 203–22.

Schuitema, G. and L. Steg (2005), 'Factors that affect the acceptability of pricing policies in transport', Paper presented at the 7th Nordic Environmental Social Science (NESS) Research Conference, Göteborg, Sweden, 15–17 June.

Small, K.A. and J.A. Gomez-Ibañez (1998), 'Road pricing for congestion management: the transition from theory to policy', in K.J. Button and E.T. Verhoef (eds), *Road Pricing, Traffic Congestion and the Environment. Issues of Efficiency and Social Feasibility*, Cheltenham, UK and Lyme, USA: Edward Elgar, pp. 213–46.

Steg, E. M. and C. Vlek (1997), 'The role of problem awareness in willingness-to-change car use and in evaluating relevant policy measures', in J.A. Rothengatter and E. Carbonell Vaya (eds), *Traffic and Transport Psychology: Theory and Application*, Oxford: Pergamon, pp. 465–75.

Steg, L. (2005), 'Car use: lust and must. Instrumental, symbolic and affective motives for car use', *Transportation Research A*, **39** (2–3), 147–62.

Steg, L. and G. Schuitema (2007), 'Behavioural responses to transport pricing: a theoretical analysis', in T. Gärling and L. Steg (eds), *Threats to the Quality of Urban Life from Car Traffic: Problems, Causes, and Solutions*, Amsterdam: Elsevier, pp. 347–66.

Transport for London (2006), *Impacts Monitoring: Fourth Annual Report*, www.tfl. gov.uk/tfl/cclondon/pdfs/FourthAnnualReportFinal.pdf, accessed February 2006.

Ubbels, B.J. (2006), 'Road pricing: effectiveness, acceptance and institutional issues', PhD thesis, Free University, Amsterdam.

Verhoef, E.T. (1996), *Economic Efficiency and Social Feasibility in the Regulation of Road Transport Externalities*, Amsterdam: Thesis Publishers.

12. Sensitivity of geographical accessibility measures under road-pricing conditions

Taede Tillema, Tom de Jong, Bert van Wee and Dirk van Amelsfort

12.1 INTRODUCTION

Accessibility indicators or measures give the opportunity to gain a quick and an interpretable insight into (accessibility) effects due to changes in the land use or transport system (for example, caused by certain policy interventions). These advantages might also make accessibility indicators a useful policy tool to assess (transport-geographical) effects due to transport pricing.

There are several categories/types of accessibility measures with which accessibility can be computed (Handy and Niemeier, 1997; Bruinsma and Rietveld, 1998; Geurs and Ritsema van Eck, 2001; Tillema et al., 2003; Geurs and van Wee, 2004). These geographical accessibility measures have in common that they generally consist of an opportunity component, on the one hand, and an impedance component, on the other. The location component indicates which, or which type of, activity location(s) is (are) central within the analysis. Examples of activity locations are jobs, shops, services, other people, amusement parks and so on. The second component, the impedance, indicates the difficulty of reaching a destination from a certain origin location. This impedance can be expressed by various factors, the most important of which are distance, time and costs.

The geographical accessibility effects of road-pricing may be evaluated in different ways, depending on the goal of the study and the argument of the impedance function. If a distance-based accessibility measure is used to evaluate road-pricing effects, accessibility is not likely to change unless, perhaps (in the longer term), toll revenues are reinvested in the infrastructure (maintenance, new infrastructure). Such a distance-based accessibility study may, therefore, hardly be useful and insightful in the evaluation of road-pricing effects. If the aim is to assess accessibility effects due to traffic changes (for example, travel-time consequences) caused by a road-pricing measure, it may be interesting to use a travel-time-based impedance function. In such a situation, generally an increase in accessibility due to road-pricing may be expected, at least if travel demand is price elastic. However, if the aim is to derive a more balanced insight into geographical accessibility effects due to road-pricing measures, other impedance components, such as toll costs, revenue rebates and so on, should also be taken into account. This can be done by using a generalized transport-cost approach. To the authors' knowledge, generalized cost-based accessibility measures have not yet been explicitly used to evaluate road-pricing effects.

But, what is the use of such a generalized cost-based accessibility analysis, given that a suitable approach to determine average welfare effects of road-pricing measures already exists: economic welfare analysis? We believe that economic welfare theory is the most useful/theoretically sound way to determine (average) welfare effects of road-pricing measures. However, one may not always be interested only in overall cost implications. An example from another field can illuminate this. The overall cost of road traffic accidents in the Netherlands in the year 2003 was estimated at €12.3 billion (Ministry of Transport, Public Works and Water Management, 2006). If policy makers develop a certain (infrastructure) plan that is planned to reduce traffic accident costs by say €15 million, it may also be worth knowing how many fewer possible injured people or fatalities there will be as a result of such a plan. In the same way, it may be interesting not only to determine average welfare effects of road pricing, but also to study how such a measure affects the accessibility of opportunities (for example, jobs, shops and so on) in general or in particular areas, and how accessibility effects differ for different groups of people living or conducting activities at certain locations. Moreover, it may be worthwhile to know how spatial effects differ by type of road-pricing measure. We believe, therefore, that a generalized cost-based accessibility approach adds value, as it combines the strengths of different approaches: (i) it uses components of economic welfare theory by considering not only the benefits but also the costs of road pricing; and (ii) it uses the advantages of accessibility measures to assess the spatial accessibility effects of pricing.

As described above, a generalized transport-cost impedance function can be used to assess cost-based accessibility effects. In such a generalized cost function, travel times can be monetarized by using time valuations. The extra toll component can then easily be added. However, using only one generalized transport function might not be sufficient to model 'realistic' accessibility effects. The generalized transport-cost function might differ for different (groups of) people and firms. Apart from the fact that different categories of travellers and firms might have dissimilar cost functions, they may also 'deal' with charging costs in an unequal way. Some types of travellers can decide to change behaviour in order to mitigate their costs. This influences accessibility. Subsequently, all these behavioural adaptations in aggregate might have an impact on travel impedances and the land-use system. Changes in impedances and locations, in their turn, again affect accessibility. Moreover, the implementation of pricing measures results in monetary gains for decision/policy makers. These 'revenues' might be reinvested in society in different ways, which can influence accessibility. Thus, realistic accessibility effects cannot be retrieved only by monetarizing some impedance components. When considering the characteristics of categories/ groups of travellers, behavioural processes and revenue reinvestments are important, too.

Thus, in modelling (cost-based) accessibility effects, several choices have to be made with regard to modelling characteristics. Modellers or decision makers have, for example, to choose a type of accessibility measure(s), the construction and level of differentiation of the generalized transport-cost function, and the level of network differentiation. The choice of such factors influences accessibility outcomes. This makes it important to gain insight into the sensitivity of accessibility outcomes to varying all kinds of (cost-related and other) characteristics. A high sensitivity to varying a certain attribute indicates, for example, that it is important to carefully implement such a characteristic when one wants to model realistic accessibility effects due to pricing measures.

Therefore, the goal of this chapter is to gain more insight into the sensitivity of computed accessibility changes due to road pricing to varying characteristics, which are particularly important in the case of road pricing: the sensitivity of accessibility outcomes to the size of the value of time, to the (number of) factors taken into account in the impedance function, and to varying price-measure characteristics (that is, price level, elastic or inelastic demand). Thereby, two types of sensitivity are discerned: (i) the 'overall' or average sensitivity of accessibility outcomes in a study area, and (ii) the 'spatial' sensitivity, meaning the extent to which accessibility effects are sensitive at specific locations/regions in the study area. If the sensitivity of accessibility measures for the generalized-cost impedance function is relatively low, a simpler impedance function might have advantages above a more detailed modelling process. This may have important implications for modelling the accessibility effects of road pricing.

We do not study the sensitivity of accessibility outcomes to (varying) revenue reinvestments, since many different types of revenue usage exist, of which not all are easy to include in a generalized transport-cost function.[1] Since revenue rebates are not included in the analysis, we clearly do not aim to determine 'realistic' (cost-based) accessibility effects; nor do we attach much value to the 'absolute size' (for example, give subjective indications whether certain accessibility effects are 'good' or 'bad'). However, in addition to studying the sensitivity of outcomes (that is, the primary aim), the accessibility results in this chapter also provide some other insights, for example: (i) the results indicate to what extent travel-time gains compensate toll costs;[2] and (ii) the outcomes make it possible[3] to compare accessibility effects for the various groups of people living at different locations, even though the actual results (without incorporating revenue rebates) may form worst-case results.

Although we primarily focus on studying the sensitivity of outcomes (without including revenue rebates), the idea is to keep (the rest of) the sensitivity study close to reality. On the one hand, this 'realism' can be achieved by taking account of important processes which might occur due to road pricing, that is, travel behaviour alterations due to a pricing measure which lead to travel-time changes. These changes are incorporated into the sensitivity analysis. On the other hand, 'realism' is operationalized as varying parameters/variables in the sensitivity analysis within reasonable limits. This means, for example, that the sensitivity of accessibility outcomes is tested for reasonably realistic price measures and values of time.

The outline of this chapter is as follows. Section 12.2 describes the methodology including the most important simulation characteristics. Section 12.3 focuses on describing travel-time benefits due to applied road-pricing measures and explores the sensitivity of accessibility outcomes when a generalized cost-based impedance function is used. Finally, conclusions follow in Section 12.4.

12.2   METHODOLOGY AND SIMULATION CHARACTERISTICS

This section describes the most important methodological issues and simulation characteristics regarding the accessibility sensitivity analysis. Section 12.2.1 explains why a simulation approach is used for the sensitivity analysis, describes the simulation models applied, and gives some features of the study area. Subsequently, Section 12.2.2 looks at the characteristics of the sensitivity analysis. Finally, in order to analyse sensitivity results in a systematic way a reference situation is described in Section 12.2.3.

12.2.1   Simulation (Models) and Study Area

As described in the previous section, there are a number of accessibility measures with which accessibility can be put into effect and computed, and simulation models are used to simulate (geographical) accessibility. Without using simulation models it is almost impossible to gain insight into the sensitivity of accessibility measure outcomes due to road pricing because of the (complexity of the) different stages that can be distinguished in computing accessibility outcomes under road-pricing conditions and the sensitivity attached to each stage. A higher price level (for the same type of charge) is likely to lead to a higher reduction of travel times at congested points in a traffic network. But it is unknown whether, for example, a charge which is made twice as high as a 'reference charge' also leads to doubling travel-time gains (for example, a linear/proportional relation in the case of using a contour measure, see Section 12.2.2). Subsequently, it is unclear how changes in travel time affect accessibility. An impedance function of an accessibility measure might, for example, not only consist of monetarized travel time (gains) but also might contain other cost components (for example, charging costs) that influence the sensitivity of accessibility outcomes to travel-time gains. Altogether, this means, for instance, that a possible linear proportional relation between price level and travel-time gain does not necessarily imply a proportional relation with accessibility change. Finally, the sensitivity might depend on the number and spatial position of opportunity locations. Overall, this means that many factors and processes might influence the sensitivity of accessibility outcomes under pricing conditions, making it, as said before, practically impossible to gain more insight into the sensitivities without using simulation models.

For the sensitivity analyses in this chapter, two simulation models are used: a dynamic traffic assignment model called 'INDY' (Bliemer et al., 2004) and a Geographical Information System-extension (GIS) called 'Flowmap'. The dynamic traffic assignment model was extended within OmniTRANS[4] to model not only a dynamic route-choice equilibrium, but also departure-time choice and elastic demand. The INDY modelling framework is used to forecast route travel times at different departure times, before and after the introduction of a road-pricing measure. Section 12.1 has already mentioned that it is important to take these benefits into account when modelling accessibility effects due to road-pricing in a realistic way. Outputs from the traffic model are used as input for Flowmap, which computes several geographical accessibility measures. The advantage of using these two models is that the strengths of two models are combined: INDY can compute changes in traffic conditions due to a road-pricing measure, and Flowmap is able to compute the geographical accessibility effects.

The study area (see Figure 12.1a) is a part of the Dutch province of North-Brabant situated in the southern part of the Netherlands. The east–west length amounts to approximately 50 kilometres. North–south,

(a)   (b)

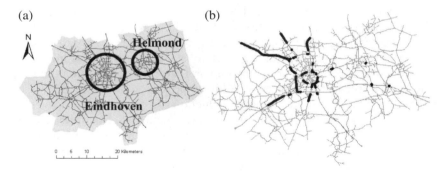

Note: Thick black lines indicate links with a speed ratio (= actual speed/free flow speed) below 0.65 (b).

Figure 12.1   Study area and network links

the size of the study area is somewhat smaller (approximately 30 kilometres). Two major cities are positioned within the boundaries of the area. The biggest is Eindhoven with about 208 000 inhabitants, and the other is Helmond with roughly 86 000 inhabitants. Several motorways cross the area, which all converge at the city of Eindhoven. The motorways around Eindhoven are known to suffer from congestion problems (see Figure 12.1b), which makes it interesting to study the road-pricing accessibility effects for this area.

The study area is regarded as a 'closed system'. This means in this case that only origin (for example, residential) and destination (for example, job) locations within the study area are considered. In reality, however, accessibility might be different, because people living in the study area might also look for opportunities beyond its boundaries.[5] This problem emerges more or less for each study area and, of course, depending on the goal of the study, it might be important to acknowledge this 'closed system' characteristic when the aim is to determine the actual accessibility effects due to road pricing. In this chapter, where the aim is rather to give an indication of the *sensitivity* of geographical accessibility results under road-pricing conditions, the closed system characteristic might not have a large influence on the sensitivity of the results. Although only opportunities within the study area are considered, the 'outside' world was in fact taken into account in order to determine realistic travel times in the network. The applied traffic assignment model INDY incorporated the effects of road pricing (i) on traffic crossing the study area; *and* (ii) on traffic with an origin outside and a destination inside the study area, and vice versa.

The total simulation period in INDY runs from 6.00 a.m. until 10.00 a.m. and in this case only simulates one user group: namely, commuters. Because traffic has to enter the network and build up in the beginning of the simulation and has to leave the network again at the end of the simulation period, it is better to leave a part of the 4 hours out of the actual analysis of results. Therefore, the period for which results are checked runs from 6.30 a.m. until 9.00 a.m. Simulation results are given for every 10-minute interval. The plan year for the simulations is 2010.

12.2.2 Characteristics of the Sensitivity Analysis

Accessibility measures and impedance parameter
On the basis of five criteria[6] (see Tillema, 2007), the suitability of different types of measures for modelling accessibility effects due to road-pricing measures was tested (ibid.). Classical location-based measures, such as the contour and potential measures, seemed to satisfy the used criteria rather well. Therefore, these two measures are employed in the simulation study.

A *contour measure* counts the number of opportunities which can be reached within a given travel time, distance or cost (fixed cost), or is a measure of the (average or total) time or cost required to access a fixed number of opportunities (fixed opportunities) (Geurs, 2006). A *potential measure* (also called a gravity-based measure), on the other hand, estimates the accessibility of zone i to all other zones (n) in which smaller and/or more distant opportunities provide diminishing influences. The measure has the following form:

$$A_i = \sum_j D_j F(c_{ij}),$$

where A_i is a measure of accessibility in zone i to all opportunities D in zone j, and $F(c_{ij})$ is the impedance function, in which c_{ij} represents the costs/impedance to travel between i and j. The cost/impedance function has a significant influence on the results of the accessibility measure and can take different forms, such as a power or exponential form (see Geurs and Ritsema van Eck, 2001).

The emphasis will be on studying variations in the generalized transport-cost function on accessibility computed with both types of measures. Jobs are chosen as the unit of analysis because an important goal of road-pricing measures is to reduce congestion. This means that the sensitivity of the accessibility of job locations is determined for people living at (origin) locations in the study area. Congestion mainly occurs during peak hours. The vast majority of people driving within these periods are on their way to or from work.

An important methodological issue not only in this study but in all geographical accessibility studies is which type of impedance parameter should be used. In this chapter, which focuses on studying the sensitivity of job accessibility results to cost aspects due to road pricing, only one impedance parameter per type of accessibility measure is used. For the contour measures, a cost equivalent[7] of 15 minutes is used. For the potential measure we use a cost sensitivity parameter of 1 (that is, a linear/proportional cost 'decay' function). For insight into the sensitivity of accessibility outcomes to different impedance parameters, see Tillema (2007).

A further consideration in the case of potential measures is the type of impedance function that is used. Power and exponential-based functions are both often applied in practice, with each function having advantages and disadvantages (see Geurs and Ritsema van Eck, 2001; Willigers, 2006). In this sensitivity analysis the power function is applied, because this type of impedance function may often be used on account of its correspondence with the 'original' Newtonian law of gravity, which forms the basis for the potential (gravity-) based measures.

To get a quick insight into the overall sensitivity of job accessibility changes of people (at different origin locations) in the case of using the contour accessibility measure, we use the following indicator: the average change (that is, over all zones) in the percentage of total jobs in the study area that can be reached from an origin location. To derive an interpretable measure to indicate the sensitivity of accessibility changes based on the potential measure, the approach of Geertman and Ritsema van Eck (1995) is used. They construct a 'modified potential measure' by computing the quotient of two classical potential formulas, whereby the impedance sensitivity parameter in the numerator is 1 point (integer value) lower than the parameter in the denominator. The outcome (in this chapter) is the average travel costs from an origin location to all surrounding zone centres. By weighting this average travel cost per origin zone with the number of houses located in a zone (that is, a proxy for the number of inhabitants), and by doing this for all zones in the study area, we can give an indication of the average travel cost (per zone) in the study area. We can then determine the relative changes in average travel costs if cost aspects are varied in the sensitivity analysis. In addition, we use a tessellated representation of the study area to show the 'spatial' sensitivity of accessibility outcomes to both the contour and the potential measure.

Price-measure characteristics

The sensitivity of accessibility outcomes is tested for a time-differentiated kilometre charge. As described in Section 12.2.1, the total simulation period runs from 6.00 a.m. until 10.00 a.m. Three different charge-level combinations are applied, with a higher charge within than outside the peak. During a one-hour period (that is, from 7.30 until 8.30 a.m.) the highest kilometre charge is levied. This period corresponds to the period with the highest traffic demand which causes traffic congestion in the network. Before and after this period a lower charge is used. The three price measures range from relatively low to high charge levels. The first measure charges 2 eurocents outside the peak period and 6 eurocents per kilometre between 7.30 and 8.30 a.m. The second charge corresponds to 11 eurocents in the highest charge period and 3.4 eurocents outside that period. The third and final differentiated charge amounts to 24 eurocents between 7.30 and 8.00 a.m. and 8 eurocents before and after this period. For all price measures the highest charge level is (approximately) three times as large as the lowest one.

As a result of the time-differentiated price measures, the expectation is that part of the traffic demand during the highest charge period will be diverted to less expensive time periods, thus improving the traffic conditions. The modelling framework also allows for the assumption of elastic demand for overall trip demand, which results in an increase or decrease in travel demand per origin–destination (OD) pair depending on the changes in generalized cost. Route-change effects might not be particularly strong when introducing a kilometre charge since all roads within the transport network are charged.

With respect to travel-demand changes, two alternatives were simulated for each price measure: one assuming inelastic, and one elastic demand. The alternative with the assumption of inelastic demand can be seen as a sort of lower boundary of possible travel-time changes: travel-time alterations only occur as a result of time and route changes. For the elastic demand, the (at the moment) default INDY cost elasticity of -0.2 was used. This means that a 10 per cent increase in transport costs leads to a 2 per cent decrease in overall traffic demand. This demand decrease might lead to an additional reduction in congestion problems within the study area. A cost elasticity of -0.2 is quite comparable to short-term cost elasticities for fuel costs (see, for example, Goodwin et al., 2004). However, a cost elasticity of -0.2 might be rather conservative in this case where the generalized transport-cost function consists of a combination of fuel costs and of a kilometre charge. First, the generalized transport-cost sensitivity is quite likely to be higher since fuel costs form only one part of the total generalized transport costs (besides the kilometre charge itself). Moreover, a road-pricing measure is more directly linked to travelling than to fuel costs, which might lead to higher travel-demand changes due to road pricing (that is, compared with the effect of equally high fuel-cost changes). Therefore, using a demand elasticity of -0.2 is likely to result in an underestimation of time gains that could be expected in reality.

Adjustment cost function and sensitivity parameters

For testing the influence of the cost function on accessibility outcomes, two stages in this simulation study are distinguished: (i) testing the effect of the size of the value of time (VOT) used; and (ii) testing the sensitivity of accessibility outcomes for adding a fuel-cost component.

VOTs are in most cases derived from data collected by stated choice experiments. Although there are certain ranges in which VOTs in general seem to fall, nevertheless substantial differences between those values can still be found. There are various reasons for these differences. First, different (groups of) individuals with different characteristics may have different VOTs (Gunn, 2001; Wardman, 2001). As a more methodological reason, the size of the VOT may depend on the type of choice experiment used to estimate these values. Route-choice experiments seem to lead to other estimated VOTs than mode-choice experiments, whose values are again different from values derived from departure-time experiments. The research method used (for example, stated or revealed preference), the type of estimation model applied (for example, multinomial or mixed logit models), and the formulation of the questions in a questionnaire are, however, also methodological aspects that might influence the VOT. Finally, VOTs may be influenced by other less easily explainable factors, such as the realism of, and the variation within, experiments.

Because of the large differences in VOTs, and the importance of those values for monetarizing the impedance function of accessibility measures, it is important to assess the effect that different VOTs (in size) may have on accessibility outcomes under pricing conditions. Changing the size of the VOT has two methodological consequences. On the one hand, the influence of the (monetarized) travel time within the cost function rises when the VOT is increased: the share of toll costs within the total cost function decreases. On the other hand, time gains are also valued more highly, leading to higher accessibility improvements when time gains are present. The net effect would quite likely be that a higher compared to a lower VOT would lead to relatively higher accessibility in the case of road pricing. However, it is hard to comment on the sensitivity of the process in advance. Therefore, the simulation study was conducted. The different VOTs that were tested in the case of the contour measure were: 5, 11 and 20 euros/hour. The average value of time estimated on the basis of data from a stated choice experiment in which respondents had to trade off different alternative commuting journeys amounted to 11 euros/hour (van Amelsfort and Bliemer, 2006). A value of 5 euros/hour was chosen because this comes quite close to low VOTs that were found on the basis of stated choice data in which people had to trade off residential locations on the basis of several house and location factors, on the one hand, and travel time and cost (that is, relative to the work location) related factors, on the other. The value of 20 euros/hour was chosen quite arbitrarily as a rounded maximum VOT. The average VOT for different commuter groups might, however, be (much) higher (see, for example, van Amelsfort and Bliemer, 2006).

At first sight, it might seem strange from a methodological point of view to determine travel-time changes with a traffic assignment model that uses a certain average VOT (in this case 11 euros/hour) and then use these travel times in an accessibility study, which studies the sensitivity to the VOT. It might, however, not be so odd. The traffic model INDY 'delivers' the average link travel times per period. And, although in reality people with, for example, a lower VOT, might change their behaviour differently from people with a higher VOT, this might on average not result in (much) different average link travel times in the network compared with the situation in which one average VOT was applied (with an average behavioural change). The accessibility (computed with Flowmap) was put into effect as the accessibility of a group of people with certain characteristics at a particular location and time period given the (average) traffic situation (that is, link travel times). Given this average travel time per link, people with a higher VOT but (living) at the same location might have another degree of accessibility change due to road-pricing than someone with a lower VOT (given the same link travel times for both persons). It might, therefore, be interesting to know how sensitive accessibility outcomes are for different groups of people with differing VOTs, given a certain traffic situation.

Apart from testing the influence of the size of the VOT used, taking other components such as fuel costs into account will also influence accessibility outcomes. By incorporating another cost component such as fuel costs (per kilometre), the relative size of the VOT in the cost function is reduced. This might influence the sensitivity of accessibility outcomes to the VOT used. A prognosis of sensitivity alterations in advance is especially hard to give in the case of using a potential measure in which the opportunities available are divided by a changing impedance coefficient (that is, a quotient). This chapter tries to gain some insight into only the sensitivity of accessibility outcomes to adding a fuel-cost component, and leaves the question whether it is wise to include a (kilometre-based) fuel-cost component unanswered. The fuel-cost component that was applied in the second stage amounts to 10.5 eurocents per kilometre. This is an average estimate of the fuel cost, taking into account the fuel prices for the different fuel types (Shell, 2006), the share of petrol, diesel and LPG cars in the Netherlands, and the average fuel consumption of these cars per kilometre (computed from data of Schellings, 2004).

Simulation period sensitivity analysis
The accessibility sensitivity analysis described in this chapter focuses on the particular 10-minute period (in the total simulation) in which travel-time gains are highest due to the kilometre charge. The idea behind this choice is that sensitivity to the VOT in such a period is largest, thus making it possible to gain better insight into the 'boundaries' of the sensitivity than if periods with smaller time benefits are used in the analysis. The largest travel-time gains are expected to occur in the 'high-charge period'. Partly depending on the traffic demand in the low-charge period, there will be a trade-off between the price level of the charge and the resulting travel-time gains. A higher charge will lead to a higher share of people who change from the high- to the low-charge period. But a point might be reached where so much demand is diverted that congestion occurs in the low-charge period, possibly affecting travel times in the high-charge period. Moreover, a high charge that leads to large travel-time gains in the 'high-demand' period might overall lead to worse traffic conditions than a lower charge if the low-charge periods are also taken into account in the analysis. But, as was explained, the aim of this chapter is to gain insight into the accessibility changes. In that respect, periods with high travel-time gains should be studied.

12.2.3 Reference Situation

The situation that is used as a reference against which the sensitivity analysis results are described is as follows: a time-differentiated kilometre charge with an average charge level and with inelastic overall traffic demand (that is, 11 eurocents from 7.30 a.m. to 8.30 a.m. and 3.4 eurocents outside that period), a contour measure with (a cost equivalent of) 15 minutes as a boundary value or a power function-based potential measure with a sensitivity parameter of 1, a VOT of 11 euros/hour, and no inclusion of a fuel-cost component.

12.3 TRAVEL-TIME BENEFITS AND SENSITIVITY OF COST-BASED ACCESSIBILITY OUTCOMES

This section focuses on studying the sensitivity of accessibility changes due to road-pricing measures for a generalized travel-cost-based impedance function in which the benefits (that is, time gains) of a road-pricing measure were included. Before presenting the actual sensitivity results, Section 12.3.1 first gives insight into the travel-time benefits that occur as a result of the time-differentiated kilometre charge(s). Then, Section 12.3.2

describes the accessibility change results due to pricing for the reference situation (see Section 12.2.3). Subsequently, Sections 12.3.3 to 12.3.5, respectively, represent the sensitivity of accessibility changes to: (i) the price measure; (ii) the VOT; and, finally, (iii) the addition of a fuel-cost component.

12.3.1 Travel-time Benefits of the Pricing Measure

Travel-time gains are a potential important benefit component of road-pricing measures. If the pricing measure does not lead to time gains and revenues are not reinvested, accessibility to jobs will inevitably decrease under pricing conditions for all groups of persons at whatever location they live. Therefore, it is important to first assess the differences in travel times between the situation with and without pricing.

For all pricing measures (that is, three price levels and assuming elastic or inelastic demand), the highest travel-time gains are found during the time interval 7.40–7.50 a.m. For the charge of 11 eurocents per kilometre with inelastic demand, the highest travel-time gain between any OD pair amounts to slightly more than 9 minutes, and, overall, around 1 per cent of the OD pairs have a gain of 5 minutes or more. As expected, time gains for the situation with elastic demand are higher: the highest benefit is approximately 14 minutes and 50 seconds, and around 1.5 per cent of the zones have a time decrease of 5 minutes or more. The highest time gains overall are observed for the situation with the charge of 24 eurocents per kilometre, and the lowest decreases occur for the 6 eurocents charge. The most extreme time benefit amounts to approximately 17–18 minutes in the case of introducing the 24 eurocents per kilometre charge (assuming elastic overall trip demand). The time-gain results also seem to point to elastic demand having a higher influence on time gains than departure time and route changes.

12.3.2 Results Reference Situation

The results for the reference situation for the contour and potential accessibility measures are presented in Figures 12.2 and 12.3, respectively. Grey and black shadings indicate the zones which have a better accessibility in the situation without road pricing: the darker the colour, the higher the differences. As can be expected in advance on the basis of economic welfare theory, Figure 12.2 shows that (in the case of using an average VOT) for all zones a deteriorating accessibility due to pricing is found. Time gains due to the kilometre charge are outweighed by the costs of 11 eurocents per kilometre. The highest deterioration in accessibility due to road pricing

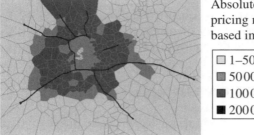

Absolute job accessibility *loss* due to pricing measured with a travel-cost-based impedance function:

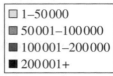

□ 1–50 000
▨ 50 001–100 000
▨ 100 001–200 000
■ 200 001+

Figure 12.2   Contour measure with impedance step cost equivalent of 15 min

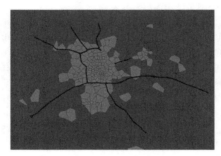

Relative accessibility *loss* due to pricing measured with a travel-cost-based impedance function:

■ 20–35%
▨ 35–50%

Figure 12.3   Potential accessibility measure with power costs sensitivity parameter of 1

occurs in the city of Eindhoven itself, but especially in its fringes and immediate surrounding area. The more rural areas just inside the boundaries of the study area experience the lowest absolute losses. A possible explanation for the more 'severe' deterioration of accessibility in the area around Eindhoven is that, with the introduction of road pricing, the large pool of jobs in the city of Eindhoven might no longer be reachable within the chosen contour impedance step, whereas without pricing these jobs can still be reached. More rural areas often cannot reach the job opportunities in Eindhoven, either with or without pricing, within a cost equivalent of 15 minutes. Therefore absolute differences in accessibility are possibly lower there. The zone that suffers most (in an absolute sense) from the kilometre charge can reach around 176 000 jobs less than it would without the charge. To give an indication, this amounts to more than 40 per cent of the job opportunities available within the study area.

Corresponding with the results for the contour measure, the potential measure also indicates a loss in accessibility for all zones due to the introduction of the kilometre charge (see Figure 12.3). However, the general spatial picture of deterioration is different. The potential measure outcomes show that the relative loss of accessibility is lowest in Eindhoven and its environs compared with the rest of the study area. In contrast, the contour measure shows the highest loss within and around the city. A possible explanation for the lower decrease in accessibility in the city when using the potential measure might be because, as mentioned before, a large number of jobs are available in close proximity in the city and travel-time gains due to the price measure are highest within and around Eindhoven. Because of the strong influence of the kilometre charging costs in the impedance function (compared with the travel-time gains), the smallest accessibility differences between the situation with and without pricing occur when distances and thus kilometre charge costs are relatively low; this leads to a smaller negative impact of the charging costs in the case of road-pricing compared with the situation without road pricing. Thus, shorter distances in and around Eindhoven, in combination with the relatively higher travel-time gains compared with the other parts of the study area result in a relatively lower accessibility decrease within the city. The highest relative decrease in job accessibility amounts to roughly 46 per cent.

In conclusion, in line with economic welfare theory, travel-time gains alone are not high enough to compensate for higher monetary costs due to the kilometre charge for people with an average VOT. More interesting is the finding that the sensitivity of results to the type of accessibility measure seems to be high. The spatial pattern of accessibility change due to road pricing differs markedly between using a contour or a potential accessibility measure. The only similarity is that both measures indicate a general accessibility decrease as a result of road pricing.

12.3.3 Sensitivity to Price-measure Characteristics

Three different kilometre charges were applied: 6, 11 and 24 eurocents per kilometre between 7.30 and 8.30 a.m.[8] As expected, the lowest charge (that is, 6 eurocents) leads to the lowest accessibility decrease. For 24 eurocents the decrease is highest. Larger travel-time gains caused by higher charges (see Section 12.3.1) do not compensate for the extra charging costs per kilometre. In reality, of course, a charge of 24 eurocents would not be very realistic and, if such a high charge were to be implemented, revenue rebates would also be higher. But the aim here is to gain insight into the *sensitivity* of accessibility changes for different price ranges. The decreases in average job accessibility for charge levels of 6, 11 and 24 eurocents are, respectively (see Figure 12.4): approximately 12.4, 17.6 and 24.8 per cent (of the total jobs) less. Thus, sensitivity to the type of price measure is quite large. Yet, accessibility changes are rather insensitive to the assumption of elastic demand. The reason for this is that, as described before, travel-time gains are not in such a range (even with elastic demand) that they compensate for charging costs.

For the potential measure, the lowest accessibility decreases again occur for the alternative of 6 eurocents/kilometre (see Figure 12.5). The average increase in mean trip costs for people living in the study area amounts to 14.0 per cent. For a charge of 11 eurocents this increase in average costs is 22.3 per cent. The highest deterioration in accessibility is found for the

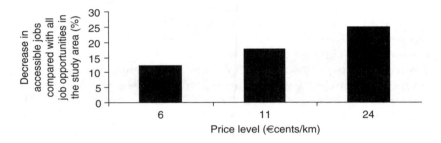

Figure 12.4   Average accessibility loss (i.e., percentage of total jobs in study area) due to pricing computed with a contour measure with a travel-cost-based impedance function for price levels of 6, 11 and 24 €cents per kilometre

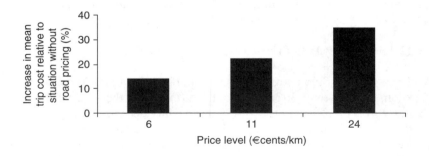

Figure 12.5   Average increase in mean trip cost due to road pricing computed with the potential accessibility measure and given for price levels of 6, 11 and 24 €cents per kilometre

highest charge of 24 eurocents per kilometre: an increase of approximately 35 per cent in average costs.

It can be concluded that the sensitivity to varying price-measure characteristics is high. Higher monetarized travel-time gains for higher charges do not compensate for higher costs due to the charge. The sensitivity of accessibility to the assumption of demand elasticity is low, at least for the time-differentiated kilometre charge.[9] Although not presented here, the 'spatial' sensitivity to varying price-measure characteristics was tested too. The spatial sensitivity to such characteristics is relatively low compared with the spatial sensitivity to the type of accessibility measure. The accessibility measure primarily determines the spatial pattern of where high or low accessibility effects can be expected.

12.3.4 Sensitivity to the Value of Time

As described in Section 12.2.2, three VOTs were applied in the sensitivity analysis. Accessibility outcomes for the contour measure are sensitive to the size of the VOT. Higher VOTs cause time gains due to the road-pricing measure having a higher monetary value. To give an indication of the sensitivity, the average decrease in job accessibility for a zone in the case of using a VOT of 5 euros/hour and a contour impedance step of (a cost equivalent of) 15 minutes amounts to 25.0 per cent (that is, 25 per cent less of the total jobs in the study area). For VOTs of 11 and 20 euros/hour, this average decrease in accessibility is, respectively, approximately 17.6 and 12.4 per cent (see Figure 12.6). However, although accessibility outcomes are sensitive to the VOT, even for people with higher than average VOTs, that is, 20 euros/hour (for example, time-constrained car commuters), monetarized travel-time gains due to the price measure do not compensate for the kilometre charge costs. Figure 12.7 shows that, for the reference situation described in Section 12.2.3, the trade-off VOT for which almost the same number of zones benefit as do not benefit from the kilometre charge of 11 eurocents is close to an unrealistic 1000 euros/hour. If elasticity of overall travel demand is assumed, the trade-off is found to be close to 250 euros/hour.

For the potential measure, the same kind of sensitivity is observed: the decreases in accessibility due to the kilometre charge become smaller with increasing VOT, but for a VOT of 20 euros/hour a decrease in accessibility for all zones is still observed. The average increase in mean trips cost due to road-pricing for someone living in the study area amounts to 22.3 per cent if a VOT of 11 euros/hour is used. For VOTs of 5 and 20 euros/hour, the mean increases are, respectively, 35.0 and 14.0 per cent (see Figure 12.8).

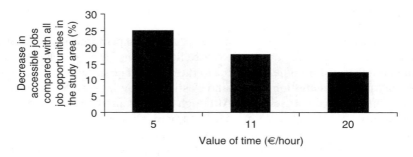

Figure 12.6   Average accessibility loss (i.e., percentage of total jobs in study area) due to pricing computed with a contour measure with a travel-cost-based impedance function for VOTs of 5, 11 and 20 € per hour

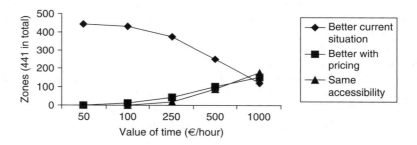

Figure 12.7   Trade-off VOT for reference situation (i.e., charge 11 €cents/kilometre, no overall elastic demand)

In conclusion, it can be said that accessibility results are rather sensitive to the VOT used. Only groups of people with extremely high (unrealistic) VOTs seem to benefit from road pricing, at least as long as only travel-time gains are incorporated as benefits into the generalized transport-cost function. Finally, in line with the previous section, it was found (but not graphically shown in this chapter) that the spatial sensitivity to the VOT is relatively small.

12.3.5   Sensitivity for Adding a Fuel Cost

To determine the sensitivity of accessibility outcomes for fuel costs, an average fuel cost of 10.5 eurocents/kilometre is added to the impedance function (see Section 12.2.2). By adding a fuel-cost component, decreases in accessibility due to the road-pricing measure seem to get smaller if a contour

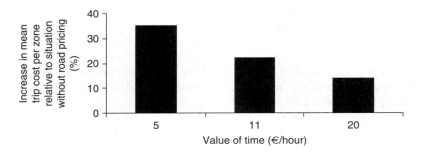

*Figure 12.8   Average increase in mean trip cost due to road pricing
computed with the potential accessibility measure and given
for values of time of 5, 11 and 20 € per hour*

measure is used. This result might be somewhat misleading. Because the
same fuel-cost component is added both with and without pricing, the cost
impedance between two zones is in fact increased by a constant value (that
is, distance * fuel cost per kilometre). Then, in order to obtain the same
accessibility change outcomes due to pricing as observed without adding a
fuel cost, the impedance step used for the contour measure should also be
increased. Thus, the sensitivity of accessibility outcomes based on a contour
measure in fact does not change as a result of the addition of an extra cost
component. It is rather a 'difference of scale problem'. For the potential
measure, however, sensitivity results are somewhat different. As a result of
the addition of a fuel-cost component, the available opportunities are
divided by a higher impedance both with and without road pricing. The
higher influence of resistance causes accessibility differences between the
situation with and without road pricing to become more local (as also
happens if a higher impedance parameter is chosen). Besides that, however,
the accessibility decrease due to pricing becomes relatively lower because the
(constant) opportunities are divided by a higher impedance.

12.4   CONCLUSIONS

This chapter has aimed to gain more insight into the *sensitivity* of job-
accessibility changes due to time-differentiated kilometre charges. Two
accessibility measures with a generalized transport-cost-based impedance
function were used: a contour and a potential accessibility measure. During
a one-hour period, in which the largest traffic demand occurred, the highest
charge was implemented. The three different price levels that were tested

were: 6, 11 and 24 eurocents per kilometre. Outside that period, the charge was (approximately) one-third of the highest charge, respectively, 2, 3.4 and 8 eurocents. For the 10-minute period with the highest travel-time gains due to the charge, sensitivity analyses were conducted. The sensitivity of accessibility changes was studied for the size of the VOT, the (number of) factors taken into account in the impedance function, and price-measure characteristics (that is, price level, elastic or inelastic demand).

It was found that the 'spatial' sensitivity of the results to the type of accessibility measure used is large: the spatial pattern of accessibility change due to road pricing was found to be very different when using either a contour or a potential measure. The only similarity is that both measures point towards a general decrease in accessibility due to road pricing. This sensitivity to the type of accessibility measure is especially related to differences in how various accessibility measures work. A contour measure, for example, uses an impedance step and determines which opportunities can be reached from a certain origin location within that impedance. A potential measure, on the other hand, does not work with fixed impedances. Instead, a more gradual impedance (decay) function is used. Such differences influence the results. Since the spatial sensitivity of accessibility to varying the type of measure is high, one must know precisely what one wants to know or express by using a particular accessibility measure. If this is not the case, it is probably better to use several indicators in order to be able to give a sort of 'bandwidth' of accessibility effects.

The general sensitivity of accessibility outcomes (that is, average effects for the study area) to price-level changes of the charge and to the VOT applied is quite high. Although higher charges lead to higher travel-time gains during congested periods, higher travel-time gains alone do not seem to compensate for the extra monetary costs due to a higher price level. Monetary pricing costs even dominate travel-time gains to such an extent that the lowest charge (that is, 6 eurocents per kilometre) leads to the lowest decrease in accessibility compared with the situation without road pricing. Moreover, three VOTs were included in the sensitivity analysis: 5, 11 and 20 euros/hour. For higher VOTs, decreases in accessibility due to pricing clearly become smaller. However, in the reference situation (that is, a kilometre charge of 11 eurocents per kilometre and assuming inelastic trip demand) a VOT of almost 1000 euros/hour is needed to trade off the higher costs of the kilometre charge. Although the overall (that is, average effects for the study area) accessibility effects due to changes in price-measure characteristics and in the VOT are high, the spatial sensitivity is relatively low. The type of accessibility measure particularly determines where in the study area the highest or lowest accessibility effects can be found. Within this given 'spatial pattern', price and VOT changes merely seem to influence the size of the changes. This low spatial sensitivity to varying cost-related aspects also has to do with the fact that the applied kilometre charge is not differentiated in space (see also Tillema, 2007).

The influence of adding a fuel-cost component was also tested. The results seem to be very sensitive to adding an extra cost component to the cost function. But, in fact, the largest part of this sensitivity is actually due to a general increase in the (measurement) scale of the cost function: for both the situation with and without the charge, an extra cost component is added. In further research, it would be interesting to study the sensitivity of accessibility changes to adding a fuel-cost component in a more differentiated way: for example, by not taking into account only one mean fuel cost per kilometre, but by making a distinction between different fuel types.

Although this chapter particularly focused on the sensitivity of geographical accessibility effects, it seems that cost-based accessibility analyses can contribute to (but not substitute for) economic welfare analyses in the way that they make it possible to determine spatial (differentiated) accessibility consequences. If the actual (welfare-based) accessibility effects of road pricing are to be assessed, it is important to not only include travel-time gains as a benefit component. In such cases the accessibility of groups of persons with an average VOT would always decrease due to pricing. This might give the (incorrect) idea that road pricing only leads to decreases in accessibility. To determine 'realistic' accessibility effects, it is therefore important to also include revenue rebates, whenever possible. Nevertheless, when only travel-time gains are incorporated, the computed accessibility effects might still be of value. Such results make it possible to compare the accessibility effects for different groups of people (for example, with a different VOT) living at different locations, even though the actual accessibility effects might form 'worst-case' scenarios where everybody in general 'loses'.

Finally, the type of procedure followed in this chapter can only correctly determine the accessibility changes for people who do not change behaviour but who benefit from time gains caused by people who do change their behaviour (for further details, see Tillema, 2007). The aggregate 'loss' of this group of people who change behaviour can be determined quite easily by using an economic welfare approach (the rule of half). The loss in consumer surplus of the group of people who change behaviour is equal to $\frac{1}{2}$*(number of car trips changed)*(increase in generalized price) (see, for example, de Borger and Proost, 1997). The increase in general price is equal to the charge level minus the monetarized benefits (for example, due to travel-time reductions).

NOTES

1. Leaving out revenue rebates in fact causes the accessibility outcomes that are presented in this chapter to be 'worst-case scenarios'.
2. On the basis of economic welfare theory, one might expect that these time gains do not fully compensate for toll costs, at least if the value of time used is not that far from that of the average driver.
3. This is true as long as we assume that every person benefits to the same extent from a revenue investment, should it be implemented.
4. OmniTRANS is a software environment for transport planning and modelling.
5. With respect to this study area, this might more strongly be the case for the opportunities outside the study area located at the north, east and west. But in the south, opportunities might be less interesting since the southern border of the study area corresponds with the 'country' border between the Netherlands and Belgium.
6. The five criteria were: realism outcomes; ability to model on a regional scale; data requirements; transferability of the modelling approach to different regions; and interpretability and communicability of outcomes.
7. A cost equivalent means that travel-time impedance steps are expressed as costs by multiplying the travel time by a value of time.
8. Lower charges were used outside this period (see Section 12.2.2).
9. For a more spatially differentiated charge (that is, not all roads are tolled), the sensitivity for the assumption of elastic demand is higher (see Tillema, 2007).

REFERENCES

Bliemer, M.C.J., H.H. Versteegt and R.J. Castenmiller (2004), 'INDY: a new analytical multiclass dynamic traffic assignment model', *Proceedings of the TRISTAN V Conference*, Guadeloupe, 13–18 June, pp. 1–8.

Bruinsma, F. and P. Rietveld (1998), 'The accessibility of European cities: theoretical framework and comparison of approaches', *Environment and Planning A*, **30**, 499–521.

de Borger, B. and S. Proost (eds) (1997), 'Mobiliteit: de juiste prijs' ('Mobility: the right price'), Leuven/Apeldoorn: Garant Uitgevers n.v.

Geertman, S.C.M. and J.R. Ritsema van Eck (1995), 'GIS and models of accessibility potential: an application in planning', *International Journal of Geographical Information Systems*, **9** (1), 67–80.

Geurs, K.T. (2006), 'Accessibility, land use and transport (Accessibility evaluation of land-use and transport developments and policy strategies)', PhD thesis, Faculty of Geosciences, Human Geography, Utrecht: Utrecht University.

Geurs, K.T. and J.R. Ritsema van Eck (2001), 'Land use, accessibility and the environment', Bilthoven, RIVM (National Institute for Public Health and the Environment), report number 114.

Geurs, K.T. and B. van Wee (2004), 'Accessibility evaluation of land-use and transport strategies: review and research directions', *Journal of Transport Geography*, **12**, 127–40.

Goodwin, P., J. Dargay and M. Hanly (2004), 'Elasticities of road traffic and fuel consumption with respect to price and income: a review', *Transport Reviews*, **24** (3), 275–92.

Gunn, H. (2001), 'Spatial and temporal transferability of relationships between travel demand, trip cost and travel time', *Transportation Research E*, **37**, 163–89.

Handy, S.L. and D.A. Niemeier (1997), 'Measuring accessibility: an exploration of issues and alternatives', *Environment and Planning A*, **29**, 1175–94.

Ministry of Transport, Public Works and Water Management (2006), 'Kosten verkeersongevallen in Nederland (ontwikkelingen 1997–2003)' ('Costs of traffic accidents in the Netherlands (developments 1997–2003)'), AVV, Rotterdam, working paper.

Schellings, R. (2004), 'Steeds meer auto's op diesel' ('More and more cars on diesel'), Webmagazine CBS.

Shell (2006), 'Shell Brandstofprijzen' ('Shell fuel prices'), www.shell.com/home/PlainPageServlet?FC=/nl-nl/html/iwgen/app_profile/nl-nl_hoeveelkost.html, April.

Tillema, T. (2007), 'Road pricing: a transport geographical perspective (geographical accessibility and short and long-term behavioural effects)', PhD thesis, Faculty of Geosciences, Human Geography, Utrecht: Utrecht University.

Tillema, T., G.P. van Wee and T. de Jong (2003), 'Road-pricing from a geographical perspective: a literature review and implications for research into accessibility', Paper presented at the 43rd European Regional Science Association (ERSA) Congress 2003, Jyväskylä, Finland, 27–30 August.

van Amelsfort, D.H. and M.C.J. Bliemer (2006), 'Alternative specifications of scheduling delay components: the effect of travel time uncertainty and departure time rescheduling', Paper presented at the 85th Transportation Research Board (TRB) Annual Meeting, Washington, DC, 22–26 January.

Wardman, M. (2001), 'A review of British evidence on time and service quality valuations', *Transportation Research E*, **37**, 107–28.

Willigers, J. (2006), 'Impact of high-speed railway accessibility on the location choices of office establishments', PhD thesis, Faculty of Geosciences, Human Geography, Utrecht: Utrecht University.

13. Firms' perception and acceptability of transport pricing

Linda Steg, Taede Tillema, Bert van Wee and Geertje Schuitema

13.1 INTRODUCTION

Motorized transport has greatly increased during the last few decades. The growing number of motorized vehicles and their frequent use causes serious problems for environmental quality, the quality of the urban life, traffic safety, traffic flows and the accessibility of various destinations. Many have stressed that the current transport system is not sustainable (for example, OECD, 1997, 2002; UNEP, 1999; EU, 2001, 2003; van Wee, 2007).

It is widely acknowledged that changes in the volumes of motorized traffic are needed to reduce the many problems it produces (for example, OECD, 1997; Gärling et al., 2002). Furthermore, problems could be reduced if people were to drive at other times or in different places. Thus, policies must target the demand for car use. Various policy measures have been proposed to manage travel demand. In general, four general travel demand management (TDM) strategies may be distinguished: information strategies and social marketing; urban planning; prohibition; and transport pricing (Steg, 2003; Gärling and Steg, 2007). These strategies differ in the way they trigger behaviour changes. The first, information strategies and social marketing, is aimed at reducing car use by changing people's perceptions, beliefs, attitudes, values and norms. The last three are designed to change conditions and structures that inhibit motorized transport and/or facilitate the use of sustainable modes of transport. Urban planning aims to facilitate or inhibit certain types of travel behaviour by changing physical structures and infrastructure. Prohibition is based on enforcing behaviour changes via laws, regulations and standards adopted by the government. Transport pricing concerns making motorized transport less attractive by increasing the price of motorized transport (in general, or at certain times or on specific routes), or by making the use of sustainable modes of transport (or driving at other times and places) relatively cheaper, thereby increasing their relative attractiveness.

Transport pricing is generally believed to be an effective and efficient way to manage problems resulting from motorized traffic (for example, Ubbels and Verhoef, 2007). Various modelling studies, but also some studies in which the actual effects of transport pricing were studied, revealed that transport pricing may be highly effective in reducing motorized transport and its associated problems (for a review, see Verhoef et al., 2004). Prominent examples are the Singapore area licence scheme (a congestion charge) and the London congestion charge (see Small and Gomez-Ibañez, 1998; Santos, 2004; Santos et al., 2004; and Santos, Chapter 14 in this volume). However, transport pricing is not easily implemented because of lack of public support, that is, in general, the public evaluates transport-pricing measures as rather unacceptable (for example, Schlag and Teubel, 1997; Jones, 1998, 2003; and, for a review, see Steg and Schuitema, 2007). In fact, many transport-pricing policies have not been implemented (yet) because of public resistance, as expressed by various lobbying and interest groups which represent the transport sector and car users. Policy makers appear quite reluctant to implement unpopular policies. Thus, an important question is whether it is possible to design pricing schemes that are acceptable. This requires knowledge of the factors that affect the acceptability of transport policies, and more specifically, transport pricing.

Recently, various (psychological) studies have been conducted on factors related to the acceptability of transport pricing among private car users (for example, Schlag and Teubel, 1997; Jakobsson et al., 2000; Schade and Schlag, 2000, 2003; Schlag and Schade, 2000; Bamberg and Rölle, 2003; Jones, 2003; Loukopoulos et al., 2005; and, for a review, see Steg and Schuitema, 2007). These studies reveal that the acceptability of transport pricing is particularly related to the perceived effects of pricing policies (Bamberg and Rölle, 2003; Jaensirisak et al., 2003; Schade and Schlag, 2003; Schuitema and Steg, 2005b; and see also Schuitema et al., Chapter 11 in this volume). In general, people appear to resist policies that are not effective in solving problems caused by car use. On the other hand, policies are not acceptable when they are quite effective in changing an individual's own behaviour and seriously affect the individual's freedom to move (Jakobsson et al., 2000; Schuitema and Steg, 2005b). Apparently, people prefer policies that help solve collective problems resulting from car use, without having serious consequences for their own travel behaviour.

Transport pricing may have negative effects for many people, and, consequently, may not be very acceptable to them. However, some groups may find ways to evade the charges, and thus price increases may not affect them. Moreover, some groups may actually benefit from transport-pricing policies: for example, if congestion levels decrease, accessibility improves, or if environmental and urban quality improve, this is advantageous to society. Thus, to the extent that people would benefit from pricing policies, they may actually be in favour of transport pricing.

Interestingly, the studies discussed above focused just on private car use. To the authors' knowledge, it has not yet been studied whether transport pricing is acceptable to firms, and what factors affect firms' acceptability ratings. This is surprising, since a substantial proportion of motorized traffic is related to business transport. Almost all transport of goods and products is business transport. More specifically, in most countries about 10 to 20 per cent of total car-kilometres is business related, for example, in the Netherlands, about 15 per cent in 2003 (Ministerie van Verkeer en Waterstaat, 2004). Therefore, it is highly relevant to study firms' opinions on transport pricing.

In this chapter, we examine whether transport pricing, and more specifically, kilometre charging, is acceptable to firms, and which factors affect these acceptability judgements. As studies on private car use have revealed that acceptability is strongly related to the extent to which people think that transport pricing will be effective, we focus on the relationships between acceptability and the perceived effectiveness of kilometre charging. Based on studies of private car use, our general hypothesis is that kilometre charging will be less acceptable the more that firms are likely to suffer from it, while kilometre charging will be more acceptable if firms benefit from it. Firms may consider various costs and benefits. We propose that the degree to which firms will benefit or be prejudiced against kilometre charging may be shown particularly in changes in travel costs and the accessibility of firms: kilometre charging will be less acceptable if (travel) costs increase and accessibility does not improve. Moreover, the extent to which the accessibility of firms can improve may be influential. After all, in this case, firms may actually profit from kilometre charging, as the charge would indeed reduce accessibility problems. Therefore, in this chapter, we focus on how factors related to the accessibility of firms and the extent to which firms expect changes in travel costs and accessibility, all affect acceptability judgements. We further break down our general hypothesis into the following three specific hypotheses.

First, the allocation of revenues from kilometre charges may affect both travel costs and perceived accessibility of firms (see Steg and Schuitema, 2007). Total travel costs will increase less or may even decrease if revenues from kilometre charging are used to reduce other costs of travel (for example, to reduce fuel levies or road taxes). Moreover, the accessibility of (at least some) firms may increase if revenues are used to construct new road infrastructure, resulting in a reduction in congestion problems. Therefore, we hypothesize that kilometre charging is more acceptable if revenues are used to (i) reduce fuel levies; (ii) abolish road taxes; or (iii) construct new road infrastructure, rather than allocating revenues to (iv) general public funds, (v) improve the quality of public transport, (vi) provide high-quality public traffic information, or (vii) decrease income taxes (Hypothesis 1).

Second, both the accessibility of business locations in the current situation and perceived changes in accessibility due to kilometre charging may affect acceptability judgements. We hypothesized that kilometre charging is more acceptable if firms experience accessibility and congestion problems (Hypothesis 2a) and if they expect their accessibility to improve when kilometre charging is implemented (Hypothesis 2b). We elaborate on the extent to which firms actually expect such charging to affect their accessibility. Accessibility may improve as travel times decrease, and the reliability of travel times increases.

Third, the extent to which kilometre charging results in cost increases may affect acceptability. Not only may travel costs increase, but also business costs, for example, when firms compensate employees for higher travel costs by offering various fringe benefits, such as reimbursement of travel costs.[1] On the other hand, firms may evade increases in travel costs by adapting firm-related travel behaviour. We hypothesized that kilometre charging is less acceptable when firms expect their travel costs to increase (Hypothesis 3a) and when firms plan to compensate employees for increased travel costs by offering various fringe benefits (Hypothesis 3b), while kilometre charging would be more acceptable when firms see opportunities to evade cost increases by changing travel patterns (Hypothesis 3c).

Besides investigating the relationships between the perceived need for, and the effectiveness and acceptability of, kilometre charging, we shall also examine to what extent expected changes in accessibility and travel costs contribute uniquely to the explanation of the acceptability of kilometre charging, and which of these factors is most important in this respect.

Finally, we shall explore differences in acceptability judgements between categories of firms. Various firm characteristics may affect the acceptability of kilometre charging, in so far as these characteristics determine the extent to which firms may face the consequences of kilometre charging. In this study, three firm characteristics are considered: sector (industry or services); firm size; and composition of the workforce (that is, mainly managerial, ancillary or executive). We do not a priori formulate hypotheses related to this but apply a more exploratory approach.

13.2   METHOD

In the second half of 2005, an Internet-based questionnaire was administered to the employees of two types of firms in the Netherlands: industrial firms and businesses in the service sector. Employees were approached by a polling agency. Some of the respondents participated in the agency's employment panel, while others were called by phone and asked to participate. Employees had to meet several criteria to be eligible for participation in the study. First, they had to be employed in the industry or services sector. Second, the establishment where they worked should employ more than 20 people. Third, they had to be acquainted with the company's location and personnel policies.

In total, 485 respondents participated in the study, of whom 246 (51 per cent) worked in the industry sector, and 239 (49 per cent) in the service sector. As may be expected, relatively few large companies were included in the study: 211 (44 per cent) employees worked in companies with 20–49 employees; 133 (27 per cent) in companies with 50–99 employees; 92 (19 per cent) in companies with 100–249 employees; 28 (6 per cent) in companies with 250–499 employees; and 21 (4 per cent) in companies with more than 500 employees.

The questionnaire comprised three parts. In this chapter, we focus on variables that are relevant for our own purposes. The first part of the questionnaire included questions on characteristics of the respondents' establishment (that is, the particular branch of the company where they work). In the second part, respondents indicated to what extent a kilometre charge would affect their establishment (again, their particular branch), and to what extent the charge would be acceptable for their establishment. Respondents were urged to reply in their capacity as a representative of their firm, and not based on personal convictions. The kilometre charge was described as follows:

> Imagine that the government introduces a kilometre charge. The level of the charge is dependent on the time of travel. On working days, charges amount to 12 eurocents per kilometre during rush hours (between 7.00 and 9.00, and between 17.00 and 19.00), and 4 eurocents per kilometre outside rush hours. Electronic devices register travel behaviour, and compute the total costs per trip. Payments may be made via automatic debit notices, credit card, giro, smart cards, or prepaid cards. The registration and payment systems have no technical defects. The privacy of travellers will not be threatened. The government decided to use the revenues for decreasing income taxes.

The third part comprised questions about the last employee who was hired by the company; these data are discussed by Tillema et al., Chapter 6 in this volume.

13.3   RESULTS

This section presents the main results of the study. First, we describe whether different types of revenue allocation affect the acceptability of kilometre charging. Second, we discuss whether the acceptability of kilometre charging is related to the extent to which firms currently encounter traffic problems, such as poor accessibility and traffic delays. Third, we indicate to what extent the kilometre charge is expected to affect the accessibility of establishments, and elaborate on relationships between expected changes in the accessibility and acceptability of kilometre charging. Fourth, we elaborate on relationships between acceptability judgements and the extent to which the kilometre charge is expected to affect firms negatively. Fifth, we report to what extent expected changes in costs and accessibility contribute to the explanation of the acceptability of kilometre charging. Finally, we discuss whether firm characteristics are related to the acceptability of kilometre charging.

13.3.1 Is the Acceptability of Kilometre Charging Dependent on Revenue Use?

After indicating the extent to which the kilometre charge would affect the firm's travel costs and congestion problems, respondents indicated to what extent the charge would be acceptable for their own establishment. Scores could vary from 'not acceptable at all' (1) to 'highly acceptable' (7). On average, the kilometre charge was evaluated as rather unacceptable ($M = 3.0$). Respondents also indicated to what extent the kilometre charge would be acceptable to their establishment if revenues were to be allocated differently. This question was included at the very end of the second part of the questionnaire. Respondents evaluated the acceptability of the kilometre charge, given the following seven types of revenue use: decreasing fuel levies; abolishing road taxes; constructing new road infrastructure; increasing the quality of public transport; decreasing income taxes; investing in high-quality traffic information systems alongside roads (for example, to warn about traffic jams ahead or suggest alternative routes); and allocating revenues to general public funds (which implies that revenues may be invested in many public goals, including health care, education and benefits). Responses were given on the same 7-point scale. The second column of Table 13.1 shows that the acceptability of a kilometre charge did indeed appear to be highly dependent on the way revenues are allocated: $F(6, 479) = 95.12, p < 0.001$. Kilometre charging is acceptable to firms if revenues are used to reduce fuel levies and to abolish road taxes. The kilometre charge is also quite acceptable if revenues are allocated to construct new road infrastructure. In contrast, allocating revenues of the kilometre charge to general public funds is not perceived to be acceptable.

Note that the respondents were asked once again to indicate to what extent they found the kilometre charge acceptable if revenues were used to

Table 13.1 Mean acceptability of different types of revenue as such, and acceptability of kilometre charge when revenues are allocated differently

	Acceptability of km charge when revenues are allocated differently	Acceptability of different types of revenue use	t
Decrease fuel levies	5.7 (1.30)	6.2 (1.12)	6.38*
Abolish road taxes	5.7 (1.24)	5.7 (1.25)	1.24
Construct new road infrastructure	5.1 (1.29)	5.5 (1.18)	7.87*
Increase quality of public transport	4.6 (1.51)	5.1 (1.54)	6.20*
Decrease income taxes	4.6 (1.67)	4.9 (1.72)	4.42*
Invest in high-quality traffic information systems alongside roads, e.g., to warn about traffic jams or suggest alternative routes	4.0 (1.46)	4.5 (1.47)	8.67*
General public funds, e.g., health care, education, benefits	3.6 (1.74)	4.0 (1.83)	6.50*

Note: * $p < 0.001$. Standard deviations are given in brackets.

decrease income taxes (this was also indicated in the description of the kilometre charge). Interestingly, the two judgements do not match. When respondents first evaluated this kilometre charge, they found the charge quite unacceptable ($M = 3.0$, see above), while the same charge was evaluated as more acceptable ($M = 4.6$) later on in the questionnaire. This suggests that the way in which questions are formulated may affect acceptability ratings. We shall come back to this issue in the Discussion section.

The finding that different ways of questioning may elicit different answers was also demonstrated in another part of our study. Before the idea of the kilometre charge was introduced, respondents had to indicate to what extent they found different ways of using the revenues from road-pricing policies acceptable in general. Thus, these acceptability ratings were given before respondents had evaluated the specific kilometre charge, and before they had considered how this charge might affect their establishment. Again, seven types of revenue use were judged (see Column 3 of Table 13.1). Although the ranking of the acceptability of different types of revenue use did not differ from the ranking presented in Column 2 of Table 13.1, significant differences were found between both acceptability ratings: $F(6, 479) = 109.24$, $p < 0.001$. The table shows that respondents judged the acceptability of different types of revenue use as such (without making any reference to a specific road-pricing policy: Column 3) more favourably, compared with the acceptability of the same allocation of revenues when it was explained that revenues were to be gathered via a kilometre charge (which would affect the respondents' establishment: Column 2). Pairwise t-tests revealed that this is true for all types of revenue use except for the allocation of revenues to abolish road taxes (Table 13.1).

13.3.2   Is Kilometre Charging More Acceptable When Firms Encounter Traffic Problems?

We explored the relationship between the extent to which firms actually encounter traffic problems and the acceptability of kilometre charging in two different ways. First, we examined the relationship between perceived accessibility problems and acceptability judgements. The respondents indicated to what extent they found it difficult to travel to and from their business location by trucks and cars, public transport, and by bicycle or foot, respectively. Accessibility was defined as the effort or trouble involved for employees, customers, buyers and suppliers when travelling to or from the establishment. It was explained that the effort may be dependent on various aspects, including travel time, reliability of travel time and travel costs. Responses about accessibility were given on a scale ranging from 'very poor' (1) to 'very good' (7). It appeared that establishments were more easily accessible by trucks and cars ($M = 5.8$; $SD = 1.13$) and non-motorized transport ($M = 5.6$, $SD = 1.43$) compared with public transport ($M = 4.3$, $SD = 1.75$). Interestingly, no significant relationship was found between perceived accessibility problems and acceptability of the kilometre charge. Acceptability problems correlated -0.01 ($p = 0.835$) with perceived accessibility by trucks and car; 0.02 ($p = 0.738$) with perceived accessibility by non-motorized transport; and 0.04 ($p = 0.349$) with perceived accessibility by public transport. Thus, the acceptability of kilometre charging is not related to the extent to which establishments actually experience accessibility problems.

Second, we examined the relationship between the extent to which firms experience congestion problems and acceptability judgements. The respondents indicated to what extent their establishment encounters traffic jams, on a scale ranging from 'very little' (1) to 'very much' (7). On average, establishments did not suffer much from traffic jams ($M = 2.9$; $SD = 1.6$). Contrary to our expectation, the kilometre charge was evaluated as slightly less acceptable the more establishments actually experienced traffic jams ($r = -0.13$, $p = 0.005$); the relationship is quite weak, though.

13.3.3   Is Kilometre Charging More Acceptable When the Accessibility of Firms Improves?

In many cases, traffic is a derived demand, because the actual demand is determined by the wish to undertake different activities at different places. Therefore, geographical accessibility, which explicitly links traffic network effects to activity locations, may be used to evaluate the effects of kilometre charging. Geographical accessibility has advantages over more specific transport network-related accessibility indicators, which do not take account of the spatial configurations of activity locations (Geurs and van Wee, 2004). Perceived geographical accessibility (changes) may influence decision making and behaviour of actors, including firms. As a result of changes in accessibility, firms may, for example, decide to change their trip patterns or, in the long term, to relocate. Not much is known about how firms perceive accessibility, and more particularly about how kilometre charging may change perceived accessibility. This section aims to study how the kilometre charge may affect the perceived accessibility of firms. Specific attention is paid to examining the effects on perceived accessibility of possible travel time or travel-time reliability gains due to the kilometre charge.

Respondents were first reminded of our definition of accessibility (see Section 13.3.2). Next, they indicated to what extent the kilometre charge would affect the accessibility of their establishment. Initially, respondents were not made aware of possible travel time or travel-time reliability gains. Next, the same question was presented, but this time respondents were asked to assume that the kilometre charge would improve the reliability of travel time, but such reliability was not further defined or quantified.[2] Subsequently, the respondents indicated to what extent the accessibility of their firm would change when assuming that the kilometre charge would result in a decrease in travel times during congestion by 25 or 50 per cent, respectively. In all four cases, responses were given on a 7-point scale ranging from 'accessibility gets much worse' (1) to 'accessibility gets much better' (7).

Column 2 of Table 13.2 shows that, in general, respondents expected that the kilometre charge would barely affect their accessibility. The majority of firms (78 per cent) indicated that the kilometre charge would not affect their accessibility at all, while 14 per cent indicated that their accessibility would deteriorate, and 8 per cent expected the accessibility of their establishment to improve. Still, in most cases, only minor changes were expected.

The respondents expected that the accessibility of their establishment would increase somewhat if the possible benefits of kilometre charges were explained. Column 3 reveals that 24 per cent of the firms expected their accessibility to improve if travel-time reliability improved, while only

Table 13.2   *Changes in perceived accessibility of firms due to the kilometre charge; percentage of respondents choosing each answer and mean scores*

	No assumptions	Improvement reliability of travel time	Travel time in congestion decreases 25%	Travel time in congestion decreases 50%
Mean scores	4	4.2	4.4	4.5
Accessibility gets . . .				
1. much worse	1	1	1	1
2. worse	5	2	2	2
3. somewhat worse	8	5	2	2
4. stays the same	78	69	56	53
5. somewhat better	7	20	33	27
6. better	1	4	6	13
7. much better	–	–	–	3
Worse (sum 1, 2, 3)	14	7	5	5
Better (sum 5, 6, 7)	8	24	39	43

7 per cent expected their accessibility to decrease, but only minor changes were expected. Some 69 per cent did not expect any changes at all. When travel times during congestion are expected to decrease, more pronounced improvements in accessibility are expected. Column 4 shows that 39 per cent of the respondents expected an improvement in the accessibility of their firm if travel time during congestion were to be reduced by 25 per cent, while only 5 per cent expected their accessibility to deteriorate. In this case, 56 per cent of the firms did not expect any changes in accessibility. If travel times during congestion were to decrease by 50 per cent, 43 per cent of the respondents expected that the accessibility of their firm would improve, 5 per cent that their accessibility would deteriorate, and 53 per cent did not expect any changes at all. Again, in most cases, only minor changes in accessibility were expected. When comparing the results presented in Columns 4 and 5, we may conclude that a further decrease in travel time during congestion would not affect the accessibility of firms much. However, looking more closely at the distribution of frequencies, the effect of a further decrease in travel time is more pronounced. More respondents expect their accessibility to get (much) better if travel time during congestion were to be reduced further (from 25 to 50 per cent).

Expected changes in accessibility appeared to be related to acceptability judgements. The kilometre charge is more acceptable, the more respondents believe that the accessibility of their establishment would improve as a result of the kilometre charge ($r = 0.25$, $p < 0.001$). Furthermore, respondents who indicated that the accessibility would improve if the reliability of travel times were to improve as a result of the kilometre charge evaluated the kilometre charge as more acceptable than respondents who did not think increased reliability of travel times would improve their accessibility ($r = 0.20$, $p < 0.001$). Finally, respondents evaluated the kilometre charge as somewhat more acceptable when they thought that the accessibility of their establishment would improve if travel times during congestion would be reduced by 25 per cent ($r = 0.11$, $p = 0.017$) or by 50 per cent ($r = 0.12$, $p = 0.006$). In sum, these results suggest that the kilometre charge is more acceptable, the more respondents expected the accessibility of their establishment to improve.

13.3.4   Is Kilometre Charging Less Acceptable When Firms Are Seriously Negatively Affected by the Kilometre Charge?

As explained in the Introduction to this chapter, we expected the kilometre charge to be less acceptable, the more firms would be negatively affected by the charge. In this section, we focus only on monetary costs. Changes in travel times and reliability were discussed in the previous section. Firms may be affected by the kilometre charge in different ways. First, the charge may result in an increase in transport, business or commuter monetary travel costs. Second, firms may compensate employees for increased travel costs by offering various fringe benefits, which also implies a cost increase. Third, firms may evade increases in travel cost by changing transport, business or commuter travel behaviour. Below, we elaborate on each of these possible effects.

First, respondents indicated to what extent the kilometre charge would result in an increase in costs associated with the transport of goods and products, business travel and commuter travel, respectively. Responses were given on a 7-point scale, ranging from 'very strongly' (1) to 'not at all' (7). In general, respondents expected considerable increases in travel costs. In particular, they expected prices for costs of business ($M = 3$, SD = 1.71) and commuter travel ($M = 3.1$, SD = 1.89) to increase, while costs for transporting goods and products ($M = 3.4$, SD = 2.03) are expected to increase somewhat less. As expected, the acceptability of the kilometre charge was related to expected increases in travel costs. This was true for all three types of travel costs: the kilometre charge was evaluated as less acceptable, the more increases were expected in costs for transporting goods and products ($r = 0.26$, $p < 0.001$), business travel ($r = 0.31$, $p < 0.001$), and commuter travel ($r = 0.28$, $p < 0.001$).

Second, respondents indicated to what extent their establishment would change the following (untaxed) fringe benefits and facilities offered to their employees: reimbursement of removal expenses; company cars; reimbursement of kilometre or fuel expenses; reimbursement of costs of public transport; flexible working hours; and teleworking. Scores could range on a 7-point scale from 'the establishment would offer this far less often' (1) to 'the establishment would offer this far more often' (7); a score of 4 means that the current policies will not change. Table 13.3 shows that, in general, firms expect to make only minor policy changes with regard to fringe benefits; and the majority of firms would not change their policies at all. Company cars and the reimbursement of kilometre or fuel expenses would be offered somewhat less often, while flexible working hours and teleworking facilities would be offered slightly more often. The table also shows that the acceptability of kilometre charging is barely related to expected changes in employment policies. Weak (but significant) positive relationships were found only for offering company cars, reimbursement of kilometre or fuel costs, and reimbursement of public transport costs, which suggests that the kilometre charge is somewhat more acceptable if firms expect to compensate their employees in these respects.

Third, respondents were asked to indicate to what extent the kilometre charge would affect the firm's travel behaviour. They first indicated to what extent the number of business trips and trips made for transporting goods and products would change. A distinction was made between trips outside and during rush hours. In addition, they indicated to what extent use of information and communication technology (ICT) as a substitute for commuting or business trips, respectively, would change. Scores varied from 'far less' (1), to 'far more' (7), with a score of 4 indicating that nothing

Table 13.3   *Mean changes in offering fringe benefits and facilities, and correlations between these changes and acceptability judgements*

	% no change	M (SD)	r	p
Reimbursement of removal expenses	73	4.0 (1.06)	0.03	0.584
Company cars	75	3.7 (0.87)	0.14	0.002
Reimbursement of kilometre or fuel expenses	70	3.8 (0.91)	0.10	0.029
Reimbursement of costs of public transport	72	4.1 (0.94)	0.12	0.011
Flexible working hours	64	4.3 (1.02)	0.06	0.209
Teleworking	65	4.3 (0.96)	0.03	0.511

Table 13.4   *Mean changes in firm's travel behaviour, and correlations between these changes and acceptability judgements*

	% no change	M (SD)	r
Business trips by car	78	3.8 (0.72)	0.06
Business trips by car outside rush hours	56	4.6 (0.92)	0.05
Business trips by car during rush hours	58	3.6 (0.89)	0.09
Trips for transporting goods and products	91	4.0 (0.52)	−0.02
Transporting goods and products outside rush hours	73	4.4 (0.80)	0.08
Transporting goods and products during rush hours	72	3.7 (0.75)	−0.00
Replace commuter trips by ICT (e.g., teleworking)	65	4.4 (0.79)	0.10
Replace business trips by ICT (e.g., teleconferencing, email)	65	4.4 (0.78)	0.13

would change. Table 13.4 shows that the number of trips for business or transport purposes was not expected to change much; the vast majority of firms would not make any changes at all. However, firms indicated that they were likely to increase the number of trips outside rush hours, and to decrease the number of trips during rush hours. Thus, they intended to change the time of travel to evade increases in travel costs. Moreover, respondents indicated that commuter and business trips would to some extent be replaced by the use of ICT. Furthermore, the table reveals that expected changes in travel behaviour are barely related to the acceptability of the kilometre charge. Some weak positive correlations were found only between acceptability judgements and expected increases in ICT use to replace commuter ($r = 0.10$, $p = 0.027$) and business trips ($r = 0.13$, $p = 0.004$), which suggests that the kilometre charge is evaluated as slightly more acceptable when firms expect to replace commuter and business trips by ICT.

13.3.5   Factors Explaining the Acceptability of Kilometre Charging

From the above, we may conclude that acceptability judgements are mainly related to expected increases in travel costs and expected changes in accessibility. To further explore the relative significance of these expected changes in order to explain acceptability judgements, we conducted a regression analysis, with acceptability of the kilometre charge as the dependent variable, and expected changes in costs for transporting goods and

Table 13.5   Regression of expected changes in travel costs and accessibility on acceptability of the kilometre charge

	β	t	p
Change in costs of transporting goods and products	0.13	2.81	0.005
Change in costs of business travel	0.15	2.80	0.005
Change in costs of commuter travel	0.15	3.03	0.003
Change in accessibility	0.20	4.77	< 0.001

Note: $R^2 = 0.17$, Adj. $R^2 = 0.17$, $F(4, 480) = 25.05$, $p < 0.001$.

products, commuter travel and business travel, and expected changes in the accessibility of establishments as predictor variables. Together, these independent variables explained 17 per cent of the variance in acceptability judgements. Table 13.5 reveals that all four variables made a significant contribution to the model: the kilometre charge was evaluated as less acceptable if costs for transporting goods and products ($\beta = 0.13$), business ($\beta = 0.15$) and commuter travel ($\beta = 0.15$) were expected to increase. Moreover, the kilometre charge was more acceptable, the more respondents believed the accessibility of their establishment would improve ($\beta = 0.20$). Since all variables made a significant contribution to the model, expected changes in accessibility are probably not strongly related to expected changes in travel costs. Indeed, correlations between expected changes in accessibility and travel costs were quite low, ranging from 0.11 to 0.15.

13.3.6   Differences in Acceptability between Firms

Finally, we explored the relationship between firm characteristics and the acceptability of kilometre charging. No differences were found in acceptability ratings between the industry ($M = 3.0$, $SD = 1.4$) and the service sector ($M = 2.9$, $SD = 1.5$). Furthermore, acceptability judgements were not related to firm size: $F(4, 480) = 1.51$, $p = 0.200$. This may be partly because few large firms were included in our study (see the Method section). Table 13.6 suggests that firms with more than 500 employees evaluated the kilometre charge somewhat more favourably compared with firms with fewer employees. Indeed, a t-test revealed significant differences between mean acceptability ratings of these large firms (> 500 employees) and the smaller firms. However, given the small number of large companies included in our study, these results should be interpreted with caution.

To explore the various relationships between workforce characteristics and the acceptability of the kilometre charge, the respondents indicated what

Table 13.6   Mean acceptability of kilometre charge for firms differing in size

	M (SD)
20–49 employees	2.9 (1.47)
50–99 employees	3.0 (1.39)
100–249 employees	2.9 (1.41)
250–499 employees	3.1 (1.46)
> 500 employees	3.7 (1.28)

percentage of employees performed managerial functions (14 per cent), ancillary functions (19 per cent) and executive functions (67 per cent). No significant relationships were found between acceptability judgements and the percentage of managerial functions ($r = -0.09$, $p = 0.054$), ancillary functions ($r = -0.04$, $p = 0.420$) and executive functions ($r = 0.08$, $p = 0.079$).

13.4   CONCLUSIONS AND POLICY IMPLICATIONS

This chapter has aimed to examine to what extent kilometre charging is acceptable to firms, and which factors affect the acceptability of kilometre charging. We found some support for our general hypothesis that, in general, kilometre charging will be less acceptable, the more that firms would suffer (and not benefit) from kilometre charging. Indeed, kilometre charging was less acceptable if firms expected no improvements in accessibility and if (travel) costs were expected to increase due to the implementation of kilometre charging, while kilometre charging was more acceptable if firms expected positive consequences in these respects. Contrary to our expectations, the extent to which firms encountered traffic problems was barely related to acceptability judgements. Below, we discuss these findings in more detail.

First, as expected, the kilometre charge was evaluated as more acceptable if revenues were of direct benefit to firms (Hypothesis 1). The kilometre charge was fairly acceptable to firms when revenues were allocated to reduce fuel levies or abolish road taxes, while the same charge was evaluated as far less acceptable when allocating revenues to general funds. These results are in line with those reported in studies focusing on private car users (for example, Schuitema and Steg, 2005a; and, for a review, see Steg and Schuitema, 2007). Of course, using revenues to reduce costs of travel may affect the total effectiveness of kilometre charging. In fact, this may be precisely the reason why this type of revenue use was evaluated rather favourably.

Second, contrary to our expectations, the extent to which firms currently experienced traffic problems was not strongly related to acceptability judgements. However, kilometre charging was evaluated as somewhat less acceptable by firms that experienced congestion problems, but this relationship is rather weak. Thus, the extent to which firms currently have accessibility problems is not very influential (Hypothesis 2a). What matters is the extent to which respondents think that the kilometre charge will alleviate accessibility problems, as will become apparent below.

The vast majority (78 per cent) of the firms did not expect the kilometre charge to affect their accessibility if no information is given about the (possible) benefits of the charge with respect to travel-time (reliability) gains. However, if possible travel-time gains and/or travel-time reliability improvements are explained, the overall picture changed. In this case, a higher proportion of firms expected their accessibility to improve, especially if travel-time during congested periods were to be reduced. This suggests that accessibility may improve (only) if kilometre charging were to result in reductions in travel time during congested periods and/or improvements in travel-time reliability. As expected (Hypothesis 2b), kilometre charging is evaluated as more acceptable when respondents expect improvements in the accessibility of their establishment.

Third, we found some support for our hypothesis that kilometre charging is likely to be less acceptable if increases in travel costs are expected. Indeed, the kilometre charge was less acceptable, the more that firms expected increases in costs for transporting goods and products, and in costs of business and commuter travel (Hypothesis 3a). Hypothesis 3b was not supported. In general, the acceptability of kilometre charging was barely related to the extent to which firms expected to change their offering of fringe benefits and facilities to employees. However, contrary to our expectation, the kilometre charge was somewhat more acceptable if firms expected to compensate their employees by more frequently offering company cars, reimbursing kilometre or fuel costs, and reimbursing travel costs. The extent to which firms may evade increases in travel costs was also not strongly related to the acceptability of kilometre charging (Hypothesis 3c). Expected changes in travel behaviour were barely related to acceptability judgements, although the kilometre charge was slightly more acceptable if firms expected to replace commuter and business trips by ICT. Interestingly, firms expected to evade significant cost increases mainly by travelling at other times or by replacing commuter and business trips by ICT. Nevertheless, the total number of trips made would not be affected much.

Both expected changes in travel costs and changes in accessibility contributed independently to the explanation of the acceptability of kilometre charging. Indeed, kilometre charging was more acceptable if firms expected that their travel costs would not increase much, and if improvements in accessibility were expected. Expected changes in travel costs were barely related to expected changes in accessibility.

Finally, hardly any differences in acceptability judgements were found between firms operating in different sectors (industry or services) and firms differing in workforce characteristics. Nor did firm size appear to be influential, although our results indicate that kilometre charging may be more acceptable to large firms. This difference was not statistically significant, which may be because only a few large firms were included in our sample. Further research, including a sufficient number of large companies, is needed to address this issue.

These findings suggest that differences between different types of firms may not be as significant as might be expected. However, our study focused only on industrial firms and businesses in the service sector. Clearly, further research is needed to examine whether results may be generalized to other sectors, including government, the public sector, the transport sector, farming, catering and health organizations.

This study has yielded some other interesting findings regarding how the way of questioning may affect study results. Respondents had to rate the acceptability of the specific kilometre charge if revenues were to be allocated to decrease income taxes at two different places in the questionnaire: almost right after the kilometre charge was introduced to them, and after they had indicated the extent to which their own establishment would be affected in detail by the kilometre charge. Interestingly, the same kilometre charge was evaluated as more acceptable when respondents had thoroughly considered the consequences of the charge for their firm.[3] Two mechanisms may account for this finding. First, when the initial acceptability judgement was given, respondents were not asked to consider other types of revenue use, while, obviously, respondents compared different types of revenue use in the case of the other question. Comparative judgements may elicit different answers. Second, and more importantly, the initial acceptability rating was given almost straight after respondents had read the description of the kilometre charge, after they indicated to what extent the charge would affect their transport, business and commuter traffic, and the extent to which they thought the charge would be effective in reducing congestion levels in the Netherlands. Thus, respondents probably did not think through the consequences of the kilometre charge for their establishment in much detail. In contrast, the next acceptability ratings were given much later. In fact, it was the final question on the consequences of the kilometre charge for their own establishment. Probably, by this time respondents had considered the many pros and cons of the kilometre charge in more detail, and their judgements were better considered. Possibly, respondents were more aware of the possible advantages of the kilometre charge. Of course, this has important implications for policy. If the acceptability of kilometre charging is higher after people think through possible consequences of the charge for their firm, the positive consequences of kilometre charging should be high-lighted, for example, via information campaigns.

The possible effects of ways of questioning were also demonstrated in another part of our study. Respondents judged the acceptability of different ways of allocating revenues in general more favourably than the acceptability of the same type of revenue use when explaining that revenues would be gathered via a kilometre charge (which would affect the respon-dents' establishment). These results are in line with earlier studies on the acceptability of transport pricing among private car users (Schuitema and Steg, 2005a; see also Steg and Schuitema, 2007). Thus, different types of revenue use are more acceptable if no reference is made to the fact that the respondents themselves would be charged. Although the absolute levels of acceptability ratings differed, preference ranking was not affected.

These results illustrate that it is important to consider carefully the way in which questions are asked, and to select methods that elicit the highest-quality data possible. To get an accurate and valid view of the acceptabil-ity of pricing policies and different types of revenue use, multiple methods should be used in order to test the robustness of results.

In conclusion, although initially firms evaluated the kilometre charge as rather unacceptable, overall, the kilometre charge was evaluated as quite acceptable, especially if revenues were to be allocated in a way that may benefit firms, thus yielding the overall picture that firms did not seem to care that much about transport pricing. These results suggest that firms may evaluate transport pricing more favourably than households do (see Schuitema et al., Chapter 11 in this volume). In general, kilometre charg-ing is more acceptable if firms expect to benefit (and not only suffer) from it. It is important to communicate clearly the possible positive (and nega-tive) effects of transport pricing, in order to promote public acceptability.

NOTES

1. By introducing fringe benefits, business expenses will increase. Moreover, firms that com-pensate employees for increased traffic costs apparently expect negative effects from road pricing, which they try to reduce by offering fringe benefits. Of course, eventually, firms will consider the extent to which they may benefit from it as well.
2. Quantifying the gain in travel-time reliability was too difficult, given the limited space available in the questionnaire.
3. More generally, after indicating the consequences of the charge in various respects, the kilometre charge was evaluated quite favourably for any type of revenue use.

REFERENCES

Bamberg, S. and D. Rölle (2003), 'Determinants of people's acceptability of pricing measures – replication and extension of a causal model', in J. Schade and B. Schlag (eds), *Acceptability of Transport Pricing Strategies*, Oxford: Elsevier Science, pp. 235–48.

European Union (EU) (2001), *White Paper: European Transport Policy for 2010: Time to Decide*, Brussels: European Commission, europa.eu.int/scadplus/leg/en/lvb/l24007/htm, accessed February 2006.

European Union (EU) (2003), *Europe at a Crossroads: The Need for Sustainable Transport*, Luxembourg: Office for Official Publications of the European Communities, see also europa.eu.int/scadplus/leg/en/lvb/l24007/htm, accessed February 2006.

Gärling, T., D. Eek, P. Loukopoulos, S. Fujii, O. Johansson-Stenman, R. Kitamura, R. Pendyala and B. Vilhelmson (2002), 'A conceptual analysis of the impact of travel demand management on private car use', *Transport Policy*, **9** (1), 59–70.

Gärling, T. and L. Steg (eds) (2007), *Threats to the Quality of Urban Life from Car Traffic: Problems, Causes, and Solutions*, Amsterdam: Elsevier.

Geurs, K.T. and B. van Wee (2004), 'Accessibility evaluation of land-use and transport strategies: review and research directions', *Transport Geography*, **12**, 127–40.

Jaensirisak, S., A.D. May and M. Wardman (2003), 'Acceptability of road user charging: the influence of selfish and social perspectives', in J. Schade and B. Schlag (eds), *Acceptability of Transport Pricing Strategies*, Amsterdam: Elsevier, pp. 203–18.

Jakobsson, C., S. Fujii and T. Gärling (2000), 'Determinants of private car users' acceptance of road pricing', *Transport Policy*, **7**, 153–8.

Jones, P. (1998), 'Urban road pricing: public acceptability and barriers to implementation', in K.J. Button and E.T. Verhoef (eds), *Road Pricing, Traffic Congestion and the Environment. Issues of Efficiency and Social Feasibility*, Cheltenham, UK and Lyme, USA: Edward Elgar, pp. 263–84.

Jones, P. (2003), 'Acceptability of road user charging: meeting the challenge', in J. Schade and B. Schlag (eds), *Acceptability of Transport Pricing Strategies*, Amsterdam: Elsevier, pp. 27–62.

Loukopoulos, P., C. Jakobsson, T. Gärling, C.M. Schneider and S. Fujii (2005), 'Public attitudes towards policy measures for reducing private car use', *Environmental Science and Policy*, **8** (1), 57–66.

Ministerie van Verkeer en Waterstaat (2004), *Kerncijfers personenvervoer* (Basic data passenger traffic), Den Haag: Ministerie van Verkeer en Waterstaat, Rijkswaterstaat, Adviesdienst Verkeer en Vervoer.

Organization for Economic Cooperation and Development (OECD) (1997), *Towards Sustainable Transportation*, Summary proceedings of an international conference held in Vancouver, March 1996, Hull (Quebec): Environment Canada.

Organization for Economic Cooperation and Development (OECD) (2002), 'Report on the OECD conference "Environmentally sustainable transport (EST): Futures, strategies and best practice" ', www.oecd.org, accessed February 2006.

Santos, G. (2004), 'Urban road pricing in the UK', in G. Santos (ed.), *Road Pricing: Theory and Evidence*, Amsterdam: Elsevier, pp. 251–82.

Santos, G., W.W. Li and T.H. Koh (2004), 'Transport policies in Singapore', in G. Santos (ed.), *Road Pricing: Theory and Evidence*, Amsterdam: Elsevier, pp. 209–35.

Schade, J. and B. Schlag (2000), *Acceptability of Urban Transport Pricing*, Helsinki: VATT.

Schade, J. and B. Schlag (2003), 'Acceptability of urban transport pricing strategies', *Transportation Research F*, **6**, 45–61.

Schlag, B. and J. Schade (2000), 'Public acceptability of traffic demand management in Europe', *Traffic Engineering and Control*, **41** (8), 314–18.

Schlag, B. and U. Teubel (1997), 'Public acceptability of transport pricing', *IATSS Research*, **21** (2), 134–42.

Schuitema, G. and L. Steg (2005a), 'Factors that affect the acceptability of pricing policies in transport', Paper presented at the 7th Nordic Environmental Social Science (NESS) Research Conference, Göteborg, Sweden, 15–17 June.

Schuitema, G. and L. Steg (2005b), 'Effects of revenue use and perceived effectiveness on acceptability of transport pricing policies', Paper presented at the 45th Congress of the European Science Association, Amsterdam, 23–27 August.

Small, K.A. and J.A. Gomez-Ibañez (1998), 'Road pricing for congestion management: the transition from theory to policy', in K.J. Button and E.T. Verhoef (eds), *Road Pricing, Traffic Congestion and the Environment. Issues of Efficiency and Social Feasibility*, Cheltenham, UK and Lyme, USA: Edward Elgar, pp. 213–46.

Steg, L. (2003), 'Factors influencing the acceptability and effectiveness of transport pricing', in J. Schade and B. Schlag (eds), *Acceptability of Transport Pricing Strategies*, Amsterdam: Elsevier, pp. 187–202.

Steg, L. and G. Schuitema (2007), 'Behavioural responses to transport pricing: a theoretical analysis', in Gärling and Steg (eds), *Threats from car traffic to the quality of urban life: problems, causes and solutions*, Amsterdam: Elsevier, pp. 347–366.

Ubbels, B. and E. Verhoef (2007), 'The economics of transport pricing', in Gärling and Steg (eds), *Threats from car traffic to the quality of urban life: problems, causes and solutions*, Amsterdam: Elsevier, pp. 325–345.

United Nations Environment Programme (UNEP) (1999), *GEO 2000: Global Environment Outlook*, London: Earthscan.

van Wee, B. (2007), 'Environmental effects of urban traffic', in Gärling and Steg (eds), *Threats from car traffic to the quality of urban life: problems, causes and solutions*, Amsterdam: Elsevier, pp. 11–32.

Verhoef, E., C. Koopmans, M. Bliemer, P. Bovy, L. Steg and B. van Wee (2004), *Vormgeving en effecten van prijsbeleid op de weg. Effectiviteit, efficiëntie en acceptatie vanuit een multidisciplinair perspectief* (Design and effects of road pricing. Effectiveness, efficiency and acceptability from a multidisciplinary perspective), Amsterdam: Vrije Universiteit/SEO; Delft: Technische Universiteit Delft; Groningen: Rijksuniversiteit Groningen.

PART IV

Past and future of road pricing

14. The London experience[1]

Georgina Santos

14.1 BACKGROUND TO THE LONDON CONGESTION CHARGING SCHEME

On 17 February 2003 the London Congestion Charging Scheme (LCCS) was implemented, after a number of public consultation exercises and with a fair amount of background research supporting its design. The legislation needed had been in place since 1999.

The Greater London Authority Act 1999 (Acts of Parliament, 1999) had created an authority for Greater London, which consisted of the Mayor of London and the London Assembly; and had, at the same time, given the Mayor powers to implement road user charging and/or workplace parking levies.

Two major research studies on congestion charging in London had also been carried out. In July 1995, the Government Office for London published the results of the London Congestion Charging Research Programme (MVA Consultancy, 1995), which examined a range of technical options. The Review of Charging Options for London (ROCOL) Working Group had been set up in August 1998 with the aim of providing an assessment of options for congestion charging in London. They also produced a report, overseen by the Government Office for London, and published in March 2000 (ROCOL, 2000), which reviewed the available options for charging, conducted and discussed public attitude surveys, and assessed the impact of illustrative charging schemes.

The introduction of congestion charging was a central part of Mayor Ken Livingstone's manifesto for election in May 2000. After being elected, Livingstone decided to take forward the ROCOL proposals for a London congestion charging scheme in Central London. A number of documents and public consultations followed his decision.

The first such document was *Hearing London's Views*, which was published in July 2000, and sent to local councils, businesses and road-user representatives in order to get feedback on the initial ideas for a charging scheme.[2] After these comments, the Mayor's draft Transport Strategy, which included proposals for a Central London congestion charging scheme, was published on 11 January 2001 and sent to public consultation until 30 March 2001. This in turn was followed by his final Transport Strategy, published on 10 July 2001.

The proposed congestion charging scheme was then sent out for public consultation in its own right from 23 July to 28 September 2001. The results of this public consultation, especially in the area of exemptions and discounts, translated into modifications to the proposed scheme. Following the publication of the proposed modifications to the scheme in November 2001, there was a further consultation period until 18 January 2002.

On 26 February 2002 the Mayor finally confirmed the Scheme Order, which was subsequently modified several times until 14 February 2003. Even after it was implemented there were a number of Variation Orders that were confirmed and incorporated into the Greater London (Central Zone) Congestion Charging Order, the most significant one being the extension of the charging zone to include Kensington and Chelsea. More variations may be introduced in the future.

14.2   THE LONDON CONGESTION CHARGING SCHEME

The LCCS, designed and managed by Transport for London (TfL), is an area licensing one. All vehicles entering, leaving, driving or parking on a public road inside the zone between 7.00 a.m. and 6.00 p.m. Monday to Friday, excluding public holidays, must pay a congestion charge. This was initially £5, but on 4 July 2005 it was increased to £8. Similarly, the original hours of charging extended until 6.30 p.m., but they were shortened by 30 minutes on 19 February 2007, when the charging zone was extended westwards.

Figure 14.1 shows the limit of the area. The northern limit follows the Grand Union Canal and Harrow Road in part, Westway A40, Eastbourne Terrace, Praed Street, Sussex Gardens, Old Marylebone Road, Marylebone Road, Park Crescent, Euston Road, Pentonville Road and City Road. The eastern limit follows Old Street, Commercial Street and Tower Bridge Road. The southern limit is determined by New Kent Road, Kennington Lane, Vauxhall Bridge Road, Grosvenor Road, Chelsea Embankment and Cheyne Walk. The western limit follows Edith Grove, Redcliffe Gardens, the southbound route of the Earl's Court One-Way System, Pembroke Road, Warwick Gardens, Addison Road, Holland Road, the West Cross Route, the Great Western Railway Line and Scrubs Lane.

No charge is made for driving on the roads that mark the limit of the charging zone, and there are two free corridors: one north to south along

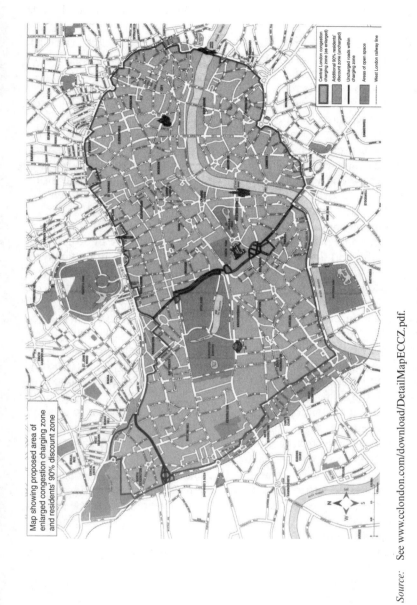

Map showing proposed area of enlarged congestion charging zone and residents' 90% discount zone

Source: See www.cclondon.com/download/DetailMapECCZ.pdf.

Figure 14.1   Map of the London congestion charging zone

275

Edgware Road, Park Lane, Grosvenor Place, Bressenden Place and Vauxhall Bridge Road; and another one north-west of the zone, east to west, as the diversion route would have been too long for drivers just wanting to cross that segment of Westway A40. The heavily-shaded roads on Figure 14.1 are all free of charge.

The charging zone is relatively small. It roughly covers 39 km² (15 mi²), representing 2.4 per cent of the total 1579 km² (617 mi²) of Greater London.

Payment can be made for a day, a week, a month and a year, up to 90 days in advance. The charge can also be paid on the day or on the day after. However, if the charge is paid on the day after, it increases to £10.

The methods of payment are online, in person at selected shops, petrol stations and car parks, by post, by telephone, by SMS from the payer's mobile phone, and at BT Internet kiosks. Paying for the previous charging day, however, can only be made via the call centre or via the TfL's website.

Businesses and other organizations operating more than 10 vehicles can use the Fleet Automated Scheme. After registering the 10 or more vehicles and paying an annual administration charge of £10 for each vehicle, the number plates of the registered Fleet vehicles are photographed by the cameras, and the corresponding charges calculated automatically. A pre-payment for the forthcoming month is drawn by direct debit from the Fleet account. The daily charge for the registered Fleet vehicles is £7, rather than £8.

There are a number of exemptions and discounts in place, which, as of February 2007, can be summarized as shown in Table 14.1. The 90 per cent discount to residents, which originally only applied to residents living inside the charging zone, has been extended beyond the charging zone boundary. The decision was made on the basis of the results of the 2004 public consultation on the Transport Strategy Revision.

The reasons for extended residents' discount zones are linked to parking and severance issues (TfL, 2005b, p. 10). For example, in some cases, the designated residents' parking is inside the extension and there are no alternative parking arrangements for these residents outside the zone. In other cases, the nearest, most accessible local services and amenities (such as hospitals, libraries and leisure centres) are inside the extension (ibid., p. 11). The areas where the extended residents' discount applies are the shaded areas just outside the bold line that shows the limits of the charging zone on the map in Figure 14.1.

Enforcement is undertaken with Automatic Number Plate Recognition (ANPR). There are camera sites located at every entry and exit to the congestion charging zone and also inside the zone. These cameras read and record the number plates of virtually all the vehicles making use of the

Table 14.1   Exemptions and discounts

Discount/status	Category
Fully exempt	Motorcycles, mopeds and bicycles Emergency vehicles Public transport vehicles with 9 or more seats Vehicles used by disabled persons who are exempt from road tax Licensed London taxis and mini-cabs National Health Service vehicles that are exempt from road tax
100% discount with free registration	Certain military vehicles Vehicles with 9 or more seats not licensed as buses (e.g., work buses, community service buses, private hire minibuses)
100% discount with a one-off £10 registration	Vehicles driven for or by individuals or institutions that are Blue Badge holders[a] Motortricycles (1 metre or less in width and 2 metres or less in length)
100% discount with £10 registration per year	Alternative fuel vehicles (requires certain emission savings for each vehicle type, as described on the TfL website) and electrically propelled vehicles Roadside assistance and recovery vehicles (e.g., motoring organizations such as the Automobile Association)
90% discount with £10 registration per year	Vehicles registered to residents of the central zone

Note: [a] Blue Badges, which existed before the scheme was implemented, are special parking permits issued to disabled people to allow them to park near shops, stations and other facilities. The badge belongs to the disabled person who qualifies for it (who may or may not be a car driver) and can be used in any vehicle they are travelling in. The discount applies to individual Blue Badge holders anywhere in the EU.

Source: See www.cclondon.com/exemptions.shtml.

zone, to subsequently send them to a processing centre with ANPR software. These number plates are then matched against the number plates that have paid, are exempt, are entitled to a 100 per cent discount, or have registered with the Fleet Scheme. The pictures of the matched number plates are then deleted. After a manual check, violators are tracked through the Driver and Vehicle Licensing Agency and issued with a Penalty Charge Notice (PCN) of £100. As of February 2007 the PCN of £100 is reduced to £50 if paid within 14 days, and increased to £150 if not paid within 28 days.

Once a penalty has increased to £150, a charge certificate is sent to the registered keeper or hirer of the vehicle. Failure to pay the outstanding charge can lead to the registration of the debt with the County Court and the eventual appointment of bailiffs to recover the debt.

Vehicles with three or more outstanding congestion PCNs may be clamped or removed, anywhere in Greater London. As of February 2007 the clamp fee is £65 and the removal fee is £150. Storage of the vehicle costs £25 a day. If a vehicle is clamped or removed, then all the outstanding charges must be paid before it is released. If the release fee is not paid, then the vehicle may be disposed of at auction or by scrapping. In this case, the registered keeper remains liable for all outstanding charges, including an £80.25 disposal fee.

14.3   IMPACTS OF THE LCCS

At the time of this chapter going to print, the western extension was still very recent and there were no actual data on the impacts, only forecasts. For this reason, the impacts are reported separately for the original zone, which is the area to the east of what is now the north to south free route, highlighted with a bold line cutting across the whole charging zone on Figure 14.1, and the extension, which is the area to the west of that route.

14.3.1   Original Zone

Impacts on traffic

Congestion   The aim of the LCCS was to reduce traffic congestion in and around the charging zone, and it succeeded in so doing in the first two years. Even in the third year congestion was lower than that observed before the scheme was introduced, although the difference was not as big.

During 2003 and 2004 there were average reductions in congestion within the charging zone of 30 per cent when compared with pre-charging levels (TfL, 2005a, p. 14). Congestion is defined by TfL as 'the difference between the average network travel rate and the uncongested (free-flow) network travel rate in minutes per vehicle-kilometre' (TfL, 2003a, Table 3.1, p. 46). Using the uncongested network travel rate of 1.9 min per km (approximately 32 km per hour) from TfL (ibid., p. 52), and 2002 and 2003/04 average travel rates of 4.2 and 3.5 min per km, respectively, it can be seen that congestion decreased from 2.3 to 1.6 min per km (TfL, 2005a, p. 15). Most of this reduction in travel times was the result of reduced queuing 'time at junctions, rather than increases in driving speeds' (ibid., p. 13).

In 2005, however, TfL (2006, p. 4) reported that average delay values were 1.8 min per km, rather than 1.6 min per km as in the previous two years. This would imply a reduction in congestion of just under 22 per cent, in contrast with the 30 per cent reported for 2003 and 2004.

Since vehicles travelling on the Inner Ring Road (which marked the limit of the original charging zone) do not pay the congestion charge, TfL expected that through-traffic, with origin and destination outside the charging zone, would divert and use the Inner Ring Road instead. However, improved traffic management arrangements were put into place on the Inner Ring Road before the scheme started, and this prevented an increase in congestion. For example, between one and two seconds were taken off green light time on radial roads, which were anticipated would have less traffic, and added on to green light time on the Inner Ring Road. That made a sufficient difference to keep the Ring Road operating satisfactorily with marginally lower levels of congestion in 2003, when compared with pre-charging conditions in 2002 (TfL, 2004a, p. 14). However, a further two surveys were undertaken in 2004 and, although the first of these still indicates a reduction in congestion, comparable to that found in 2003, the second survey, conducted in Autumn 2004, indicates similar levels of congestion to those that prevailed in 2002, before the LCCS was implemented.

Congestion on main radial routes approaching or leaving the charging zone decreased in 2003 and increased in 2004, with TfL (2005a, p. 18) concluding that the level of congestion in that year was only marginally lower than in 2002, before charging. In 2005, conditions on the main radial routes were similar to those observed in 2004 (TfL, 2006, p. 4). Main roads in inner London also had higher levels of congestion in 2005 than in 2002, before the scheme was implemented (ibid., p. 4).

Vehicle counts The total volume of traffic entering the charging zone during charging hours in 2003 and 2004 was 18 per cent lower than in 2002. Table 14.2 gives the percentage changes in the number of different vehicle types entering and leaving the charging zone in 2003 and 2004. As expected, there was a reduction of potentially chargeable vehicles and an increase in exempt vehicles.

While the number of certain vehicle types will decrease, the kilometres they are driven may increase. Depending on the relative magnitude of these changes, the total vehicle-kilometres driven may increase or decrease. Chargeable vehicles in London have, however, all decreased their vehicle-kilometres, which indicates that the reduction in their number was not compensated by the potentially longer distances driven.

TfL reports a decrease of 15 per cent in vehicle-kilometres driven by vehicles with four or more wheels inside the charging zone during charging

Table 14.2   Percentage change in number of vehicles entering and leaving the charging zone in 2003 and 2004

	Change inbound 2003 vs 2002	Change outbound 2003 vs 2002	Change inbound 2004 vs 2003	Change outbound 2004 vs 2003
Cars	−33	−35	−1	−2
Taxis	+17	+8	−1	0
Buses and coaches	+23	+21	+8	+4
Vans	−11	−15	−1	−1
Lorries and other	−11	−12	−5	−5
Pedal cycles	+19	+6	+8	+8
Powered two-wheelers	+12	+5	−3	−4

Source: TfL (2005a, Fig. 11, p. 25).

times in the first year of the LCCS and a further 6 per cent reduction in the second year (TfL, 2005a, p. 28). Table 14.3 gives the changes in vehicle-kilometres by vehicle type.

Public transport   Table 14.4 summarizes the number of buses and bus passengers crossing the charging zone in 2002 and 2003. Up to half of the increase in bus passengers was provisionally assessed as being primarily due to the LCCS, with the remainder probably reflecting the long-term background growth in bus patronage, as a result of service improvements (ibid., p. 44).

In 2004 the number of passengers crossing the charging zone by bus inbound between 7.00 a.m. and 10.00 a.m. increased by a further 12 per cent compared with 2003 (ibid., p. 45).

In the first full year after the introduction of the LCCS there were substantial reductions in excess waiting time, the additional waiting time at bus stops caused by service irregularity or missing buses. This reduction was 24 per cent overall across Greater London and over 30 per cent in and around the charging zone (ibid., p. 50). In the period from March to December 2004, there was a further reduction in excess waiting time of 18 per cent in and around the charging zone (ibid., p. 50).

In the first year of the LCCS there was a decrease in patronage of the London Underground. This was mainly due to the slowdown of the economy, the decrease in tourism in London, which in turn might have been linked to the war in Iraq, and the temporary closure of the Central Line for

Table 14.3 Vehicle-kilometres (vkm) driven within the charging zone during charging hours, including percentage share of traffic

Vehicle type	2002 vkm (millions)		2003 vkm (millions)		2004 vkm (millions)		% change 02 to 03	% change 03 to 04
All vehicles	1.64	100%	1.45	100%	1.38	100%	−12%	−5%
Four or more wheels	1.44	88%	1.23	84%	1.16	84%	−15%	−6%
Potentially chargeable	1.13	69%	0.85	58%	0.80	58%	−25%	−6%
Cars	0.77	47%	0.51	35%	0.47	34%	−34%	−7%
Vans	0.29	18%	0.27	19%	0.26	19%	−5%	−4%
Lorries and other	0.07	4%	0.07	5%	0.06	5%	−7%	−8%
Licensed taxis	0.26	16%	0.31	21%	0.29	21%	+22%	−7%
Buses and coaches	0.05	3%	0.07	5%	0.07	5%	+21%	+5%
Powered two-wheelers	0.13	8%	0.14	9%	0.13	10%	+6%	−2%
Pedal cycles	0.07	4%	0.09	6%	0.09	7%	+28%	+4%

Note: Annualized weekday for 2002, 2003 and 2004.

Source: TfL (2005, Fig. 15, p. 29).

Table 14.4 Bus passengers and buses crossing the charging zone boundary

| | AM peak (7.00–10.00 a.m.) | | | Charging hours (7.00 a.m.–6.30 p.m.) | | | | | |
| | Inbound | | | Inbound | | | Outbound | | |
	Passengers	Buses	Passengers per bus	Passengers	Buses	Passengers per bus	Passengers	Buses	Passengers per bus
Autumn 2002	77 000	2400	32	193 000	8 280	23	163 000	7800	21
Autumn 2003	106 000	2950	36	264 000	10 500	25	211 000	9 900	21
Percentage difference	+38%	+23%	+12%	+37%	+27%	+8%	+29%	+26%	+2%

Source: TfL (2005, Fig. 27, p. 45).

almost three months, following a derailment at Chancery Lane station (TfL, 2003b, points 2.2 and 5.4). In the second year of the LCCS this trend was reversed. Although inside the charging zone, patronage of the Underground during 2004 was still lower than in 2002, across the whole Underground network, patronage was roughly similar to that of 2002, before the introduction of charging (TfL, 2005a, p. 52).

No change was registered in the use of national rail following the implementation of the LCCS (TfL, 2004a, p. 39; TfL, 2005a, p. 53).

Economic impacts
The impacts of the LCCS on the economy in Central London have been neutral (TfL, 2005a, p. 68). The scheme started in February 2003, when the economy was slowing down, after four quarters of negative growth (ibid., p. 71). The economy picked up, however, at the end of 2003 and during 2004.

A number of studies and databases were used to compare business performance in terms of variables such as number of businesses or sites, numbers of employees, sales and profits, inside and outside the congestion charging zone and before and after the introduction of the LCCS. The conclusion of these comparisons is that, overall, businesses have not been significantly affected by the congestion charge (ibid., p. 73). Commercial and residential property markets do not show any impacts from the congestion charge either (ibid., p. 68).

Ernst and Young conducted an independent review, which concluded that the £5 charge had had a neutral impact on the Central London economy (TfL, 2006, p. 68).

Impacts on accidents and the environment
TfL (2005a, p. 5; 2006, p. 6) claims that the LCCS is responsible for between 40 and 70 fewer accidents per year within the charging zone and on the Inner Ring Road in comparison with the background trend. They estimate the monetary costs of accident savings at £15 million per year. Assuming that there have indeed been between 40 and 70 accidents saved per year,[3] the monetized value of £15 million seems to be too high.

From all traffic accidents in London involving personal injury, around 87 per cent are slight, 13 per cent are serious, and just under 1 per cent are fatal (TfL, 2001, Table 16, p. 28; 2004b, Table 6.1.1, p. 50; 2005a, Figure 78, p. 106).[4] Applying these shares to the upper bound of 70 accidents saved, as reported by TfL (2005b, 2006), together with the total cost per accident by severity as calculated in the Highways Economics Note 1 (DfT, 2007, Table 3, p. 11), yields an estimate of just over £4 million at 2005 prices.[5] This is much lower than the £15 million reported by TfL.

Despite the increase in the use of bicycles and motorcycles, accidents involving them have decreased, in line with the long-term background trend (TfL, 2005a, p. 5). Higher average speeds have not resulted in more accidents because most of the time savings are experienced at junctions, where there is less queuing (ibid., p. 5). Driving speeds themselves have not increased.

Emissions of nitrogen oxides and particulate matter within the charging zone have been reduced by 18 and 22 per cent, respectively, due to the effect of both charging and vehicle technology (TfL, 2006, p. 118). On the Inner Ring Road, the reductions were approximately 12 per cent for nitrogen oxides and 13 per cent for particulate matter (ibid., p. 118).

The reduction in emissions of carbon dioxide inside the zone in the first year of operation is estimated at 15.7 per cent inside the charging zone and 8.5 per cent on the Inner Ring Road (ibid., Table 6.3, p. 117). No estimates are available for later years.

14.3.2   Western Extension

The western extension is different from the original charging zone. The impacts from congestion charging are therefore expected to be different. Table 14.5 presents the numbers of employees, business units and residents in the two zones, showing how these differ. The benefits in general will be lower because the expected reductions in traffic are smaller than those experienced with the original scheme. The reasons for this are as follows:

1.   Drivers in the extension who already pay the charge because they use the original charging zone, will continue to travel regardless of charging inside the extension or not (TfL, 2005b, p. 66, point 6.1.7).
2.   Residents within the extension are entitled to a 90 per cent discount and will probably be attracted onto the roads. By paying the discounted

Table 14.5   Employees, business units and residents in the original charging zone and in the western extension

	Original zone	Western extension
Employees[a]	1 235 257	218 477
Business units[a]	81 667	21 692
Residents[b]	148 000	230 000

Sources: (a) TfL (2006, Table 11.2, p. 206); (b) TfL (2005b, Table 7.1, p. 95) and TfL (2004b, p. 3).

charge they are able to drive not only in the extension but also in the original charging zone. Some residents who did not drive may start driving, including those who initially made alternative arrangements after the LCCS was first introduced (ibid., points 6.4.11 and 6.4.12, p. 72).

3. There is a greater proportion of car travel by residents in the extension than there is in the original zone, and therefore a higher proportion of households are able to take advantage of a residents' discount. The number of cars registered for a resident discount may thus increase by more than 150 per cent (TfL, 2004c, p. 3).

A reduction in vehicle-kilometres of between 10 and 14 per cent within the extension is expected. Average speeds are also projected to increase by between 10 and 14 per cent (TfL, 2005b, point 6.4.10, p. 72).

Traffic on the free corridor north to south (the western limit of the original charging zone) is expected to increase by between 1 and 2 per cent, and traffic on the other limits of the original zone is expected to decrease by between 1 and 2 per cent (ibid., point 6.4.14, p. 73). Traffic on the boundary of the western extension (other than the free corridor north to south) is projected to increase by between 3 and 5 per cent (ibid., 2005b, point 6.4.16, p. 73).

The extension will also cause an increase in vehicle-kilometres in the original charging zone of roughly 2 per cent, mainly because, as explained in point (2) above, residents will be priced onto the roads. As a result of this, average speeds in the original charging zone are expected to decrease by 2 per cent (ibid., points 6.4.17 and 6.4.19, p. 74).

With the end time brought forward to 6.00 p.m., inbound traffic to the enlarged zone between 6.00 p.m. and 6.30 p.m. is expected to increase to pre-charging levels. The increase could be even higher if drivers who used to enter the original charging zone earlier in the day change their travel time to enter it after 6.00 p.m. and those who used to arrive after 6.30 change their travel time to arrive earlier but after 6.00 p.m., when charging now finishes (ibid., point 6.4.21, p. 74).

An increase of between 2 and 3 per cent in public transport passengers is expected, 75 per cent of which will affect buses (ibid., point 6.4.47, p. 84).

As shown in Table 14.7 in the section that follows, TfL believes that as a result of the extension there will be fewer accidents, which they value at £5 to £10 million per year. However, Santos and Fraser (2006, pp. 287–8) are suspicious of those estimates, which either attribute too many accidents prevented to the extension or assume an excessive proportion of severe injuries and fatalities prevented, or both.

14.4   COSTS, BENEFITS AND REVENUES

14.4.1   Original LCCS

The capital costs of the LCCS were approximately £200 million at 2002 prices, most of which were provided by the central government.[6]

The annual costs and benefits of the LCCS are presented in Table 14.6. The figures are in 2005 values and prices. 'Charge-payer compliance costs', listed as disbenefits, are resources consumed by charge payers (not the scheme operators) to comply with the scheme. These estimates include, for

Table 14.6   Annual operating costs and benefits of the London scheme (£ million at 2005 prices and values, charge at £5)

Costs and benefits	£m
Costs	
TfL administration	5
TfL contractors	85
Additional bus costs	20
Total	110
Benefits	
Time savings and reliability benefits to car occupants, business trips	65
Time savings and reliability benefits to car occupants, journey to work and other trips	45
Time savings and reliability benefits to taxi occupants, business trips	30
Time savings and reliability benefits to taxi occupants, journey to work and other trips	10
Time savings and reliability benefits to commercial vehicle occupants	35
Time savings and reliability benefits to bus passengers, business trips	2
Time savings and reliability benefits to bus passengers, journey to work and other trips	40
Charge-payer compliance costs to car occupants, business trips	−10
Charge-payer compliance costs to car occupants, journey to work and other trips	−10
Charge-payer compliance costs to commercial vehicle occupants	−10
Vehicle fuel and operating savings	10
Accident savings	15
Disbenefit to deterred trip makers, business trips	−5
Disbenefit to deterred trip makers, journey to work and other trips	−20
Reduced CO_2 emissions	3
Total	200

Source: TfL (2006, Table 9.1, p. 172).

example, the time consumed in actually paying charges, such as in making the telephone call, walking to the retail outlet, or logging on to the Internet. They do not include the financial transaction as this is deemed to be a transfer payment.

The scheme generated net revenues of roughly £122 million in 2005/06, including the increase experienced after the change from £5 to £8. From these revenues, £100 million have been spent on improving bus services (TfL, 2006, p. 174).

14.4.2 Western Extension

The capital costs of the extension are projected to be between £113 and £118 million at 2005 values and prices (TfL, 2005b, Table 7.8, p. 108).

Table 14.7 gives costs and benefits of the extension for the first year of operation. The values are in 2005 values and prices. The lower sensitivity

Table 14.7 Costs and benefits of the western extension for the first year of operation (£ million at 2005 values and prices)

	High sensitivity	Low sensitivity
Costs		
Service provider costs (operating)	9.9	11.8
Enforcement infrastructure costs (operating)	6.1	6.1
Contracted enforcement costs (operating)	4.6	4.6
Business operations costs (operating)	3.0	3.6
Additional bus costs	15.0	11.0
6.00 p.m. finish: reduced operating costs to existing scheme	−1.0	−1.0
Total	37.6	36.1
Benefits		
Time savings to vehicle occupants	63	44
Increased journey time reliability to vehicle occupants	6	4
Time savings and increased reliability for bus users	21	15
Reduced fuel consumption	2	2
Reduced number of accidents	10	5
Disbenefits to deterred car occupants	−16	−12
Charge-payer compliance costs	−6	−7
6.00 p.m. finish: loss of benefits to existing scheme	−12	−7
Total	68	44

Source: TfL (2005b, Tables 7.4, 7.6 and 7.7, pp. 100, 104 and 105, respectively).

values reflect a 'relatively inelastic response to the introduction of charging', and the higher sensitivity values reflect a more elastic response (ibid., p. 71). The corresponding reductions in vehicles with four or more wheels entering the extension are projected to be 13 per cent under the low sensitivity assumption and 17 per cent under the high sensitivity assumption.

The net revenues from the extension, after including operating costs but not implementation costs or additional bus costs in the calculations, are projected to be between £25 and £40 million per year (ibid., point 7.5.26, p. 102).

It is interesting to note the very high annual costs of the extension, which result in relatively small benefits – between £7.9 and £30.4 million per year. Santos and Fraser (2006) model the extension using a spreadsheet traffic model and find similar results to TfL's, and a benefit–cost ratio of around 1. This cost–benefit analysis includes capital and operating costs and benefits, discounted over a 10-year period.

Unfortunately Tables 14.6 and 14.7, which are virtually reproduced from TfL's reports, contain information that cannot be checked. The author would have preferred to check the reliability and validity of the data, methods and assumptions in more detail. However, TfL were unable to answer any of her questions or provide any data within a reasonable time span.

14.5   WINNERS AND LOSERS

In the case of London, the original charging zone has clearly yielded social gains by reducing levels of traffic and travel times. With heterogeneous travellers, who have different values of time, use different modes of transport, and have different journey purposes, the distributional impacts are, however, necessarily complicated to assess.

Using vehicle counts pre- and post-charging and their occupancy rates, Santos (2004, p. 273) estimates that 52 per cent of all people travelling to or from the charging zone used buses before the LCCS was introduced. If taxi and pedal and motorcycle users are added as well, the total share of people who did not use a chargeable mode of transport before the LCCS rises to 63.9 per cent. These are winners, in the sense that they are enjoying the benefits from the scheme (higher speeds and lower travel times) without paying anything and without undergoing the disutility of making alternative travel arrangements.

From a very conservative point of view, the remaining 36.1 per cent would be car users, who are probably losers. These car users are mostly worse off either because they have had to switch mode or change time or suppress their trip, or because the benefits they get from lower travel times are lower than the cost of the charge. The exceptions are commuters with a very high value of time and car users who travel during working hours, or are either exempt or entitled to a discount.

Santos and Bhakar (2006, p. 29) estimate that the minimum income for a car commuter to benefit from a £5 charge is £1400 per week. They do this exercise assuming that the value of time is lower in uncongested conditions in comparison with congested conditions.[7]

This weekly salary of £1400 is roughly equivalent to an annual salary of just under £75 000. Given that on average, the richest 10 per cent of full-time workers in London earn over £65 450 per year (Office for National Statistics, 2004a, Table 7.7a), it is not unreasonable to think that quite a number of car commuters would have benefited from the £5 congestion charge.

Using the same methodology reported in Santos and Bhakar (2006), if an £8 charge is assumed instead of a £5 charge, the minimum weekly salary for a car commuter to benefit from the scheme increases to £2348, roughly equivalent to an annual salary of £122 000. This casts doubt on what proportion of car commuters would actually benefit. Although it can be ascertained that it will be less than 10 per cent, the smallest quantiles reported by the Office for National Statistics (2004a, Table 7.7a) are deciles, and so it is impossible to pinpoint the exact percentage of Londoners with an annual salary higher than £122 000. In any case, it would be difficult to determine what proportion of those high earners use the charging zone on a daily basis. It should be borne in mind, however, that these estimates refer to commuting values of time, and not to working values of time. There is no doubt that business trips by car benefit from the charge, even if the same values of time are assumed during congested and free-flow conditions.

14.6   CONCLUSIONS

The London congestion charge is not a first-best (Pigouvian) charge and it is not a second-best charge either. It is rather a practical, unsophisticated charge, equal for all vehicle types, despite their different congestive effects. It does not vary in time or location, except for the fact that it applies in a specific area between 7.00 a.m. and 6.00 p.m.

Even though the costs of running the scheme are very high, the economic benefits are positive. In general, it is seen as a success story. The only aim of the LCCS was 'to reduce traffic congestion in and around the charging zone' (TfL, 2004a, p. 7). It has, no doubt, succeeded in so doing, and as expected, is contributing to four of the Mayor's 10 priorities for transport as set out in his Transport Strategy (Greater London Authority, 2001): 'to reduce congestion, to make radical improvements in bus services, to improve journey time reliability for car users, and to make the distribution of goods and services more reliable, sustainable and efficient' (TfL, 2004a, p. 7).

Santos and Fraser (2006, p. 296) note that important decisions regarding the scheme design such as: (a) the level of the charge, and whether it was going to differ by vehicle type or time of the day; (b) the times when the scheme was going to operate; and (c) the exact limits of the charging zone, were not based on economic principles. Instead, they were based on political considerations, and the results of an extensive consultation process in which TfL engaged before the Mayor confirmed the final Scheme Order. Interestingly, this did not prevent the LCCS from achieving the objective of reducing congestion.

The western extension, on the other hand, may yield negative economic benefits. The benefit–cost ratio that TfL (2005b, p. 108) calculates is only positive under an optimistic set of assumptions. Given the limited scope for decreases in congestion in the extension (due to the very different composition of traffic and the attractiveness that the extension will present to residents who might be priced onto the roads) and the very high implementation and operation costs, the prospects are not promising.

When the LCCS was implemented in 2003, the Mayor managed to surpass the most important obstacle, which was public and political acceptability. Proof of that is that, if no one had paid the charge, the scheme would simply not have worked. The enforcement system, not designed to deal with no one paying the charge, would have collapsed.

Banking on that success, the Mayor extended the charging zone westwards, despite the low benefit–cost ratios forecast by TfL. This decision was really a political one, not an economic one, as the net social gains will be negligible, if not negative. Environmentalists, supporters of sustainable transport and users of non-chargeable modes of transport are probably on his side. A situation like this can only happen in London, where car dependency is the lowest in the UK. Data averaged over the years 2003 and 2004 (Office for National Statistics, 2006, Table 10.05) show that the miles travelled by car per person per year is 63 per cent in London,[8] in contrast with an average of 84 per cent for the UK as a whole. No other region in England is below 80 per cent. Scotland and Wales are also above 79 per cent.

The London experience is therefore not easily transferable to other towns and cities in the UK, and care should be taken when trying to apply a similar policy in other places around the world, especially those with poor public transport and/or high car dependency.

NOTES

1. Georgina Santos gratefully acknowledges financial support from the Rees Jeffrey's Fund. Any views and errors in this chapter are the author's own.
2. Despite several phone and e-mail attempts over three months, TfL were unable to provide the author with information on the proportion of people who replied to *Hearing London's Views* in favour of the scheme before it was implemented. As of February 2007, no information on the matter is available on the Transport for London website.
3. TfL (2006, pp. 112–14) summarizes the results obtained by an independent statistical study, which confirms that congestion charging has led to these additional net reductions.
4. Figure 78 (TfL, 2004b) corresponds to traffic accidents on the Inner Ring Road and within the charging zone only, but the shares are the same as those derived from Table 16 in TfL (2001) and Table 6.1.1 in TfL (2004b), which cover the whole of Greater London.
5. The average values per accident, by severity of accident, are £1 644 790 for fatal accidents, £188 920 for serious accidents, and £19 250 for slight accidents (DfT, 2007, Table 3, p. 11). These estimates include lost output, medical and ambulance costs, human costs to reflect the pain, grief and suffering, police costs, insurance and administration costs, and damage to property. These estimates correspond to average accidents. For example, in 2005, a fatal accident on average involved 1.10 fatalities, 0.36 serious casualties and 0.54 slight casualties (DfT, 2007, paragraph 6, p. 4).
6. Information provided by TfL on request.
7. MVA et al. (1987, p. 176) estimate that the value of time in congested conditions can be up to 40 per cent higher; Wardman (2001, p. 125) concludes that it can be 50 per cent higher; and Steer Davies Gleave (2004, p. 19) concludes that it can be almost 100 per cent higher. TfL (2005b, point 7.5.4, p. 99), however, assumes a uniform value of time, regardless of the prevailing traffic conditions.
8. This was 67 per cent in the 1999–2001 period (Office for National Statistics, 2004b, Table 10.6). The reduction is probably caused by both the LCCS and the improvements in bus services.

REFERENCES

Acts of Parliament (1999), *Greater London Authority Act 1999 c. 29*, London: HMSO, www.hmso.gov.uk/acts/acts 1999/19990029.htm, accessed 20 January 2006.

Department for Transport (DfT) (2007), *Highways Economics Note No.1, 2005 Valuation of the Benefits of Prevention of Road Accidents and Casualties*, London, January, www.dft.gov.uk/pgr/roadsafety/ea/pdfeconnote105, accessed 2 May 2006.

Greater London Authority (2001), *The Mayor's Transport Strategy*, www.london.gov.uk/mayor/strategies/transport/trans_strat.jsp, accessed 5 April 2006.

MVA Consultancy (1995), *The London Congestion Charging Research Programme: Final Report*, London: HMSO.

MVA Consultancy, ITS University of Leeds, and TSU University of Oxford (1987), *Value of Travel Time Savings*, Newbury, Berks: Policy Journals.

Office for National Statistics (2004a), First release: 2004 Annual Survey of Hours and Earnings, Table 7.7a, www.statistics.gov.uk/downloads/theme_labour/ASHE_2004_inc/tab7_7a.xls, accessed 2 June 2006.

Office for National Statistics (2004b), *Regional Trends 38 – Data*, www.statistics.gov.uk/statbase/Product.asp?vlnk=11614&image.x=7&image.y=9, accessed 2 June 2006.

Office for National Statistics (2006), *Regional Trends 39 – Data*, www.statistics. gov.uk/statbase/Product.asp?vlnk=14356, accessed 2 June 2006.

ROCOL Working Group (2000), *Road Charging Options for London: A Technical Assessment*, London: The Stationery Office, www.gos.gov.uk/gol/transport/ 161558/228862/228869/, accessed 3 May 2006.

Santos, G. (2004), 'Urban road pricing in the UK', in Georgina Santos (ed.), *Road Pricing: Theory and Evidence*, Oxford: Elsevier, pp. 251–82.

Santos, G. and J. Bhakar (2006), 'The impact of the London Congestion Charging Scheme on the generalised cost of car commuters to the City of London', *Transport Policy*, **13** (1), 22–33.

Santos, G. and G. Fraser (2006), 'Road pricing: lessons from London', *Economic Policy*, **21** (46), 264–310.

Steer Davies Gleave (2004), *The Effect of Road Congestion on Rail Demand*, Report to the Passenger Demand Forecasting Council, London, July.

Transport for London (TfL) (2001), *Transport Statistics for London 2001*, London, www.tfl.gov.uk/tfl/pdfdocs/stats2001.pdf, accessed 9 September 2005.

Transport for London (2003a), *Impacts Monitoring Programme: First Annual Report*, Transport for London, London, June, www.tfl.gov.uk/tfl/cclondon/cc_ monitoring-1st-report.shtml, accessed 4 July 2005.

Transport for London (2003b), *Congestion Charging: Six Months On*, Transport for London, London, October, www.tfl.gov.uk/tfl/downloads/pdf/congestion-charging/cc-6monthson.pdf, accessed 4 July 2005.

Transport for London (2004a), *Congestion Charging Central London – Impacts Monitoring: Second Annual Report*, April, www.tfl.gov.uk/tfl/cclondon/cc_ monitoring-2nd-report.shtml, accessed 4 July 2005.

Transport for London (2004b), *London Travel Report 2004*, London, www.tfl.gov.uk/tfl/pdfdocs/ltr/london-travel-report-2004.pdf, accessed 4 July 2005.

Transport for London (2004c), *Report to the Mayor – Annex E: Economic Assessment*, July, www.tfl.gov.uk/tfl/cclondon/cc_report_mayor2005.shtml, accessed 4 July 2005.

Transport for London (2005a), *Congestion Charging Central London – Impacts Monitoring: Third Annual Report*, April, www.tfl.gov.uk/tfl/cclondon/pdfs/ ThirdAnnualReportFinal.pdf, accessed 4 July 2005.

Transport for London (2005b), *Proposed Western Extension of the Central London Congestion Charging Scheme*, Report to the Mayor following consultation with stakeholders, businesses, other organisations and the public, September, www.tfl.gov.uk/tfl/cc-ex/tfl-report.shtml, accessed 12 October 2005.

Transport for London (2006), *Congestion Charging Central London – Impacts Monitoring: Fourth Annual Report*, June, www.tfl.gov.uk/tfl/cclondon/pdfs/ fourthAnnualReportFinal.pdf, accessed 30 June 2006.

Wardman, M. (2001), 'A review of British evidence on time and service quality valuations', *Transportation Research E*, **37** (2–3), 107–28.

15. Transport infrastructure pricing: a European perspective

Chris Nash[1]

15.1 INTRODUCTION

It is now 10 years since the European Commission put forward proposals to base transport infrastructure pricing on sound economic principles including the internalization of externalities. In that time there has been much activity in terms of research, proposals and debate, but actual achievement in terms of pricing reform has been slow.

The aim of this chapter is to give an overview of progress on European Union (EU) transport pricing policy, and of the research to which it has led. We shall concentrate on road and rail transport, as the modes on which legislative activity has centred. The next section outlines the development of the policy. We then consider current legislation on rail and road infrastructure charges. Following this, we discuss reasons for the lack of progress, before considering research on these issues, and finally reach our conclusions.

15.2 DEVELOPMENT OF EC POLICY

European Commission policy is built on the principle of subsidiarity, which means broadly that issues should be left to the member states unless there is good reason for dealing with them at the European level. Thus, historically, the European interest in infrastructure charging has come from a wish to establish principles that avoid unfair competition. Unfair competition could arise in a number of ways: the most blatant form comprises charging transport operators different amounts for use of the infrastructure according to where they are registered, and this has been a concern particularly in road haulage. More generally, a failure to charge appropriately for the use of infrastructure might give one country an unfair competitive advantage over others. Thus the key interest of the Commission has been in international transport, particularly freight, and in transport by commercial operators. A charge for the use of roads by cars has been seen as a matter for the member states; although the Commission does promote research and best practice on this issue, it has never legislated on it.

The current interest in infrastructure charging really dates back to the publication of a Green Paper: *Towards Fair and Efficient Pricing in Transport* (CEC, 1995). This argued that charges for the use of transport infrastructure should reflect not just the costs of providing and maintaining the infrastructure but also congestion, environmental and accident externalities. The policy was more precisely set out in a White Paper: *Fair Payment for Infrastructure Use* (CEC, 1998), which put forward a phased programme for moving to basing infrastructure charges on marginal social cost. Setting out an infrastructure charging policy was particularly urgent for rail, where the introduction of open access for new operators, and for operators based in one country to run trains in another, required legislation to prevent discrimination. Thus it was that rail was really the first mode to which the new approach was applied in a directive in 2001 (2001/14). In the meantime there was already a directive on charging road haulage designed to prevent discrimination by nationality, and in 2003 a proposal was brought forward to amend this (CEC, 2003). We discuss these measures below.

Short-run marginal social cost (SMC) pricing ensures that prices are set to reflect the additional costs to society associated with an additional kilometre travelled or an additional trip made, given that the capacity of the transport network is held constant. In an ideal world, capacity would then be adjusted until SMC also equalled long-run marginal social cost (LMC) (the cost of carrying extra traffic, given that capacity is appropriately adjusted) (Jansson, 1997). However, there are many reasons why this may not be achieved. Major infrastructure projects require large amounts of money; they take a decade or more to plan and build; there are major indivisibilities involved; and environmental considerations lead to proposed developments frequently being highly controversial. Thus, for instance, progress on the EU-supported Trans-European Network has been slow. When time lags or constraints prevent the optimal capacity from being achieved, SMC pricing makes the best use of the available capacity. On the other hand, it is often argued that LMC pricing provides more appropriate investment incentives. With SMC pricing, the infrastructure manager has an incentive to restrict capacity to drive up price. However, this argument seems to presume that the infrastructure manager is driven by commercial incentives and that either competition or regulation holds the price at the level of expenditure actually incurred – otherwise infrastructure managers might still charge LMC but fail to provide the appropriate level of investment. Whether these issues are also relevant where governments are directly responsible for both infrastructure charges and infrastructure investment is more open to debate. In this case, the principle generally followed is that SMC pricing should be accompanied by investment decisions based on social cost–benefit analysis, although there are certainly those who suspect that governments have motives for favouring high charges that are not based purely on economic efficiency (for example, Evans, 1992).

The debate between LMC and SMC pricing might remain prominent in academic circles, but in terms of practical politics the key debate remains whether to implement marginal cost pricing at all. It has been argued that marginal cost pricing is a textbook concept whose assumptions (that resulting deficits may be funded by distortion-free lump-sum transfers, and that prices throughout the rest of the economy equal marginal cost) render it irrelevant to real-world decisions (Rothengatter, 2003). The typical response of supporters of marginal cost pricing is to accept that these factors require second-best modifications to pure marginal cost pricing, but to argue that marginal cost remains the centrepiece of appropriate pricing. However, the practical political argument remains, with a widespread view that only full cost pricing is both efficient and fair. Neither theoretical second-best literature nor empirical evidence offer support for the view that full cost pricing is efficient (tests in the UNITE study suggested that, while there were substantial benefits to be achieved by marginal social cost pricing, full cost pricing would actually be worse than the current situation: Mayeres et al., 2005), or indeed that it is fair (it frequently requires rather arbitrary allocations of costs between groups of users, rendering it difficult to prove this proposition). Interestingly, supporters of full cost pricing include those who believe that it should be combined with the internalization of externalities by charging the full cost of those externalities to users. (Obviously, if the capital costs of providing the infrastructure are already included, then it would not be appropriate to include charging for congestion. The latter, while being in part an external cost at the level of the individual user, is internalized within the group of users as a whole.) Arguments based on the club good principle are often invoked to suggest that full cost pricing, including for externalities, will bring appropriate incentives to members of the club to take full social costs into account in their decisions, although whether such incentives would exist in a club of all road users – surely most of the population – seems doubtful.

In the case of the road system, the traditional approach to charging users has been through annual taxes and through taxes on fuel. In some European countries (France, Italy, Spain, Portugal), these taxes have been supplemented by tolls on specific motorways, while more recently others have introduced a time-based 'vignette' for the use of motorways (a supplementary charge per day, week or year). None of these pricing mechanisms is able fully to reflect the variations in marginal social cost with vehicle type, time and space. Thus, when the infrastructure pricing policy was restated in the 2001 White Paper on Transport Policy (CEC, 2001), it argued: 'The thrust of Community action should therefore be gradually to replace existing transport system taxes with more effective instruments for integrating infrastructure costs and external costs'.

The White Paper envisaged that new instruments would be introduced to recover maintenance and capital costs, and also to charge for congestion and other environmental impacts. This would then leave the role of fuel tax being solely to control the emissions of carbon dioxide. In these circumstances, fuel tax could be harmonized throughout the EU.

The centrepiece of the proposals on charging was a new framework directive, to set out the principles for charging for transport infrastructure on all modes. This was to have been accompanied by a methodology paper, setting out methodologies for calculating the components of the infrastructure charge. It was anticipated that the methodology paper and framework directive would be followed by a series of four separate directives dealing in detail with the practical implementation of pricing for road, sea, rail and air modes.

The draft framework directive was proposed for publication during 2002, but did not emerge that year and has not emerged since. Progress on infrastructure charging has, nevertheless, been made over the period since 2001, though this has been confined to rail and road rather than, as was envisaged in the framework directive, across all modes. The directive on rail infrastructure charging – Directive 2001/14 – has been implemented throughout the EU and has been incorporated into member state law since Spring 2003. A proposed directive, amending Directive 1999/62 on charges for heavy goods vehicles was published in mid-2003; an amended version of that proposed directive was approved by the European Parliament in Spring 2004, and agreement with the Council of Ministers was reached late in 2005 (CEC, 2006). The next two sections consider each of these directives in turn.

15.3 THE RAIL INFRASTRUCTURE CHARGING DIRECTIVE

Directive 2001/14, on the allocation of railway infrastructure capacity and levying of charges, enshrined the proposals on railway infrastructure charging emerging from the 1998 railways package. In summary, the directive determines that charges must be based on 'costs directly incurred as a result of operating the train service'. They may include:

- scarcity, although where a section of track is defined as having a scarcity problem, the infrastructure manager must examine proposals to relieve that scarcity, and undertake them unless they are shown, on the basis of cost–benefit analysis, not to be worthwhile;
- environmental costs, but only where these are levied on other modes;
- recovery of the costs of specific investments where these are worthwhile and could not otherwise be funded;
- discounts, but only where justified by costs; large operators may not use their market power to get discounts;
- reservation charges for scarce capacity, which must be paid whether the capacity is used or not;
- compensation for unpaid costs on other modes; and
- non-discriminatory mark-ups for financial purposes, but these must not exclude segments of traffic which could cover direct cost.

In other words, this directive reflects some sensible second-best economics. It seems clear from the list of elements that may be included in the charges that 'the direct cost of operating the service' is to be interpreted as an SMC. Typically, this is thought of as a very low charge, but provision is made for reservation fees for scarce capacity and for heavily used parts of the network. These may need to be substantial to regulate demand. However, the arguments that this form of pricing may lead infrastructure managers to artificially restrict capacity or to be unable to fund their activities in total or particular investments are all addressed by special provisions. In particular, the need to attract private investment or to fund fixed costs for which governments fail to provide adequate funding may lead to a need for prices that exceed marginal cost, but these mark-ups should be non-discriminatory in terms of operation and lose as little traffic as possible. This appears to encourage Ramsey–Boiteux pricing, whereby mark-ups are larger, the less sensitive the segment of the market is to price. Moreover, there is allowance for second-best pricing in the face of distorted prices on other modes. However, the effect of these provisions, all sensible in themselves, is to considerably water down the likely effect of the directive by permitting a continued high degree of variation in both the structure and level of charges (particularly as the proportion of infrastructure costs that governments are willing to fund continues to vary enormously). In particular, the degree to which competitive charges for slots involving several countries, based on comparable pricing regimes, will be achieved will inevitably be limited. In practice, a wide diversity of structures and levels of rail infrastructure charges exist (Nash, 2005), with some (particularly in Scandinavia) actually below marginal social cost but many (especially in Central and Eastern Europe) substantially above it, especially for freight.

15.4   HEAVY GOODS VEHICLE USER CHARGES

Charges for the use of roads by heavy goods vehicles became an important issue when liberalization made it possible for vehicles registered in one country to compete in another. It is also, of course, a major issue in terms of competition between road and rail, where the White Paper (CEC, 2001) sought to stabilize rail market share.

As has been explained above, the original reason for the interest of the European Commission in heavy goods vehicle charges is the danger that the wide range of structures and levels of charges might distort competition between member states. This led to legislation imposing minima and maxima on the levels of annual vehicle taxes and fuel taxes. However, this did not stop allegations of unfair competition between road hauliers based in different countries, with those based in countries with low annual taxes (and to an extent low fuel taxes, since they could fill their tanks at their base and often avoid refuelling in high tax countries) having an unfair advantage over those based where taxes were high. In the early 1990s, Germany sought to deal with this problem by imposing a time-related charge on all users of its motorways. This in due course became the 'Eurovignette', implemented also by the Benelux countries, Sweden and Denmark. The original Eurovignette directive in 1993 was designed to prevent this system from exploiting foreign hauliers by charging them more than it cost to provide and maintain the roads in question or by discriminating by nationality in the charge. The directive was amended in 1999, and – as stated above – agreement on further amendments was reached late in 2005. These amendments will still tie the average level of charges to average infrastructure costs (costs are to be allocated between vehicle types according to vehicle-kilometres, with the possibility of using objectively supported equivalence factors to allow, for instance, for the additional wear and tear caused by high axle-weight vehicles). However, they permit charges on all roads (the previous legislation applied to motorways only), and permit charges to be differentiated in time and space according to levels of congestion, environmental and accident costs, and according to the emission characteristics of the vehicle (indeed, the last is required by 2010). A further significant development was the agreement of an explicit cross-subsidy between modes in the case of environmentally sensitive areas. In these circumstances, a surcharge of up to 25 per cent will be permitted in order to fund alternative transport infrastructure, including, where appropriate, rail.

The decision to tie the average level of charges to average infrastructure costs limits the extent to which the proposed charges can reflect marginal social costs, in particular environmental and congestion costs (although there is provision for separate regulatory charges to deal with these problems). Nevertheless, the new directive represents a clear advance on the existing directive in a number of respects. In terms of many of the decisions open to freight vehicle operators (type of vehicle, route, time of day), it is toll differentiation rather than the average level of toll that is the crucial factor. Moreover, it also requires the Commission to review the evidence on measurement of marginal social cost and on the implications of implementing charges based on it within two years, for further consideration of the issue. However, in terms of overall levels of freight transport and inter-modal competition, the absolute level of charges is clearly important.

It should be noted that the new legislation permits such charges but does not require them. In practice, the first European country to introduce a kilometre-based charge on all roads was Switzerland in 2001. Switzerland is not a member of the EU and not therefore bound by EU legislation, so it was able to base the charge on an explicit calculation of infrastructure and external costs. Austria and Germany have also introduced charges on motorways only, Germany using global positioning system (GPS) technology which is capable of extension to all roads, as permitted by the new legislation. A number of other countries, including Sweden and Britain, are interested; Britain indeed was well advanced in the procurement of the technology for a kilometre-based charging system for heavy goods vehicles on all roads when it decided to postpone such a system until it was ready to introduce nationwide road pricing for all vehicle types.

15.5 REASONS FOR LACK OF PROGRESS

It is clear that progress on the Commission's policy on transport pricing has been disappointingly slow. In the rail sector, a directive has been introduced that is consistent with the principles, but this has not prevented a wide range of pricing structures and levels from persisting. In the road sector, even the proposed amendments to legislation actually tie average charges to average infrastructure cost rather than to marginal social cost. In other sectors no relevant legislation at the European level exists.

What are the major reasons for this situation? Obviously the interests of the different stakeholders vary. Some of the most hotly contested issues in the debate have been the following:

1. *What proportion of infrastructure costs varies with use, and how can this be allocated between different vehicle types?* It might be thought that this was an issue resolved by engineering studies decades ago. However, when the approach of different European countries to allocating road infrastructure costs to vehicle types was compared, major differences

were found. In the rail sector there was little research on which to draw. Thus there was plenty of potential for argument about the degree to which costs were variable and the extent to which these costs should be allocated to heavy goods vehicles or rail freight.

2. *Is it possible to value external costs, especially environmental costs, or are all valuations essentially arbitrary?* Despite the amount of research the Commission itself had sponsored on this issue, this was given as a major reason for excluding externalities from heavy goods vehicle charges in the preamble to the 2003 proposals (CEC, 2003).

3. *What would be the impact of marginal social cost pricing on the economy? Would it particularly harm peripheral states?* In many, though not all, countries marginal social cost pricing would lead to higher charges for road haulage. The roads and, indeed, the industrial lobby in general argued that this would damage European competitiveness. This was a particular concern in the peripheral countries, whose freight faced long lengths of haul with much of the distance in congested core European countries where it was feared that charges would be high.

4. *Should all revenues be earmarked for investment in the mode from which they accrue or in the transport system as a whole?* The 2001 White Paper (CEC, 2001) specifically saw marginal social cost pricing of road haulage as a way of funding necessary new infrastructure on both road and rail modes. Indeed the Trans-European Network investment proposals gave high priority to new rail infrastructure. But the roads lobby was adamant that what its members paid in taxes should be ploughed back into the road system.

The European Commission has sponsored extensive research on all these issues as part of its framework programmes and we consider the implications of that research in the next section.

15.6   RESEARCH

In this section we try to answer the questions raised about marginal cost pricing in the previous section on the basis of European Commission sponsored research. We shall address the four questions raised in turn.

15.6.1   Variability of Infrastructure Costs

Traditional approaches to the allocation of infrastructure cost have relied on cost allocation formulae, driven by a mix of engineering knowledge and judgement as to what seems reasonable. For instance, Table 15.1 shows the cost allocation formula for road infrastructure costs used in Britain for many years, in which different categories of maintenance cost are allocated to vehicle miles, maximum permitted gross tonne miles, average actual gross tonne miles, and standard axle miles (a standard axle is a single pass of a 10-tonne axle, and standard axle miles are computed weighting axles of different weights by the fourth power of their axle load, based on test results which show that pavement wear is related to the fourth power of the axle load). In the table, those elements of cost which are variable with use have been distinguished from those that are fixed on the basis of what seems reasonable. However, a comparison of the formulae used in different European countries shows that judgement as to what seems reasonable differs substantially from country to country (Link et al., 1999). It would be preferable to have some hard evidence based on actual data.

The UNITE project (Nash and Matthews, 2005a) was responsible for econometric studies of road and rail infrastructure costs, in which data on the actual costs of maintenance and renewal of individual sections of road

Table 15.1   Road wear and tear costs (%)

Description	PCU-km	Av.gwt-km	Sa-km	Include in MC?
Long-life pavements			100	✓
Resurfacing			100	✓
Overlay			100	✓
Surface dressing	20	80		✓
Patching and minor repairs		20	80	✓
Drainage	100			✓
Bridges and remedial earthworks		100		
Footways, cycle tracks and kerbs		100		
Fences and barriers	33	67		
Verges, traffic signs and crossings	100			
Sweeping and cleaning	100			
Road markings	10	90		✓
Winter maintenance & misc.	100			
Street lighting	100			
Policing and traffic wardens	100			

Notes: av.gwt: average gross vehicle weight; pcu: passenger car unit (a standard size car equals 1 pcu); sa: standard axles (a measure of the relative damage due to axle weights). The costs attributed to pedestrians for roads other than motorways (50% of the categories from fences and barriers through to street lighting) are removed prior to allocation to motorized vehicles.

Source: Sansom et al. (2001).

or railway line were regressed on various cost drivers including traffic levels. The results of these and a small number of other studies are summarized in Table 15.2 and were somewhat variable, but it appears that, for road, the cost elasticity is generally somewhat less than 1 and, for rail, greatly less than 1. Full cost allocation procedures will greatly overstate the marginal cost of use, particularly in the case of rail.

However, econometric analysis of this sort assumes that expenditure actually reflects the impact of wear and tear in the year in question. This is particularly problematic in the case of renewals, where deferral is a possibility, usually at the expense of increased maintenance cost. Moreover, it is not usually possible to get data to test the impact of the number of standard axles using a stretch of road, or to identify different types of vehicle (although for rail, gross tonne kilometres was the measure used, so this does take account of differences in vehicle weight). Thus it remains necessary to blend econometric evidence on the overall degree of cost variability with engineering evidence on the relevant impact of different vehicle types.

15.6.2   Measurement and Valuation of External Costs

The measurement and valuation of external costs has traditionally been undertaken mainly by 'top-down' procedures which estimated the total costs for a particular country and then allocated them to different types of traffic. There are several reasons why this approach may be inadequate. First, for congestion, accident and noise costs in particular, the relationship between costs and volume is non-linear so marginal cost is not equal to average cost. But, second, all these costs vary greatly in time and space. Simple national averages are far from adequate for pricing purposes.

In the case of congestion, it is common to assume that there is no congestion up to a certain proportion of capacity utilization, after which journey time rises exponentially as capacity utilization increases. Thus the marginal external cost of congestion (the difference between marginal and average cost) rises exponentially over this range.

Something of the variation of the results can be seen in Table 15.3, taken from Sansom et al. (2001).

In the case of accidents, there are two key issues in determining the external element of costs (Lindberg, 2005). The first is the degree to which costs are borne by the state or third parties, for instance in the form of health service or police costs, as opposed to being borne directly by the individual involved either directly or through insurance. The second is the extent to which increased traffic volumes add to the risk to other road users. There is increasing evidence that, in many cases, increased traffic actually makes the

Table 15.2 Results of marginal infrastructure wear and tear cost estimation for road

	Country	Study	Costs considered	Elasticities	Costs		
					Mean	Trucks	Passenger cars
Road					Costs per vehicle km (in eurocents)		
	Germany	Link (2006)	Renewal	0.05–1.17 (Mean 0.87)		0.08–1.87	
	Austria	Herry and Sedlacek (2002)	Maintenance and renewals	1.046	0.16	2.17	0.07
	Switzerland	Schreyer et al. (2002)	Maintenance, renewals and upgrades	0.8	0.67–1.15	3.62–5.17	0.42–0.50
	Sweden	Lindberg (2002)	Renewals	0.1–0.8		0.77–1.86	
Rail					Costs per 1000 gross tonne km (in eurocents)		
	Sweden	Johannson and Nilsson (2004)	Maintenance	0.169		0.127	
	Finland	Johannson and Nilsson (2004)	Maintenance	0.167		0.239	
	Finland	Tervonen and Idstrom (2004)	Maintenance	0.133–0.175		0.179–0.246	
	Austria	Munduch et al. (2002)	Maintenance	0.27		0.55	
	France	Gaudry and Quinet (2003)	Maintenance	0.37		n.a.	
	Finland	Tervonen and Idstrom (2004)	Maintenance and renewals	0.267–0.291		0.77–0.87	

Source: Ricci et al. (2006a).

Table 15.3   Estimates of the marginal external costs of congestion by road types (pence per vehicle km, 1998 prices and values)

Categories	Values
Central London	
Motorway	53.75
Trunk & principal	71.09
Other	187.79
Inner London	
Motorway	20.10
Trunk & principal	54.13
Other	94.48
Outer London	
Motorway	31.09
Trunk & principal	28.03
Other	39.66
Inner conurbation	
Motorway	53.90
Trunk & principal	33.97
Other	60.25
Outer conurbation	
Motorway	35.23
Trunk & principal	12.28
Other	0.00
Urban > 25 km^2	
Trunk & principal	10.13
Other	0.72
Urban 15–25 km^2	
Trunk & principal	7.01
Other	0.00
Urban 10–15 km^2	
Trunk & principal	0.00
Other	0.00
Urban 5–10 km^2	
Trunk & principal	2.94
Other	0.00
Urban 0.01–5 km^2	
Trunk & principal	1.37
Other	0.00
Rural	
Motorway	4.01
Trunk & principal	8.48
Other	1.28

Source: Sansom et al. (2001).

Table 15.4   *Range of environmental cost estimates (euros/1000 pkm/tkm)*

	Car UNITE*	INFRAS/IWW	HGV UNITE*	INFRAS/IWW
Noise	0.13–1.27	0.1–13.0	0.11–5.06	0.25–32.0
Air pollution	1.46–3.13	5.7–45.0	2.20–7.32	33.5
Climate change	2.40–2.93	1.7–27	2.16–2.74	1.8–13

Note: * Inter-urban case studies using the Impact Pathway Assessment approach; cars use petrol. Assumes mean passengers per car = 1.5, and mean tonnes per hgv 10. Emissions standards of vehicles are at the Euro 2 level.

Sources: INFRAS/IWW (2004); Bickel et al. (2005).

road safer for other road users, presumably by slowing traffic. However, this is not the case for increases in heavy goods vehicles which may be involved in accidents with lighter vehicles, or for increases in vehicular traffic in situations in which there are many vulnerable road users (pedestrians or cyclists).

For environmental externalities, the issues are more complex. Table 15.4 shows the contrast between the environmental costs estimated in two studies, UNITE and INFRAS/IWW (2004). Both used the bottom-up impact pathway assessment approach, whereby the emission, dispersion and final deposition of the pollutant are modelled; its impact in terms of health, building deterioration, crop reduction and so on is forecast; and then this is valued. For greenhouse gases, the impact is unaffected by the location or time of emission, while for local air pollution, population density and direction and strength of wind speed are important; in the case of noise, population density, background noise and time of day are important (noise causes much more nuisance at night than in the daytime). UNITE used a single monetary valuation so the variation in results depends entirely on external circumstances, whereas INFRAS/IWW used upper and lower values.

For climate change, the uncertainty is almost entirely a matter of the value placed on greenhouse gases. UNITE assumed that for Europe the Kyoto agreement would form a binding constraint. Thus the impact of a change in transport emissions would be a change in emissions elsewhere in the economy in order to remain at the target level, and it is the cost of achieving this change in emissions elsewhere that is the relevant valuation. On these assumptions, the emission of greenhouse gases in total is unaffected by the level of transport emissions. On the basis of a number of studies this valuation was estimated at around $20 per tonne of carbon.

However, many commentators argue for a much higher level of reduction of greenhouse gases, and the higher INFRAS/IWW estimates assumed that this would be achieved, leading to much higher costs.

For local air pollution and noise nuisance, the differences are also partly a matter of valuation but there are also differences in the effects taken into account and in the assumed dose-response functions. In general, UNITE used only well-established results, whereas INFRAS/IWW included some more speculative relationships.

On all these issues it seems reasonable to treat the UNITE estimates as lower-bound estimates. It is unlikely that the true value is lower than these figures, but it may well be higher. Thus, if prices do not at least allow for the UNITE estimates of external costs, then it is highly likely that they are below marginal social cost.

15.6.3 Impacts of Marginal Social Cost Pricing

There have been many studies of the impacts of marginal social cost pricing for transport in Europe. Here we shall confine ourselves to comments on the results of two Europe-wide attempts to model its impacts – the IASON (Tavasszy et al., 2004) and TIPMAC projects (Kohler et al., 2003). Both used the SCENES transport model, but while IASON linked this to a computable general equilibrium model, TIPMAC used an input–output type macroeconomic model to predict the economic impact.

In terms of transport impacts, it should be noted that in IASON far more than simply a diversion between modes was predicted. While some 6 per cent of road haulage tonne-kilometres were predicted to switch to more environmentally friendly modes, there was also a shift in traffic from urban to inter-urban and rural roads and a switch to larger but also cleaner vehicles (although, on average, larger vehicles of the same emissions rating impose more externalities per vehicle-kilometre, they impose less per tonne-kilometre). But something like half the overall impact of the change in transport prices on road traffic levels came from changes in the pattern of economic activity, with more industrial inputs and consumer goods sourced locally.

In IASON, the regional impact of the higher charges was modelled without assuming that the revenue would be recycled, thus leading to a general decline in economic activity which was indeed slightly greater in peripheral areas. It was the case that the highest revenues and greatest relief from externalities were experienced in the core countries which are generally the most congested. Traffic passing through these countries, to or from peripheral countries, would have to pay more but the peripheral countries would not benefit (except from reduced congestion on the transit routes). TIPMAC, however, assumed that revenues would be recycled by reduction of income tax. This produced a 'double dividend' in that externalities were reduced and so was a distorting tax. The net impact on gross domestic product and on employment in this case was forecast to be positive in every EU country, although in some cases it was much greater than in others.

15.6.4 Earmarking

Earmarking of revenues has also been a very controversial issue. The argument is simple, earmarking may prevent governments from using revenues in an optimal way; on the other hand, earmarking rules which constrain governments' freedom of action may actually lead to revenues being used in a better way than would otherwise occur. Plenty of studies, for example, MC-ICAM (Niskanen and Nash, 2004) and REVENUE (Ricci et al., 2006b) have produced evidence in favour of the former proposition, while a few models attempt to explain the dynamics of government behaviour and thus are able to tackle the latter. One model which does is ASTRA, and it has produced arguments in favour of earmarking (see Ricci op.cit.).

What does appear clear is the following. Transport taxes designed to internalize externalities avoid the distorting effects of general taxation, and thus are a better way of funding transport expenditure than is general taxation. On the other hand, it is quite possible that efficient transport charges will produce more revenue than is needed to fund efficient transport infrastructure investment. In this case, it is clearly better that the surplus should be used to offset other distorting taxes such as income tax rather than investing excessively in the transport sector.

There is, however, an added issue, that of equity. A case study of road haulage pricing in the UK examined this issue in the MC-ICAM project (Niskanen and Nash, 2004). It was found that using transport taxes to reduce income tax had a regressive impact. Using the revenue instead to boost social security payments would favour poorer sectors of the community, but was less efficient. Nevertheless, transport infrastructure pricing reform was still worthwhile, although the optimal charge was lower when the use of revenue was less efficient.

There is good evidence that the use of revenue is a key element in gaining acceptability for new higher transport infrastructure charges (Schade and Schlag, 2003). If it is the only way to make them acceptable, then earmarking may be worthwhile even if it reduces the overall welfare gains from the pricing reforms, provided that they are still positive. But the question arises whether taxes have to be earmarked for use in the same sector as the revenue is raised in order to make them acceptable, or whether earmarking part of them to other favoured uses that are more efficient might also achieve acceptability.

15.7   CONCLUSIONS

It appears that, despite the proposals of the White Paper, actual progress towards more efficiency in transport pricing has been slow. For rail, the relevant directive bases pricing on marginal social cost but allows for the need to charge for scarcity; to charge mark-ups for financial reasons; and to adopt the principles of second-best pricing in the light of distortions on other modes. This commendable flexibility does, however, mean a continuing wide variety of structures and levels of charges, with adverse consequences for the competitive position of rail in those countries with high charges, and for international routes to, from and through those countries. The agreed reform of charging of heavy goods vehicles would improve on the current position in terms of the degree of differentiation, but actually run counter to declared EU policy in not permitting full internalization of externalities. (However, it should be noted that the 1998 White Paper foresaw a situation in which average charges equalled average infrastructure costs, though charges were differentiated according to marginal social cost as an intermediate position while acceptability for more radical change was built up, and the legislation does indeed require the commission to re-examine the evidence and bring forward further proposals.) This change would presumably achieve benefits in terms of time of day, route and type of vehicle used, all of which appear to be significant benefits of the reform of heavy goods vehicle charging, but not in terms of incentives for modifying mode split or for more local sourcing of goods.

Why has faster progress not been made? Major arguments against marginal social cost pricing are: the difficulty of measuring marginal wear and tear costs of different types of vehicle; the difficulty of measuring and valuing external costs; fears of the impact of marginal social cost pricing particularly in peripheral countries; and the need to earmark revenues. Much research on these topics has been sponsored by the European Commission in recent years. It is argued that it is possible on the basis of this research to identify lower bounds below which it is unlikely that marginal social cost will fall, although it is certainly possible to argue for higher prices. Provided that the revenue is used sensibly, it does not appear that, marginal social cost pricing would harm any country in Europe, although certainly the net benefits would be uneven, and acceptability might be improved by measures to redistribute them. However, there is a problem in that the most efficient use of any surplus of revenues over that which can be efficiently invested in the transport sector may be to reduce income tax and the impact of this would be regressive; yet if the revenue is used in a way which helps poorer sectors of the economy then the efficiency benefits may be less. Earmarking may well reduce the benefits of marginal social cost pricing, although if it is the only way to implement it then it may be worthwhile. It may be possible to earmark revenues for popular uses which are not purely within the mode in question or the transport sector as a whole if the entire revenue cannot be used efficiently in the transport sector.

NOTE

1.   This chapter draws heavily on work conducted for the Imprint-Europe and Imprint-Net coordination actions, which were funded under the fifth and sixth framework programmes of the EC, and I wish to thank my colleagues involved in these projects, in particular Bryan Matthews and Batool Menaz, for their contribution to this work.

REFERENCES

Bickel, P., S. Schmid and R. Friedrich (2005), 'Environmental costs', in Nash and Matthews (eds), pp. 185–209.
Commission of the European Commission (CEC) (1995), *Towards Fair and Efficient Pricing in Transport–Policy Options for Internalising the External Cost of Transport in the European Union*, Brussels: CEC (COM(95)691).
Commission of the European Communities (CEC) (1998), *White Paper: Fair Payment for Infrastructure Use: A Phased Approach to a Common Transport Infrastructure Charging Framework in the European Union*, Brussels: CEC.
Commission of the European Communities (CEC) (2001), *White Paper: European Transport Policy for 2010: Time to Decide*, Brussels: CEC.
Commission of the European Communities (CEC) (2003), *Proposal for a Directive of the European Parliament and of the Council amending Directive 1999/62/EC on the charging of heavy goods vehicles for the use of certain infrastructures*, Brussels: CEC.
Commission of the European Communities (CEC) (2006), *Directive of the European Parliament and of the Council amending Directive 1999/62/EC on the charging of heavy goods vehicles for the use of certain infrastructures*, Brussels: CEC.
Evans, A.W. (1992), 'Road congestion pricing: when is it a good policy?', *Journal of Transport Economics and Policy*, **26** (3), 213–43.
Gaudry, M. and E. Quinet (2003), 'Rail track wear-and-tear costs by traffic class in France', Montréal: Université de Montréal, Publication AJD–66.
Herry, M. and N. Sedlacek (2002), 'Road econometrics – case study Austria', Deliverable 10, Annex A1c, UNITE (UNIfication of accounts and marginal cost for transport efficiency), funded by EU 5th Framework RTD Programme, Institute for Transport Studies: University of Leeds.

INFRAS/IWW (2004), *External Costs of Transport: Accident, Environmental and Congestion Costs of Transport in Western Europe*, Zurich/Karlsruhe: Union of International Railways and Community of European Railways.

Jansson, J.O. (1997), 'Theory and practice of transport infrastructure and public transport pricing', in Gines de Rus and Chris Nash (eds), *Recent Developments in Transport Economics*, Aldershot: Ashgate, pp. 74–134.

Johansson, P. and J. Nilsson (2004), 'An economic analysis of track maintenance costs', *Transport Policy*, **11** (3), 277–86.

Kohler, J., H. Pollitt, N. Raha and P. Cuthbertson (2003), TIPMAC Deliverable 4, Results of the Combined SCENES/E3ME model system analysis, WSP Cambridge (formerly ME&P consultancy).

Lindberg, G. (2002), 'Marginal cost of road maintenance for heavy goods vehicles on Swedish roads', Deliverable 10, Annex 2, UNITE (UNIfication of accounts and marginal cost for transport efficiency), funded by EU 5th Framework RTD Programme, Institute for Transport Studies: University of Leeds.

Lindberg, G. (2005), 'Accidents', in Nash and Matthews (eds), pp. 155–83.

Link, H. (2006), 'An economic analysis of motorway renewal costs in Germany', *Transportation Research Part A*, **40** (1), 19–34.

Link, H., J. Dodgson, M. Maibach and M. Herry (1999), *The Costs of Road Infrastructure and Congestion in Europe*, Heidelberg: Physica/Springer.

Mayeres, I., S. Proost and K. van Dender (2005), 'The impacts of marginal social cost pricing', in Nash and Matthews (eds), pp. 211–43.

Munduch, G., A. Pfister, L. Sogner and A. Stiassny (2002), *Estimating Marginal Costs for the Austrian Railway System*, working paper 78, Department of Economics Working Paper Series, Vienna University of Economics & BA, Vienna.

Nash, C.A. (2005), 'Rail infrastructure charges in Europe', *Journal of Transport Economics and Policy*, **39** (3), 259–78.

Nash, C.A. and B. Matthews (eds) (2005a), *Research in Transportation Economics*, Vol. 14, Oxford: Elsevier.

Nash, C.A. and B. Matthews (2005b), 'Measuring the marginal social cost of transport', Oxford, UK: Elsevier.

Niskanen, E. and C.A. Nash (2004), *Final Report for Publication*, MC-ICAM, Implementation of Marginal Cost Pricing in Transport – Integrated Conceptual and Applied Model Analysis. Funded by 5th Framework RTD Programme, Institute for Transport Studies, University of Leeds.

Ricci, A., P. Fagiani, C.A. Nash, B. Matthews, B. Menaz, D. Johnson, P.E. Wheat, A. Burgess, W. Savenije, R. de Jong, K. Tanczos, F. Meszaros and J. Schade (2006a), *Pricing for Sustainable Transport Policies – State of the Art*, IMPRINT-NET deliverable 1, Rome: ISIS.

Ricci, A., C. Sessa, C.A. Nash, R. Macario, M. van der Hoofd, M. Carmona, S. Proost and A. de Palma (2006b), *Synthesis and Policy Conclusions*, REVENUE Project deliverable 6, Rome: ISIS.

Rothengatter, W. (2003), 'How good is first best? Marginal cost and other pricing principles for user charging transport', *Transport Policy*, **10**, 121–30.

Sansom, T., C.A. Nash, P.J. Mackie, J.D. Shires and P. Watkiss (2001), *Surface Transport Costs and Charges, Great Britain 1998*, A Report for the UK Department of the Environment, Transport and the Regions.

Schade, J. and B. Schlag (2003), *Acceptability of Transport Pricing Strategies*, Oxford: Elsevier.

Schreyer, C., N. Schmidt and M. Maibach (2002), 'Road econometrics – case study motorways Switzerland', Deliverable 10, Annex A1b, UNITE (UNIfication of accounts and marginal costs for transport efficiency), funded by EU 5th Framework RTD Programme, Institute for Transport Studies: University of Leeds.

Tervonen, J. and T. Idström (2004), *Marginal Rail Infrastructure Costs in Finland 1997–2002*, report from the Finnish Rail Administration, available at: www.rhk.fi.

Tavasszy, L., G. Renes and A. Burgess (2004), *Final report for publication: Conclusions and recommendations for the assessment of economic impacts of transport projects and policies*, Deliverable 10, IASON (Integrated Appraisal of Spatial, Economic and Network Effects of Transport Investments and Policies), Funded by 5th Framework RTD Programme, TNO Inro, Delft, Netherlands.

16. Conclusions and directions of further research

Bert van Wee, Michiel Bliemer, Linda Steg and Erik Verhoef

The various chapters in this book have provided deeper insight into the design and effects of road-pricing schemes, focusing on different aspects of pricing, and taking different perspectives to study them. In this final chapter, we shall not try to repeat all the conclusions from the previous chapters. Rather, we draw some more general conclusions. Furthermore, we identify some possible directions of further research.

16.1   GENERAL CONCLUSIONS

A first conclusion is that multidisciplinary and interdisciplinary transport research, as we had hoped, does indeed often produce new insights and fresh perspectives, especially so in studies of multifaceted phenomena with direct policy relevance, such as transport pricing. Several of the chapters in this book are based on multidisciplinary research that aims to integrate the insights of economists, psychologists, civil engineers and geographers. Partly based on this experience, we consider such multidisciplinary research as very fruitful. The collaboration between scientists with different backgrounds has resulted in rewarding interactions, and even cross-fertilization. For example, civil engineers aim to implement in practice theoretical optimal pricing schemes proposed by economists, thereby taking practical second-best limitations explicitly into account. Additionally, the psychologists contribute in furthering the way in which travel behaviour can be put into models, by questioning the rationale of making certain assumptions on travellers' behaviour responses, such as the economists' and engineers' natural starting-point of assuming rational, utility-maximizing agents. This was not only inspiring for the researchers, but we think that such multidisciplinary research is an important step in the right direction to better understand the many aspects surrounding pricing in transport, and their interactions. Needless to say, it is important to extend multidisciplinary research to other fields of transport research.

A second general conclusion is that, for the implementation of a policy such as transport pricing, a large number of – often interrelated – questions are relevant, which need addressing not only for the successful technical and practical implementation of road pricing but also to achieve an optimal benefit–cost ratio, and to secure maximum, or at least sufficient, support from the public and from particular stakeholders. These questions relate to the many design options for road pricing (for example, when, where, for whom and how much to charge). They also relate to acceptability issues, revenue use and several types of effects, such as transport demand in multimodal networks, accessibility effects, and social costs and benefits. Further questions arise concerning the relations with other policies, and the process of design, implementation, refinement and evaluation. In this book, we have tried to shed light on some of these questions, but many questions still remain open.

To assist policy makers in decision making, analysts develop and apply models that forecast the impacts of specific pricing designs on a multitude of aspects. This book confirms that elaborate models are needed in order to investigate the long-term effects of road pricing. First, travel choice behaviour needs to be modelled in a way that encompasses a wide range of choices, such as trip choice, route choice, departure-time choice and mode choice. Then, traffic simulation models are used to analyse the effect of travel demand on traffic conditions, which in turn will feed back into travel choice behaviour. Finally, longer-run choices such as location choice behaviour, car ownership and technology choice also need to be modelled. All these (sub)models generate feed back to other (sub)models, making a full modelling system extremely complex. Moreover, the calibration of all these models depends heavily on available data, particularly to estimate the behavioural models. The complexity of the whole modelling and calibration process means that research into road pricing is very challenging.

This book aimed to provide an overview of road pricing from different perspectives. The various chapters clearly present the complexities in the analyses and applications of pricing in transport, and indicate that much research still needs to be done.

16.2   DIRECTIONS OF FURTHER RESEARCH

In this section we address possible directions of further research. We do not claim complete coverage, but we discuss several options, because we think that – despite the scientific progress in recent years – many challenges remain.

16.2.1   Interdisciplinary Research

From multidisciplinary to interdisciplinary research
This book has emphasized the importance of multidisciplinary research. We define multidisciplinary research as research in which researchers from different disciplines work together to study a specific object of study, combining their views and reflecting on these, but not yet necessarily integrating them. A next step may be interdisciplinary research in which the various views and methods from different disciplines are more fully integrated. This may need the assimilation of theories and concepts, but also the integration of research methods.

16.2.2   Effects of Pricing

Goods transport and logistics
It appears that, in the area of pricing in transport, much more is known about passenger transport compared with freight transport. Although some of the chapters in this book did focus on freight transport, future research might study the impact of pricing on the supply chain and supply chain management, reactions of firms that produce or transport goods, and perceptions of directors and logistic managers of firms in more depth. For such research, there is a clear need for data. In addition, assessing the implications of pricing for goods transport over the supply chain raises many modelling challenges, as does combining freight and passenger transport network models. For the long-term effects, including relocations, and regional economic development, insights from various theories of agglomeration, including new economic geography, may prove helpful.

Accessibility effects
Many challenges remain related to the use of indicators designed to express the accessibility impacts of road pricing. Some important questions include first, what is 'the best' way to express accessibility changes in the case of road-pricing measures, given various possible purposes of the analysis and second, to what extent does the use of different accessibility measures result in different pictures of the changes in accessibility?

Valuing external costs
If pricing policy aims to regulate external costs, more research into unit values for various external cost categories appears to be in order. This relates not only to the value of time, but also to the valuation of the reliability of travel times, environmental and nature impacts, safety, and wear

and tear of infrastructure. The number of primary studies in these areas for some of these costs is quite small, resulting in a rather limited basis for determining unit costs as used in policy-related research, including *ex ante* evaluation studies such as cost–benefit analysis.

Employers' reactions
Another area of empirical research includes employers' reactions to road pricing in their employee-related strategies. Will they change their policy on lease cars, and will they compensate employees for the road-pricing charges they have to pay? Will there be effects on (tele-)working at home, on compensation for residential relocations, or on other fringe benefits? Some of the chapters in this book provided some initial insights into these issues, but more research is definitely warranted.

16.2.3   Empirical Research

Revealed preferences
Now that road pricing has been introduced in several countries, and probably will be implemented in other regions and countries in the near future, more options for revealed preference (RP) research will become available. Such RP research is highly important in order to understand the actual opinions about, and the effects of, transport pricing. Moreover, the results of RP research should be compared with the outcomes of previously carried out stated preference (SP) and modelling studies, including the research presented in some of the chapters of this book, in order to examine to what extent SP and modelling studies yield valid assessments of opinions on, and the effects of, transport pricing.

Long-term responses
Most empirical research focuses on short-term behavioural responses, such as trip frequency, destination choice, mode choice, time of day choice and route choice. This book also explored some longer-term responses, including residential choice, job changes and vehicle choice (based on SP data). As long-term effects are of main interest to policy makers, more research into these effects is important. Clearly, obtaining empirical RP data on these long-term responses to road pricing is more difficult than on short-term responses, which are more readily available.

Cross-country comparisons
Related to the recent successful implementation of road pricing and possible future implementations, it would be worthwhile to make cross-country comparisons – not only focusing on the opinions about, and the effects of,

pricing but also on the process, and the technologies used. In addition, it is important to include not only cases of successful implementations but also examples of failures. This should help to identify the determinants for success and failure. Many factors could be considered in this respect, such as differences in infrastructural, economic, technological, cultural and psychological factors between countries.

Opinions of the public
Also related to successful implementation, it is important to carry out research into the opinions expressed by the public: how do they change over time, and why, and to what extent are these opinions influenced by the media, experiences, actual effects on travel behaviour and environmental conditions, or other factors?

Data
A final area of empirical research is related to data. As a result of technology installed for road pricing, what data will become available for what purposes? What data can be useful for road infrastructure managers, or for route-guiding devices? What about privacy issues: what problems might occur, and how can they be handled? Can arrangements be made so that people providing data will benefit from giving permission to use their data?

16.2.4 Modelling

Behavioural models
For modelling travel behaviour, activity-based modelling has recently received some attention, and important progress has been made in the past decade. A challenge is to link activity- to trip-based modelling and models for the use of infrastructure. This requires both methodological advances to be made, and also the design of sufficiently rapid solution algorithms for spatial-dynamic activity-based transport network models.

Model implementations and applicability
Another challenge in the area of modelling is to translate new scientific insights into models that can be used for practical purposes, like those that large and medium-sized cities and towns have, as well as the model packages often used by consultants. More and more (commercial) software is becoming available that can be used to analyse the effects of road-pricing strategies. However, these software programs have their methodological and theoretical drawbacks, as well as practical limitations. Combining the current scientific knowledge and the available practical

implementations will be an important step in improving the applicability of the models.

16.2.5 Design of Road Pricing

Optimal design of road-pricing schemes
It is clear that different objectives will lead to different optimal designs for road pricing. As such, the natural starting-point for designing a road-pricing scheme should be to determine which objectives are most important to the policy maker. Then, a road-pricing scheme can be determined that is essentially a design problem. However, designing an optimal scheme for a full dynamic network can be difficult, particularly for the more practical second-best pricing strategies, mainly because the number of possible designs is very large. Evaluating each design can be very time-consuming. Even if the charging locations and the charging time periods have already been chosen, determining the optimal charges for the given objective(s) is a difficult task. For each instance of charging levels, a model needs to be run, which at least includes trip choice, route choice, departure time choice, and mode choice together with a (dynamic) traffic simulator. Nowadays such models exist and can be used to evaluate a given road-pricing scheme. However, optimizing the design of such a scheme requires the systematic evaluation of a large number of schemes. Raw computation power is not enough. Rather, an intelligent way of constructing such an optimal design should be sought, which is one of the most challenging research topics for transport engineers and economists active in this field.

The land-use–transport link and pricing
An important issue is the relationship between the land-use–transport configuration and the design and effects of pricing options. In Central London, a cordon-based toll system may be an obvious option, but in polynuclear regions, such as the Randstad area (Netherlands), the German Ruhr area, or West Belgium, a kilometre-based charge may be the only option. These considerations need to be taken into account when creating a road-pricing design.

Charging versus rewarding
Most studies of price incentives in road transport focus on taxes, a starting-point that is consistent with the possible objective of road prices to internalize external costs. However, some theoretical studies describe credit-based systems, in which credits can be earned for travelling off-peak and can be spent for travelling during the peak period. For future research it would be very interesting to investigate the opinions about, and effects

of, rewarding compared with charging in more detail, as there is a clear lack of knowledge in this area. Again, this is an example of a second-best measure, where prices are set under the restriction that some prices be negative (that is, subsidies).

16.2.6   Technology

Technology dynamics
Technology is of course a dynamic phenomenon. Important research questions surround technology dynamics, including changes in technology performance over time, but also cost changes, partly due to scale and learning effects. An important question here is whether and (if so) how one can avoid being locked into a non-optimal technology. More generally, a trade-off between the social costs and benefits of competing technologies seems important, even more so if different countries coordinate their choices so as to guarantee interoperability.

GPS
Advanced technologies enable the tracking of vehicles. For example, GPS systems can be used for road pricing, as recently introduced in Germany, and therefore extensive use of GPS systems for road pricing can be expected. In fact, road pricing is one of the specific applications of the European 'Galileo' positioning system, which is scheduled to become available in a few years. While this enables the application of very advanced road-pricing schemes, it may also worry travellers, as it may intrude upon privacy. Solving privacy problems requires creative thinking and a careful development of tracking systems, so that these systems will be accepted by the public. How this can best be achieved is still an open question. Scientifically, GPS data are very valuable for evaluating the behavioural effects of road pricing, as they provide detailed information on actual travel behaviour. Moreover, behavioural models can be significantly improved using such RP data.

16.2.7   Policy and Process

Interaction between pricing and other policies
An important policy-associated research question relates to interactions between pricing and other policies, including the construction of new infrastructure, and parking, land-use and intermodal transport policies. The same holds for non-transport policies, such as those for spatial planning and tax.

Lease and insurance companies

A second area for policy-associated research relates to the reactions of lease and insurance companies, which are increasingly interested in the possibilities of new technologies in the area of driving behaviour, and distance driven, both in general and related to place and time.

Structural changes in society

An important question relates to the position of pricing policies, given structural changes in society in the long term, such as a decreasing population size, a decrease in the labour force, the ageing society, and an increase in ICT-related possibilities of avoiding congestion periods or periods with high tariffs. What impacts will such changes have on the long-term perspectives of pricing? Clearly, all these impacts have to be examined together with the impacts of pricing.

Second-best pricing

Another issue we mention concerns the use of second-best policies when first-best charges would be too complex to be understood by most drivers – with the potential danger of limiting the behavioural responses. Besides this being another potential source for second-best policies, it raises the question of just how much complexity in pricing schedules can be imposed upon road users. Here, the answer may obviously depend on whether such complexity is phased in gradually – but then the next question would be how such phasing-in trajectories could be best designed.

The process

In general, we think that the process of design, implementation, refining and evaluation of pricing policies is an under-researched area. Politicians and researchers alike have long held that introducing road pricing almost implies political suicide, because of public resistance. Ken Livingstone, the Mayor of London, who announced that he would introduce the congestion charge if he were elected to office, and who was elected and even re-elected after the successful implementation of the charge, has shown that this is not necessarily true. In general, we think that the complex interactions among actors, stakeholders and institutions are an important area of research. Game theory might prove an interesting way of researching in this area. Major challenges include the linking of theory to practice. Partly inspired by the role of Livingstone in London, research into the role of the 'champions' in road pricing may be important. A particular kind of research related to this issue would investigate public involvement: which options for public involvement have which impacts, under which conditions, and does public involvement yield better policies that are both effective and acceptable?

16.3   IN CONCLUSION . . .

Although we consider that the chapters in this book have clarified many questions related to transport pricing, from the above discussion it is clear that many questions remain. We hope that in 10 years this book will have become outdated in several respects because new, challenging research will have answered at least some of these questions.

Index